Toward a Safer and More Secure Cyberspace

Seymour E. Goodman and Herbert S. Lin, *Editors*

Committee on Improving Cybersecurity Research in the United States

Computer Science and Telecommunications Board

Division on Engineering and Physical Sciences

NATIONAL RESEARCH COUNCIL *AND*
NATIONAL ACADEMY OF ENGINEERING
OF THE NATIONAL ACADEMIES

THE NATIONAL ACADEMIES PRESS
Washington, D.C.
www.nap.edu

THE NATIONAL ACADEMIES PRESS 500 Fifth Street, N.W. Washington, DC 20001

NOTICE: The project that is the subject of this report was approved by the Governing Board of the National Research Council, whose members are drawn from the councils of the National Academy of Sciences, the National Academy of Engineering, and the Institute of Medicine. The members of the committee responsible for the report were chosen for their special competences and with regard for appropriate balance.

Support for this project was provided by the Defense Advanced Research Projects Agency (award number N00174-03-C-0074), the National Science Foundation (award number CNS-0221722), the National Institute of Standards and Technology (contract number SB1341-03-C-0028), the Department of Homeland Security through the National Science Foundation (award number CNS-0344585), the National Academy of Engineering, the National Research Council Fund (no award number), and F. Thomas Leighton and Bonnie Berger Leighton. Any opinions, findings, conclusions, or recommendations expressed in this publication are those of the author(s) and do not necessarily reflect the views of the organizations, agencies, or individuals that provided support for the project.

Back cover: Summarized in the right-hand column of the chart is the new mind-set advocated in this report as essential to achieving a more generally secure cyberspace.

Library of Congress Cataloging-in-Publication Data

Toward a safer and more secure cyberspace / Committee on Improving Cybersecurity Research in the United States, Computer Science and Telecommunications Board, Division on Engineering and Physical Sciences, National Research Council of the National Academies ; Seymour E. Goodman and Herbert S. Lin, editors.
p. cm.
Includes bibliographical references.
ISBN 978-0-309-10395-4 (pbk.) -- ISBN 978-0-309-66741-8 (pdf) 1. Computer security. 2. Computer networks--Security measures. 3. Cyberterrorism--Prevention. I. Goodman, Seymour E. II. Lin, Herbert. III. National Research Council (U.S.). Committee on Improving Cybersecurity Research in the United States.
QA76.9.A25T695 2007
005.8--dc22

2007037982

This report is available from
Computer Science and Telecommunications Board
National Research Council
500 Fifth Street, N.W.
Washington, DC 20001

Additional copies of this report are available from the National Academies Press, 500 Fifth Street, N.W., Lockbox 285, Washington, DC 20055; (800) 624-6242 or (202) 334-3313 (in the Washington metropolitan area); Internet, http://www.nap.edu.

Printed in the United States of America

THE NATIONAL ACADEMIES

Advisers to the Nation on Science, Engineering, and Medicine

The **National Academy of Sciences** is a private, nonprofit, self-perpetuating society of distinguished scholars engaged in scientific and engineering research, dedicated to the furtherance of science and technology and to their use for the general welfare. Upon the authority of the charter granted to it by the Congress in 1863, the Academy has a mandate that requires it to advise the federal government on scientific and technical matters. Dr. Ralph J. Cicerone is president of the National Academy of Sciences.

The **National Academy of Engineering** was established in 1964, under the charter of the National Academy of Sciences, as a parallel organization of outstanding engineers. It is autonomous in its administration and in the selection of its members, sharing with the National Academy of Sciences the responsibility for advising the federal government. The National Academy of Engineering also sponsors engineering programs aimed at meeting national needs, encourages education and research, and recognizes the superior achievements of engineers. Dr. Charles M. Vest is president of the National Academy of Engineering.

The **Institute of Medicine** was established in 1970 by the National Academy of Sciences to secure the services of eminent members of appropriate professions in the examination of policy matters pertaining to the health of the public. The Institute acts under the responsibility given to the National Academy of Sciences by its congressional charter to be an adviser to the federal government and, upon its own initiative, to identify issues of medical care, research, and education. Dr. Harvey V. Fineberg is president of the Institute of Medicine.

The **National Research Council** was organized by the National Academy of Sciences in 1916 to associate the broad community of science and technology with the Academy's purposes of furthering knowledge and advising the federal government. Functioning in accordance with general policies determined by the Academy, the Council has become the principal operating agency of both the National Academy of Sciences and the National Academy of Engineering in providing services to the government, the public, and the scientific and engineering communities. The Council is administered jointly by both Academies and the Institute of Medicine. Dr. Ralph J. Cicerone and Dr. Charles M. Vest are chair and vice chair, respectively, of the National Research Council.

www.national-academies.org

COMMITTEE ON IMPROVING CYBERSECURITY RESEARCH IN THE UNITED STATES

SEYMOUR (Sy) E. GOODMAN, Georgia Institute of Technology, *Chair* (from August 2006)
JOEL S. BIRNBAUM, Hewlett-Packard Company, *Chair* (until August 2006)
DAVID AUCSMITH, Microsoft Corporation
STEVEN M. BELLOVIN, Columbia University
ANJAN BOSE, Washington State University
BARBARA FRASER, Cisco Systems, Inc.
JAMES GOSLER, Sandia National Laboratories
WILLIAM GUTTMAN, Carnegie Mellon University
RUBY B. LEE, Princeton University
FERNANDO (FRED) LUIZ, Hewlett-Packard Company (retired)
TERESA F. LUNT, Palo Alto Research Center
PETER G. NEUMANN, SRI International
STEFAN SAVAGE, University of California, San Diego
WILLIAM L. SCHERLIS, Carnegie Mellon University
FRED B. SCHNEIDER, Cornell University
ALFRED Z. SPECTOR, Independent Consultant
JOHN WANKMUELLER, MasterCard International
JAY WARRIOR, Agilent Laboratories

Staff

HERBERT S. LIN, Senior Scientist and Study Director (from September 2005)
CHARLES N. BROWNSTEIN, Study Director (until September 2005)
KRISTEN BATCH, Associate Program Officer
JENNIFER M. BISHOP, Program Associate (until November 2006)
JANICE M. SABUDA, Senior Program Assistant
TED SCHMITT, Consultant

Preface

In the past several years, cybersecurity has been transformed from a concern chiefly of computer scientists and information system managers to an issue of pressing national importance. The nation's critical infrastructure, such as the electric power grid, air traffic control system, financial system, and communication networks, depends extensively on information technology (IT) for its operation. Concerns about the vulnerability of this infrastructure have heightened in the security-conscious environment after the September 11, 2001, attacks. National policy makers have become increasingly concerned that adversaries backed by substantial resources will attempt to exploit the cyber-vulnerabilities in the critical infrastructure, thereby inflicting substantial harm on the nation.

Today, there is an inadequate understanding of what makes IT systems vulnerable to attack, how best to reduce these vulnerabilities, and how to transfer cybersecurity knowledge to actual practice. For these reasons, and in response to both legislative and executive branch interest, the National Research Council (NRC) established the Committee on Improving Cybersecurity Research in the United States (see Appendix A for biographies of the committee members). The committee was charged with developing a strategy for cybersecurity research in the 21st century. To develop this strategy, the committee built on a number of previous NRC reports in this area, notably, *Computers at Risk* (1991), *Trust in Cyberspace* (1998), and *Information Technology for Counterterrorism* (2003).[1] Although

[1]National Research Council, 1991, *Computers at Risk*, National Academy Press, Washington, D.C.; National Research Council, 1998, *Trust in Cyberspace*, National Academy Press, Washington, D.C.; National Research Council, 2003, *Information Technology for Counterterrorism: Immediate Actions and Future Possibilities*, The National Academies Press, Washington, D.C.

these reports were issued some years ago, the committee found that they contained valuable points of departure for the present effort. In addition, the committee undertook a set of hearings and briefings that provided information about present-day concerns and responses to those concerns. The report of the President's Information Technology Advisory Committee on cybersecurity—*Cyber Security: A Crisis of Prioritization*—which lays out a research agenda and makes recommendations on how to implement it, provided a useful point of departure as well.[2]

Box P.1 contains the full charge to the committee. The committee's survey of the current cybersecurity research landscape is described in Appendix B. As requested in the charge, Section B.5 contains a survey of the research effort in cybersecurity and trustworthiness to assess the current mix of topics; Sections B.4 and B.6 address level of effort, division of labor, and sources of funding; Section B.3 addresses quality. The issue related to the timescales of cybersecurity research is addressed in Section 10.2.2. Structural dimensions of a program for cybersecurity research are addressed in Section 3.3.

Two elements in the committee's statement of task were not fully addressed. First, although Part II provides general guidance regarding appropriate areas of programmatic focus, this report does not provide a detailed explication of research priorities within or among these areas (that is, the research areas meriting federal funding). The reason, explained at greater length in Section 3.4.4, is that in the course of its deliberations, the committee concluded that the nation's cybersecurity research agenda should be broad and that any attempt to specify research priorities in a top-down manner would be counterproductive. Second, the study's statement of task calls for it to address appropriate levels of federal funding for cybersecurity research. As discussed in Section 10.2.2, the committee articulates a specific principle for determining the appropriate level of budgets for cybersecurity research: namely, that such budgets should be adequate to ensure that a large fraction of good ideas for cybersecurity research can be explored. It further notes that the threat is likely to grow at a rate faster than the present federal cybersecurity research program will enable us to respond to, and thus that in order to execute fully the broad strategy articulated in this report, a substantial increase in federal budgetary resources devoted to cybersecurity research will be needed.

It is important to delineate the scope of what this report does and to

---

[2]President's Information Technology Advisory Committee. February 2005. *Cyber Security: A Crisis of Prioritization*, National Coordination Office for Information Technology Research and Development, Washington, D.C.; available at www.nitrd.gov/pitac/reports/20050301_cybersecurity/cybersecurity.pdf.

specify what it does not do. The committee recognizes that cybersecurity is only one element of trustworthiness, which can be defined as the property of a system whereby it does what is required and expected of it—despite environmental disruption, human user and operator errors, and attacks by hostile parties—and that it does not do other things. Trust-

BOX P.1
Statement of Task

This project will involve a survey of the research effort in cybersecurity and trustworthiness to assess the current mix of topics, level of effort, division of labor, sources of funding, and quality; describe those research areas that merit federal funding, considering short-, medium-, and long-term emphases; and recommend the necessary level for federal funding in cybersecurity research. Technologies and approaches conventionally associated with cybersecurity and trustworthiness will be examined to identify those areas most deserving of attention in the future and to understand the research baseline. In addition, this project will also seek to identify and explore models and technologies not traditionally considered to be within cybersecurity and trustworthiness in an effort to generate ideas for revolutionary advances in cybersecurity. Structural alternatives for the oversight and allocation of funding (how to best allocate existing funds and how best to program new funds that may be made available) will be considered and the project committee will provide corresponding recommendations. Finally, the committee will offer some guidance on the shape of grant-making research programs.

Consistent with legislative language, the committee will consider:

1. Identification of the topics in cybersecurity research that deserve emphasis for the future. As discussed with congressional staff, this analysis will build on past work within CSTB [Computer Science and Telecommunications Board] and elsewhere, which has identified many important and often enduring topics.
2. The distribution of effort among cybersecurity researchers. The emphasis will be on universities, in part to address the link between the conduct of researchers and the education and training of cybersecurity experts, to ensure that there are enough researchers to perform the needed work. Comparisons between academic and industry activities will be made.
3. Identification and assessment of the gaps in technical capability for critical infrastructure network security, including security of industrial process controls.
4. The distribution, range, and stability of support programs among federal funding organizations.
5. Issues regarding research priorities, resource requirements, and options for improving coordination and efficacy in the national pursuit of cybersecurity research. Opportunities for cross-sector (and intra-sector) coordination and collaboration will be considered

worthiness has many dimensions, including correctness, reliability, safety, and survivability, in addition to security. Nevertheless, the charge of this report is to focus on security, and other issues are addressed only to the extent that they relate to security.

This report is not confined to technical topics alone. A number of policy issues related to cybersecurity are discussed. These policy issues provide an overarching context for understanding why greater use has not been made of cybersecurity research to date. In addition, because the report concludes that cybersecurity research should not be undertaken entirely in a domain-independent manner, the report also discusses briefly a number of problem domains to which cybersecurity research is applicable.

The committee assembled for this project included individuals with expertise in the various specialties within computer security and other aspects of trustworthiness, computer networks, systems architecture, software engineering, process control systems, human-computer interaction, and information technology research and development (R&D) programs in the federal government, academia, and industry. In addition, the committee involved individuals with experience in industrial research.

The committee met first in July 2004 and four times subsequently. It held several plenary sessions to gather input from a broad range of experts in cybersecurity. Particular areas of focus included then-current federal research activity, the state of the art in usable security, and current vendor activity related to advancing the state of cybersecurity. The committee did its work through its own expert deliberations and by soliciting input from key officials at sponsoring agencies, numerous experts at federal agencies, academic researchers, and hardware and software vendors (see Appendix C). Additional input included perspectives from professional conferences, the technical literature, and government reports studied by committee members and staff (see Appendix B).

The committee appreciates the support of its sponsoring agencies and especially the numerous inputs and responses to requests for information provided by Jaynarayan Lala and Lee Badger at the Defense Advanced Research Projects Agency (DARPA), Carl Landwehr and Karl Levitt at the National Science Foundation (NSF), Edward Roback at the National Institute of Standards and Technology (NIST), Douglas Maughan at the Department of Homeland Security (DHS), and Robert Herklotz at the Air Force Office of Scientific Research (AFOSR).

PERSONAL NOTE FROM THE CHAIR

A large fraction of the American population now spends a great deal of time in cyberspace. We work and shop there. We are educated and entertained there. We socialize with family, friends, and strangers in cyberspace. We are paid and we pay others through this medium. Millions of commercial enterprises and local, state, and federal government agencies do their business there. It has become a critical infrastructure in its own right, and it is embedded in almost all other critical infrastructures. We rely on cyberspace to help keep electricity flowing, public transportation running, and many other basic services working at levels that we have come to regard as essential elements of our society. These functions, expectations, and resulting dependencies are with us now, have been growing rapidly, and are expected to continue to grow well into the future.

The people, businesses, and governments of the rest of the world are following suit. On a per capita basis, some are even more committed to this infrastructure than the United States is. The Internet alone is now used by about a billion people and comes to ground in about 200 countries. And they are all connected to us and to one another.

It is thus very much in the public interest to have a safe and secure cyberspace. Yet cyberspace in general, and the Internet in particular, are notoriously vulnerable to a frightening and expanding range of accidents and attacks by a spectrum of hackers, criminals, terrorists, and state actors who have been empowered by unprecedented access to more people and organizations than has ever been the case with any infrastructure in history. Most of the people and organizations that increasingly depend on cyberspace are unaware of how vulnerable and defenseless they are, and all too many users and operators are poorly trained and equipped. Many learn only after suffering attacks. These people, and the nation as a whole, are paying enormous costs for relying on such an insecure infrastructure.

The Committee on Improving Cybersecurity Research in the United States was established by the National Research Council of the National Academies with the financial support of NSF, DARPA, NIST, DHS, the National Academy of Engineering, and F. Thomas and Bonnie Berger Leighton. The basic premise underlying the committee's task is that research can produce a better understanding of why cyberspace is as vulnerable as it is and that it can lead to new technologies and policies and their effective implementation to make things better.

Cybersecurity is not a topic that is new to the national agenda. Indeed, a number of earlier reports have addressed this subject from different perspectives. Many of these reports have been concerned with specific threats (e.g., terrorism), missions (e.g., critical infrastructure protection), government agencies (e.g., how they might better protect themselves), or specific sectors (e.g., banking and finance). This study tackles the problem from the perspective of protecting all legitimate users of cyberspace, including the individual citizens, small commercial concerns, and government agencies that are particularly vulnerable to harassment and injury every time they use the Internet or connect to other networks. The committee strongly believes that a more generally secure cyberspace would go a long way toward protecting critical infrastructure and national security.

What would a safer and more secure cyberspace look like? To address this question, the committee has formulated a Cyberspace Bill of Rights (CBoR). It consists of 10 basic provisions that the committee believes users should have as reasonable expectations for their online safety and security. The CBoR articulated in this report is distinctly user-centric, enabling individuals to draw for themselves the contrast between that vision and their own personal cyberspace experiences.

Unfortunately, the state of cyberspace today is such that it is much easier to state these provisions than it is to achieve them. No simple research project will lead to the widespread reality of any of these provisions. Indeed, even achieving something that sounds as simple as eliminating spam will require a complex, crosscutting technical and nontechnical R&D agenda. Accordingly, this report goes on to propose a comprehensive R&D agenda and to show how that agenda would help realize the provisions of the CBoR. The report also warns that there will be no shortcuts and that realizing the CBoR vision will take a long, sustained, and determined effort. There is much to accomplish.

Many of this report's technical R&D recommendations build on and support those of earlier reports. However, they give particular emphasis to problems that have handicapped the more extensive practice of cybersecurity in the past. Thus, the report focuses substantial attention on the very real challenges of incentives, usability, and embedding advances in cybersecurity into real-world products, practices, and services.

On behalf of the committee, I would like to thank those who took the time and trouble to contribute to our deliberations by briefing the committee. This group of individuals is listed in Appendix C. In addition, those who reviewed this report in draft form played a critical and indispensable role in helping to improve the report (see "Acknowledgment of Reviewers" on page xiii). On the Computer Science and Telecommunications Board (CSTB), Ted Schmitt's work as program officer on his first NRC project was exemplary, and Janice Sabuda provided administrative and logistical support beyond compare. Special recognition is due to Herbert S. Lin, who became the CSTB study director about halfway through the committee's lifetime, and who worked so hard to pull this report together. His tenacity, determination, and expertise were indispensable.

Seymour E. Goodman, *Chair*
Committee on Improving Cybersecurity
Research in the United States

Acknowledgment of Reviewers

This report has been reviewed in draft form by individuals chosen for their diverse perspectives and technical expertise, in accordance with procedures approved by the National Research Council's Report Review Committee. The purpose of this independent review is to provide candid and critical comments that will assist the institution in making its published report as sound as possible and to ensure that the report meets institutional standards for objectivity, evidence, and responsiveness to the study charge. The review comments and draft manuscript remain confidential to protect the integrity of the deliberative process. We wish to thank the following individuals for their review of this report:

Eric Benhamou, Benhamou Global Ventures, LLC,
Earl Boebert, Sandia National Laboratories (retired),
William R. Cheswick, AT&T Research,
David D. Clark, Massachusetts Institute of Technology,
Richard A. DeMillo, Georgia Institute of Technology,
Samuel H. Fuller, Analog Devices, Inc.,
Paul A. Karger, IBM Thomas J. Watson Research Center,
Pradeep Khosla, Carnegie Mellon University,
Butler Lampson, Microsoft Corporation,
Brian Lopez, Lawrence Livermore National Laboratory,
William Lucyshyn, University of Maryland,
Clifford Neuman, University of Southern California,
Eugene Spafford, Purdue University,

Philip Venables, Goldman Sachs,
Jesse Walker, Intel Corporation, and
Jeannette M. Wing, Carnegie Mellon University.

Although the reviewers listed above have provided many constructive comments and suggestions, they were not asked to endorse the conclusions or recommendations, nor did they see the final draft of the report before its release. The review of this report was overseen by Lewis Branscomb and Brian Snow. Appointed by the National Research Council, they were responsible for making certain that an independent examination of this report was carried out in accordance with institutional procedures and that all review comments were carefully considered. Responsibility for the final content of this report rests entirely with the authoring committee and the institution.

Contents

PART III
CONCLUSION

APPENDIXES

Boxes

Executive Summary

BACKGROUND

Given the growing importance of cyberspace to nearly all aspects of national life, a secure cyberspace is vitally important to the nation, but cyberspace is far from secure today. The United States faces real risks that adversaries will exploit vulnerabilities in the nation's critical information systems, thereby causing considerable suffering and damage.

In this context and in response to a congressional request, the National Research Council (NRC) established the Committee on Improving Cybersecurity Research in the United States. The committee was charged with developing a strategy for cybersecurity research at the start of the 21st century. The basic premise underlying this report is that research can produce a better understanding of why cyberspace is as vulnerable as it is and that such research can lead to new technologies and policies and their effective implementation, making cyberspace safer and more secure. The report also addresses the nature of the cybersecurity threat, explores some of the reasons that previous cybersecurity research efforts and agendas have had less impact on the nation's cybersecurity posture than desired, and considers the human resource base needed to advance the cybersecurity research agenda.

Society ultimately expects computer systems to be trustworthy—that is, that they do what is required and expected of them despite environmental disruption, human user and operator errors, and attacks by hostile parties, and that they not do other things. Trustworthiness has many dimensions, including correctness, reliability, safety, and survivability, in addition to security. However, the scope of this report, consistent with the committee's charge, is somewhat narrower: it focuses on security and addresses other trustworthiness issues only to the extent that they relate to security.

WHAT IS AT STAKE

Information technology (IT) is essential to the day-to-day operations of companies, organizations, and government. People's personal lives also involve computing in areas ranging from communication with family and friends to online banking and other household and financial management activities. Companies large and small are ever more reliant on IT to support diverse business processes, ranging from payroll and accounting, to tracking of inventory, operation of sales, and support for research and development (R&D)—that is, IT systems are increasingly needed for companies to be able to operate at all. Critical national infrastructures—such as those associated with energy, banking and finance, defense, law enforcement, transportation, water systems, and government—and private emergency services also depend on IT-based systems and networks; of course, the telecommunications system itself is a critical infrastructure for the nation.

Such dependence on IT will grow. But in the future, computing and communications technologies will also be embedded in applications in which they are essentially invisible to their users. A future of "pervasive computing" will see IT ubiquitously integrated into everyday objects in order to enhance their usefulness, and these objects will be interconnected in ways that further multiply their usefulness. In addition, a growing focus on innovation in the future will require the automation and integration of various services to provide rapid response tailored to the needs of users across the entire economy.

The ability to fully realize the benefits of IT depends on these systems being secure—and yet nearly all indications of the size of the threat, whether associated with losses or damage, type of attack, or presence of vulnerability, indicate a continuously worsening problem. Moreover, it is almost certainly the case that reports understate the actual scope of the threat, since some successful attacks are not noticed and others noticed but not reported.

The gaps between commercial practice and vulnerabilities in critical infrastructure are still wide. Meanwhile, the ability of individuals, organizations, or even state actors to attack the nation's institutions, its people's identities, and their online lives in cyberspace has grown substantially. Industry trends toward commoditization have resulted in clear targets for focused attacks, making coordinated attacks by hundreds of thousands of co-opted cooperating agents practical for the first time in history.

The potential consequences of a lack of security in cyberspace fall into three broad categories. First is the threat of catastrophe—a cyberattack, especially in conjunction with a physical attack, could result in thousands of deaths and many billions of dollars of damage in a very short time. Second is frictional drag on important economic and security-related processes. Today, insecurities in cyberspace systems and networks allow adversaries (in particular, criminals) to extract billions of dollars in fraud and extortion—and force businesses to expend additional resources to defend themselves against these threats. If cyberspace does not become more secure, the citizens, businesses, and governments of tomorrow will continue to face similar pressures, and most likely on a greater scale. Third, concerns about insecurity may inhibit the use of IT in the future and thus lead to a self-denial of the benefits that IT brings, benefits that will be needed for the national competitiveness of the United States as well as for national and homeland security.

THE BROAD RANGE OF CAPABILITIES AND GOALS OF CYBERATTACKERS

A very broad spectrum of actors, ranging from lone hackers to major nation-states, poses security risks to the nation's IT infrastructure. Organized crime (e.g., drug cartels) and transnational terrorists (and terrorist organizations, perhaps state-sponsored) occupy a region in between these two extremes, but they are more similar to the nation-state than to the lone hacker.

High-end attackers are qualitatively different from others by virtue of their greater resources—money, talent, time, organizational support and commitment, and goals. These adversaries can thus target vulnerabilities at any point in the IT supply chain from hardware fabrication to end uses. Furthermore, they are usually highly capable of exploiting human or organizational weaknesses over extended periods of time. The bottom line is that the threat is growing in sophistication as well as in magnitude, and against the high-end attacker, many current best practices and security technologies amount to little more than speed bumps—thus requiring additional fundamental research and new approaches, such as a greater emphasis on mitigation and recovery.

THE CYBERSECURITY BILL OF RIGHTS

The committee believes that individual users, organizations, and society at large are entitled to use and rely on information technologies whose functionality does not diminish even when they are under attack. This vision for a safe and secure cyberspace can be expressed as the committee's Cybersecurity Bill of Rights (CBoR).

Following is a list of the 10 provisions in this CBoR. Explanations and additional discussion of each provision are presented in the main body of the report.

The first three provisions relate to properties of holistic systems, including availability, recoverability, and control of systems:

I. Availability of system and network resources to legitimate users.
II. Easy and convenient recovery from successful attacks.
III. Control over and knowledge of one's own computing environment.

The next three provisions relate to the traditional security properties of confidentiality, authentication (and its extension, provenance), and authorization:

IV. Confidentiality of stored information and information exchange.
V. Authentication and provenance.
VI. The technological capability to exercise fine-grained control over the flow of information in and through systems.

The next three provisions relate to crosscutting properties of systems:

VII. Security in using computing directly or indirectly in important applications, including financial, health care, and electoral transactions and real-time remote control of devices that interact with physical processes.
VIII. The ability to access any source of information (e.g., e-mail, Web page, file) safely.
IX. Awareness of what security is actually being delivered by a system or component.

The last provision relates to justice:

X. Justice for security problems caused by another party.

How are the goals of the CBoR to be achieved? As the discussion in the remainder of this report indicates, a different way of thinking about cybersecurity will be necessary regarding the ways in which secure systems are designed, developed, procured, operated, and used. In the long run, this different way of thinking will entail new directions in education, training, development practice, operational practice, oversight, liability laws, government regulation, and so on.

REALIZING THE VISION

Compared with what exists today, this vision of a secure cyberspace is compelling. However, for two distinct but related reasons, the nation is a long way from meeting this goal. The first reason is that much about cybersecurity technologies and practices is known but not put into practice. Even the deployment of cybersecurity measures that are quite unsophisticated can make a difference against casual attackers. Thus, the cybersecurity posture of the nation could be strengthened substantially if individuals and organizations collectively adopted current best practices and existing security technologies that are known to improve cybersecurity.

The second reason is that, even assuming that everything known today was immediately put into practice, the resulting cybersecurity posture—though it would be stronger and more resilient than it is now—would still be inadequate against today's threat, let alone tomorrow's. Closing this gap—a gap of knowledge—will require both traditional and unorthodox approaches to research.

Traditional research is problem-specific, and there are many cybersecurity problems for which good solutions are not known. (A good solution to a cybersecurity problem is one that is effective, is robust against a variety of attack types, is inexpensive and easy to deploy, is easy to use, and does not significantly reduce or cripple other functionality in the system of which it is made a part.) Research will be needed to address these problems.

But problem-by-problem solutions, or even problem-class by problem-class solutions, are highly unlikely to be sufficient to close the gap by themselves. Unorthodox, clean-slate approaches will also be needed to deal with what might be called a structural problem in cybersecurity research now, and these approaches will entail the development of new ideas and new points of view that revisit the basic foundations and implicit assumptions of security research.

Addressing both of these reasons for the lack of security in cyberspace is important, but it is the second goal—closing the knowledge gap—that is the primary goal of cybersecurity research and the primary focus of this report.

Research is needed both to develop new knowledge and to make such knowledge more usable and transferable to the field. Furthermore, cybersecurity will be a continuing issue: threats evolve (both on their own and as defenses against them are discovered), and new vulnerabilities often emerge as innovation changes underlying system architectures, implementation, or basic assumptions. And, because there are growing incentives to compromise the security of deployed IT systems, research will always be needed. Personal gain, organized crime, terrorism, and national interests are superseding (and, in the eyes of many, have superseded) personal fame and curiosity as incentives.

PRINCIPLES TO DRIVE THE ONGOING RESEARCH AGENDA

The committee identified several principles that should shape the cybersecurity research agenda:

- *Conduct cybersecurity research as though its application will be important.* The scope of cybersecurity research must extend to understanding how cybersecurity technologies and practice can be applied in real-life contexts. Consequently, fundamental research in cybersecurity will embrace organizational, sociological, economic, legal, and psychological factors as well as technological ones.
- *Hedge against uncertainty in the nature and severity of the future cybersecurity threat.* It seems prudent to take a balanced approach that hedges against the eventuality that a high-end cybersecurity threat emerges and becomes manifestly obvious to all. That hedge is an R&D agenda in cybersecurity that is both broader and deeper than might be required if only low-end threats were at issue. (Because of the long lead time for large-scale deployments of any measure, part of the research agenda must include research directed at reducing those long lead times.)
- *Ensure programmatic continuity.* A sound research program should also support a substantial effort in research areas with a long time horizon for payoff. This is not to say that long-term research cannot have intermediate milestones, although such milestones should be treated as midcourse corrections rather than "go/no-go" decisions that demoralize and make researchers overly conservative. Long-term research should engage both academic and industrial actors, and it can involve collaboration early and often with technology-transition stakeholders, even in the basic science stages.
- *Respect the need for breadth in the research agenda.* Cybersecurity risks will be on the rise for the foreseeable future, but few specifics about those risks can be known with high confidence. Thus, it is not realistic to imagine that one or even a few promising approaches will prevent or even substantially mitigate cybersecurity risks in the future, and cybersecurity research must be conducted across

a broad front. In addition, because qualitatively new attacks can appear with little warning, a broad research agenda is likely to decrease significantly the time needed to develop countermeasures against these new attacks when they appear. Priorities are still important, but they should be determined by those in a position to respond most quickly to the changing environment—namely, the research constituencies that provide peer review and the program managers of the various research-supporting agencies. Notions of breadth and diversity in the cybersecurity research agenda should themselves be interpreted broadly as well, and might well be integrated into other research programs such as software and systems engineering, operating systems, programming languages, networks, Web applications, and so on.

- *Disseminate new knowledge and artifacts (e.g., software and hardware prototypes) to the research community.* Dissemination of research results beyond one's own laboratory is necessary if those results are to have a wide impact—a point that argues for cybersecurity research to be conducted on an unclassified basis as much as possible. Other information to be shared as widely as possible includes threat and incident information that can help guide future research.

IMPORTANT CATEGORIES OF RESEARCH FOCUS

A research agenda can be laid out to make progress toward the vision embedded in the Cybersecurity Bill of Rights. This agenda has six primary areas of focus. Although these categories identify important areas of focus, they are broad in scope. This breadth reflects a recognition of the holistic nature of cybersecurity—attackers will attack at any technological or procedural weak point, so no single or even small number of silver bullets can "solve the cybersecurity problem." A good cybersecurity research portfolio recognizes the importance of diversity in an uncertain threat environment, which is true even if several areas of focus warrant emphasis.

1. *Category 1—Blocking and limiting the impact of compromise.* This category includes secure information systems and networks that resist technical compromise; convenient and ubiquitous encryption that can prevent unauthorized parties from obtaining sensitive or confidential data; containment, backup, mitigation, and recovery; and system lockdowns under attack.

   One illustrative example of research in this category is secure design, development, and testing. Research is needed that will facilitate the design of systems that are "secure by design." Research is also needed for security evaluation, for good implementation practices and tools that reduce the likelihood of program flaws (bugs) and make it easier for developers to implement secure systems, and for improved testing and evaluation for functionality that has not been included in the specification of a system's requirements and that may result in security vulnerabilities.

2. *Category 2—Enabling accountability*. This category includes matters such as remote authentication, access control and policy management, auditing and traceability, maintenance of provenance, secure associations between system components, intrusion detection, and so on. In general, the objective is to hold anyone or anything that has access to a system component—a computing device, a sensor, an actuator, a network—accountable for the results of such access.

   One illustrative example of research in this category is attribution. Anonymous attackers cannot be held responsible for their actions and do not suffer any consequences for the harmful actions that they may initiate. But many computer operations are inherently anonymous, which means that associating actors with actions must be done explicitly. Attribution technology enables such associations to be easily ascertained, captured, and preserved. At the same time, attribution mechanisms do not solve the important problem of the unwittingly compromised or duped user, although these mechanisms may be necessary in conducting forensic investigations that lead to such a user.

3. *Category 3—Promoting deployment*. This category is focused on ensuring that the technologies and procedures in Categories 1 and 2 are actually used to promote and enhance security. Category 3 includes technologies that facilitate ease of use by both end users and system implementers, incentives that promote the use of security technologies in the relevant contexts, and the removal of barriers that impede the use of security technologies.

   One illustrative example of research in this category is usable security. Security functionality is often turned off, disabled, bypassed, and not deployed because it is too complex for individuals and enterprise organizations to manage effectively or to use conveniently. Thus, an effort to develop more usable security mechanisms and approaches would have substantial payoff. Usable security has social and organizational dimensions as well as technological and psychological ones. Other illustrations are provided in the main text of this report.

4. *Category 4—Deterring would-be attackers and penalizing attackers.* This category includes legal and policy measures that could be employed to penalize or impose consequences on cyberattackers, and technologies that support such measures. In principle, this category could also include technical measures to retaliate against a cyberattacker.

   One illustrative example of research in this category would facilitate the prosecution of cybercriminals across international borders. Many cybercrime perpetrators are outside of U.S. jurisdiction, and the applicable laws may not criminalize the particulars of the crime perpetrated. Even if they do, logistical difficulties in identifying a perpetrator across national boundaries may render him or her practically immune to prosecution. Research is needed to further harmonize laws across many national boundaries to enable international prosecutions and to reduce the logistical difficulties involved in such activities. Other illustrations are provided in the main text of the report.

5. *Category 5—Illustrative crosscutting problem-focused research areas.* This category focuses elements of research in Categories 1 through 4 onto specific important problems in cybersecurity. These include security for legacy systems, the role of secrecy in cyberdefense, coping with the insider threat, and security for new computing environments and in application domains.

6. *Category 6—Speculative research.* This category focuses on admittedly speculative approaches to cybersecurity that are unorthodox, "out-of-the-box," and also that arguably have some potential for revolutionary and nonincremental gains in cybersecurity. The areas described in this report are merely illustrative of such ideas—of primary importance is the idea that speculative ideas are worth some investment in any broad research portfolio.

WHY HAS CYBERSECURITY ACTION TAKEN TO DATE BEEN INSUFFICIENT?

The committee believes that the cybersecurity threat is ominous. Moreover, as one of the most IT-dependent nations in the world, the United States has much to lose from the materialization of this threat. But this committee is not the first committee—and this report is not the first report—to make this claim. After more than 15 years of reports pointing to an ominous threat, and in fact more than 15 years in which the threat has objectively grown, why is there not a national sense of urgency about cybersecurity? Why has action not been taken to close the gap between the nation's cybersecurity posture and the cyberthreat?

The notion that no action to promote cybersecurity has been taken in the past 15 years is somewhat unfair. In recent years, most major IT vendors have undertaken significant efforts to improve the security of their products in response to end-user concerns over security, and many of today's products are by many measures more secure than those that preceded these efforts. In addition, the sentinel events of September 11, 2001, spurred public concerns about security, and some of that concern has spilled over into the cybersecurity domain.

Nevertheless, these changes in the environment, important though they are, do not change the fact that the degree of awareness and action taken in the past 15 years is nowhere near what is necessary to achieve a robust cybersecurity posture.

The committee believes that the lack of adequate action in the cybersecurity space can be largely explained by three factors:

- Past reports have not provided the sufficiently compelling information needed to make the case for dramatic and urgent action. If so, perhaps it is possible to paint a sufficiently ominous picture of the threat in terms that would inspire decision makers to take action. Detailed and specific information is usually more convincing than information couched in very general terms, but unfortunately, detailed and specific information in the open literature about the scope and nature of the cyberthreat is lacking. Many corporate victims of cyberattack, for example, are reluctant to identify themselves as being victims for fear of being cast in a bad light relative to their competitors.
- Even with the relevant information in hand, decision makers discount future possibilities so much that they do not see the need for present-day action. That being the case, nothing short of a highly visible and perhaps ongoing cyber-disaster will motivate actions. Decision makers weigh the immediate costs of putting into place adequate cybersecurity measures, both technical and procedural, against the potential future benefits (actually, avoided costs) of preventing cyber-disaster in the future—and systematically discount the latter as uncertain and vague.
- The costs of inaction are not borne by the relevant decision makers. The bulk of the nation's critical infrastructure is owned and operated by private-sector companies. To the extent that these companies respond to security issues, they generally do so as one of the risks of doing business. But they do much less to respond to the

threat of low-probability, high-impact (i.e., catastrophic) threats, although all of society at large has a large stake in their actions.

The first factor above suggests the necessity of undertaking a truly authoritative assessment of the cybersecurity threat that draws on the best industry and intelligence data available and that is made public for all to see. The second and third factors suggest that the cybersecurity problem results not from a failure to recognize the threat but from a failure to respond sufficiently to it. (In other words, awareness is not enough—there are potential solutions that have not been deployed widely and many problems for which practical solutions are not known today.) These factors suggest the need for putting into place mechanisms that change the calculus used to make decisions about cybersecurity.

As for the impact of research on the nation's cybersecurity posture, it is not reasonable to expect that research alone will make any substantial difference at all. Indeed, there is a very large gap between a successful "in principle" result or demonstration and its widespread deployment and use; closing this gap is the focus of research in Category 3—Promoting deployment, above. But many other factors must also be aligned if research is to have a significant impact. Specifically, IT vendors must be willing to regard security as a product attribute that is coequal with performance and cost; IT researchers must be willing to value cybersecurity research as much as they value research into high-performance or cost-effective computing; and IT purchasers must be willing to incur present-day costs in order to obtain future benefits.

PRIORITIES FOR ACTION TODAY

The committee has identified the following five action items for policy makers as warranting the highest priority:

- *Create a sense of urgency about the cybersecurity problem.* One element will be to provide as much information as possible about the scope and nature of the threat. A second element will be to change the decision-making calculus that excessively focuses vendor and end-user attention on short-term costs of improving their cybersecurity postures.
- *Commensurate with a rapidly growing cybersecurity threat, support a broad, robust, and sustained research agenda at levels which ensure that a large fraction of good ideas for cybersecurity research can be explored.* Discretionary budgets for the foreseeable future will be very tight, but even in such times, program growth is possible if the political will is present to designate these directions as priorities. Both the

scope and scale of federally funded cybersecurity research are seriously inadequate. To execute fully the broad strategy articulated in this report, a substantial increase in federal budgetary resources devoted to cybersecurity research will be needed. Nor should cybersecurity research remain in the computer science domain alone, and additional funding might well be used to support the pursuit of cybersecurity considerations in other closely related research endeavors, such as those related to creating high-assurance systems and the engineering of secure systems and software across entire system life cycles.

- *Establish a mechanism for continuing follow-up on a research agenda.* Today, the scope and nature of cybersecurity research across the federal government are not well understood, least of all by government decision makers. An important first step would be for the government to build on the efforts of the National Coordination Office for Networking and Information Technology Research and Development to develop a reasonably complete picture of the cybersecurity research efforts that the government supports from year to year. To the best of the committee's knowledge, no such coordinated picture exists.
- *Support research infrastructure.* Making progress on any cybersecurity research agenda requires substantial attention to infrastructural issues. In this context, a cybersecurity research infrastructure refers to the collection of open testbeds, tools, data sets, and other things that enable research to progress and which allow research results to be implemented in actual IT products and services. Without an adequate research infrastructure, there is little hope for realizing the full potential of any research agenda.
- *Sustain and grow the human resource base.* When new ideas are needed, human capital is particularly important. For the pool of cybersecurity researchers to expand to a sufficiently large level, would-be researchers must believe that there is a future to working in this field, a point suggesting the importance of adequate and stable research support for the field. Increasing the number of researchers in a field necessarily entails increased support for that field, since no amount of prioritization within a fixed budget will result in significantly more researchers. In addition, potential graduate students see stable or growing levels of funding as a signal about the importance of the field and the potential for professional advancement.

Part I
Setting the Stage

Part I of this report consists of three chapters. Chapter 1, "Introduction," provides a brief overview of the report and describes how this study came into being.

Chapter 2, "What Is at Stake?," describes what is at stake in realizing (or failing to realize) a more secure cyberspace. Specifically, it notes today's dependence on computing and communications technologies for myriad applications, and it projects a future of "pervasive computing" in which information technology will be ubiquitously integrated into everyday objects in order to enhance their usefulness and in which these "smart objects" will be interconnected in ways that further multiply their usefulness. In this context, the chapter addresses the nature of cybersecurity vulnerabilities, explores some of their consequences, and characterizes various parties that pose a threat to cybersecurity.

Chapter 3, "Improving the Nation's Cybersecurity Posture," characterizes the vision of the National Research Council's Committee on Improving Cybersecurity Research in the United States—embodied in the Cybersecurity Bill of Rights—of what a more secure cyberspace would look like, and it underscores the key role that research will necessarily play in achieving such a vision. Most importantly, Chapter 3 lays out a set of principles driving an ongoing research agenda.

1

Introduction

1.1 THE REPORT IN BRIEF

Given the growing importance of cyberspace to nearly all aspects of national life, a secure cyberspace is vitally important to the nation, but cyberspace is far from secure today. The United States faces real risks that adversaries will exploit vulnerabilities in the nation's critical information systems. The basic premise underlying this report is that research can produce a better understanding of why cyberspace is as vulnerable as it is, and that such research can lead to new technologies and policies and their effective implementation to make cyberspace safer and more secure.

Cybersecurity is not a topic new to the national agenda. But previous efforts to examine cybersecurity have addressed the subject from the standpoint of dealing with specific threats (e.g., terrorism), missions (e.g., critical infrastructure protection), government agencies (e.g., how they might better protect themselves), or specific sectors (e.g., banking and finance). This report focuses on the value of addressing cybersecurity from the perspective of protecting all legitimate users of cyberspace, including individual citizens and small commercial establishments and government agencies, which are particularly vulnerable to harassment and injury every time they log on to the Internet or use some other commercial network. The Committee on Improving Cybersecurity Research in the United States believes that a more generally secure cyberspace will go a long way toward protecting critical infrastructure and national security.

The committee's vision for a safer and more secure cyberspace is reflected in a "Cybersecurity Bill of Rights" (CBoR), consisting of 10 basic provisions that users should have as reasonable expectations for their safety and security in cyberspace. The CBoR articulated in this report is user-centric, enabling individuals to draw for themselves the contrast between the vision contained in the CBoR and their own personal cyberspace experiences. Unfortunately, the state of cyberspace today is such that it is much easier to state these provisions than it is to achieve them. No simple research project, no silver bullet, no specific critical cybersecurity research topic will lead to the widespread reality of any of these provisions. Indeed, even achieving something that sounds as simple as eliminating spam will require a complex, crosscutting technical and nontechnical research and development (R&D) agenda.

The committee's proposal for action focuses attention on a number of research areas identified as important in earlier reports (Appendix B, Section B.5). It also focuses on understanding why important and helpful cybersecurity innovations developed in the past have not been more widely deployed in today's information technology (IT) products and services, thus bringing the very real challenges of incentives, usability, and embedding advances in cybersecurity squarely into the research domain.

The committee's action agenda for policy makers has five elements. The first is to create a sense of urgency about the cybersecurity problem, as the cybersecurity policy failure is not so much one of awareness as of action. The second, commensurate with a rapidly growing cybersecurity threat, is to support a broad, robust, and sustained research agenda at levels which ensure that a large fraction of good ideas for cybersecurity research can be explored. The third is to establish a mechanism for continuing follow-up on a research agenda that will provide a coordinated picture of the government's cybersecurity research activities across the entire federal government, including both classified and unclassified research. The fourth is to support research infrastructure, recognizing that such infrastructure is a critical enabler for allowing research results to be implemented in actual IT products and services. The fifth is to sustain and grow the human resource base, which will be a critical element in ensuring a robust research agenda in the future.

1.2 BACKGROUND OF THE STUDY

Policy makers, and to a lesser extent, the public, have given attention to cybersecurity issues for some time now, but cybersecurity problems have continued to fester. For example, in 1997, the President's Commission on Critical Infrastructure Protection noted the importance of cybersecurity for the systems that operate the nation's critical infrastructure, such as the electric power grid and the air traffic control system as well as the communications and processing backbones that are increasingly essential to the operation of the entire economy, including distribution, finance, and manufacturing. In the wake of the attacks of September 11, 2001, there is a rising concern that adversaries, backed by substantial resources, will attempt to exploit the vulnerabilities in the information systems of the nation, both private and public.

It is a long way between knowing that there are vulnerabilities and fixing them. First and foremost, the will to fix them must be present—a will that has been all too often absent in the committee's judgment. Presuming the will to do so, more and better application of existing knowledge and cybersecurity technologies and practices to information system vulnerabilities would help to mitigate many of them. In some cases, such application is straightforward. In other cases, the understanding of the vulnerabilities or of how to deal with them is incomplete or inadequate. And in still other cases, as with cybersecurity in the power grid and in health care, the specific applications context frames how such existing knowledge can be helpful, even when that knowledge is very relevant.

Against this backdrop, the National Research Council established the Committee on Improving Cybersecurity Research in the United States, charged with developing a coherent strategy for cybersecurity research at the start of the 21st century. The committee's strategy is laid out in this report. To frame this strategy in an appropriate context, this report also considers the nature of the cybersecurity threat, reasons why previous cybersecurity research efforts and agendas have had less impact than hoped for on the nation's cybersecurity posture, and the human resource base needed to advance the cybersecurity research agenda.

To put this report into context, it is helpful to consider the findings and conclusions from a number of other reports and activities on cybersecurity from the past several years. Described in greater detail in Appendix B, these reports and activities have made a number of points that will be reprised in this report. The following are key conclusions that can be drawn from past studies.

First, there are no silver bullets for "fixing" cybersecurity. The threats are evolving and will continue to grow, meaning that gaining ground requires a broad and ongoing society-wide effort that focuses on cybersecurity vulnerabilities. A culture of security must pervade the entire life cycle of IT systems operations, from initial architecture, to design, development, testing, deployment, maintenance, and use. A number of focus areas are particularly important to achieving such a culture: collaboration among researchers; effective coordination and information sharing between the public and private sector; the creation of a sufficient core of research specialists necessary to advance the state of the art; the broad-based education of developers, administrators, and users, making security-conscious practices second nature just as optimizing for performance or functionality is; making it easy and intuitive for users to "do the right thing"; the employment of business drivers and policy mechanisms to facilitate security technology transfer and diffusion of R&D into commercial products and services; and the promotion of risk-based decision making (and metrics to support this effort).

Second, the earlier reports have identified as meriting research investment a number of important areas that are consistent with those identified in this report, including authentication, identity management, secure software engineering, modeling and testbeds, usability, privacy, and benchmarking and best practices. Understanding the intersection between critical infrastructure systems and the IT systems increasingly used to control them is another common theme for research needs.

Third, taken together the activities reviewed give an overall sense that—unless we as a society make cybersecurity a priority—IT systems are likely to become overwhelmed by cyberthreats of all kinds and eventually to be limited in their ability to serve society. This future is avoidable, but precluding it requires the effective coordination and collaboration of private and public sector; continuous, comprehensive, and coordinated research; and appropriate policies to promote security and deter attackers.

2

What Is at Stake?

2.1 INTERCONNECTED INFORMATION TECHNOLOGY EVERYWHERE, ALL THE TIME

For many people today, the information revolution is represented by the most visible and salient interactions they have with information technology (IT)—typing at the keyboard of their computers at work or at home or talking on their cellular telephones. People's personal lives also involve computing through social networking, home management, communication with family and friends, and management of personal affairs. But a much larger collection of information technology embodied in computing, software, and networking deployments is instrumental to the day-to-day operations of companies, organizations, and government. Companies large and small rely on computers for diverse business processes, ranging from payroll and accounting to the tracking of inventory and sales, to support for research and development (R&D). The distribution of food and energy from producer to retail consumer relies on computers and networks at every stage. Nearly everyone (in everyday society, business, government, and the military services) relies on wireless and wired communications systems. Information technology is used to execute the principal business processes both in government and in many of the largest sectors of the economy, including financial services, health care, utilities, transportation, and services. Indeed, the architecture of today's enterprise IT systems is the very embodiment of the critical business logic in complex enterprises. It is impossible to imagine the Wal-Marts, the FedExes, and the Amazons of today without information technology. In short, many computing and communications systems are themselves infrastructure and serve as components of the infrastructure of other organizations.

In the future, computing and communications technologies (collectively, information technologies) are likely to be found in places where they are essentially invisible to everyday view: in cars, wallets, clothing, refrigerators, keys, cabinets, watches, doorbells, medicine bottles, walls, paint, structural beams, roads, dishwashers, identification (ID) cards, telephones, and medical devices (including some embedded in human beings). Computing will be embedded in myriad places and things or will be easily transported in pockets or on wrists. Computing devices will be coupled to multiple sensors and effectors. Computing and communications will be seamless, enabling the tight integration of personal, family, and business systems. Sensors, effectors, and computing will be networked together so that they pass relevant information to one another automatically.

In this vision of truly pervasive computing, the ubiquitous integration of computing and communications technologies into common everyday objects enhances their usefulness and makes life easier and more convenient. Understanding context, personal information appliances will make appropriate information available on demand, enabling users to be more productive in both their personal and professional lives. And, as has been true with today's desktops and mainframes, interconnections among all of these now-smart objects and appliances will multiply their usefulness many times over.

2.2 THE NATURE OF CYBERSECURITY VULNERABILITIES

A security vulnerability in an IT artifact (e.g., a part, hardware component, software module, data structure, system, and so on) exists if there is a way to manipulate the artifact to cause it to act in a way that results in a loss of confidentiality, integrity, and availability.

- *Confidentiality*. A secure system will keep protected information away from those who should not have access to it. Examples of failures that affect confidentiality include the interception of a wireless signal and identity theft.
- *Integrity*. A secure system produces the same results or information whether or not the system has been attacked. When integrity is violated, the system may continue to operate, but under some circumstances of operation, it does not provide accurate results or information that one would normally expect. The alteration of data

in a database or in a sensor data stream or an instruction stream to a mechanical effector, for example, could have this effect.
- *Availability*. A secure system is available for normal use even in the face of an attack. A failure of availability may mean that the e-mail does not go through, or the computer simply freezes, or response time becomes intolerably long (possibly leading to catastrophe if a physical process is being controlled by the system).

These types of damage may be inflicted without the victim even being aware of the attack. For example, a system may be compromised by the obtaining of information ostensibly protected by that system (e.g., encrypted information may be intercepted and decrypted without the owner realizing it). Or, an attack may be used to support a selective denial of services (i.e., the allowing of access for most connections, but denying or corrupting some particular critical connections). If improper alteration occurs in small amounts in large, seldom-referenced databases, the fact of such corruption may never be discovered.

Note also the impact of any such damage on the user's psychology. A single database that is found to be corrupted, even when controls are in place to prevent such corruption, may throw into question the integrity of all of the databases in a system. A single data stream that is compromised by an eavesdropper may lead system operators and those who depend on the system to be concerned that all data streams are potentially compromised. In such cases, the potential harm from any of these incidents goes far beyond the actual corrupted database or compromised data stream, since enormous amounts of effort need to be made to ensure that other databases or data streams have not been corrupted or compromised. Those other databases may be perfectly good, but may not be considered reliable under such circumstances.

Denial of service, corruption, and compromise are not independent—for example, an attacker could render a system unavailable by compromising it. An attacker could seek to inflict such damage in several ways.

- An attack can be remote—one that comes in "through the wires," for example, as a virus or a Trojan horse program introduced via e-mail or other communication or as a denial-of-service attack over a network connection. As a general rule, remote attacks are much less expensive, much less risky, and much easier to conduct than are the second and third types listed below.
- Some IT element may be physically destroyed (e.g., a critical data center or communications link could be blown up) or compromised (e.g., IT hardware could be surreptitiously modified in the

distribution chain). Such attacks generally require close access (i.e., requiring physical proximity).

- A trusted insider may be compromised or may be untrustworthy in the first place (such a person, for instance, may sell passwords that permit outsiders to gain entry); such insiders may also be conduits for hostile software or hardware modifications that can be inserted at any point in the supply chain, from initial fabrication, to delivery to the end user. Compromising a trusted insider can be accomplished remotely or locally. Not all compromises are the result of insider malice; phishing attacks are one example of how a trusted insider can be tricked into providing sensitive information.

Of course, these three ways of causing damage are not mutually exclusive, and in practice they can be combined to produce even more destructive effects than any one way alone. Additionally, attackers can easily "pre-position" vulnerabilities to facilitate the timing of later attacks. This pre-positioning could be in the form of trap doors left behind from previous virus infections, unintentional design vulnerabilities,[1] or compromised code left by a compromised staff member or by a break-in to the developer's site.[2]

2.3 SYSTEMS AND NETWORKS AT RISK

What IT systems and networks are at risk? Key elements of information technology fall into three major categories: the Internet; embedded/real-time computing (e.g., avionics systems for aircraft control; air traffic control; Supervisory Control and Data Acquisition [SCADA] systems controlling the distribution of electricity, gas, and water; the switching systems of the conventional telecommunications infrastructure; bank teller machine networks; floodgates); and dedicated computing devices (e.g., desktop computers). Each of these elements plays a different role in national life, and each is subject to different kinds of attack.

---

[1]An example is the recent episode during which Sony's BMG Music Entertainment surreptitiously distributed software on audio compact discs (CDs) that was automatically installed on any computers that played the CDs. This software was intended to block the copying of the CD, but it had the unintentional side effect of opening security vulnerabilities that could be exploited by other malicious software such as worms or viruses. See Iain Thomson and Tom Sanders, "Virus Writers Exploit Sony DRM," vnunet.com, November 10, 2005; available at http://www.vnunet.com/vnunet/news/2145874/virus-writers-exploit-sony-drm.

[2]P.A. Karger and R.R. Schell, *Multics Security Evaluation: Vulnerability Analysis*, ESD-TR-74-193, Vol. II, June 1974, HQ Electronic Systems Division, Hanscom Air Force Base; available at http://csrc.nist.gov/publications/history/karg74.pdf.

2.3.1 Attacks on the Internet

The infrastructure of the Internet is a possible target, and given the Internet's public prominence and ubiquity, it may appeal to terrorists or criminals as an attractive target. The Internet can be attacked in two (not mutually exclusive) ways—physically or "through the wires."

Physical attacks might destroy one or a few parts of the Internet infrastructure. But the Internet is a densely connected network of networks that automatically routes around portions that become unavailable,[3] which means that a large number of important nodes would have to be destroyed simultaneously to bring it down for an extended period of time. Destruction of some key Internet nodes could result in reduced network capacity and slow traffic across the Internet, but the ease with which Internet communications can be rerouted would minimize the long-term damage.[4]

An attack that comes through the wires rather than via physical attack can have much higher leverage. The Internet crosses borders and its reach is extended throughout the globe. But the global Internet was not designed to operate in a hostile environment where information systems and networks can be attacked from inside. Indeed, it is an unfortunate result of Internet history that the protocols used by the Internet today are derived from the protocols that were developed in the early days of the Advanced Research Projects Agency Network, where there were only a few well-respected researchers using the infrastructure, and they were trusted to do no harm. Consequently, security considerations were not built in to the Internet, which means that all cybersecurity measures taken today to protect the Internet are add-on measures that do not remedy the underlying security deficiencies.

One type of attack is directed against Internet operations. Such attacks are often based on self-replicating programs (worms and viruses) that are transmitted from system to system, consuming prodigious amounts of router processing time and network channel bandwidth. In recent years, some of these worms and viruses have been transmitted without explicitly destructive payloads and yet have been able to disrupt key Internet backbone subnetworks for several days. Another kind of attack on Inter-

---

[3]National Research Council. 2001. *The Internet's Coming of Age.* National Academy Press, Washington, D.C. Note, however, that the amount of redundancy is limited primarily by economic factors.

[4]This comment applies largely to U.S. use of the Internet. It is entirely possible that other nations—whose traffic is often physically routed through one or two locations in the United States—would fare much worse in this scenario. See National Research Council. 2003. *The Internet Under Crisis Conditions: Learning from September 11.* The National Academies Press, Washington, D.C.

net operations seeks to corrupt the routing tables that determine how a packet should travel through the Internet. In both cases, the intent of the attack is to reduce the normally expected functionality of the Internet for some significant portion of its users—that is, it is a denial-of-service attack in intent, although not one necessarily based on flooding traffic.

An attacker might also target the Internet's Domain Name System (DNS), which translates domain names (e.g., "example.com") to specific Internet Protocol (IP) addresses (e.g., 123.231.0.67) denoting specific Internet nodes. A relatively small number of "root name servers" underpins the DNS. Although the DNS is designed to provide redundancy in case of accidental failure, it has some vulnerability to an attack that might target all name servers simultaneously. Although Internet operations would not halt instantly, an increasing number of sites would, over a period of time measured in hours to days, become inaccessible without root name servers to provide authoritative translation information. Physical replacement of damaged servers would be achievable in a matter of days, but changing the IP addresses of the root name servers and promulgating the new IP addresses throughout the Internet—a likely necessary step if the name servers are being attacked repetitively in an automated fashion—would be much more problematic.[5]

A through-the-wires attack is possible because of Internet-enabled interconnection. Thus, a hostile party using an Internet-connected computer 10,000 miles away can launch an attack against an Internet-connected computer in the United States just as easily as if the attacker were next door. Criminals and adversaries located all over the globe may nonetheless communicate and partly coordinate their activities through the network, without ever having to meet or cross national boundaries, especially in countries were they can operate without a serious fear of surveillance or aided by insider accomplices. By contrast, the planet is a world of sovereign nation-states, with different laws and regulations governing computer activities—a point that makes traditional responses of military retaliation or criminal prosecution much more problematic.

Dependence on the Internet for the performance of core business functions is increasingly a fact of life for a growing number of businesses and government agencies, as well as citizens in private life. It is obvious that a disruption to the Internet would be a major disruption to an electronic commerce company such as Amazon.com. But what is less obvious is that in the last couple of years, many large companies have come to depend on the Internet and other networks running Internet protocols

[5]National Research Council. 2005. *Signposts in Cyberspace: The Domain Name System and Internet Navigation*. The National Academies Press, Washington, D.C.

for internal voice and data communications and other key functions—and these trends will only accelerate in the future as pressures for cost reduction grow. A good example is the fact that Voice-Over-IP (VOIP) connections are increasingly replacing conventional telephony. Thus, it is only a matter of a relatively short time before today's independence of voice communications from the Internet no longer exists to any significant degree—and this will be true for business, government, and the general civilian population.

Finally, it is an unfortunate fact of life today that in many cases, when a system or a network connected to the Internet is under attack, the only feasible protective action is to disconnect from the Internet. Such an action may eliminate the attack (unless a rogue program has been successfully inserted into the targeted system or network before the connection is cut), but it also renders the attack maximally successful in a certain sense, since now for all practical purposes the disconnected system or network does not exist on the Internet.

2.3.2 Attacks on Embedded/Real-Time Computing and Control Systems

Embedded/real-time computing in specific systems could also be attacked. For example, many embedded computing systems could be corrupted over time or be deployed with hidden vulnerabilities.[6] Of particular concern could be avionics in airplanes, collision-avoidance systems in automobiles, and other transportation systems. Such attacks would require a significant insider presence in technically responsible positions in key sectors of the economy, likely but not necessarily over long periods of time. Another example is that sensors, which can be important elements of counterterrorism or anticrime precautions, could be the target of an attack or, more likely, precursor targets of a terrorist or criminal attack.

Another possible attack on embedded/real-time computing would be an attack on the systems controlling elements of the nation's critical infrastructure—for example, the electric power grid, the air traffic control system, the railroad infrastructure, water purification and delivery, or telephony. For example, attacks on the systems and networks that control and manage elements of the nation's transportation infrastructure could introduce chaos and disruption on a large scale that could drastically reduce the capability of transporting people and/or freight (including food and fuel).

[6]An inadvertent demonstration of this possibility was illustrated with the year-2000 (Y2K) problem that was overlooked in many embedded/real-time systems designed in the 1980s and earlier.

To illustrate, electric generation plants are controlled by a variety of IT-based SCADA systems. Attacks on these SCADA systems could obviously result in local disruptions in the supply of electrical power. But two other scenarios are more problematic. The electric power distribution grid, also controlled by IT-based SCADA systems and being necessary for electric power generated in one location to be useful in another location hundreds of miles away, is also a conduit through which a failure in one location can cascade to catastrophic proportions before the local failure can be dealt with.[7] (In this context, the distribution grid includes both the transmission lines that carry electricity and their control channels.) In addition, because SCADA systems are used to control physical elements of the grid, attacks on SCADA systems can also result in irreversible physical damage to unique equipment that may require many months to replace. Although causing such consequences requires inside or expert knowledge rather than just random attacks, the consequences are severe in terms of economic damage to the country.

Similar concerns arise with conventional telecommunications and the financial system (including the Federal Reserve banking system, which is a system for handling large-value financial transactions, and a second system for handling small-value retail transactions [including the Automated Clearing House, the credit-card system, and paper checks]). Although these systems are also largely independent of the public Internet, they are utterly dependent on computers, and thus they are subject to a variety of security vulnerabilities that do not depend on Internet connectivity.

2.3.3 Attacks on Dedicated Computing Facilities

In many of the same ways that embedded computing could be attacked, dedicated computers such as desktop computers could also be corrupted in ways that are hard to detect. One possible channel comes from the use of untrustworthy IT talent by software vendors.[8] The con-

---

[7]For example, the cause of the blackout of August 2003—lasting 4 days and affecting 50 million people in large portions of the midwestern and northeastern United States and Ontario, Canada—was traced to a sequence of cascading failures initiated by the shutdown of a single 345 kV transmission line. Admittedly, the grid was in a stressed state in northeastern Ohio when this occurred, but the grid often faces such stress during heat waves and storms. See U.S.-Canada Power System Outage Task Force, *Final Report on the August 14, 2003 Blackout in the United States and Canada: Causes and Recommendations*, April 2004; available at https://reports.energy.gov/BlackoutFinal-Web.pdf.

[8]Although security concerns are often raised about the offshoring of IT development, untrustworthy talent may be foreign or domestic in origin. Foreign IT workers—whether working in the United States (e.g., under an H1-B visa or a green card) or offshore on outsourced work—are generally not subject to thorough background investigations; therefore, an obvious route is available through which foreign terrorist organizations can gain insider

cern is that once working on the inside, these individuals would be able to introduce additional but unauthorized functionality into systems that are widely used. Under such circumstances, the target might not be just any desktop computer (e.g., any computer used in the offices around the country) but rather the desktop computers in particular sensitive offices or in critical operational software used in corporate or government computer centers (e.g., a major bank or the classified and unclassified systems of the Department of Defense).

Another possible channel for attacking dedicated computing facilities results from the connection of computers through the Internet; such connections provide a potential route through which terrorists or criminal organizations might attack computer systems that do provide important functionality for many sectors of the economy. Examples of widely used Internet-based vectors that, if compromised, would have a large-scale effect in a short time include appealing Web pages and certain shareware programs, such as those for sharing music files. An appealing Web page might attract many viewers in a short period of time, and viewers could be compromised simply by viewing the page. Shareware programs might contain viruses or other "malware." In principle, channels for distributing operating systems upgrades could be corrupted as well, but because of their critical nature, these channels are in general much more resistant to security compromise.

It is likely that Internet-connected computer systems that provide critical functionality to companies and organizations are better protected through firewalls and other security measures than is the average system on the Internet. Nevertheless, as press reports in recent years make clear, such measures do not guarantee that these large systems are immune to the hostile actions of outsiders.[9]

2.4 POTENTIAL CONSEQUENCES OF EXPLOITS

The possible consequences of successful exploits of cyber vulnerabilities cover a broad spectrum, from causing annoyance to an individual to causing catastrophic consequences for society. It is, of course, possible that the existence of a vulnerability—even if widespread—will not lead to

---

access. Reports of American citizens having been successfully recruited by foreign terrorist organizations add a degree of believability to the scenario of domestic IT talent's being used to compromise systems for terrorist purposes.

[9]For example, the Slammer worm attack reportedly resulted in a severe degradation of the Bank of America's automatic teller machine network in January 2003. See Aaron Davis, "Computer Worm Snarls Web: Electronic Attack Also Affects Phone Service, BOFA's ATM Network," *San Jose Mercury News*, January 26, 2003; available at http://www.bayarea.com/mld/mercurynews/5034748.htm+atm+slammer+virus&hl=en.

disaster (see Box 2.1), but making this possibility the basis for an effective cybersecurity response is clearly not a sensible thing to do today.

- If a virus attacks a home computer and erases all of the files on it, the consequences range from mere annoyance to emotional trauma (e.g., if irreplaceable pictures were stored). If the user had made a recent backup, the hassle factor involved in recovering the files may be only a matter of an hour or two—though removing the virus may be more involved than that. If the "home" computer involved belongs to a small business, critical business records could be lost.
- If a cybersecurity breach enables a hostile party to impersonate an individual, the result may be highly problematic for the individual. Victims of identity theft suffer for years under a cloud of uncertainty about their finances and credit records even as they try to clear their records.[10] No one dies because someone has impersonated him or her, although the compromise of personal information such as home addresses can certainly lead to serious harm.[11] If the identities of many individuals are compromised and identity theft results, serious economic losses to financial institutions may occur.[12]
- If consumers are not confident of online security, they will be more reluctant to engage in online activities and electronic commerce. For example, the Gartner Group estimated that $1.9 billion in e-commerce sales would not occur in 2006 because of consumer concerns about the security of the Internet.[13]
- If a company's trade secrets or confidential business plans are compromised, its viability as a business entity may be placed at risk (most likely if it is a small company) or its competitiveness in the

---

[10]The term "identity," as used in "identity theft," is somewhat misleading in this context. Some observers point out that in a deep philosophical sense, an individual's identity is inextricably associated with that individual. They thus suggest that a more precise term may be "credential theft" or "theft of personal information," either of which allows the possessor of the credential or personal information to impersonate the individual to whom that credential refers or with whom that personal information is associated. However, customary usage refers to "identity theft," and in the interests of clarity for the reader, this report continues that usage.

[11]In 1989, actress Rebecca Schaeffer was stalked and murdered by a fan who allegedly retrieved her name and address from the California motor vehicle department. Her death inspired the passage of the federal Driver's Privacy Protection Act of 1994, 18 U.S.C. 2721.

[12]Gartner Press Release, "Gartner Says Number of Phishing E-Mails Sent to U.S. Adults Nearly Doubles in Just Two Years," November 9, 2006; available at http://www.gartner.com/it/page.jsp?id=498245.

[13]Gartner Press Release, "Gartner Says Nearly $2 Billion Lost in E-Commerce Sales in 2006 Due to Security Concerns of U.S. Adults," November 27, 2006; available at http://www.gartner.com/it/page.jsp?id=498974.

marketplace reduced. Millions of dollars might be lost, but people rarely die from the theft of trade secrets.

- If the fly-by-wire controls of a modern passenger airplane are compromised, the pilot might lose control and be unable to land safely. Hundreds of lives aboard the plane may be placed at risk.
- If the computer systems controlling the operation of a railroad are compromised, extensive physical damage may be caused in train crashes.
- If electronic medical records are compromised by the unauthorized alteration of data, medical and pharmaceutical decisions that rely on the integrity of those data are placed at risk, and improper treatment may result. If these alterations are not detected, thousands of lives may be placed at risk.
- If the Department of Defense's logistics systems are compromised, large-scale military deployments could become quite difficult or impossible to conduct in a timely manner.
- If the communications systems used by emergency responders in a city are compromised so that communications capabilities are greatly diminished, police, fire, and medical personnel would be crippled in responding to emergencies.
- If the computerized controls for an industrial plant are compromised, an adversary might be able to cause a major industrial accident. For example, if a chemical plant near a major metropolitan area were involved, a Bhopal-like accident might occur.
- If the electric power grid is compromised and attackers are able to cause blackouts over a wide area, public safety may be endangered through collateral consequences, such as rioting and looting. Widespread blackouts that last for more than a few days—entirely possible if the appropriate attack strategy is used—go beyond mere nuisance and begin to threaten economic livelihoods and personal health and safety on a large scale.

Even worse, the latter scenarios cannot be considered in isolation. Indeed, if launched as part of a broader terrorist attack, they might be accompanied by physical "kinetic" attacks on vital national interests, either domestically or abroad. Cyberattacks conducted as part of a multipronged attack scenario that also includes physical attacks, rather than cyberattacks alone, could have the most catastrophic consequences.[14] For example, cyberattacks conducted as part of a larger scenario could result in greater opportunity to widen the damage of a physical attack (e.g., by providing false information that drives people toward, rather than away

---

[14]National Research Council. 2003. *Information Technology for Counterterrorism: Immediate Actions and Future Possibilities.* The National Academies Press, Washington, D.C.

BOX 2.1
Lack of Exploitation Does Not Indicate Nonvulnerability

Skeptics have often asked the following question: If information technology is so vulnerable, why hasn't there been a "digital Pearl Harbor" yet? The rhetorical logic is that since a digital Pearl Harbor hasn't happened yet, the nation's cybersecurity posture must not be as bad as is claimed. In the view of the Committee on Improving Cybersecurity Research in the United States, the premise could reasonably be questioned, but stipulating the premise for the moment, such rhetoric does raise an interesting question: How might an observer distinguish which of the following statements is true: "There are no serious vulnerabilities in today's information technology" or "There are serious but unseen vulnerabilities"?

A story from the early days of computer security is a good place to begin. An experimental time-sharing system at a major university, to which users could connect using dial-up modems, was subject to attack by hackers who would try to bring the system down. Using these dial-up connections, the hackers were successful from time to time. The system administrators responded to this threat by changing the system command structure. In particular, they added a command, called CRASH, that any user could invoke. The command was documented as follows: "If you use this command, you will crash the system. Everyone will lose their work, and be really mad at you. Please don't do this." This security innovation turned out to be successful, because the existence of the CRASH command took all the intellectual challenge out of crashing the system, and the system administrators—themselves of a hacker mind-set—understood the motivations of their adversaries very, very well.

Obviously, such an approach would not work today. But this story illustrates the point that nondisaster does not necessarily mean that no vulnerabilities are present. Given the existence of systemic vulnerabilities and the capability to exploit them, which essentially every cybersecurity expert recognizes, the question neces-

from, the point of attack); interfering with timely responses to an attack (e.g., by disrupting the communications systems of first responders); or increasing terror in the population through misinformation (e.g., by providing false information about the nature of a threat). And, of course, it is possible for information technology controlling the operation of physical systems to cause physical damage to those systems.

Note also that the nation's information technology might be either a target of an attacker or a weapon for an attacker to use. In the first case, an element of the IT infrastructure itself (e.g., the means for people to communicate or to engage in financial transactions) might be a target to be destroyed. In the second case, the target of an adversary might be another kind of critical infrastructure (e.g., the electric power grid), and the adversary could either launch or exacerbate the attack by exploiting the IT infrastructure.

sarily turns to one of motivation. Why might a hostile party with the capability to exploit a vulnerability not do so?

It is instructive to consider an analogous situation in the intelligence community. Sensitive and important information about Nation A may be gathered by (adversary) Nation B from a well-placed but covert source. Under what circumstances might Nation B refrain from using that information against Nation A? The answer depends on the value that Nation B places on protecting the source of the information versus the value that it places on using the information at that time. Protecting sources and methods is a task of paramount importance in the intelligence community, because many sources and methods of collecting intelligence would be difficult to replace if their existence became known—and thus, certain types of information are not used simply because their use would inevitably disclose the source.

Similarly, in the shadowy world of cyberthreat and cybersecurity, a hostile party with the capability to exploit a vulnerability would be well-advised to wait until the time was advantageous for it to launch an attack. In fact, one might well imagine that such a party would conduct exercises to probe weaknesses and lay the groundwork for an attack without actually taking overly hostile action. For example, such a party might use a virus that simply replicated itself but did not carry a payload that did any damage at all to prove to itself that such an attack was possible in principle.

The cybersecurity community knows of incidents (such as rapidly propagating viruses without destructive payloads and the active compromise of many network-connected computers that can be used to launch a variety of distributed attacks) that are consistent with the likely tactics of intelligent hostile parties. And it knows of intelligent parties whose intentions toward the United States are hostile. These factors do not constitute a logical proof of extensive cyberthreat, but they do underlie the committee's judgment that the vulnerabilities with which it is concerned are not merely theoretical.

Taken together, these scenarios suggest that a lack of security in cyberspace has three potential consequences. First is the threat of catastrophe—a cyberattack, especially in conjunction with a physical attack, could result in thousands of deaths and many billions of dollars of damage in a very short time. Second is frictional drag on important economic and security-related processes. Today, insecurities in cyberspace systems and networks allow adversaries (in particular, criminals) to extract enormous sums of money in fraud and extortion—and force businesses to expend additional resources to defend themselves against these threats. If cyberspace does not become more secure, tomorrow's businesses will continue to face similar pressures, and most likely on a greater scale. Third, concerns about insecurity may inhibit the use of information technologies in the future and thus lead to self-denial of the benefits they bring, benefits that will be needed for the national competitiveness of the United States as well as for national and homeland security.

2.5 THE MAGNITUDE OF THE THREAT AGAINST TODAY'S TECHNOLOGIES

The previous sections in this chapter describe what might be possible through a cyberattack. In the absence of quantitative threat information, these possibilities might well be regarded as speculative or isolated instances. But nearly all indicators of frequency, impact, scope, and cost of cybersecurity incidents show a continuously worsening picture. This is true whether one considers the losses due to IT-based fraud and theft, identity theft and attacks on personal information, incidence of viruses and malicious code, number of compromised systems, or other types of impact. The discussion below reviews some of the publicly available evidence about the impacts of cyberattacks.

In February 2005, the President's Information Technology Advisory Committee (PITAC) released a report entitled *Cybersecurity: A Crisis of Prioritization* containing several data points indicating the size and scope of the threat, drawn from various sources.[15] Reexamining those data points and a number of others 2 years later offers a point of direct comparison for measuring recent trends in cybersecurity:

- The PITAC report noted that in the Deloitte 2004 *Global Security Survey*, 83 percent of financial service organizations experienced compromised systems in 2004. This compares with 28 percent in 2005 and 82 percent in 2006. In 2003, the figure was 39 percent.[16]
- The PITAC report noted that the *9th Annual Computer Virus Prevalence Survey 2003* of ICSA Labs (formerly known as the International Computer Security Association) reports that the monthly percentage of personal computers infected by a virus grew from 1 percent in 1996 to over 10 percent in 2003. The *10th Annual Computer Virus Prevalence Survey 2004* reports *a continued increase of 0.8 percent*, approaching 12 percent.[17]

---

[15]President's Information Technology Advisory Committee. February 2005. *Cyber Security: A Crisis of Prioritization*, National Coordination Office for Information Technology Research and Development, Washington, D.C.; available at www.nitrd.gov/pitac/reports/20050301_cybersecurity/cybersecurity.pdf.

[16]Deloitte, *Global Security Survey*, annual reports on the global financial services industry, 2002 to 2006. The 2006 report explained the huge differences as resulting from changes in the respondent pool, specifically their size and geographic distribution; see Deloitte, 2006, *2006 Global Security Survey*, Deloitte Touche Tohmatsu, p. 26; available at http://www.deloitte.com/dtt/cda/doc/content/us_fsi_150606globalsecuritysurvey(1).pdf.

[17]ICSA Labs, *9th Annual Computer Virus Prevalence Survey 2003* (2004); and ICSA Labs, *10th Annual Computer Virus Prevalence Survey 2004* (2005); see http://www.icsalabs.com/icsa/

- The PITAC report noted that the January to June 2004 *Symantec Internet Security Threat Report* showed that the rate of computers incorporated into bot armies rose from under 2,000 per day to over 30,000. Symantec's January to June 2006 report shows *a rising rate* of compromised computers, from over 40,000 to over 60,000, with an average over the period of 57,717.[18]
- The 2003 ICSA Labs report noted that 92 of 300 respondents (31 percent) reported virus disasters. The 2004 ICSA Labs report shows an *increase of 6 percent* over 2003, from 92 of 300 to 112 of 300 respondents.[19]
- The PITAC report noted that the ICSA Labs surveys show an upward trend for each of the past 9 years for cost, downtime, and days to recover from significant virus events. This trend continued in 2004, with a *25 percent increase* in recovery time over the 2003 figure and a significant jump in cost related to recovery.
- New vulnerabilities reported to the Computer Emergency Response Team Coordination Center (CERT/CC) *more than doubled* again from the 3,780 recorded in 2004 to 8,064 recorded in 2006.[20]
- The Symantec report noted that in the first half of 2004, the average time between the public disclosure of a vulnerability and the release of an associated exploit was 5.8 days. The report showed that in the first half of 2006, an average exploit time was 3 days, continuing the trend of quicker exploitation and cutting exploit time by almost half.[21]

Since the release of the PITAC cybersecurity report, a number of other reports have highlighted the increasing sophistication of attacks. Overall, these reports suggest that less-sophisticated attacks are now being

---

icsahome.php. The 2003 rate is 108/1,000, or 10.8 percent. The 2004 rate is 116/1,000, or 11.6 percent.

[18]Symantec Corporation, *Symantec Internet Security Threat Report: Trends for January 06–June 06*, Vol. X, September 2006. The report warns that new methodologies were implemented to obtain and record attack data, including bot activity. It says that as a consequence of these changes "any comparison with the attack data gathered in previous periods would be invalid." See p. 40.

[19]The ICSA Labs report defines a virus disaster as an incident in which 25 or more personal computers or servers are infected at the same time with the same virus, or an incident causing significant damage or monetary loss to the organization. See ICSA Labs, *10th Annual Computer Virus Prevalence Survey 2004* (2005), p. 1.

[20]Computer Emergency Response Team Coordination Center, CERT Statistics; available at http://www.cert.org/stats/.

[21]The Symantec report for January-June 2006 (Vol. X) also notes that vendors are dramatically reducing the patch development and release time, so that the overall window of exposure fell from 60 days in January 2006 to 28 days in June 2006. See Symantec Corporation, *Symantec Internet Security Threat Report: Trends for January 06–June 06*, Vol. X, September 2006, pp. 58-59.

thwarted by the increased use of virus protection software, spyware, and spam filters and other security products, but the attacks that are succeeding have greater impact—and are more difficult to protect against. For example, the Deloitte *2006 Global Security Survey* noted the "exponential increase in the sophistication of threats and their potential impact across an organization."[22] The *2006 E-Crime Watch Survey* found that 55 percent of all organizations in the survey had at least one incident of an insider attack, up from 39 percent the previous year.[23] The *Symantec Internet Security Threat Report*, Volume X, published in September 2006, concludes that "the threat environment continues to be populated by lower-profile, targeted attacks as cyber criminals identify new ways to steal information or provide remote access to user systems. The attacks propagate at a slower rate in order to avoid detection and increase the likelihood of successful compromise before security measures can be put in place."[24]

The documentation of the nature of cybersecurity incidents provided in these reports is fragmented and incomplete. For example, the Department of Justice notes that there is "currently [in February 2006] no national baseline measure . . . on the extent of cybercrime."[25] Yet, the available data are sufficient to make assertions about the seriousness of the threat that are more than just statements to be taken on faith. (Box 2.2 lists some of more significant sources.) Some efforts focus on counting the frequency, nature, and trends of attacks. Others focus on measuring the impacts and costs of incidents by surveying organizations and individuals. Taken together, they paint a clear picture of growing impacts, including lost production, operational disruptions, and direct economic costs from fraud and lost business, measured on the scale of several billions of dollars annually.[26] The impact is already very large and is growing, and the threat is expanding.

It is also likely that the reported level of security incidents understates

---

[22]Deloitte, *2006 Global Security Survey* (2006), p. 13.

[23]CSO magazine, U.S. Secret Service, CERT Coordination Center, Microsoft Corp., *2006 E-Crime Watch Survey;* available at http://www2.csoonline.com/info/release.html?CID=24531.

[24]Symantec Corporation, *Symantec Internet Security Threat Report: Trends for January 06–June 06*, Vol. X, September 2006, p. 4.

[25]Department of Justice, Bureau of Justice Statistics, *National Computer Security Survey Announced*, February 9, 2006; available at http://www.ojp.usdoj.gov/bjs/pub/press/ncsspr.htm. The survey is also supported by a number of trade associations and industry groups.

[26]For example, the 2006 Javelin Strategy and Research report on identity fraud estimated the total cost of ID fraud in 2004 at $56.6 billion. Approximately 9 percent of these cases were attributable to phishing, hacking, computer viruses, or spyware on home computers; another 6 percent resulted from data breaches at businesses holding personal information. Assuming that the average cost of an incident of computer-based ID fraud is comparable with the cost of other kinds of ID fraud (an assumption that seems roughly consistent with other data presented in the report), these cases account for $8 billion to $9 billion in losses.

the actual level. For example, the *2006 CSI/FBI Computer Crime and Security Survey* found that the negative publicity from reporting incidents to law enforcement is a major concern of many organizations, noting that only 25 percent of firms report incidents to authorities.[27]

Some incidents would routinely go unreported for benign reasons (e.g., they were not severe enough). But there is also a systematic bias against reporting, because targets of cyberattacks such as government agencies and large corporations are often concerned that widespread disclosure of their victimization would shake public confidence in their operations and integrity. Whether they are concerned about embarrassment, loss of confidence, giving competitors an advertising advantage over them, or drops in market share, agencies and corporations have few incentives to report these events in a public forum. In some cases, successful cyberattacks may never be noticed at all (as might be the case if valuable secrets were stolen).

How significant is the underreporting? This magnitude is hard to estimate, but one widely cited article from 2002 claims that "only about 10% of all cybercrimes committed are actually reported and fewer than 2% result in a conviction." The article offers two reasons for this: institutions feel that they have more to lose by reporting computer security breaches, and they assume that law enforcement will provide little or no assistance.[28]

2.6 AN OMINOUS FUTURE

The committee believes that security will be a continuing issue because there will always be incentives to compromise the security of deployed systems, and that these incentives will only increase over time as organizations and individuals increasingly depend on information technology. Personal gain, organized crime, terrorism, and national interests are superseding personal fame and curiosity as incentives for cyberattacks, and thus the threat picture is coming to include increasingly sophisticated actors who possess significant resources to execute attacks. Moreover, threats evolve (both on their own and as defenses against them are discovered), and new vulnerabilities often emerge as innovation changes underlying system architectures, implementation, or basic assumptions.

See Javelin Strategy and Research, *Identity Fraud Survey Report, Consumer Version,* January 2006; available at www.javelinstrategy.com/products/AD35BA/27/delivery.pdf.

[27]Lawrence A. Gordon, Martin P. Loeb, William Lucyshyn, and Robert Richardson, *2006 CSI/FBI Computer Crime and Security Survey*, Computer Security Institute, 2006; available at http://i.cmpnet.com/gocsi/db_area/pdfs/fbi/FBI2006.pdf.

[28]Chris Hale, "Cybercrime: Facts and Figures Concerning the Global Dilemma," *Crime and Justice International*, 18(65): 5-6, 24-26, September 2002.

BOX 2.2
Major Sources of Data Characterizing the Cyberthreat

There are many sources of data characterizing the nature of the cybersecurity threat. The sources of data and analysis described in this box are (or are planned to be) updated on an ongoing (e.g., annual) basis. (In a few instances reports have been issued consistently for more than 10 years.) Sponsoring organizations include academic institutions, federal agencies, and a range of private-sector companies working either alone or in collaboration.

The first two sources listed here focus on the frequency of incidents and the type of attacks observable through the monitoring of Internet traffic. The others are surveys measuring the scope, impact, and cost of incidents to organizations and firms, although the purpose, scope, and methods of these surveys vary considerably.

- *CERT/CC Statistics:* The Computer Emergency Response Team Coordination Center (CERT/CC) has collected statistics on vulnerabilities and incidents since 1988. CERT is a center of Internet security expertise located at the Software Engineering Institute, a federally funded research and development center operated by Carnegie Mellon University. In addition to maintaining incident and vulnerability statistics, CERT/CC works with US-CERT to coordinate defense against and response to cyberattacks. Further information is available at http://www.cert.org/stats/cert_stats.html.
- *Symantec Internet Security Threat Report:* First published in January 2002 by Riptech, Inc. (acquired by Symantec in July 2002), this report has been published twice annually since 2002, for a total of 10 reports. Using network data collected by sensors monitoring network activity globally, these reports summarize and analyze network attack trends, vulnerability trends, and malicious code trends. Metrics used to measure the "threat landscape" have continued to evolve along with the types of attacks. All of the reports are available at http://www.symantec.com/enterprise/threatreport/index.jsp.
- *E-Crime Watch Survey:* This annual survey, started in 2004, is conducted by *CSO* (Chief Security Officer) magazine in cooperation with the U.S. Secret Service's Electronic Crimes Task Force, CERT/CC, and Microsoft Corporation. The purpose of the survey is to identify electronic-crime trends and techniques and to gather data on their impact. The 2006 report is available at http://www.cert.org/archive/pdf/ecrimesurvey06.pdf.
- *FBI Computer Crime Survey:* Conducted in 2005, the purpose of this survey is to "gain an accurate understanding of what computer security incidents are being experienced by the full spectrum of sizes and types of organizations within the United States."[1]

- *Internet Fraud Crime Report:* Prepared by the National White Collar Crime Center and the Federal Bureau of Investigation (FBI), the 2005 edition is the fifth annual compilation of "information on complaints received and referred by the Internet Crime Complaint Center (IC3) to law enforcement or regulatory agencies for appropriate action."[2] The report outlines many of the current trends and patterns in Internet crime; it is available at http://www.ic3.gov/media/annualreport/2005_IC3Report.pdf.
- *CSI/FBI Computer Crime and Security Survey:* Conducted by the Computer Security Institute (CSI) with the participation of the San Francisco, California, FBI Computer Intrusion Squad, this survey is now in its 11th year, having produced a report every year since 1996. Its primary focus is on the economic impacts of incidents, the economic decisions that organizations make regarding computer security, and how they manage risk associated with security breaches. See http://www.gocsi.com/.
- *Deloitte's Global Security Survey:* Published annually since 2003, this survey reports on the outcome of focused discussions with information technology executives from the global financial services institutions designed to identify perceived levels of risks, the types of risks that are the focus of concern, the resources being used to mitigate these risks, the security technologies being employed, and the value gained from the security investments made. The 2006 report is available at http://www.deloitte.com/dtt/cda/doc/content/Deloitte%202006%20Global%20Security%20Survey(2).pdf.
- *ICSA (formerly known as the International Computer Security Association) Labs Annual Computer Virus Prevalence Survey:* Conducted every year from 1996 through 2004, the objectives of this survey are "to examine the prevalence of computer viruses in mid- and large-sized organizations; describe the computer virus problem in computer networks, including desktop computers; application and file servers; and perimeter devices such as firewalls, gateways, and proxy servers; and observe trends in computer virus growth, infection methodologies, and attack vectors."[3] The 10th annual report, published in 2005, is available at http://www.icsalabs.com/icsa/docs/html/library/whitepapers/VPS2004.pdf.

---

[1]Federal Bureau of Investigation, *2005 FBI Computer Crime Survey*, Washington, D.C., p. 1. Key findings of this report may be found at http://www.fbi.gov/page2/jan06/computer_crime_survey011806.htm; the entire report is available at http://www.digitalriver.com/v2.0-img/operations/naievigi/site/media/pdf/FBIccs2005.pdf.

[2]National White Collar Crime Center, Federal Bureau of Investigation, The Internet Crime Complaint Center 2005 Internet Crime Report: January 1, 2005–December 31, 2005, Washington, D.C., p. 3.

[3]ICSA Labs, *10th Annual Computer Virus Prevalence Survey 2004*, 2005, p. 3.

2.6.1 The Evolution of the Threat

In 1992, the World Wide Web had not yet been invented. Cybersecurity efforts were focused primarily on enhancing the security of individual, un-networked systems. Even then, security had been raised as an important issue (as discussed in Section 10.1). But 15 years later, information technology has advanced dramatically in almost all fields—except for cybersecurity. Consider that in the past 15 years:

- The increasingly ubiquitous interconnection of the world's computers provides many avenues for cyberattackers to exploit, and these will only proliferate.
- Increasing standardization and homogeneity of communications protocols, programming interfaces, operating systems, computing hardware, and routers allow for a single developed attack to be used against vast numbers of systems.
- Distinctions between data and program have been eroded. "Active content" is now quite common in programming paradigms; pictures, word processing files, and spreadsheets can and often do contain programs embedded within them in order to increase their functionality. (For example, a spreadsheet can contain macros that are integral to the use of that spreadsheet.) The consequence is that the computing environment is no longer under the complete control of the user of these files.
- As systems evolve they tend to become more complex. The greater the complexity, the more difficult it is to verify the operation of the system before it is put into use, and the more difficult it may be to detect that the system's defenses have been penetrated. Dramatic increases in complexity make the jobs of both attacker and defender more difficult, but the increase in difficulty affects the defender much more than the attacker.
- User demands for backward compatibility often mean that older and less secure components cannot be replaced with newer components that reduce or mitigate the old vulnerabilities. Furthermore, the complexities of the ensuing extra software to accommodate compatibility tend to introduce further flaws.
- Use of Web-based services (see Section 8.4.3) proliferates the opportunities for adversaries to attack important service providers. Web services may depend on other Web services, so the ability to predict, or even comprehend, the impact of attacks may be very low.
- The great difficulties of associating individuals with specific destructive or hostile actions, coupled with an uncertain and ambiguous legal and policy framework for dealing with such incidents (especially when they involve communications and information passed across national boundaries), make it highly unlikely that

adversaries will suffer significant negative consequences for their actions, thus increasing the likelihood that others will take actions with similar intent.

Widespread networking of computers was a signal event in the evolution of information technology, with significant implications for cybersecurity. As one example, consider the problem of botnets. A botnet (also known as a zombie-net) is a collection of computers on a network that are under the remote control of an unauthorized party, often obtained through the use of a worm or a Trojan horse that exploits some system vulnerability. (Box 2.3 describes botnets in greater detail.)

Botnets are one of the most pernicious Internet security problems today (that is, in mid-2007). For example, Symantec reported that in the first 6 months of 2006, it identified 6,337 command-and-control servers (i.e., botnet controllers) and 4,696,903 individual computers that had been compromised ("zombied") at some point during that time period.[29] Some reports indicate that approximately 250,000 new compromises occur daily, although this figure includes a large number of compromises occurring on previously compromised systems (i.e., a vulnerable computer is likely compromised by multiple botnets).[30] David Dagon of the Georgia Institute of Technology has reported that the total number of compromised computers is in the tens or hundreds of millions,[31] and the Messaging Anti-Abuse Working Group estimated that in 2006, about 7 percent of all Internet-connected computers (some 47 million) had been compromised.[32] The size of individual botnets has grown as well, with some reports suggesting the existence of botnets with as many as hundreds of thousands or even 1.5 million zombies.[33]

A similarly profound shift is likely as computing becomes increas-

---

[29]Symantec Corporation, *Symantec Internet Security Threat Report: Trends for January 06–June 06*, Vol. X, September 2006; available at http://www.symantec.com/specprog/threatreport/ent-whitepaper_symantec_internet_security_threat_report_x_09_2006.en-us.pdf.

[30]Rick Wesson, "Abuse and the Global Infection Rate," presentation at Defcon, August 14, 2006; more information is available at http://www.defcon.org/html/defcon-14/dc-14-speakers.html.

[31]David Dagon, "The Network Is the Infection," available at http://www.caida.org/projects/oarc/200507/slides/oarc0507-Dagon.pdf.

[32]Byron Acohido and Jon Swartz, "Malicious-Software Spreaders Get Sneakier, More Prevalent," *USA Today*, April 23, 2006; available at http://www.usatoday.com/tech/news/computersecurity/infotheft/2006-04-23-bot-herders_x.htm.

[33]In late 2005, a man was indicted by a federal grand jury on charges that he had compromised nearly 400,000 Windows computers (see Robert Lemos, "Suspected Bot Master Busted," *SecurityFocus*, November 3, 2005; available at http://www.securityfocus.com/news/11353). Also in late 2005, Dutch prosecutors alleged that three suspects had compromised 1.5 million computers as part of a worldwide botnet (see Toby Sterling, "Dutch Say Suspects Hacked 1.5M Computers," Associated Press newswire, October 20, 2005; available at http://www.usatoday.com/tech/news/computersecurity/2005-10-20-dutch-hack_x.htm).

BOX 2.3
On Botnets

Botnets (also known as *zombie-nets*) are collections of compromised computers that are remotely controlled by a malevolent party. A *compromised computer* is connected to the Internet, usually with an "always-on" broadband connection, and is running software introduced by the malevolent party. Malevolent software can be introduced through a number of channels; they include clicking on a link that takes the user to a certain Web page, downloading an attachment that executes a program, forcing entry into a computer through an unprotected port (e.g., one typically used for file sharing across the Internet), and so on. Using up-to-date security software such as antivirus programs and firewalls helps to reduce the threat of such "malware," but today most personal computers—even protected ones—are at least somewhat vulnerable to such threats.

An individual compromised computer (a *zombie* or a *bot*) can be used for many purposes, but the threat from botnets arises from the sheer number of computers that a single malevolent party can control—often tens of thousands and as many as a million. (Note also that an individual unprotected computer may be part of multiple botnets as the result of multiple compromises.) When the zombied computers are connected to the Internet through broadband connections, the aggregate bandwidth of the botnets is enormous (e.g., a small botnet of 1,000 zombies times a 300 kilobit Digital Subscriber Line connection is 300 megabits per second). A further property of botnets is that they can be controlled remotely by an adversary, which means that the apparent perpetrator of a hostile act is a zombie computer—making it difficult to trace a hostile act to its initiator. Indeed, an adversary may be located in a nation other than the home country of the zombies.

Typically, an adversary builds a botnet by finding a few machines to compromise. The first hostile action that these initial zombies take is to find other machines to compromise—a task that can be undertaken in an automatic manner. But botnets are capable of undertaking a variety of other actions that have significant impact on the botnet operator's target(s). For example, botnets can be used to conduct the following actions:

- *Distributed denial-of-service attacks.* A denial-of-service attack on a target renders the target's computer resources unavailable to service legitimate requests by requesting service itself and blocking others from using those resources. But if these requests for service come from a single source, it is easy to simply drop all service requests from that source. However, a distributed denial-of-service attack can flood the target with multiple requests from many different machines, each of which might, in principle, be a legitimate requester of service.
- *Spam attacks.* Botnets can be used to send enormous amounts of spam e-mail. Since spam is illegal in many venues and is regarded as antisocial by most, it is in a spammer's interest to hide his or her identity. Some botnets also search for e-mail addresses in many different locations.
- *Traffic-sniffing attacks and key-logging.* A zombie can examine clear-text data passing by or through it. Such data might be sensitive information such as usernames and passwords, and it might be contained in data packets or in various input channels, such as the keyboard channel.

- *Click fraud.* A great deal of advertising revenue comes from individuals clicking on ads. A botnet can easily be used to generate a large volume of clicks on ads that do not correspond to any individual's legitimate interest in those ads. Further, because each zombie appears to be legitimate, it is difficult for the party being defrauded to know that a botnet is being used to perpetrate click fraud.
- *Probes.* It is widely reported that only a few minutes elapse between the instant that a computer attaches to the Internet and the time that it is probed for vulnerabilities and possibly compromised itself. Without botnets in operation, finding open and vulnerable machines would be a much more difficult process.
- *Acting as hosts for information exfiltration.* Botnets could be used as *recipients* of clandestinely gathered information—a kind of "dead drop" for Trojan horses planted to gather information secretly that mask the ultimate destination of such information.

Botnets would be (and are) a logical vehicle of choice for many malevolent parties. Botnets can be dormant for a long time before being activated. Once activated, the botnet owner or operator can stay in the background, unidentified and far away from any action, while the individual bots—mostly belonging to innocent parties—are the ones that are visible to the party under attack. And botnets are highly flexible, capable of being upgraded on the fly just like any other piece of software.

Thus, it is not surprising to see that botnets can be used as the basis of an underground service to unethical end users. A botnet owner could rent the botnet to Party A to send spam, Party B to extort money from an online business, and Party C to sniff traffic and collect online identification credentials. A typical price might be "$0.50 per zombie per hour of use." Today, it is known that botnets are used for criminal purposes such as cyber-extortion, but the extent to which they are used by terrorists or adversary nations is unknown.

SOURCE: Adapted in part from Honeynet Project and Research Alliance, "Know Your Enemy: Tracking Botnets," March 13, 2005; available at http://www.honeynet.org.

ingly pervasive and embedded in all manners of devices. These embedded computers are themselves likely to be in communication with one another when they are in range (with all of the security issues that such communication implies). They are also likely to be much larger in number: an ordinary room at home could conceivably contain tens or hundreds of such devices. These developments—pervasive computing and adaptive (dynamic) ubiquitous networked systems—will call for the development of new security models and architectures.

If continued expansion of the use and benefits of IT is to be realized, the information technology systems and networks must be adequately protected. Otherwise, individuals and organizations throughout society will deem it unacceptably risky to increase their reliance on insecure technologies. Even today, cybersecurity issues have not been addressed adequately, and individuals and organizations throughout society find themselves under an increasingly dark and threatening cloud. In short, cybersecurity is increasingly important, both as a pillar of today's critical computing and communications applications and as an enabler of future advances in computing and information technology.

2.6.2 The Broad Range of Capabilities and Goals of Cyberattackers

The committee believes that a very broad spectrum of actors, ranging from lone hackers at one extreme to major nation-states at the other, pose security risks to the nation's information technology infrastructure. Organized crime (e.g., drug cartels) and transnational terrorists (and terrorist organizations, some of them state-sponsored) occupy a region between these two extremes, but they are closer to the nation-state than to the lone hacker.[34]

Attackers have a range of motivations. Some are motivated by curiosity. Some are motivated by the desire to penetrate or vandalize for the thrill of it, others by the desire to steal or profit from their actions. And still others are motivated by ideological or nationalistic reasons.

Today, the most salient cybersecurity threat emanates from hackers and criminals, although there is growing realization that organized crime is seeing increasing value in exploiting and targeting cyberspace. Thus, most cybersecurity efforts taken across the nation in all sectors—both in research and in deployment—are oriented toward defending against these low- and mid-level threats.

Much more work remains to be done to address even these lower-level threats. The state of security practice today is such that even casual attackers can find many vulnerabilities to exploit. The deployment of even quite unsophisticated cybersecurity measures can make a difference against casual attackers. Thus, the cybersecurity posture of the nation could be strengthened if individuals and organizations collectively adopted "best practices" that are known to improve cybersecurity.

The research and development (R&D) activities addressed in much of this report will ultimately lead to significant progress against these low- to mid-level threats. However, against the high-end attacker, efforts oriented

[34]In certain ways, it could be argued that organized crime constitutes a more potent threat than many nation-states do. One reason is that the resources available to organized crime syndicates for supporting cyberthreat activities may exceed those available to a nation-state. A second reason is that the operations of nation-states are often constrained within a bureaucratic context that may be more cumbersome than in a syndicate.

toward countering the casual attacker or even the common cybercriminal amount to little more than speed bumps. The reason is that the high-end cyberthreat, as described below, is qualitatively different from other threats.

First and foremost, high-end actors usually have enormous resources. Major nation-states, for example, are financed by national treasuries; they can exploit the talents of some of the smartest and most motivated individuals in their national populations; they often have the luxury of time to plan and execute attacks; and they can draw on all of the other resources available to the national government, such as national intelligence, military, and law enforcement services. Organized crime syndicates, such as drug cartels, may operate hand in hand with some governments; when operating without government cooperation, their human and financial resources may not be at the level available to governments, but they are nevertheless quite formidable. State-sponsored terrorist groups by definition obtain significant resources from their state sponsors.

As a result, the high-end cyberattacker can be relatively profligate in executing its attack and in particular can target vulnerabilities at any point in the IT supply chain from hardware fabrication to user actions (Box 2.4). In particular, the resources of the high-end cyberattacker facilitate attacks that require physical proximity. For example, a major nation-state threat raises questions about the nations in which it is safe to design software or to manufacture chips.[35]

The availability of such resources widens the possible target set of high-end attackers. Low- and mid-level attackers often benefit from the ability to gain a small profit from each of many targets. Spammers and bot harvesters are the best examples of this phenomenon—an individual user or computer is vulnerable in some way to a spammer or a bot harvester, but the spammer or bot harvester profits because many such users or computers are present on the Internet. However, because of the resources available to them, high-end attackers may also be able to target a specific computer or user whose individual compromise would have enormous value ("going after the crown jewels"). In the former case, an attacker confronted with an adequately defended system simply moves on to another system that is not so well defended. In the latter case, the attacker has the resources to escalate the attack to a very high degree—perhaps overwhelmingly so.

It is also the case that the resources available to an adversary—especially high-end adversaries—are not static. This means that for a sufficiently valuable target, a high-end adversary may well be able to deploy

[35]Defense Science Board. 2005. *High Performance Microchip Supply*, Office of the Under Secretary of Defense for Acquisition, Technology, and Logistics, Washington, D.C., February; available at http://www.acq.osd.mil/dsb/reports/2005-02-HPMS_Report_Final.pdf.

BOX 2.4
Possible Points of Vulnerability in Information Technology Systems and Networks

An information technology system or network has many places where an operationally exploitable vulnerability can be found; in principle, a completely justifiable trust in the system can be found only in environments that are completely under the control of the party who cares most about the security of the system. As discussed here, the environment consists of many things—all of which must be under the interested party's control.

The software is the most obvious set of vulnerabilities. In a running operating system or application, exploitable vulnerabilities may be present as the result of faulty program design or implementation, and viruses or worms may be introduced when the system or network comes in electronic contact with a hostile source. But there are more subtle paths by which vulnerabilities can be introduced as well. For example, compilers are used to generate object code from source code. The compiler itself must be secure, for it could introduce object code that subversively and subtly modifies the functionality represented in the source code. A particular sequence of instructions could exploit an obscure and poorly known characteristic of hardware functioning, which means that programmers well versed in minute behavioral details of the machine on which the code will be running could introduce functionality that would likely go undetected in any review of the code.

The hardware constitutes another set of vulnerabilities, although less attention is usually paid to hardware in this regard. Hardware includes microprocessors, microcontrollers, firmware, circuit boards, power supplies, peripherals such as printers or scanners, storage devices, and communications equipment such as network cards. On the one hand, hardware is physical, so tampering with these components requires physical access at some point in the hardware's life cycle, which may be difficult to obtain. On the other hand, hardware is difficult to inspect, so hardware compromises are hard to detect. Consider, for example, that graphics display cards often have onboard processors and memory that can support an execution stream entirely separate from that running on a system's "main" processor. Also, peripheral devices, often with their own microprocessor controllers and programs, can engage in bidirectional communications with their hosts, providing a possible vector for outside influence. And, of course, many systems rely on a field-upgradable read-only memory (ROM) chip to support a boot sequence—and corrupted or compromised ROMs could prove harmful in many situations.

The communications channels between the system or network and the "outside" world present another set of vulnerabilities. In general, a system that does not interact with anyone is secure, but it is also largely useless. Thus, communications of some sort must be established, and those channels can be compromised—for example, by spoofing (an adversary pretends to be the "authorized" system), by jamming (an adversary denies access to anyone else), or by eavesdropping (an adversary obtains information intended to be confidential).

Operators and users present a particularly challenging set of vulnerabilities. Both can be compromised through blackmail or extortion. Or, untrustworthy operators and users can be planted as spies. But users can also be tricked into actions that compromise security. For example, in one recent exploit, a red team used inexpensive universal serial bus (USB) flash drives to penetrate an organization's security. The red team scattered USB drives in parking lots, smoking areas, and other areas of high traffic. In addition to some innocuous images, each drive was preprogrammed with software that would collect passwords, log-ins, and machine-specific information from the user's computer, and then e-mail the findings to the red team. Because many systems support an "auto-run" feature for insertable media (i.e., when the medium is inserted, the system automatically runs a program named "autorun.exe" on the medium) and the feature is often turned on, the red team was notified as soon as the drive was inserted. The result: 75 percent of the USB drives distributed were inserted into a computer.

Given the holistic nature of security, it is also worth noting that vulnerabilities can be introduced at every point in the supply chain: that is, systems (and their components) can be attacked in design, development, testing, production, distribution, installation, configuration, maintenance, and operation. On the way to a customer, a set of CD-ROMs may be intercepted and a different set introduced in its place; extra functionality might be introduced during chip fabrication or motherboard assembly; a default security configuration might be left in an insecure state—and the list goes on.

Given the dependence of security on all of these elements in the supply chain, it is not unreasonable to think of security as an emergent property of a system, as its architecture is implemented, its code instantiated, and as the system itself is embedded in a human and an organizational context. In practice, this means that the actual vulnerabilities that a system must resist are specific to that particular system embedded in its particular context. This fact should not discourage the development of generic building blocks for security that might be assembled in a system-specific way, but it does mean that an adversary could attack many possible targets in its quest to compromise a system or a network.

SOURCES:

Information on compilers based on Ken Thompson, "Reflections on Trusting Trust," *Communications of the ACM,* 27(8): 761-763, August 1984. See also P.A. Karger and R.R. Schell, "Thirty Years Later: Lessons from the Multics Security Evaluation," pp. 119-126 in *Proceedings of the 18th Annual Computer Security Applications Conference*, December 9-13, 2002, Las Vegas, Nev.: IEEE Computer Society. Available at http://www.acsa-admin.org/2002/papers/classic-multics.pdf.

Information on USB drive: See Steve Stasiukonis, "Social Engineering, the USB Way," *Dark Reading*, June 7, 2006. Available at http://www.darkreading.com/document.asp?doc_id=95556&WT.svl=column1_1.

Information on chip fabrication based on Defense Science Board, *High Performance Microchip Supply,* Department of Defense, February 2005; available at http://www.acq.osd.mil/dsb/reports/2005-02-HPMS_Report_Final.pdf.

additional resources in its continuing attack if its initial attacks fail. In other words, capabilities that are infeasible for an adversary today may become feasible tomorrow. This point suggests that systems in actual deployment must continually evolve and upgrade their security.

A corollary issue is the value of risk management in such an environment. If indeed an adversary has the resources to increase the sophistication of its attack and the motivation to keep trying even after many initial attempts fail, it raises the question of whether anything less than perfect security will suffice. This question in turn raises understandable doubts about the philosophy of managing cybersecurity risks that is increasingly prevalent in the commercial world. Yet, doing nothing until perfect security can be deployed is surely a recipe for inaction that leaves one vulnerable to many lower-level threats.

High-end cyberattackers—and especially major nation-state adversaries—are also likely to have the resources that allow them to obtain detailed information about the target system, such as knowledge gained by having access to the source code of the software running on the target or the schematics of the target device or through reverse-engineering. Success in obtaining such information is not guaranteed, of course, but the likelihood of success is clearly an increasing function of the availability of resources. For instance, a country may obtain source code and schematics of a certain vendor's product because it can require that the vendor make those available to its intelligence agencies as a condition of permitting the vendor to sell products within its borders.

Concerns about a high-end cyberattacker surfaced publicly in congressional concerns about the Department of State's use of computers manufactured in China (Box 2.5). Although there is no public evidence that the nondomestic origin of IT components has ever compromised U.S. interests in any way, there is concern that it might in the future, or that such compromises in the past may have gone undetected.

Second, high-end attackers sometimes do not wish their actions to be discovered. For example, they may hope that their adversaries do not gain a full picture of their own capabilities or do not take defensive actions that might reduce their capabilities in the future.[36] (See Box 2.6.) In such situations, and unlike a successful hacker who seeks glory and fame in the eyes of his or her peers, the successes of high-end cyberattackers may well never be known outside a very small circle of individuals. A related point is that sophisticated attackers are very well capable of appearing to be less skilled hobbyist-hackers, when in fact they are actually laying the groundwork for future attacks. Put differently, under such circumstances, it might well be surprising to see actual direct evidence of the high-end attacker, since such evidence would likely be masked. Indirect evidence and inference thus become necessary to make the case that such an attacker even exists, even though such a case is necessarily weaker from an evidentiary standpoint.

[36]This is not to say that a high-end attacker would *never* want to be discovered. In some cases, an attacker may find it desirable to leave some evidence behind so that the damage that an attack causes cannot be attributed to an error or a glitch but instead points to the fact that the attacker is present and is a force to be reckoned with.

BOX 2.5
Foreign Sourcing of Information Technology Used in the United States

In March 2006, the U.S. Department of State announced that it would purchase 16,000 Lenovo computers and related equipment for use throughout the department. (Lenovo, Inc., is the Chinese company to which IBM sold its laptop and desktop personal computer [PC] business in 2005. Lenovo was incorporated in Hong Kong but is currently headquartered in the United States, and is reported to have ties to the Chinese government as well.) About 900 of the 16,000 PCs were designated for use in the network connecting U.S. embassies and consulates. In May 2006, and after objections had been raised in the U.S. Congress concerning the use of computers made by Lenovo in a classified network, the State Department agreed not to use Lenovo computers for such classified work.

The use of computers made by a Chinese company for classified work was bound to raise a number of security concerns. But the State Department–Lenovo incident is symptomatic of a much larger issue. As computers and other information technology (IT) systems are assembled with components manufactured or provided by vendors in many nations, even an "American" computer is not necessarily "Made in the USA" in anything but name. Similar concerns arise with software components or applications that have been designed or coded or are maintained overseas but are being used in the United States.

The nations that supply IT components include many—not just China—that might well have an interest in information on U.S. national security or economic matters. In addition, as "American" companies increasingly send some of their work offshore or use foreign citizens in the United States to work on IT, it is easy to see many possible avenues of foreign threat to the integrity of the security of information technology used in the United States.

Of course, the committee also recognizes that threats to the integrity of information technology used by the United States do not emanate from foreign sources alone, and there is no evidence known today that the nondomestic origin of IT components has compromised U.S. interests in any way. But there is concern that compromises might occur in the future, or that such compromises in the past may have gone undetected. (As a saying in the intelligence community goes, "We have never found anything that an adversary has successfully hidden.")

Third, the high-end cyberattacker is generally indifferent to the form that its path to success takes, as long as that path meets various constraints such as affordability and secrecy. In particular, the high-end cyberattacker will compromise or blackmail a trusted insider to do its bidding or infiltrate a target organization with a trained agent rather than crack a security system if the former is easier to do than the latter. Many hackers are motivated by the fame that they gain from defeating technological security mechanisms (sometimes by social engineering means rather than by technology exploitation).

Fourth, the motivation of a high-end cyberattacker is unambiguously

BOX 2.6
The Silence of a Successful Cyberattack

Given the existence of systemic vulnerabilities and a party with the capability and intent to exploit them, it is important to consider the motivations of such a party. In particular, it is important to ask why a hostile party with the capability to exploit a vulnerability would *not* do so.

Consider first an analogous situation in the intelligence community. Say that sensitive and important information about Nation A is gathered by (adversary) Nation B from a well-placed but covert source. Under what circumstances might Nation B refrain from using that information against Nation A? The answer depends on the value that Nation B places on protecting the source of the information versus the value it places on using the information at that time. "Protecting sources and methods" is a task of paramount importance in the intelligence community, because many sources and methods of collecting intelligence would be difficult to replace if their existence became known—and thus, certain types of information are not used simply because their use would inevitably disclose the source.

Similarly, in the shadowy world of cyberthreat and cybersecurity, a hostile party with the capability to exploit a vulnerability might be well advised to wait until the time is right for it to launch an attack. In fact, one might well imagine that such a party would conduct exercises to probe weaknesses and lay the groundwork for an attack, without actually taking overly hostile action. For example, such a party might use a virus that simply replicated itself but did not carry a payload that did any damage at all in order to prove to itself that such an attack is possible in principle.

The cybersecurity community knows of incidents (such as rapidly propagating viruses without destructive payloads and the active compromise of many network-connected computers that can be used to launch a variety of distributed attacks) that are consistent with the likely tactics of intelligent hostile parties. And it knows of intelligent parties whose intentions toward the United States are hostile. These factors do not constitute a logical proof of a high-end cyberthreat, but they do underlie the committee's judgment that the vulnerabilities with which it is concerned are not merely theoretical.

and seriously hostile. For example, a high-end cyberattacker may use IT in an attack as a means to an end and not as an end itself for a high-impact attack, much as the terrorists on September 11, 2001 (9/11), commandeered four airplanes to use as weapons. That is, for a high-end adversary, a cyberattack may be most effective as an amplifier of a physical attack.[37]

Fifth, as a military strategy (a point relevant mostly to nation-states),

[37]National Research Council. 2003. *Information Technology for Counterterrorism: Immediate Actions and Future Possibilities*. The National Academies Press, Washington, D.C.

offensive operations in cyberspace—especially against U.S. national interests—may offer considerable advantages for adversaries.[38] The United States is, as a nation, far more dependent on information technology than its potential adversaries are, and thus a hostile nation-state might well seek to exploit this asymmetry. Preparations for conducting cyberwarfare can be undertaken with minimal visibility, thus complicating the efforts of the United States to gather intelligence on the scope and nature of potential threats. Finally, in cyberwarfare, the advantages tend to favor attackers over defenders. For these reasons, adversary nation-states are likely to have strong incentives for developing capabilities to exploit weaknesses in the U.S. cybersecurity posture.

How likely is it that a high-end cyberthreat will emerge? Today, it is primarily knowledge of the threat emanating from hobbyists and sophisticated hackers that is widespread and that largely drives present cybersecurity efforts. Losses from these threats are known, though not with any kind of precision, and widespread real-life experience demonstrates their significance to business operations.

By contrast, information about the high-end threat emanating from organized crime and hostile nation-states is not easily available. With a lack of specific information, the high-end threat can be easily dismissed by systems owners and operators as one that is hypothetical and undocumented (at least in a public sense); such owners and operators thus might contend that there is an inadequate business case for the further investments that would be needed to counter the high-end threat. However, some analysts, notably those with access to classified information, assert in the strongest possible terms that the high-end cyberthreat is here today, that it is growing, and that the incidents reported publicly only hint at the severity and magnitude of that threat.[39]

Although the Committee on Improving Cybersecurity Research in the United States itself contained members with varying views on the seriousness or immediacy of the nation-state threat, the committee as a whole concluded that high-level threats—spawned by motivated, sophisticated, and well-resourced adversaries—could increase very quickly on a very

---

[38]Military analysts in the People's Republic of China are known to be considering such matters. See, for example, L. Qiao and X. Wang, *Unrestricted Warfare*, 1999, PLA Literature and Arts Publishing House, Beijing, People's Republic of China; available at http://www.terrorism.com/documents/TRC-Analysis/unrestricted.pdf.

[39]See, for instance, Bill Gertz, "Chinese Hackers Prompt Nave College Site Closure," *The Washington Times*, November 30, 2006, available at http://www.washtimes.com/national/20061130-103049-5042r.htm; Dawn S. Onley and Patience Wait, "Red Storm Rising: DOD's Efforts to Stave Off Nation-State Cyberattacks Begin with China," *Government Computer News*, August 21, 2006, available at http://www.gcn.com/print/25_25/41716-1.html; and Nathan Thornburgh, "Inside the Chinese Hack Attack," *Time*, August 25, 2005, available at http://www.time.com/time/nation/article/0,8599,1098371,00.html.

short timescale, potentially leading to what some dub a "digital Pearl Harbor" (that is, a catastrophic event whose occurrence can be unambiguously traced to flaws in cybersecurity)—and that the nation's IT vendors and users (both individual and corporate) would have to respond very quickly if and when such threats emerged. Therefore, a robust research program that addresses both current and future possible threats driven by the high-end threat is necessary to provide the technological underpinnings of such a response. Moreover, it suggests a research agenda that is necessarily broader and deeper than would otherwise be the case if the threat were known with high confidence to be limited to that posed by hackers and ordinary criminals.

3

Improving the Nation's Cybersecurity Posture

Given the scope and nature of the cybersecurity threat as discussed in Chapter 2, what should the nation do about it? This chapter begins with a committee-developed "Cybersecurity Bill of Rights" (Section 3.1) that characterizes what it would mean for cyberspace to be safe and secure. Building on this characterization, Section 3.2 describes the information technology (IT) landscape into which cybersecurity research flows. It describes the twin needs for research that would lead to improved deployment of today's cybersecurity technologies and the emergence of new cybersecurity technologies in the future. Section 3.3 explains the rationale for cybersecurity research, placing such research in the larger context of the cybersecurity problem, and Section 3.4 concludes the chapter with five principles that should guide that research.

3.1 THE CYBERSECURITY BILL OF RIGHTS

The Cybersecurity Bill of Rights (CBoR) describes a vision for a safe and more secure cyberspace. In the most general sense, individual users, organizations, and society at large are entitled to use and rely on information technologies whose functionality does not diminish even when these technologies are under attack. Although there are 10 provisions in the CBoR that articulate desirable security properties of information technology writ large, it is likely that as information technology evolves, other provisions will need to be added and the existing ones modified.

3.1.1 Introduction to the Cybersecurity Bill of Rights

The Cybersecurity Bill of Rights is a statement of security goals or expectations—what is it that society should reasonably expect in the way of security in its information technologies, and what should technologists and organizations strive to achieve? Since many or most of today's information technologies are not designed or implemented with the goals of the CBoR in mind, the Cybersecurity Bill of Rights also illustrates the enormous gap between what information technologies should do and what they now do. Serious efforts directed at achieving these goals would greatly decrease—but never eliminate—the security risks associated with using information technology. As importantly, the availability of information technologies designed and implemented with these goals in mind would expand the policy choices available to society about the functionality that it deserves and should expect from its technologies.

As a statement of expectations, the security provisions of the CBoR are neither absolute nor unconditional. When an information technology system or component does not embed a provision that should be provided, users have a right to know that the technology they are using does not meet that expectation so that they can act accordingly. Moreover, the way in which the provisions of the CBoR are realized for any given system will depend on many contextual factors. For example, the cybersecurity needs of an individual end user are different from those of a bank or the electric power grid.

In constructing the CBoR, the committee derived the provisions by considering four categories that are important to cybersecurity. These categories involve the following: (1) holistic systems properties relating to availability, recoverability, and control of systems; (2) traditional security properties relating to confidentiality, authentication, and authorization; (3) crosscutting properties such as safe access to information, confident invocation of important transactions, including those that will control physical devices, and knowledge of what security will be available; and (4) matters relating to jurisprudence: that is, appropriate justice for victims of cyberattack. (Some of the categories and provisions within them overlap.)

Finally, the CBoR is user-centric, but "user" should be interpreted broadly. Users include individual end users, organizations, and—most importantly—programs and system components that use (invoke or call on) other information technology systems or components. But taken together and viewed overall, the CBoR should be seen as a societal bill of rights, because the use of information technology in society has ramifications reaching far beyond a single individual or organization. Because critical societal functions depend on information technology, the security of the information technologies involved in those functions is of paramount importance.

3.1.2 The Provisions of the Cybersecurity Bill of Rights

- *The first three provisions relate to holistic systems properties including availability, recoverability, and control of systems:*

I. Availability of system and network resources to legitimate users.

Users of information technology systems (from individuals to groups to society, and including programs and applications[1]) should be able to use the computational resources to which they are entitled and systems that depend on those resources. Attacks intended to deny, seriously degrade, or reduce the timeliness of information technology-based services should not succeed.

II. Easy and convenient recovery from successful attacks.

Because cybersecurity measures will sometimes fail, recovery from a security compromise will be necessary from time to time. When necessary, such recovery should be easy and convenient for individual users, systems administrators, and other operators. Recovery is also an essential element of survivability and fault tolerance. Recovery should be construed broadly to include issues related to long-term availability in the face of "bit rot" and incompatible upgrades.[2]

III. Control over and knowledge of one's own computing environment.

Users expect to be in control of events and actions in their own immediate environment, where control refers to taking actions that influence what happens in that environment. Knowledge refers to knowing how things that are happening compare to user expectations about what is happening. To the extent that events and actions are occurring that are not initiated by the user, a breach in security may be occurring.

---

[1]Groups and societies are effectively aggregations of users, and computer programs and applications are proxies of users.

[2]"Bit rot" refers to the phenomenon in which a program (or features of a program) will suddenly stop working after a long time, even though "nothing has changed" in the environment. In fact, the environment has changed, although perhaps in subtle and unnoticed ways.

- *The next three provisions relate to the traditional security properties of confidentiality, authentication (and its extension, provenance), and authorization:*

IV. Confidentiality of stored information and information exchange.

One central function of information technology is the communication and storage of information. Just as most people engage in telephone conversations and store paper files with some reasonable assurance that the content will remain private even without their taking explicit action, users should expect electronic systems to communicate and store information in accordance with clear confidentiality policies and with reasonable and comprehensible default behavior. Systems for application in a particular problem domain should be able to support the range of privacy policies relevant to that domain.

As for systems that communicate with one another, some or all of the information that they pass among themselves belongs to someone, at least in the sense that someone has a confidentiality interest in it. In other cases, the information may not be particularly sensitive, but there is almost never any affirmative reason for that information to be shared with other parties unbeknownst to the owner—suggesting that external access to normally confidential data should normally be done with explicit permission.

As a particularly important way of ensuring confidentiality, responsible parties should have the technical capability to delete or expunge selected information that should not be permanently stored. This is important in the context of removing erroneous personal information from cyberspace. Today, electronically recorded information can be difficult to remove from the databases in which it is stored. For example, "deleted" information may be retained in a backup—and it should be possible to delete information from backups as well as from the original recording medium.

Whether or not—in a particular situation—it is appropriate to delete all instances of a given datum is a policy issue. But even if a policy choice were made that asserted that such deletions were appropriate, the technology of today is largely incapable of supporting that choice.

V. Authentication and provenance.

Mutual authentication of the senders and receivers involved in an information exchange is an essential part of maintaining confidentiality, since passing information to the wrong party or device is an obvious way in which confidentiality might be violated.

As an extension of traditional authentication, users should have access to reliable and relevant provenance (that is, knowledge of the responsible parties) for any electronic information or electronic event, commensurate with their need for security and assurance.

Provision V does not rule out anonymous speech, for example—but it does mean that any given user should be able to refuse to accept information from or participate in events initiated by anonymous parties. Information originating from untrustworthy sources should not be able to masquerade as information originating from known trustworthy sources. When information has no explicit provenance, users and their software agents should be able to determine this fact and make decisions regarding trust accordingly. Information sources and events in cyberspace should be construed broadly, so that deliberately hostile or antisocial sources and actions should have provenance as well. Provenance should be reliable and nonrepudiable.

VI. The technological capability to exercise fine-grained control over the flow of information in and through systems.

Authorized parties should be technically able to exercise fine-grained control over flows of information. For example, it should be technologically possible for an individual to conduct certain online transactions with technologically guaranteed anonymity, and for putative partners in such transactions to decline to participate if anonymity is offered. It should also be technologically possible for individuals to know who collects what information about them. And, they should have the technical ability to restrict the types, amounts, and recipients of personal information.

Access privileges determine the functionality that an information technology system or network offers to a user or other entity. Circumstances may change in such a way that privileges need to be revoked—for example, when a user is terminated or determined to be a threat, or when a service has been compromised. Revocation of privileges at various granularities is a necessary security capability.

Whether or not individuals *should* have legal rights to exercise fine-grained control over the flow of information in and through systems is a policy issue. But even if a policy choice were made that asserted the propriety of such legal rights, the technology of today is largely incapable of supporting that choice.

- *The next three provisions relate to crosscutting properties of systems such as safe access to information, confident invocation of important transactions, including those that will control physical devices, and knowledge of what security will be available:*

VII. Security in using computing directly or indirectly in important applications, including financial, health care, and electoral transactions and real-time remote control of devices that interact with physical processes.

Security is especially important in certain kinds of transactions, such as those involving financial, medical, or electoral matters. Further, computational devices increasingly control physical processes as well as information processes, and such devices may have the potential to act dangerously in the physical world. It is thus especially important that cyberattackers be precluded from impairing the safe operation of physical devices.

In this context, security refers to the availability, integrity, appropriate privacy controls on information, sufficient guarantees about the identities of involved parties to prevent masquerading and other attack, and nonrepudiation guarantees so that parties can be assured of their interactions.

VIII. The ability to access any source of information (e.g., e-mail, Web page, file) safely.

Today, many security vulnerabilities are exploited as the result of some user action in accessing some source of information. In this context, safe access means that nothing unexpected happens and that nothing happens to compromise the expected confidentiality, integrity, and availability of the user's information or computational resources. Safety cannot be assured with 100 percent certainty under any circumstances (for example, a user may take an allowed but unintended action that results in compromised confidentiality), but with proper attention to technology and to usability, the accessing of information can be made much less risky than it is today.

IX. Awareness of what security is actually being delivered by a system or component.

Users generally have expectations about the security-relevant behavior of a system, even if these expectations are implicit, unstated, or unfounded. System behavior that violates these expectations is often responsible for security problems. Thus, users have a right to know what security policies and assurances are actually being delivered by a system or component so that they can adjust their own expectations and subsequent behavior accordingly. As an illustration, nonexpert users need to know how security settings map onto policies being enforced, as well as how settings need to be specified in order to achieve a particular policy.

Such awareness also implies the ability to make informed judgments about the degree of security that different systems provide. If individuals and organizations are to improve their cybersecurity postures, they need to know how to compare the security of different systems and the impact of changes on those systems. To a great degree, quantitative risk assessments, rational investment strategies, and cybersecurity insurance all depend on the ability to characterize the security of systems.

- *The last provision relates to justice:*

X. Justice for security problems caused by another party.

In most of society, there is an expectation that victims of harm are entitled to some kind of justice—such as appropriate punishment of the perpetrator of harm. But today in cyberspace, there is no such expectation owing largely to the difficulty of identifying perpetrators and the lack of a legal structure for pursuing perpetrators. In addition, individuals who are victimized or improperly implicated because of cybersecurity problems should have access to due process that would make them whole. Society in its entirety should also have the ability to impose legal penalties on cyberattackers regardless of where they are located.

3.1.3 Concluding Comments

Every set of rights has responsibilities associated with it. Because the CBoR defines a set of security expectations for information technology, it has implications for every party that creates or uses information technology. Designers and developers of information technologies for end users will have obligations to produce systems whose security behavior is consistent with the CBoR unless otherwise explicitly noted to be inconsistent. Designers and developers of information technology systems and components on which other systems depend are also affected, because the CBoR defines for system designers and developers a set of expectations for what can happen on either side of an interface between two components. That is, because information technology systems today are crafted and deployed in a modular fashion, the CBoR also has design and implementation implications for the functionality of those two components, regardless of the side of the interface on which each resides. To the extent that the CBoR can be relied on to set security expectations for components developed by different parties, the result will be a more orderly world that supports composability of the building blocks in the IT infrastructure. The CBoR would also require end users to be sufficiently knowledgable to ascertain whether and to what extent the information technology that they use in fact delivers on the CBoR's security obligations.

How should the goals of the CBoR be achieved? As the discussion in the remainder of this report indicates, a new way of thinking about security—a drastic cultural shift—will be necessary regarding the ways in which secure systems are designed, developed, procured, operated, and used. In the long run, such a shift will entail new directions in education, training, development practice, operational practice, oversight, liability laws, and government regulation.

3.2 REALIZING THE VISION

Compared to what is available today, the foregoing vision of a secure cyberspace is quite compelling. However, for two distinct though related reasons, we are a long way away from meeting this goal. The first reason is that there is much about cybersecurity technologies and practices that is known but not put into practice. As an example, according to the senior information security officer at a major financial institution, the codification and dissemination of best practices in cybersecurity policy at the level of the chief executive officer or the chief information officer have been particularly challenging, because incentives and rewards for adopting best practices are few. Box 3.1 indicates the limited scope of threats against which certain common commercial products defend.

The second reason is that even assuming that everything known today was immediately put into practice, the resulting cybersecurity posture—though it would be stronger and more resilient than it is today—would still be inadequate against today's threats, let alone tomorrow's. Closing this gap—a gap of knowledge—will require research, as discussed below.

3.3 THE NECESSITY OF RESEARCH

Framing the issue of necessary research requires understanding the larger context of which such research is a part. Today, the vast majority of actual cybersecurity efforts is devoted to a reactive catch-up game that fixes problems as they are discovered (either in anticipation of attack as

BOX 3.1
What Firewalls and Antivirus Products Protect Against

Firewalls—whether implemented with hardware or software—are used to prevent malicious or unwanted traffic from reaching protected resources or to allow only authorized traffic (e.g., from specific network addresses). Antivirus products generally scan files or file systems looking for known computer viruses or malicious code, usually relying on a frequently updated virus definition file.

Below is a short list of some of the vulnerabilities that firewalls and antivirus products attempt to address:

- *Worms.* Both firewalls and antivirus products can be used to identify and slow (or halt) the propagation of computer worms, which, unlike viruses, can act independently once released.
- *Viruses.* Antivirus products can scan for, remove, and often repair damage done by viruses obtained from opening infected e-mails or other means.
- *Trojans.* Antivirus products can identify and remove Trojan horse software (i.e., malicious software that masquerades as legitimate software), while firewalls can be used to spot and prevent network traffic associated with Trojan horse software.
- *Vulnerability scans.* Firewalls can be used to prevent automated port-scanning tools from outside the firewall from uncovering open ports on (or otherwise learning about) potentially vulnerable machines behind the firewall.
- *Denial-of-service attacks.* Firewalls can often assist in mitigating denial-of-service attacks by blocking traffic from offending network addresses.
- *Insider misbehavior.* Firewalls are often used to block specific kinds of network traffic (or requests) from those inside the firewall as well—for example, by not allowing traffic over specific ports used by applications deemed inappropriate for a given setting (e.g., P2P file-sharing applications in an office setting) or by blocking access to specific Web sites that an organization has deemed inappropriate for a given setting.

the good guys find them or in response as the bad guys find them). Moreover, end users often do not avail themselves of known cybersecurity technologies and practices that could significantly improve their individual resistance to cyberattack of various kinds. For example, they often do not install patches to systems that could close known security holes in their design, implementation, or configuration. Vendors of IT products and services often do not use technologies and development practices that could reduce the number of security vulnerabilities embedded in them. For example, they do not use known technologies that might prevent the buffer overflows that continue to account for roughly half of all

Computer Emergency Response Team Coordination Center (CERT/CC) advisories.[3]

Reactive efforts are essential because it is impossible to replace the existing IT infrastructure in one fell swoop (and even if it were possible, we would not know what to replace it with) and because the security of any given system will require upgrading throughout its life cycle as new threats emerge and new vulnerabilities are found. Still, continuously reacting to cybersecurity problems—without new approaches to developing and deploying a stronger and more secure technological foundation—is a poor way to make progress against escalating or new threats. By their very nature, reactive efforts are incremental; vulnerabilities that flow from basic system design and architectural concepts cannot be fixed by such means, and often patching introduces additional security flaws. A focus on patching also tends to draw interest and attention away from more fundamental architectural problems that cannot be simply fixed with a patch.

Security add-ons will always be necessary to fix individual security problems as they arise, and R&D is needed to develop improved tools and techniques for dealing with near-term fixes (e.g., configuration management, audit, patch management), but ultimately there is no substitute for system- or network-wide security that is architected from initial design through deployment, easy to use, and minimally intrusive from the user's standpoint.

Furthermore, for all practical purposes, the cybersecurity risks (the combination of adversary threats and technical or procedural vulnerabilities) of the future are impossible to predict in any but the most general terms. Because it is difficult to anticipate innovation (which changes the architecture or implementation underlying specific systems) and to comprehend complex systems (which makes understanding the systems in place today very hard), it is almost guaranteed that unforeseen applications will result in unforeseen security concerns and human beings will be unable to anticipate all of the security issues that accompany complex systems.

In short, in many ways security is an emergent property of a complex IT system that depends on both the underlying system architecture and its implementation. Consider, for example, the relatively common practice of building an application on top of an off-the-shelf operating system. Although the applications builder can in principle know all there is to know about the application, its relationship to the operating system is known only through the various application programming interfaces (APIs) of the operating system. But since the input-output behavior of

[3]For more on the CERT/CC advisories, see http://www.cert.org/advisories/.

these APIs is usually incompletely specified (e.g., it may not be documented how the system responds when inputs are provided that are not of the expected variety), the overall relationship between application and operating system cannot be known completely. Much research is needed on the properties, practices, and disciplines to drive this emergence—just as research in the nascent complexity sciences is addressing similar problems of understanding emergence in other problem domains characterized by sensitive dependence on initial conditions.

This does not mean that it is impossible to identify areas of focus, but it does imply that within those areas of focus the nation's research strategy should seek to develop a broad and diverse technological foundation that would enable more rapid responses to new and currently unforeseen threats as they emerge as well as to yield unanticipated advances.

As for the character of the research needed, both traditional and unorthodox approaches will be necessary. Traditional research is problem-specific, and there are many cybersecurity problems for which good solutions are not known. (A good solution to a cybersecurity problem is one that is effective, is robust against a variety of attack types, is inexpensive and easy to deploy, is easy to use, and does not significantly reduce or cripple other functionality in the system of which it is made a part.) Research is and will be needed to address these problems.

But problem-by-problem solutions, or even problem-class by problem-class solutions, are highly unlikely to be sufficient to close the gap by themselves. Unorthodox, clean-slate approaches will also be needed to deal with what might be called a structural problem in cybersecurity research now, and these approaches will entail the development of new ideas and new points of view that revisit the basic foundations and implicit assumptions of security research.

Addressing both of these reasons for the lack of security in cyberspace is important, but it is the second—closing the knowledge gap—that is the primary goal of cybersecurity research and the primary focus of this report.

3.4 PRINCIPLES TO SHAPE THE RESEARCH AGENDA

This section describes a set of interrelated principles that the committee believes should shape the research agenda. Some are principles intended to drive specific components of the research agenda, while others are intended to change the mind-set with which the agenda is carried out. Individually, none of these principles is new, but in toto they represent the committee's best understanding of what should constitute a sound philosophical foundation for cybersecurity research.

3.4.1 Principle 1: Conduct cybersecurity research as though its application will be important.

3.4.1.1 The Rationale

The committee's view on conducting cybersecurity research is shaped by two essential points. First, much of today's cybersecurity research is limited to creating "building blocks" for security that could be incorporated into various applications. Today's dominant perspective is that basic research entails the creation or in-principle demonstration of a new cybersecurity concept or mechanism, and that bringing this concept or mechanism into real-world use is somehow less demanding or intellectually less worthy than the "basic" or "fundamental" research that led to the innovative concept or mechanism.

But research that results only in a proof of concept or a feasibility demonstration is often far from practical application, and an innovation, original though it may be, is not a tool or a system. Indeed, there is an enormous distance between the development of a good idea and its widespread use (whether by end users or by system designers and developers), and traversing that distance often entails additional research activity that is significant in its own right.

For example, the committee believes that the likelihood of a good idea succeeding in the marketplace is enhanced if it is scalable, adoptable, and composable.

- *A scalable idea* works on real-world problems of reasonable size in reasonable time.
- *An adoptable idea* is one whose benefits can easily be seen by its potential users, and it can be easily used by parties other than its creator.
- *A composable idea* can be integrated into a system without necessitating full-scale re-analysis and retesting. Composability is desirable because any system of significant size is usually developed in pieces by separate groups and at separate times, and is complicated by the fact that users may configure a system so that different components are active. Without composability, the "complete" system must be tested as one big and maximally complex lump.

Much additional research may be necessary to make a given concept scalable, composable, and adoptable. However, such considerations are often not taken seriously in the basic science stage, as many researchers believe they can defer such issues until the technology is ready for delivery. This attitude has inhibited the development of practical tools even though the underlying science had promise.

Formal verification methods provide an example. Formal methods such as model checking have been successfully applied to hardware on an economically significant scale. Nonetheless, much of the early work on formal verification methods for software resulted in technologies that required large amounts of training or radical changes to engineering practice, or that were based on unrealistic ideas about requirements gathering, or that were too costly and unable to interoperate, or that required hardware capabilities for undertaking verification that were not easily available. In many cases, these methods could operate only when the entire program to be verified was available, and could not operate on well-defined subunits. Researchers on formal methods did not have the benefit of effective metrics for assessing the benefits that might flow from adopting these methods.

In recent years, some of these problems have been overcome, with the result that formal methods do have some genuine utility in software development, and the use of formal methods is a hotbed of activity in research and in companies like Microsoft. One example is Microsoft's Static Driver Verifier (SDV) tool. The SDV is a static code-analysis tool for formally verifying that device drivers comply with various application programming interface rules about how the driver interfaces with an operating system. Box 3.2 provides more details.

Second, the committee believes that a view of cybersecurity research as being devoted only to the creation of building blocks is far too narrow, and is one of the primary reasons that the benefits of past cybersecurity research have not been fully realized. While the creation of new cybersecurity building blocks is an essential and primary component of any research agenda in cybersecurity, the span of cybersecurity research must be broadened in several interrelated dimensions to encompass—indeed, embrace—the application of known and future approaches to specific application domains, development of cybersecurity tools for every part of the IT life cycle, and multidisciplinary approaches to cybersecurity problems.

A related point is that focusing research attention on questions of deployment will help to reduce the time needed to deploy innovations. Large-scale deployments of any kind inevitably take a long time, and even small reductions in lead time could make a big difference should the need arise for the deployment of cybersecurity measures in an emergency.

In addition, it is important for research to consider and decision makers to take into account the enormous political pressures to "do something" in the wake of a catastrophe. Indeed, it is not unknown that measures hastily put into place after a disaster have subsequently proven to be ineffective, or even worse, harmful. It is thus appropriate to focus some research attention on how to sensibly deploy emergency measures

BOX 3.2
Lessons Learned from the Technology-Transfer Effort Associated with Microsoft's Static Driver Verifier

The Static Driver Verifier (SDV) systematically analyzes Windows device drivers against a set of rules that define what it means for a device driver to properly interact with the Windows operation system kernel. The SDV is based on a code-analysis engine known as SLAM, which incorporates type checking, model checking, program analysis, and automated deduction. SLAM was the result of research to create methodologies and tools to check the correctness of partial specification of program behavior—specifically the use of the device driver interface to the Windows kernel. The SDV provides an automated environment for running SLAM that incorporates rules for the Windows Driver Model; a well-articulated environment model of the Windows kernel and other drivers; scripts to configure the SDV with driver-specific information; and a graphical user interface to present results.

Intellectually, the primary lesson learned in the transition from the SLAM research to the working SDV tool is to focus on problems rather than technology. The problem must be recognized as critical by product developers and end users, and not just technically interesting to researchers. It must also be bounded sufficiently to provide a tangible solution with measurable success criteria. All parties involved, including product developers, end users, and researchers, must see clearly the link between the problem at hand and the solution—which is what the implementation of the SDV framework made clear in the case of the SLAM research.

From an organizational point of view, the primary lesson is that leaving the scaling up of a prototype research as an exercise for the development group is likely to result in lack of acceptance and adoption, since the development group will not necessarily make the "obvious" leap from technology solution to useful and viable product. Successful technology transfer is, at least in part, a research team responsibility, and involves considerable effort on the part of researchers to understand how product teams operate, how they allocate resources, how they make decisions, and what it takes to turn a prototype into a product.

SOURCE: Adapted from Thomas Ball, Byron Cook, Vladimir Levin, and Sriram K. Rajamani, *SLAM and Static Driver Verifier: Technology Transfer of Formal Methods Inside Microsoft*, Microsoft Research Technical Report, MSR-TR-2004-08, January 2004.

under such circumstances. In addition, because post-catastrophe deployments often change the boundaries of what is politically feasible, research should also consider what sensible things might be done if and when such opportunities arise.

3.4.1.2 New Computing Paradigms and Applications Domains

Cybersecurity problems in an environment of large-scale distributed computing, embedded computing, batch processing and mainframe computing, desktop computing, Web services (see Section 8.4.3), and pervasive computing (see Section 8.4.4) may be different from one another, even when meaningful analogs among these paradigms can be identified. Contexts of use matter as well: Internet services support http Web browsing and remote log-in, but the security issues associated with Web browsing are far greater than those associated with remote log-in simply because the former is used far more than the latter.

At a deep technical level, the types of attacks that may be launched in these different environments are not so different from one another, and the fundamental research issues needed to address these attacks were identified in the early 1970s and have not changed significantly since then. But these environments do differ significantly in their exposure to a wide range of anonymous attackers. As a result, the opportunities for launching different types of attack do vary significantly, suggesting the need for research on the scope and nature of those opportunities in the different environments and how those opportunities might be limited or circumscribed.

But what is less well appreciated is that similar issues apply in applications domains, and understanding how a particular cybersecurity approach is relevant to a particular application domain can be and often is as challenging as developing that approach in the first place. Cybersecurity research is most likely to be relevant to an application domain if it is conducted with deep knowledge of and insight into the issues that arise in that domain. An explicit consideration of the application domain serves both to inspire cybersecurity research based on the security problems associated with the domain and to increase the likelihood that the research will be used to solve real problems in the application domain. Examples of such application domains include cybersecurity for health care applications (see Section 8.4.1) and for the electric power grid (see Section 8.4.2).

Since most cybersecurity researchers do not have domain-specific expertise, collaboration with others who do becomes a sine qua non for success in this kind of research. Moreover, these collaborations must be undertaken as enterprises among co-equals—and in particular the computer scientist as cybersecurity researcher cannot view the problem domain as "merely" the applications domain, must refrain from jumping to conclusions about the problem domain, must be willing to learn the facts and contemplate realities and paradigms in the problem domain seriously, and must not work solely on the refined abstract problem that characterizes much of computer science research. Similarly, applications experts cannot view security as a mere annoyance to be brushed aside as quickly as possible, must refrain from jumping to conclusions about cybersecurity, must be willing to learn the facts and contemplate realities and paradigms in cybersecurity seriously, and must not work in complete isolation from the abstractions of computer science research.

The need for collaboration between domain experts and cybersecurity specialists can also be seen in the issue of how to make security functionality more usable by nonspecialists. Addressed at greater length in Section 6.1, the research area of usable security entails the development of security technologies that can be integrated seamlessly into how people already do their work, thereby increasing the likelihood that they will actually be used in everyday life.

3.4.1.3 Attending to Security Throughout a System's Life Cycle

For many years, tensions between security and other desirable system attributes or functionality have generally not been resolved in ways that have improved security. While these kinds of tension may never disappear, and indeed in some cases (e.g., in the absence of a serious observed threats) it can make good economic and business sense to resolve these tensions in such a manner, the committee believes strongly that cybersecurity must be regarded as an essential element throughout the entire life cycle of an IT product or service and that cybersecurity efforts should focus much more on creating inherently secure products. Security products that retroactively attempt to apply security to systems will always be needed, and security-related afterthoughts will always be necessary (simply because the good guys cannot anticipate every possible move by the bad guys), but the reality of security is that it is important in every phase of a system's life cycle, including requirements specification, design, development and implementation, testing and evaluation, operations, maintenance, upgrade, and even retirement. Whether different foci of research are needed to address security issues in each of these phases is an open question, but it is clear that the needs for security are not identical in each phase—and so researchers and funders should be open to the idea of phase-specific cybersecurity research.

As an example of thinking implied by this principle, consider a search for alternatives to the notion of perimeter defense, which has been a common approach to security for many years. Under perimeter defense, what is "inside" a vital information system or network is protected from an outside "attacker" who may try to "penetrate" the system to gain access to or acquire control over data and system resources on the inside.

Perimeter defense has the major advantage of being scalable. That is, defensive perimeters such as firewalls are deployed because it is much easier to secure one machine than several thousand. Scalability comes from the fact that adding a machine inside the perimeter imposes little if any additional burden on the defense.

However, in practice, perimeter defense is often implemented in ways that require no changes to systems on the inside of the perimeter. That is, defensive efforts are focused primarily on one perimeter—the perimeter that encompasses the entire system—with little defensive attention to components inside. (One familiar example of this is a firewall that protects all of the computers on a local area network—with the result that an attacker who compromises the firewall has rendered all of the computers on that network vulnerable.) The mind-set of perimeter defense is that "those inside the perimeter need not be concerned about security in any significant way."

In a world of increasingly interconnected and numerous computers and networks, this notion of perimeter defense is no longer realistic (if it ever was). Definitions of "inside" and "outside" change fluidly with business strategy and partnerships, and yesterday's business partner may be tomorrow's insider threat. In coalition operations involving U.S. military forces, an ally today may be an adversary tomorrow—implying that the implementation of security policies must be continually updated, since the categories of friend and foe are essentially arbitrary. The growing proliferation of wireless technologies and the reliance on employees working from home or while traveling makes the notion of "outside" a slippery concept. Trusted insiders may also be compromised. Most importantly, when the perimeter is breached (whether by virtue of a technical weakness such as buffer overflow or an operational weakness such as an employee being bribed to reveal a password), the attacker has entirely free rein inside.

3.4.1.4 Engaging a Multidisciplinary Approach to Cybersecurity

Any meaningful cybersecurity research program should be understood as a highly multidisciplinary enterprise for two related reasons. First, adversaries can focus their efforts on any weak point in a system, whether that weak point is technological, organizational, sociological, or psychological. Interactions related to these factors may influence the technical agenda (e.g., consideration of how to make audit trails valuable evidence in court proceedings), but a technical agenda—that is, one limited to technology alone—will almost certainly be insufficient to solve real-world problems. Put differently, cybersecurity must be regarded holistically if real-world security is to be improved. Second, solutions to cybersecurity problems may also have some relationship to law enforcement authorities, insurance companies, customers, users, international governments, and so on. Solutions developed without recognizing these relationships may prove to be unusable for practical purposes in the face of real-world deployment problems.

Understanding why certain "technically promising" research may be inadequate or unusable is necessarily multidisciplinary, involving matters of economics, law and regulation, organization theory, psychology, and sociology, as well as deep insights into technology. To illustrate, consider that applications-in-practice require attention to a range of nontechnical issues:

- *Persuading operators and developers to adopt best practices* in areas such as patch management, configuration management, audit and logging, and organizational and management processes. Also in scope are software engineering techniques, architecture, and network configuration through awareness, codification of those practices, and education programs.
- *Developing the value proposition and business case for the deployment of security,* which includes economic models and measurement techniques to facilitate models for estimating costs and benefits, testbeds, field trials, and case studies to demonstrate and assess value when in situ. This point is discussed further in Section 6.4.
- *Easing changes to established business and engineering practices* that may be associated with the introduction of cybersecurity functionality.
- *Ensuring that the application-in-practice is organizationally scalable.* For example, a small pilot program to test the suitability of a security application may not reveal the range of exceptional cases that must be handled when the application is deployed throughout the organization. Large-scale deployments are almost always organizationally stressful, and procedures tested in a small-scale environment often need debugging and optimization when an application is scaled up.
- *Providing incremental benefit for incremental deployment.* It is difficult to adopt cybersecurity solutions that provide benefit only when they are widely deployed, if only because the burden of proof is large under these circumstances. Conversely, "early gratification"—that is, when an increment of additional work or attention to cybersecurity resulting in some relatively immediate reward that relates to the current ongoing development activity—can obviate or dramatically reduce the need to use a manager-imposed "force majeure" that coerces the development team into adopting a security measure or technology.
- *Ensuring robustness against changing attacks.* A specific cybersecurity solution may protect against the exploitation of a particular vulnerability, but be rendered ineffective by a small change in the nature of that exploit. Unless the nature of that change can be kept secret (a very hard condition to meet), such "solutions" will be rendered ineffective very quickly as attackers seek to counter it.

- *Managing tensions between security and operational resilience.* Although certain tensions between security and other desirable properties have often been noted (e.g., tensions between security and ease of use), the connection between security and organizational resilience has often been overlooked. For example, operational compliance with any given organizational security policy is facilitated by standardization, but standardization often increases the risk of common-mode failures. Security is often enhanced by physical security—sensitive activities being undertaken in protected locations—but organizational resilience in crisis often relies on distribution of processing and mobile access to information. Security is enhanced by encryption and tight access controls, but in crisis or emergency, decryption keys and the small number of individuals with the necessary access are often unavailable.

These points suggest a need for problem-oriented research in addition to traditional discipline-oriented research. The latter tends to characterize research in most computer science academic departments and universities. Problem-oriented research, on the other hand, will require close collaboration among cybersecurity researchers and experts from other disciplines, and as suggested in Section 3.4.1.2, collaborations with application domain experts as well.

Because of the stovepiped nature of many academic disciplines, including computer science, special efforts will be needed to nurture problem interdisciplinary efforts that will encourage and incentivize the interaction of academic cybersecurity researchers with researchers with other specialties, both in university departments and nonacademic research institutes.

3.4.2 Principle 2: Hedge against uncertainty in the nature of the future threat.

It is unknown if a significant high-end cyberthreat will in fact emerge into public view, and judgments about the likelihood of such an emergence vary. But given the potential damage that such an adversary could inflict, it seems prudent to take a balanced approach that provides a hedge against that possibility. In the absence of substantial evidence about the existence of a high-end threat, a "Manhattan Project" approach to strengthening the nation's cybersecurity posture is likely unwarranted because of the enormous cost of such an effort, to say nothing of how one would know if such an effort had been successful.

At the same time, it is reasonable to construct a research agenda in cybersecurity that is both broader and deeper than might be required if only low-end threats were at issue. The development of stronger technological foundations for computer and network security is, of course, highly relevant to threats across the entire spectrum, but because a high-end threat may well be capable of undertaking more sophisticated or more subtle technical attacks, the technological research agenda must be correspondingly deeper. Because high-end adversaries would be perfectly happy to target nontechnological elements of a system, a broader research agenda will be needed to develop approaches to defending those elements as well.

Note that this hedge against uncertainty refers to R&D rather than deployment. That is, deployment costs are often large—and organizations may have sound reasons for not deploying various cybersecurity measures if a threat has not obviously manifested itself. Whatever the downside of a reactive approach, decision makers are often reactive because they do not see the value of certain proactive measures in the absence of a manifestly obvious threat. But it is undeniable that should a threat become manifestly obvious, decision makers will want to have options "off the shelf" that can be deployed in a short time so as to minimize the possible damage—and the very purpose of R&D is to expand the number of options available should high-end threats materialize.

Of course, the term "short" is a relative one—and the time in question is "shorter than would be possible if R&D had not been conducted." Research results cannot be deployed instantaneously, nor on a wide scale in less than a few years. In the face of the sudden emergence of a manifestly obvious high-end threat, it might be possible to deploy research prototypes on a scale of a few weeks or months for critical systems (and the likelihood of being able to do so would be higher if research had been conducted in accordance with Principle 1). For the majority of other systems, an emergency response might well be to put into place draconian procedural and technical measures that would mitigate the high-end attack but also would have the effect of drastically reducing the operational utility of those systems. As relevant research results were deployed to protect these systems, the original mitigation measures could be scaled back and the original operational utility of these systems gradually returned to normal.

3.4.3 Principle 3: Ensure programmatic continuity in the research agenda.

A research program should support a substantial effort in areas with a long time horizon for payoff. Such support would necessarily extend for timescales long enough to make meaningful progress on hard problems (5 years to investigate a promising technology is not unreasonable, for example) and in sufficient amounts that new technologies might be developed and tested in reasonably realistic operating environments.[4] Historically, such investigations have been housed most often in academia, which can conduct research with fewer pressures for immediate delivery on a bottom line.

This is not to say that long-term research cannot have intermediate milestones, though the purpose of such milestones should be to make midcourse corrections rather than go/no-go decisions that can demoralize researchers and make them overly conservative. Long-term research can also involve collaboration early and often with technology transition stakeholders and can engage both academic and industrial actors, even in the basic science stages. Those stakeholders get an early planning view and an opportunity to influence the course of research and development.

Private industry has important roles to play as well. Today, industrial research and development in cybersecurity is a significant component of the nation's cybersecurity R&D efforts, and meaningful cybersecurity results emerge from this effort. In addition, industrial participation, or at least the involvement of product developers, is essential for developing prototypes and mounting field demonstrations. Thus, it is highly appropriate to support academic/industrial cooperation in efforts oriented toward development.

Possible synergies between government and academia/private industry deserve support as well. For example, both the National Institute of Standards and Technology and the National Security Agency (NSA) have very deep expertise regarding certain aspects of cybersecurity that could be valuable in the conduct of even unclassified research undertaken in the civilian sector.

Finally, program managers—and more importantly, funders—of such research must be tolerant of research directions that do not appear to promise immediate applicability. Research programs, especially in IT, are often—even generally—more "messy" than research managers would like. The desire to terminate unproductive lines of inquiry is understandable, and sometimes entirely necessary, in a constrained budget environment. On the other hand, it is frequently very hard to distinguish between (A) a line of inquiry that will never be productive and (B) one that may take some time and determined effort to be productive. While an intel-

[4]Note, however, that it is a long way from a prototype or conceptual proof-of-principle that is usable only by its creator to a tool that might be tested or deployed in such environments. In his classic text *The Mythical Man-Month*, Frederick P. Brooks, Jr. (Reading, Mass.: Addison-Wesley, 1995) estimates that the effort necessary to create a programming systems product from a program is an order of magnitude larger than for creating the program itself.

lectually robust research program must be expected to go down some blind alleys occasionally (indeed, even frequently), the current political environment punishes such blind alleys as being of Type A, with little apparent regard for the possibility that they might be Type B.[5]

Most researchers, regardless of field, would argue that programmatic continuity is needed in any research program. But such continuity is particularly relevant to cybersecurity. As noted in Section 2.6, cybersecurity problems will endure as long as bad guys have incentives to compromise the security of IT-based systems and networks, and thus cybersecurity research will always be needed to deal with some new and unanticipated exploit. Moreover, because the underlying technology evolves (quite rapidly, in fact), solutions crafted in one IT environment may well no longer be useful in a different one.

3.4.4 Principle 4: Respect the need for breadth in the research agenda.

One of the most frequent complaints from federal policy makers regarding reports that lay out research agendas is that such reports do not set priorities. Policy makers argue that in an environment of limited financial resources, they look to the research community to set priorities so that limited dollars can be spent most effectively. The committee understands the persuasiveness of and rationale for this perspective, and for this reason it has identified important areas of research focus (grouped into six categories and explored in detail in Chapters 4 through 9). Nevertheless, the committee is still quite concerned that an excessively narrow focus on priority areas would result in other important topics or promising avenues being neglected and that such a focus would run significant risks of leaving the nation unprepared for a rapidly changing cybersecurity environment.

Broad research agendas are often regarded as "peanut butter spread"—a pejorative term used among policy makers to refer to spreading resources more or less evenly among a large number of programs or efforts. It is pejorative because the implication is that no thought has gone into deciding whether these efforts are necessary at all, and that the "spread" simply reflects the unwillingness of the agenda's creators to set priorities. But the need for breadth in this case reflects the simple reality that there is no silver bullet, or even a small number of silver bullets, that will solve "the cybersecurity problem," and a broad research agenda helps to ensure that good ideas are not overlooked.

---

[5]National Research Council. 2003. *Information Technology for Counterterrorism: Immediate Actions and Future Possibilities.* The National Academies Press, Washington, D.C.

The basic canon of priority setting is that one identifies the most important problems and allocates resources preferentially to solve those problems. "Importance" is related both to frequency of occurrence and by severity of the impact of any given occurrence. But severity is very difficult to ascertain in general, as it depends on the details and the significance of particular systems attacked. As for frequency, the deployment of a defense that addresses the threat of a highly likely Attack A may well lead to a subsequent increase in the likelihood of a previously less likely Attack B. In short, adversaries may not behave in accordance with expectations that are based on static probability distributions, and thus it is very difficult to prioritize a research program for countering terrorism in the same way that one might, for example, prioritize a program for dealing with natural disasters. (Section 6.4.2 describes some of the issues related to quantitative risk assessment.)

The fundamental asymmetry between attacker and defender also affects the research agenda. The cyberdefender must be successful at every point in the defense, whereas the cyberattacker must succeed only once. Even if one vulnerability is closed, a serious attacker will seek another vulnerability to exploit. This search will cost the attacker some time, and this other vulnerability may be more difficult to exploit—these factors make it worthwhile to close the original vulnerability. But there is no sense in which closing the original vulnerability can be said to be a final solution.

Consequently, new exploitations of vulnerabilities can appear with very little warning. In many cases, these new exploitations are merely variations on a theme, and the defense can easily adjust to the new attack. But in other cases, these new exploitations are qualitatively different, of a nature and character not seen before. Although such cases are hopefully rare, it is safe to bet that the rate at which they appear will not be zero. If qualitatively new attacks suddenly manifest themselves, considerable time will elapse before techniques and technologies can be developed to handle them. Conducting a broad research agenda is likely to decrease significantly the time needed to develop countermeasures against these new attacks when they appear.

Cybersecurity is analogous to developing a defense against con men and fraudsters, who are infinitely creative or at least very clever in adapting old attacks to new technologies. There are, of course, basic high-end principles that enable one to guard against con men and fraudsters. But it is not realistic to imagine that there is one or even a few promising approaches that will prevent or even substantially mitigate fraud in the future. Rather, a good cybersecurity research agenda is more like a good strategy for investing in the stock market, both of which are driven by a multitude of unpredictable factors. Although there are basic principles of investment about which any investor should be cognizant, ultimately a diversified portfolio of investments is a foundational element of any good overall strategy—even if one is willing to place bets on a few very promising stocks.

These comments should not be taken to mean that all topics are equally important in an absolute sense—only that the committee believes that any top-down articulation of research priorities is bound to be overtaken by events (e.g., new technologies, new threats, new kinds of exploits) very rapidly. Rather, decisions about what areas or topics should be supported should be made by those in a position to respond most quickly to the changing environment—namely, the research constituencies that provide peer review and the program managers of the various research-supporting agencies.

Finally, notions of breadth and diversity in the cybersecurity research agenda should themselves be interpreted broadly. A great deal of experience suggests that cybersecurity considerations are not easily separated from other engineering issues, and in particular go hand-in-hand with the design and engineering of secure systems. Cybersecurity is relevant to research, education, and practice for every component of the IT system's development life cycle, and research focused on these components should itself embrace a cybersecurity aspect to such work. By tacitly accepting the current practice of fencing off "cybersecurity research" into separate programs, research programs have a tendency to focus primarily on those areas that are more "purely cybersecurity" such as crypto protocols and other aspects of cybersecurity that are easily separable from basic system design and implementation and to neglect those areas where integration is a principal concern, principally the engineering of software and cyber-physical systems. Integrating cybsersecurity considerations into related programs (software and systems engineering, operating systems, programming languages, networks, Web applications, and so on) will help program managers in these areas to better integrate cybsersecurity into the overall engineering context. Because of the inability to achieve perfection in our engineering practices, it is necessary to pursue—simultaneously—a wide variety of kinds of interventions across a broad front. Section 4.3 (Software and Systems Assurance) explores these comments in somewhat greater depth.

3.4.5 Principle 5: Disseminate new knowledge and artifacts.

University research activities are an important crucible in which new ideas are discovered, invented, and explored. But publication or other dissemination of research results is also a sine qua non for progress, and it is necessary to disseminate results to a community broader than one's own research laboratory for research to have a wide impact, a point that argues for cybersecurity research to be conducted on an unclassified basis as much as possible. As argued in the 2005 cybersecurity report of the President's Information Technology Advisory Committee, "the vast majority of the Nation's academic researchers do not hold the security clearances needed to undertake classified work [and furthermore] many research universities regard classified research as incompatible with their role as producers of knowledge benefiting society as a whole."[6] Almost by definition, broad dissemination is incompatible with classified research. (See also the discussion in Section B.6.4.2.)

As a logical point, it would be possible to expand the number of researchers with clearances or to make more research unclassified. Although the committee acknowledges that there are some circumstances in which cybersecurity research should be classified, it also believes that these circumstances are narrow. Furthermore, a significant expansion in the number of cybersecurity researchers with security clearances does not seem feasible in the present political environment. Thus, the committee believes that as a general rule, the nation would be better served by the latter course.

A related point is that the cybersecurity expertise and talent developed in the classified world are likely to be quite relevant to the civilian world, and mechanisms to share ideas about technology and training with the public, and in particular with students in the field, should be encouraged. A notable example of such technology sharing is the National Security Agency's Domestic Technology Transfer Program, established for the purpose of openly sharing NSA-developed technologies with the non-NSA community.[7] NSA has also worked with at least one major IT vendor to enhance the security of its products.[8]

It is also worth noting that the declassifying of cybersecurity research has some parallels with the 1990s debate—since resolved—over restricting the export of strong cryptography.[9] Under the restrictions in effect at the time, the export of products embedding strong cryptography and

---

[6]President's Information Technology Advisory Committee, *Cyber Security: A Crisis of Prioritization*, National Coordination Office for Information Technology Research and Development, Washington, D.C., February 2005; available at www.nitrd.gov/pitac/reports/20050301_cybersecurity/cybersecurity.pdf.

[7]For more information on this program, see http://www.nsa.gov/techtrans/index.cfm for a description of the program and http://www.nsa.gov/techtrans/techt00004.cfm for a description of tools and technologies related to cybersecurity.

[8]Alec Klein and Ellen Nakashima, "For Windows Vista Security, Microsoft Called in Pros," *Washington Post*, January 9, 2007; available at http://www.washingtonpost.com/wp-dyn/content/article/2007/01/08/AR2007010801352.html.

[9]National Research Council. 1996. *Cryptography's Role in Securing the Information Society*, Kenneth W. Dam and Herbert S. Lin (eds.). National Academy Press, Washington, D.C.

even basic knowledge about cryptography was regulated as part of the munitions trade. At the time, the rationales on export related to the undesirability of allowing strong cryptography to be used by adversaries, both nation-states and criminals. But ultimately, decision makers realized that national security and economic security needs could not be easily disentangled, and that in an increasingly globalized economic environment, the ability of commercial firms to keep information confidential was important indeed. Beginning in the late 1990s, export controls on cryptography were gradually relaxed.

Finally, in many fields of scientific research, the primary means of disseminating discoveries is through presentations at conferences or publication in refereed journals. However, in much of computer science, important research knowledge and insight are conveyed through the dissemination and use of software and/or hardware artifacts. Because cybersecurity has experimental dimensions, those responsible for academic human resource decisions should expect that significant research results in cybersecurity will be broadly disseminated through software downloads at least as much as through published papers or conference proceedings.[10]

---

[10]National Research Council. 1994. *Academic Careers for Experimental Computer Scientists and Engineers.* National Academy Press, Washington, D.C. This report addresses the conflict between standard academic metrics of merit (i.e., published papers) and the practice of disseminating artifacts as is done in experimental computer science.

Part II
An Illustrative Research Agenda

Part II presents one illustrative research agenda that might be constructed to further the goals described in Part I. The first four categories of the agenda (Chapters 4 through 7) constitute what might be regarded as primary areas of programmatic focus. The fifth category (Chapter 8) is a broad, crosscutting category that draws on parts of the first four categories but focuses on bringing them together in the context of specific cybersecurity problems. The sixth category (Chapter 9) contains what might be regarded as speculative ideas that are worth some effort to investigate. Table II.1 maps the topics described in this research agenda to the provisions of the Cybersecurity Bill of Rights described in Chapter 3.

The areas of programmatic focus were selected on the basis of their high importance. (Here, "importance" is characterized by the enormous benefits that would flow from progress in those domains.) Fruitful results in these areas would significantly increase the security of the technology base on which information technology (IT) applications are built and increase the likelihood of incorporating those results into these applications. Such incorporation, on a large scale, would in turn significantly improve the nation's cybersecurity posture.

At the same time, the research described within each area of programmatic focus is fairly broad. This breadth is based on the committee's belief that excessive priority setting in the cybersecurity research field runs significant risks of leaving the nation unprepared for a rapidly changing cybersecurity environment. The committee cautions policy makers strongly against neglecting potentially important topics in their quest to prioritize research. Moreover, because there will always be incentives and opportunities to attack IT-based systems in the future, it would be a profound mistake to believe that the committee's specific research agenda—or any other one that any other group might create—can "solve the problem" of cybersecurity once and for all. The committee emphasizes that the specific topics covered in Part II constitute representative examples of possible research within the four areas of programmatic focus and not specific priorities within those areas.

TABLE II.1 Mapping Research Topics to the 10 Provisions of the Committee's Cybersecurity Bill of Rights

Research Topics[a]	I Availability	II Recovery	III Control	IV Confidentiality
Category 1—Blocking and Limiting the Impact of Compromise				
4.1-Secure design, development, and testing	X	X	X	X
4.2-Graceful degradation and recovery	X	X	X	
4.3-Software and systems assurance	X		X	X
Category 2—Enabling Accountability				
5.1-Attribution				X
5.2-Misuse and anomaly detection systems	X	X		
5.3-Digital rights management				X
Category 3—Promoting Deployment				
6.1-Usable security				X
6.2-Exploitation of previous work	X	X	X	X
6.3-Cybersecurity metrics			X	
6.4-The economics of cybersecurity	X	X	X	X
6.5-Security policies	X		X	X
Category 4—Deterring Would-Be Attackers and Penalizing Attackers				
7.1-Legal issues related to cybersecurity	X	X	X	X
7.2-Honeypots			X	
7.3-Forensics			X	

V Authentication	VI Flow Control	VII Application	VIII Access	IX Awareness	X Justice
X	X	X	X	X	X
		X	X		
X		X	X	X	
X	X	X	X		X
		X			X
	X				X
X	X	X	X		
X	X	X	X	X	X
				X	X
X	X	X	X	X	
X	X	X		X	X
X	X	X	X	X	X
				X	X
				X	X

TABLE II.1 Continued

Research Topics[a]	I Availability	II Recovery	III Control	IV Confidentiality
Category 5—Illustrative Crosscutting Problem-Focused Research Areas				
8.1-Security for legacy systems	X	X	X	X
8.2-The role of secrecy in cyberdefense	X	X	X	X
8.3-Insider threats			X	
8.4-Security in nontraditional computing environments and in the context of use	X	X	X	X
8.5-Secure network architectures	X		X	X
8.6-Attack characterization	X		X	
8.7-Coping with denial-of-service attacks	X	X		
8.8-Dealing with spam			X	
Category 6—Speculative Research				
9.1-A cyberattack research activity	X	X	X	X
9.2-Biological approaches to security	X	X	X	X
9.3-Using attack techniques for defensive purposes	X	X	X	X
9.4-Cyber-retaliation	X	X	X	X

NOTE: Some imprecision in this mapping is freely acknowledged, in the sense that a number of the specific mappings mentioned are the result of judgment calls that might be different if a different set of individuals were to make those judgments.

As presented in Chapter 3 of this report, the 10 provisions of the Cybersecurity Bill of Rights are as follows:

I. Availability of system and network resources to legitimate users.
II. Easy and convenient recovery from successful attacks.
III. Control over and knowledge of one's own computing environment.
IV. Confidentiality of stored information and information exchange.
V. Authentication and provenance.
VI. The technological capability to exercise fine-grained control over the flow of information in and through systems.

V Authentication	VI Flow Control	VII Application	VIII Access	IX Awareness	X Justice
X	X	X	X	X	
X	X	X	X	X	
X		X			X
X	X	X	X	X	X
X	X	X	X	X	
		X		X	X
		X	X		
		X	X		X
X	X	X	X	X	X
X	X	X	X	X	
X	X	X	X	X	
X	X	X	X	X	X

VII. Security in using computing directly or indirectly in important applications, including financial, health care, and electoral transactions, and real-time remote control of devices that interact with physical processes.
VIII. The ability to access any source of information (e.g., e-mail, Web page, file) safely.
IX. Awareness of what security is actually being delivered by a system or component.
X. Justice for security problems caused by another party.

[a]The numbering of each research topic corresponds with the numbering of the section on that topic in Chapter 4 through Chapter 9.

4

Category 1—Blocking and Limiting the Impact of Compromise

The goal of requirements in Category 1 of the committee's illustrative research agenda is that of ensuring that the impact of compromises in accountability or system security is limited. This broad category—blocking and limiting the impact of compromise—includes secure information systems and networks that resist technical compromise; technological and organizational approaches that reveal attempts to compromise information technology (IT) components, systems, or networks; containment of breaches; backup and recovery; convenient and ubiquitous encryption that can prevent unauthorized parties from obtaining sensitive or confidential data; system lockdowns under attack; and so on.

A basic principle underlying Category 1 is that of defense in depth. A great deal of experience in dealing with cybersecurity issues suggests that no individual defensive measure is impossible to circumvent. Thus, it makes sense to consider defense in depth, which places in the way of a cyberattacker a set of varied hurdles, all of which must be penetrated or circumvented if the cyberattacker is to achieve its goal. When different hurdles are involved, an attacker must have access to a wider range of expertise to achieve its goal and also must have the increased time and resources needed to penetrate all of the defenses.

4.1 SECURE DESIGN, DEVELOPMENT, AND TESTING

The principle that security must be a core attribute of system design, development, and testing simply reflects the point that it is more effective to reduce vulnerabilities by not embedding them in a system than to fix the problems that these vulnerabilities cause as they appear in operation.[1] Vulnerabilities can result from design, as when system architects embed security flaws in the structure of a system. Vulnerabilities also result from flaws in development—good designs can be compromised because they are poorly implemented. Testing for security flaws is necessary because designers and implementers inevitably make mistakes or because they have been compromised and have deliberately introduced such flaws.

4.1.1 Research to Support Design

4.1.1.1 Principles of Sound and Secure Design

In the past 40+ years, a substantial amount of effort has been expended in the (relatively small) security community to articulate principles of sound design and to meet the goal of systems that are "secure by design." On the basis of examinations of a variety of systems, researchers have found that the use of these principles by systems designers and architects correlates highly to the security and reliability of a system. Box 4.1 summarizes the classic Saltzer-Schroeder principles, first published in 1975, that have been widely embraced by cybersecurity researchers.

Systems not built in accord with such principles will almost certainly exhibit inherent vulnerabilities that are difficult or impossible to address. These principles, although well known in the research community and available in the public literature, have not been widely adopted in the mainstream computer hardware and software design and development community. There have been efforts to develop systems following these principles, but observable long-term progress relating specifically to the multitude of requirements for security is limited. For example, research in programming languages has resulted in advances that can obviate whole classes of errors—buffer overflows, race conditions, off-by-one errors, format string attacks, mismatched types, divide-by-zero crashes, and unchecked procedure-call arguments. But these advances, important though they are, have not been adopted on a sufficient scale to make these kinds of error uncommon.

Nonetheless, the principles remain valid—so why have they had so little impact in the design and development process? In the committee's

[1]For example, Soo Hoo et al. determined empirically that fixing security defects after deployment cost almost seven times as much as fixing them before deployment. Furthermore, security investments made in the design stage are 40 percent more cost-effective than similar investments in the development stage. See K. Soo Hoo, A. Sudbury, and A. Jaquith, "Tangible ROI Through Secure Software Engineering," *Secure Business Quarterly*, Quarter 4, 2001.

view, three primary reasons account for the lack of such impact: the mismatch between these principles and real-world software development environments, short-term expenses associated with serious adherence to these principles, and potential conflicts with performance.

4.1.1.1.1 *The Mismatch with Current Development Methodologies*

One reason for the lack of impact is the deep mismatch between the principles of system design in Box 4.1 and real-world software development environments. Even a cursory examination of the principles discussed in Box 4.1 suggests that their serious application is predicated on a thorough and deep understanding of what the software designers and architects are trying to do. To apply these principles, software designers and architects have to know very well and in some considerable detail just what the ultimate artifact is supposed to do.

The software development model most relevant to this state of affairs is often called the waterfall model, explicated in considerable detail by Boehm.[2] This model presumes a linear development process that proceeds from requirements specification, to design, to implementation/coding, to integration, to testing/debugging, to installation, to maintenance, although modified versions of the model acknowledge some role for feedback between each of these stages and preceding ones.

But despite its common use in many software development projects (especially large ones), the waterfall model is widely viewed as inadequate for real-world software development. The reason is that many—perhaps even most—software artifacts grow organically. The practical reality is that large software systems emerge from incremental additions to small software systems in ways entirely unanticipated by the designers of the original system. If the original system is successful, users will almost certainly want to add new functionality. The new functionality desired is by definition unanticipated—if the designers had known that it would be useful, they would have included it in the first place.

Indeed, it is essentially impossible in practice for even the most operationally experienced IT applications developers to be able to anticipate in detail and in advance all of a system's requirements and specifications. (Sometimes users change their minds about the features they want, or even worse, want contradictory features! And, of course, it is difficult indeed to anticipate all potential uses.) Thus, system requirements and specifications are always inherently incomplete, even though they underlie and drive the relationships among various modules and their inter-

[2] Barry Boehm, *Software Engineering Economics*, Prentice-Hall, Englewood Cliffs, N.J., 1981.

BOX 4.1
The Saltzer-Schroeder Principles of Secure System Design and Development

Saltzer and Schroeder articulate eight design principles that can guide system design and contribute to an implementation without security flaws:

- *Economy of mechanism: The design should be kept as simple and small as possible.* Design and implementation errors that result in unwanted access paths will not be noticed during normal use (since normal use usually does not include attempts to exercise improper access paths). As a result, techniques such as line-by-line inspection of software and physical examination of hardware that implements protection mechanisms are necessary. For such techniques to be successful, a small and simple design is essential.
- *Fail-safe defaults: Access decisions should be based on permission rather than exclusion.* The default situation is lack of access, and the protection scheme identifies conditions under which access is permitted. The alternative, in which mechanisms attempt to identify conditions under which access should be refused, presents the wrong psychological base for secure system design. This principle applies both to the outward appearance of the protection mechanism and to its underlying implementation.
- *Complete mediation: Every access to every object must be checked for authority.* This principle, when systematically applied, is the primary underpinning of the protection system. It forces a system-wide view of access control, which, in addition to normal operation, includes initialization, recovery, shutdown, and maintenance. It implies that a foolproof method of identifying the source of every request must be devised. It also requires that proposals to gain performance by remembering the result of an authority check be examined skeptically. If a change in authority occurs, such remembered results must be systematically updated.
- *Open design: The design should not be secret.* The mechanisms should not depend on the ignorance of potential attackers, but rather on the possession of specific, more easily protected, keys or passwords. This decoupling of protection mechanisms from protection keys permits the mechanisms to be examined by many reviewers without concern that the review may itself compromise the safeguards. In addition, any skeptical users may be allowed

faces, inputs, state transitions, internal state information, outputs, and exception conditions.

Put differently, the paradox is that successful principled development requires a nontrivial understanding of the entire system in its ultimate form before the system can be successfully developed. Systems designers need experience to understand the implications of their design choices. But experience can be gained only by making mistakes and learning from them.

to convince themselves that the system they are about to use is adequate for their individual purposes. Finally, it is simply not realistic to attempt to maintain secrecy for any system that receives wide distribution.

- *Separation of privilege: Where feasible, a protection mechanism that requires two keys to unlock it is more robust and flexible than one that allows access to the presenter of only a single key.* The reason for this greater robustness and flexibility is that, once the mechanism is locked, the two keys can be physically separated and distinct programs, organizations, or individuals can be made responsible for them. From then on, no single accident, deception, or breach of trust is sufficient to compromise the protected information.
- *Least privilege: Every program and every user of the system should operate using the least set of privileges necessary to complete the job.* This principle reduces the number of potential interactions among privileged programs to the minimum for correct operation, so that unintentional, unwanted, or improper uses of privilege are less likely to occur. Thus, if a question arises related to the possible misuse of a privilege, the number of programs that must be audited is minimized.
- *Least common mechanism: The amount of mechanism common to more than one user and depended on by all users should be minimized.* Every shared mechanism (especially one involving shared variables) represents a potential information path between users and must be designed with great care to ensure that it does not unintentionally compromise security. Further, any mechanism serving all users must be certified to the satisfaction of every user, a job presumably harder than satisfying only one or a few users.
- *Psychological acceptability: It is essential that the human interface be designed for ease of use, so that users routinely and automatically apply the protection mechanisms correctly.* More generally, the use of protection mechanisms should not impose burdens on users that might lead users to avoid or circumvent them—when possible, the use of such mechanisms should confer a benefit that makes users want to use them. Thus, if the protection mechanisms make the system slower or cause the user to do more work—even if that extra work is "easy"—they are arguably flawed.

SOURCE: Adapted from J.H. Saltzer and M.D. Schroeder, "The Protection of Information in

For these reasons, software development methodologies such as incremental development, spiral development, and rapid prototyping have been created that presume an iterative approach to building systems based on extensive prototyping and strong user feedback. Doing so increases the chances that what is ultimately delivered to the end users meets their needs, but entails a great deal of instability in "the requirements." Moreover, when such "design for evolvability" methodologies are used with modularity, encapsulation, abstraction, and well-defined interfaces, development and implementation even in the face of uncertain requirements are much easier to undertake. The intellectual challenge—and thus the research question—is how to fold security principles into these kinds of software development processes.

4.1.1.1.2 The Short-Term Expense

A second reason that adherence to the principles listed in Box 4.1 is relatively rare is that such adherence is—in the short term—almost always more expensive than ignoring the principles. If only short-term costs and effort are taken into account, it is—today—significantly more expensive and time-consuming to integrate security from the beginning of a system's life cycle, compared with doing nothing about security and giving in to the pressures of short-timeline deliverables.

This reality arises from a real-world environment in which software developers often experience false starts, and there is a substantial amount of "playing around" that helps to educate and orient developers to the task at hand. In such an environment, when many artifacts are thrown away, it makes very little sense to invest up front in that kind of adherence unless such adherence is relatively inexpensive. The problem is further compounded by the fact that the transition from the "playing around" environment to the "serious development" environment (when it makes more sense to adhere to these principles) is often unclear.

An example is the design of interfaces between components. Highly constrained interfaces increase the stability of a system incorporating such components. At the same time, that kind of constraining effort is inevitably more expensive than the effort involved when an interface is only lightly policed. In this context, a constrained interface is one in which calling sequences and protocols are guaranteed to be valid, meaningful, and appropriate. Guarantees must be provided that malformed sequences and protocols will be excluded. Providing such guarantees requires resources and programming that are unnecessary if the sequences and protocols are simply assumed to be valid.

A second example arises from cooperative development arrangements. In practice, system components are often developed by different parties. With different parties involved, especially in different organizations, communications difficulties are inevitable, and they often include incompatibilities among interface assumptions, the existence of proprietary internal and external interfaces, and performance degradations resulting from the inability to optimize across components. This point suggests the need for well-defined and carefully analyzed specifications for the constituent components, but it is obviously easier and less expensive to simply assume that specifications are unambiguous.

In both of these examples, an unstructured and sloppy design and implementation effort is likely to "work" some of the time. Although such an effort can provide insight to designers and offer an opportunity for them to learn about the nature of the problem at hand, transitioning successfully to a serious production environment generally requires starting over from scratch rather than attempting to evolve an unstructured system into the production system. But in practice, organizations pressed by resources and schedule often believe—incorrectly and without foundation—that evolving an unstructured system into the production system will be less expensive. Later, they pay the price, and dearly.

4.1.1.1.3 The Potential Conflict with Functionality and Ease of Use

A third important reason that adherence to the principles in Box 4.1 is relatively rare is the potential conflict with functionality. In many cases, introducing cybersecurity to a system's design slows it down or makes it harder to use. Implementing the checking, monitoring, and recovery needed for secure operation requires a lot of computation and does not come for free. At the same time, commodity products—out of which many critical operational systems are built—are often constrained by limited resources and cost, even while the market demands ever-higher performance and functionality.

4.1.1.2 The Relevant Research

In light of the issues above and the historically well-known difficulties in conventional computer system development (and especially the software), research and development (R&D) should be undertaken aimed at adapting the design principles of Box 4.1 for use in realistic and common software development environments that also do not make excessive sacrifices for performance or cost. Today, there are well-established methodologies for design-to-cost and design-for-performance but no comparable methodologies for designing systems in such a way that security functionality can be implemented systematically or even that the security properties of a system can be easily understood. Indeed, security reviews are generally laborious and time-consuming, a fact that reduces the attention that can be paid to security in the design process.

In general, the design process needs to consider security along with performance and cost. One essential element of a "design-for-security evaluation" will be approaches for dealing with system complexity, so that genuinely modular system construction is possible and the number of unanticipated interactions between system components is kept to a bare minimum, as discussed in Box 4.1. In any given case, the right balance will need to be determined between reducing the intrinsic complexity of a system (e.g., as expressed in the realistic requirements for security, reliability, availability, survivability, human safety, and so on) and using architectural means that simplify the interfaces and maintainability (e.g., through abstraction, encapsulation, clean interface design, and design tools that identify and enable the removal of undesired interactions and incompatibilities and hindrances to composability). This point also illustrates the need to address security issues in the overall architecture of applications and not just as added-on security appliances or components to protect an intrinsically unsafe design.

Another important element is the tracing of requirements to design decisions through implementation. That is, from a security standpoint (as well as for other purposes, such as system maintenance), it is important to know what code (or circuitry) in the final artifact corresponds to what requirements in the system's specification. Any code or circuitry that does not correspond to something in the system specification is inherently suspect. (See also Section 4.1.3.1.) Today, this problem is largely unsolved, and such documentation—in those rare instances when it does exist—is generated manually. Apart from the labor-intensiveness of the manual generation of such documentation, a manual approach applied to a complex system virtually guarantees that some parts of the code or circuitry will remain untraced to any requirement, simply because it has been overlooked. Moreover, for all practical purposes, a manual process requires that the original designers and implementers be intimately involved, since the connections between requirement and code or circuitry must be documented in near real time. Once these individuals are no longer available for consultation, these connections are inevitably lost.

With respect to the issue of short-term expense, R&D might develop both technical and organizational approaches to reducing short-term costs. From a technical perspective, it would be desirable to have tools that facilitate the reuse of existing design work. From an organizational perspective, different ways of structuring design and development teams might enable a more cost-effective way of exploiting and leveraging existing knowledge and good judgment.

Finally, it is worth developing design methods that proactively anticipate potential attacks. *Threat-based design* is one possible approach that requires the identification and characterization of the threats and potential attacks, finding mechanisms that hostile parties may employ to attack or gain entry to a computing system, and redesigning these mechanisms to eliminate or mitigate these potential security vulnerabilities. A further challenge is that of undertaking such design in a way that does not compromise design-to-cost and design-for-performance goals, such as high performance, low cost, small footprint, low energy consumption, and ease of use.

4.1.2 Research to Support Development

4.1.2.1 Hardware Support for Security

Today, systems developers embody most of the security functionality in software. But hardware and computer architecture can also support more secure systems. In the past two to three decades, computer and microprocessor architects have focused on improving the performance of computers. However, in the same way that processing capability has been used in recent years to improve the user experience (e.g., through the use of compute-intensive graphics), additional increases in hardware performance (e.g., faster processors, larger memories, higher bandwidth connections) may well be usable for improving security.

Compared with software-based security functionality, hardware-based support for security has two primary advantages. One advantage is that new hardware primitives can be used to make security operations fast and easily accessible, thus eliminating the performance penalty often seen when the same functionality is based in software and increasing the likelihood that this functionality will be used. A second advantage is that it tends to be more trustworthy, because it is much harder for an attacker to corrupt hardware than to corrupt software.

Some critics of implementing security in hardware believe that security is inflexible and cannot adapt to changes in the environment or in attacker patterns. But hardware support for security need not imply that the entire security function desired must be implemented in hardware. Research is needed to determine the fundamental hardware primitives or features that should be added to allow flexible use by software to construct more secure systems.

Hardware support can be leveraged in several ways. First, faster computing allows software to do more checking and to do more encrypting. Increases in raw processing performance can be large enough to allow more modular, more trustworthy software to run at acceptable speeds—that is, special-purpose software tricks used to enhance performance that also violated canons of secure program construction are much less necessary than they were in the past.

Second, specific checking capability can be added to the processor itself, supporting a kind of "hardware reference monitor." This is especially easy to contemplate at the moment, given the current trend to multicore architectures—some cores can be used for checking other cores.

The checks possible can be quite sophisticated, monitoring not only what actions are being requested but checking those actions in the context of past execution.[3] Such checking can be used to ensure that applications, middleware, and even privileged operating system software do not perform actions that violate security policies. Hardware can also provide a safety net for potentially harmful actions taken by software, such as executing code that should be considered data. Since the hardware processor executes all software code, it can provide valuable "defense-in-depth" support in preventing software from compromising system security and integrity.

Third, security-specific operations can be added into hardware. For example, processors can be designed in which data that are written to memory are encrypted leaving the processor and decrypted when they return to the processor. Or, instructions can be stored in memory in encrypted form and then decrypted by the hardware just prior to execution. Some proposals for hardware-implemented security operations even go so far as to make the operations of these special operations invisible to other computations that occur on that processor.

Hardware can also implement a trustworthy and protected memory for storing secrets (typically, a small number). These secrets cannot be retrieved by software (so they are guaranteed to remain secret no matter what software is running); rather, they are used—for example, to encrypt data—by invoking hardware primitives that use those secrets and return the result. This approach was first implemented in smart cards some years ago, but smart cards have often proved slow and inconvenient to use. Smart cards were followed by a succession of other positionings of the functionality, including outboard secure co-processors and modified microprocessors.

The desirability of any given positioning depends, at least in part, on the nature of the threat. For example, if the hardware support for security appears on additional chips elsewhere on a board, then an attacker with physical access to the computer board might succeed without very sophisticated equipment. Placing the support on the microprocessor chip itself significantly complicates such attacks.

An example of embedding security-specific features into hardware to protect a user's information is provided by Lee et al.,[4] who have developed a secret-protected (SP) architecture that enables the secure and con-

[3]Paul Williams and Eugene H. Spafford, "CuPIDS: An Exploration of Highly Focused, Coprocessor-Based Information System Protection," *Computer Networks*, 51(5): 1284-1298, April 2007.

[4]R. Lee, P. Kwan, J.P. McGregor, J. Dwoskin, and Z. Wang, "Architecture for Protecting Critical Secrets in Microprocessors," *Proceedings of the 32nd International Symposium on Computer Architecture*, IEEE Computer Society, Washington, D.C., pp. 2-13, June 2005.

venient protection of a user's sensitive information stored in an online environment, by providing hardware protection of critical secrets such as cryptographic keys belonging to a given user. In the SP architecture, keys follow their users and are not associated with any particular device. Thus, a given user can securely employ his or her keys on multiple devices, and a given device can be used by different users.

The SP architecture is based on several elements. One element is the existence of a concealed execution mode in an SP-enhanced microprocessor, which allows a process to execute without its state being tampered with or observed by other processes, including the main operating system running on the processor. It includes a very efficient mechanism for runtime attestation of trusted code. A second element is a trusted software module running in concealed execution mode that performs the necessary protected computations on users' secret keys, thus protecting all key information (the keys themselves, the computations, and intermediate states) from observation and tampering by adversaries. A third element is a chain of user cryptographic keys that are needed for accessing, and the protecting by encryption of any amount of sensitive information. This chain is stored in encrypted form (and thus can be resident anywhere), but it can be decrypted with a master key known only to the user. Similarly, user data, programs, and files encrypted by these keys can be stored safely in public online storage and accessed over public networks. A fourth element is a secure input/output (I/O) channel that enables the user to pass the master key to the SP hardware and the trusted software module without the risk that other modules may intercept the master key. (SP architecture also requires a variety of specific hardware and operating system enhancements for implementing these elements.)

Lee et al. suggest that SP architecture may be valuable for applications other than protecting cryptographic keys—applications such as digital rights management and privacy protection systems. Also, different scenarios, such as those requiring "transient trust" in providing protected data to crisis responders, can be supported with small extensions to the SP architecture. Lee et al. also note that while various proposals exist for secure I/O and secure bootstrapping, more research is needed to study alternatives that can be integrated into SP-like architectures for commodity computing and communications devices. SP architecture demonstrates that security-enhancing hardware features can be easily added to microprocessors and flexibly employed by software applications without degrading a system's performance, cost, or ease of use.

Another example of recent work in this area is the new generation of hardware being shipped with secure co-processors that can store encryption keys and can perform encryption and hash functions. Specifically, the Trusted Computing Group is an industry consortium that has proposed a Trusted Platform Module (TPM) that is added to the I/O bus of a computing device to enable the measurement of the bits of the software stack that is installed, in order to detect changes in the software.[5] It can provide useful security functionality that can be leveraged by many applications. TPM is a step forward in hardware-based security, but there are some limitations, such as the fact that the TPM definition of "remote attestation" enables checking the integrity of the bits on the entire software stack on program launch, but it does not do any checks after that for dynamic hostile code insertion and modification. TPM also has a threat model limited to software attacks and does not provide any coverage for even simple physical attacks like bus or memory probing; these probably should be considered because of the easy theft or loss of mobile or personal computing devices. TPM is available in some personal computers.

A system with tamper-proof hardware, or with hardware features that support the tamper-proofing of software, has the potential to radically change the way that operating systems enforce security. In particular, such a system provides a basis for doing secure attestation of programs and data—both locally and remotely. For example, a program might be accompanied by an attestation that describes its hash, thereby preventing modified programs (with the same name) from being executed. (In general, an attestation can refer to almost any property of a program and not just to the specific machine code realization of a program.) To ensure that a given software module is unaltered, one might digitally sign it—however, maintaining the binding between the hash and the software can be problematic without hardware support. In the longer run, operating systems might support programs accompanied by attestations which assert that some analyzer has checked the program (along with attestations that give a basis for trusting the analyzer and trusting the environment in which it executed) or asserting that some program has been "wrapped" in a reference monitor which ensures that certain policies are enforced.[6]

Much fundamental research remains to be done to determine what kinds of attestations will be useful to users and how difficult it will be for such attestations to be developed. There are also new legal issues to be addressed, since basic questions of ownership and control over computational resources come to the fore. (For example, the notion of hardware-based restrictions on certain uses of programs and data stored on one's computer is inconsistent with the tradition that one has unlim-

---

[5]Trusted Computing Group, "Trusted Platform Module (TPM) Specifications," April 2006; available at https://www.trustedcomputinggroup.org/specs/TPM.

[6]Alan Shieh, Dan Williams, Emin Gun Sirer, and Fred B. Schneider, "Nexus: A New Operating System for Trustworthy Computing," Work in Progress Session, *20th Symposium on Operating System Principles*, October 2005; available at http://www.cs.cornell.edu/fbs/publications/NexusSOSPwip.pdf.

ited technical freedom to do as one pleases with programs and data on one's computer.)

Another example is the recent introduction of multicore processors. These processors allow security checking to be done in parallel with other instruction processing, but the dominant application is support of code safety rather than checking access-control privileges. Today, it is not known how best to use multicore processors, and devoting some of their resources to security checking may have significant security advantages. New architectures in operating systems will be necessary to fully leverage the potential for such hardware.

Still another security function that may be more appropriately implemented in hardware is the generation of random numbers, which can be used for cryptographic keys or for nonces.[7] Random numbers generated through software are much more guessable by an opponent, since the opponent must be presumed to have access to the same software. Thus, since poor choice of random numbers leads to vulnerabilities, hardware implementation of random number generators—strictly speaking, generators for random seeds to be used as inputs into (pseudo) random number generators—allows for the continuing injection of randomness into the pool. Protection of the random seed generator and the pseudo-random number generator is more effectively accomplished in hardware.

Finally, the processor is not the only hardware element in a computing system. How other hardware elements might contribute to security is as yet almost entirely unexplored.

4.1.2.2 Tamper Resistance

The tamper resistance of an IT artifact (which includes resistance to inspection and to alteration) is also an important property. Improving the tamper resistance of hardware can increase the robustness of a system, because security functionality implemented at a high level of abstraction (in software) can often be subverted by tampering at lower levels (in hardware). Improving the tamper resistance of such artifacts is especially important in a world of pervasive computing, in which hardware devices with networked connectivity will proliferate in an unconstrained manner and thus may well be available for adversaries to examine and modify.

[7] A nonce is a number that is used in a protocol only once. For example, it can be used in an authentication protocol to ensure that an old message cannot be reused in a replay attack. Since an authentication protocol will typically require a nonce as an input variable, a replay attack is virtually impossible because the infinitesimally small likelihood that any given nonce will be identical to a previous one.

Research in both the creation of tamper-resistant components and how they can be effectively exploited is valuable.

For example, Lie et al. have developed a hardware implementation of a form of execute-only memory that allows instructions stored in memory to be executed but not otherwise manipulated.[8] In particular, software cannot be copied or modified without detection. A machine supporting internal compartments is required, in which a process in one compartment cannot read data from another compartment. All data that leave the machine are encrypted, since it must be assumed that external memory is not secure. There are trade-offs among security, efficiency, and flexibility, but the analysis of Lie et al. indicates that it is possible to create a normal multitasking machine in which nearly all applications can be run in an execute-only mode.

A second dimension of tamper resistance is that of increasing the difficulty of reverse-engineering a given object code. This can be problematic, as the object code must ultimately be read in its original form to be executed. One might encrypt object code, and decrypt it only when necessary for execution. However, in the absence of special-purpose hardware to carry out such decryption,[9] it might be possible for an adversary to intercept the code as it is being decrypted and run.

Another class of techniques is known as code obfuscation, which refers to processes through which object code can be rewritten and/or stored in forms that are hard to transform into meaningful source code.[10] Code obfuscation is intended to transform the object program in ways that do not alter its function but make it more difficult to understand. The new transformed program may have slower execution times or exhibit behavior not found in the original program, and managing this trade-off between undesirable behavior and degree of obfuscation remains a key challenge in developing code-obfuscation techniques.

Finally, a degree of tamper resistance can be obtained by adding code ("guards") that monitor for changes to the code and take action if tamper-

[8]D. Lie, C. Thekkath, M. Mitchell, P. Lincoln, D. Boneh, J. Mitchell, and M. Horowitz, "Architectural Support for Copy and Tamper Resistant Software," *Proceedings of the 9th International Conference on Architectural Support for Programming Languages and Operating Systems*, pp. 168-177, 2000.

[9]See, for example, Amir Herzberg and Shlomit S. Pinter, "Public Protection of Software," *ACM Transactions on Computer Systems*, 5(4): 371-393, November 1987.

[10]Boaz Barak, "Can We Obfuscate Programs?," available at http://www.math.ias.edu/~boaz/Papers/obf_informal.html#obfpaper; Douglas Low, "Protecting Java Code Via Code Obfuscation," available at http://www.cs.arizona.edu/~collberg/Research/Students/DouglasLow/obfuscation.html.

ing is detected.[11] Such an approach is the foundation behind at least one commercial enterprise.[12]

4.1.2.3 Process Isolation

A third interesting area is that of process isolation and separation. The ability to virtualize multiple processes running on the same processor has been in hand since the early 1960s on the PDP-1 and in the mid-1960s on IBM mainframe computers. In more recent times, early microprocessors such as the Intel 8086 lacked an instruction set architecture that could support virtualization, and this deficiency persisted through the instruction set architecture of the Pentium.[13] As the instruction set evolved to be more capable and processor speeds rose, virtualization of these microprocessors became feasible—and was useful as well, because of the increasing needs for isolation in a changing threat environment.

The basic requirements for virtualization were described in 1974 by Popek and Goldberg.[14] The basic work on virtualization to run multiple operating systems was done at IBM for the 7044,[15] the 360/40,[16] and the first product CP/67 for the 360/67.[17] Virtualization makes it possible to run multiple operating systems (and their applications) on a single server, reducing overall hardware costs. Production and test systems can run at the same time in the same hardware, and different operating systems such as Windows and Linux can share the same server. Virtualization may also have particular relevance to improving security in operating systems that are designed to be backward compatible with earlier versions. Virtualization can increase the load factor on servers and other systems, thus

---

[11]See Hoi Chang, 2003, "Building Self-Protecting Software with Active and Passive Defenses," Ph.D. dissertation, Department of Computer Science, Purdue University.

[12]For an example of a commercial enterprise based on products using this approach, see http://www.arxan.com.

[13]J.S. Robin and C.E. Irvine, "Analysis of the Intel Pentium's Ability to Support a Secure Virtual Machine Monitor," 9th USENIX Security Symposium, August 14-17, 2000, Denver, Colo.: USENIX, The Advanced Computing Systems Association, pp. 129-144; available at http://www.usenix.org/events/sec2000/robin.html.

[14]G.J. Popek and R.P. Goldberg, "Formal Requirements for Virtualizable Third Generation Architectures," *Communications of the ACM*, 17(7): 412-421, July 1974.

[15]R.W. O'Neill, "Experience Using a Time-Shared Multi-Programming System with Dynamic Address Relocation Hardware," pp. 611-621 in Vol. 30, *Proceedings of the 1967 Spring Joint Computer Conference*, April 18-20, 1967, Atlantic City, N.J.: Thompson Books.

[16]A.B. Lindquist, R.R. Seeber, and L.W. Comeau, "A Time-Sharing System Using an Associative Memory," *Proceedings of the IEEE*, 54(12): 1774-1779, December 1966.

[17]R.A. Meyer and L.H. Seawright, "A Virtual Machine Time-Sharing System," *IBM Systems Journal*, 9(3): 199-218, 1970; available at http://www.research.ibm.com/journal/sj/093/ibmsj0903D.pdf.

utilizing central processing unit cycles that would otherwise be wasted unproductively.

The major challenge today in process separation is that of achieving the capability to allow selected interactions between processes (that is, in defining and enforcing policies for information flow), and of course interactions between processes mean that independence and separation can no longer be guaranteed. Consider, for example, that a mailer and a Web browser might run on separate virtual machines. That would prevent downloaded malware from a Web site from having a harmful effect on the mailer. But what should be done if the user wants to mail a Web page? Or if the user wants to view the Web page corresponding to a URL in a received e-mail? The general problem, not solvable in the abstract, is in deciding whether any proposed interaction between processes will be harmful or not. Put differently, the issue is unanticipated consequences of interactions that are allowed and designed into the system, rather than failures in the isolation of a virtual machine in the first place. Note also that when large-scale storage devices must also be shared between processes for storing the data associated with each process, these processes must interact implicitly as they seek and obtain access to such devices, even if such interactions are not explicitly allowed by whatever security policy is in place.

Finally, the integration of higher-level components that have not been optimized for use in a secure kernel environment remains a challenge. Isolation is a relatively easily exploitable benefit, in that a component should be able to run in a virtual environment just as easily as in a real one. But other services can exploit the services provided by secure kernels as well. For example, security services can benefit from isolation because they are less easily subverted in that configuration and have greater tamper resistance. In addition, because they are isolated, they are likely to have different failure modes than if they were run in the main system. Some examples include the following: antivirus services that depend on trustworthy databases to identify viruses, provenance services that securely store the provenance of every file out of reach of the main operating system, network services that check provenance metadata prior to forwarding real data to applications, event-monitoring and -logging services for detecting problems or to support subsequent forensic investigation, and automated recovery services that enable recovery to a system state captured at some point prior to some security failure.

A different approach to process separation is to isolate functionality on multiple processors. The theory underlying this approach is that processing power is increasingly inexpensive, thus putting a lower premium on maximizing the efficiency of computational capability. Especially with multicore processors available, it becomes possible in principle for one processor to run a single application, thus increasing its immunity from flaws in other applications. The operating system for that application can thus be written in a way that supports only that application, which implies that it can be made much simpler than an operating system designed for general-purpose use. Further, from a security standpoint, the behavior of a simpler and more specialized system is easier to specify, and hence deviations from normal behavior are easier to detect.[18]

4.1.2.4 Language-Based Security

Language-based security is an approach to security that is based on techniques developed in the programming-language community to ensure that programs can be relied on not to violate some policy of interest.[19] The techniques involved include analysis and transformation. One well-known form of analysis is "type checking," whereby the fact that a program does certain unsafe things is detected before the program is run. One well-known form of program transformation is the addition of runtime checks to a program, whereby a program is instrumented in a way that prevents the (instrumented) program from making a problematic (i.e., policy-violating) transformation.[20]

These techniques are applicable to a wide variety of systems: systems written in high-end languages, legacy systems, and systems whose code is represented only as machine language today. These techniques also have special relevance to writing systems that enforce information flow and integrity policies, which are "end to end" and far more general than the usual "access-control policies" that today's operating systems enforce, and for creating "artificial diversity" (by program rewriting) so that different instances of a program are not subject to common attacks.

4.1.2.5 Component Interfaces

Sound interface design must be integrated into system architecture. A basic goal of interface design should be to encourage the development and analysis of system requirements, policies, architectures, and interfaces that will greatly enhance the understandability of computer

---

[18]Eric Bryant et al., "Poly^2 Paradigm: A Secure Network Service Architecture"; available at http://www.acsac.org/2003/abstracts/72.html.

[19]Fred B. Schneider, Greg Morrisett, and Robert Harper, "A Language-Based Approach to Security," pp. 86-101 in *Informatics: 10 Years Back, 10 Years Ahead*, Lecture Notes in Computer Science, Vol. 2000, Reihnard Wilhelm (ed.), Springer-Verlag, Heidelberg, 2000.

[20]Fred B. Schneider, "Enforceable Security Policies," *ACM Transactions on Information and System Security* 3(1): 30-50, February 2000.

systems and their behavior as observed by application developers, system administrators, and users.

The achievement of sound interfaces can have enormous benefits in the development, procurement, operation, and use of those computer systems and associated networks. This effort has user- and system-oriented aspects, particularly in trying to reduce the semantic gap between what can be derived from specific interfaces and what can be obtained by detailed examination of source code, libraries, compilers, interpreters, operating system environments, networking, and system administration tools.

Particular emphasis is also needed on the use of analysis techniques for defining and analyzing system interfaces so that the desired behavior that they represent and the dependencies among different interfaces can be more easily understood and controlled. The approach should be both constructive (in terms of developing or modifying systems to achieve more understandable behavior) and analytic (in terms of trying to figure out what is happening dynamically, especially when something unusual occurs), and it should be applicable to interfaces for operating systems, applications, and system administration.

As an illustration, consider what it means to specify a component interface. These interfaces typically describe how a component is supposed to respond to certain inputs (or a range of inputs). But many component designers fail to specify the behavior for other inputs, and this is exactly the space within which attackers search for inputs that will make the component act outside its specification.

Composability is particularly relevant in the design of interfaces. For example, combining two components with well-designed interfaces may introduce unwanted side effects that are not evident from either interface. This is clearly undesirable and needs to be avoided through sound interface and system design.

Research and development areas specifically oriented to interface design might include the following:

- *The development of models and static-analysis tools for evaluating interface specifications and determining their composability, interdependencies, and ability to enforce security requirements.* Of considerable interest to the development of secure systems would be the following:

  —The ability to analyze individual interfaces for logical consistency, completeness with respect to functionality that must be included, uniformity of interface conventions, consistency with documentation, understandability, and ease of use;
  —The ability to analyze the interactions among different interfaces, as part of the ability to create systems as predictable composi-

tions of carefully analyzed components, with analysis of how the properties of the individual interfaces are affected; and
—The ability to determine the minimal subsets of systems whose functionality is sufficient to satisfy the given requirements, and to identify any hidden dependencies on unvalidated functionality.

In addition, extensive guidelines should be developed for perspicuous interfaces, for use with various software development methodologies and programming languages.

- *The establishment of systematic approaches for handling exception conditions, concurrency, and remediation under adverse conditions.* For example, it is important to avoid bad system behavior where possible and to be able to respond rapidly to potentially complex system misbehavior or attacks, and to ensure that appropriate handles are accessible in the visible interfaces without cluttering up normal use and creating more opportunities for human error.
- *The development and constructive use of metrics for usability, particularly with respect to security issues such as access controls, authentication protocols, system administration, and so on.* Usability metrics for visible interfaces must be an integral part of the development process. They must also be incorporated into any evaluation processes, such as those built into the Common Criteria process.[21]
- *The supplementing of the design and development process with assurance techniques specifically relevant to the interfaces, including the ability to identify additional hidden and detrimental functionality that can be accessed through the interface in undocumented or unspecified ways.* For example, an interface might include a test function inserted during debugging that exposes cryptographic keys. Although such a function should be removed before release, its actual removal may be overlooked.

Note that these areas may require semantic knowledge of the underlying components (such as specifications or implementations) and cannot be based solely on the interfaces themselves.

4.1.2.6 Cryptology

Today, with many advances already made in cryptography, it is tempting to believe that cryptography is well enough understood that it does not warrant further research. Nevertheless, as the recent success in break-

[21] For more information on the Common Criteria process, see http://www.commoncriteriaportal.org/.

ing the SHA-1 hash algorithm suggests,[22] the intellectual infrastructure of cryptography for commercial and other nonmilitary/nondiplomatic use is not as secure as one might believe. Growing computational power (which led to the vulnerability of the Data Encryption Standard to brute-force decryption) and increasingly sophisticated cryptanalytic tools mean that the study of even these very basic cryptographic primitives (encryption and hash algorithms) has continuing value. Moreover, what had been viewed as esoteric cryptographic primitives and methods of mostly theoretical interest—threshold cryptography, proactive security, and multiparty computation—are now being seen as exactly the right primitives for building distributed systems that are more secure.

Nor are interesting areas in cryptology restricted to cryptography. For example, the development of secure protocols is today more of an art than a science, at least in the public literature, and further research on the theory of secure protocols is needed. A related point is that real-world cryptosystems or components can be implemented in such a way that the security which they allegedly provide can be compromised through unanticipated information "leakages" that adversaries can exploit or cause.[23] In addition, despite the widespread availability of encryption tools, most electronic communications and data are still unencrypted—a point suggesting that the infrastructure of cryptology remains ill-suited for widespread and routine use. Many practical problems, such as the deployment of usable public-key infrastructures, continue to lack scalable solutions. The conceptual complexity of employing encryption and the potential exposures that come

---

[22]More precisely, an attack against the SHA-1 algorithm has been developed that reduces its known run-time collision resistance by a factor of 2^{11} (from 2^{80} to 2^{69}) (Xiaoyun Wang, Yiqun Lisa Yin, and Hongbo Yu, "Finding Collisions in the Full SHA-1," *Advances in Cryptology—Crypto'05*; available at http://www.infosec.sdu.edu.cn/paper/sha1-crypto-auth-new-2-yao.pdf). In addition, Adi Shamir announced during the Rump Session at Crypto'05 (on August 15, 2005) that Wang and other collaborators had demonstrated the possibility of finding a collision in SHA-1 in 2^{63} operations, although no actual collisions had been found. This result applies only to collision resistance, which means that digital signatures are placed at risk, but the result does not affect constructions for key derivation, message authentication codes, or random function behavior (i.e., it does not affect any construction in which specific content may be at issue).

[23]For example, Paul Kocher has developed attacks on certain real-world systems that can reveal secret keys in much less time than would be required by brute-force techniques, even though the cryptography in these systems has been implemented perfectly. Kocher's attacks are based on timing and/or power measurements of the systems involved. See, for example, Paul Kocher et al., "Timing Attacks on Implementations of Diffie-Hellman, RSA, DSS, and Other Systems," December 1995, available at http://www.cryptography.com/resources/whitepapers/TimingAttacks.pdf; and Paul Kocher et al., "Introduction to Differential Power Analysis and Related Attacks," 1998, available at http://www.cryptography.com/dpa/technical/.

with doing it wrong strongly suggest the need for research to understand where, how, and when it fits into security architecture.

As an example of bringing cryptographic theory into practice, consider multiparty computations. Here, a collection of parties engages in computing some function of the values that each has, but no party learns values that the others have. Moreover, some protocols defend against having a fraction of the participants be compromised.

Threshold digital signatures are a simple example of a multiparty computation. This functionality is useful (though it has not yet enjoyed widespread practical use) when a service is implemented by a replicated set of servers. (Any majority of the servers can together create a signature for responses from the service, but no individual server is capable of impersonating the service.) However, more sophisticated multiparty computation algorithms have not yet made the transition from theory to practice. So-called proactive cryptographic protocols are another area of interest. These protocols call for the periodic changing of secrets so that information that an attacker gleans from successfully compromising a host is short-lived. Effecting the transition of this cryptographically supported functionality from theory to practice will change the toolbox that systems builders use and could well enable systems that are more secure through the clever deployment of these new cryptographic primitives.

Finally, as new mathematical methods are discovered and as new computing technology becomes available, what is unbreakable today may be penetrable next week. As one example, consider that quantum computing, if made practical, would invalidate several existing methods thought to be unbreakable. Likewise, it has not yet been proven that prime factorization is an NP problem, and that NP is not reducible to P. Thus, it is possible that future discoveries could change a number of the current assumptions about systems such as the RSA algorithm—suggesting that work on developing new basic cryptographic primitives is useful as a hedge against such possibilities.

4.1.3 Research to Support Testing and Evaluation

Testing and evaluation (T&E) are necessary because of the nature of information technology artifacts as things designed and implemented by people, who make mistakes. T&E generally consumes half or more of the overall cost for a software system. T&E occurs at every level of granularity in a system (unit to subassembly, to overall system, to deployed system in situ), and at all process phases, starting with requirements.

Traditional testing involves issues of coverage. Testing every statement may not be enough, but it may nonetheless be difficult to achieve. Testing every branch and path is even harder, since there is generally a combinatorially large number of paths. How much coverage is needed, and what are the metrics of coverage?

4.1.3.1 Finding Unintended Functionality

One of the most challenging problems in testing and evaluation is that of auditing a complex artifact for functionality that has not been included in the specification of requirements and that may result in security vulnerabilities. In a world of outsourced and offshore chip fabrication and/or code development and given the possibilities that trusted designers or programmers might not be so trustworthy, it is an important task to ensure that functionality has not been added to a hardware or software system that is not consistent with the system's specifications.

However, the complexity of today's IT artifacts is such that this task is virtually impossible to accomplish for any real system, and the problem will only get worse in the future. Today, the best testing methodologies can be divided into two types: (1) efforts to find the problems whose presence is a priori known, and (2) directed but random testing of everything else that might reveal an "unknown unknown." Formal methods may also offer some promise for finding unintended functionality, although their ability to handle large systems is still quite limited.

These considerations suggest that comprehensive cybersecurity involves both secure hardware and secure software at every level of the protocol stack, from the physical layer up. This is not to say that every IT application must be run on hardware or software that has been designed and fabricated by trustworthy parties—only that the sensitivity of the application should determine what level of concern should be raised about possible cybersecurity flaws that may have been deliberately embedded in hardware or software.

4.1.3.2 Test Case Generation

A second dimension of testing is to ensure that testing is based on a "good" set of test cases. For example, it is well known that test cases should include some malformed inputs and some that are formally derived from specifications and from code, and in particular, cases that go outside the specification and break the assumptions of the specification. Such cases will often reveal security vulnerabilities if they do exist.

Testing can focus on particular attributes beyond just functional behavior. For example, a security test might focus on behavior with out-of-specification inputs, or it might occur when the system is under load beyond its declared range, and so on. Similarly, unit or subsystem testing could focus on the "robustness" of internal interfaces as a way to assess how an overall system might contain an error, keeping an error within the confines of a subsystem by tolerating and recovering.

A related point is the development of test suites for commonly used software for which there are multiple implementations. For example, Chen et al. documented the existence of different semantics in three different versions of Unix (Linux, Solaris, and FreeBSD) for system calls (the uid-setting system calls) that manage system privileges afforded to users.[24] Their conclusion was that these different semantics were responsible for many security vulnerabilities. Appropriate test suites would help to verify the semantics and standards compliance of system calls, library routines, compilers, and so on.

4.1.3.3 Tools for Testing and Evaluation

A third important dimension of testing and evaluation is the real-world usability of tools and approaches for T&E, many of which suffer from real-world problems of scalability, adoptability, and cost. For example:

- Tools for static code analysis are often clumsy to use and sometimes flag an enormous number of issues that must be ignored because they are not prioritized in any way and because resources are not available to address all of them.
- Dynamic behavior analysis, especially in distributed asynchronous systems, is poorly developed. For example, race conditions—the underlying cause of a number of major vulnerabilities—are difficult to find, and tools oriented toward their discovery are largely absent.
- Model checking, code and program analysis, formal verification, and other "semantics-based" techniques are becoming practical only for modestly sized real-system software components. Considerable further work is needed to extend the existing theory of formal verification to the compositions of subsystems.

All of these T&E techniques require some kind of specification of what is intended. With testing, the test cases themselves form a specification, and indeed agile techniques rely on testing for this purpose. Inspection allows more informal descriptions. Analysis and semantics-based

---

[24] Hao Chen, David Wagner, and Drew Dean, "Setuid Demystified," *Proceedings of the 11th USENIX Security Symposium*, pp. 171-190, 2002; available at http://www.cs.berkeley.edu/~daw/papers/setuid-usenix02.pdf.

techniques rely on various focused "attribute-specific" specifications of intent.

Inspection is another important technique related to testing and evaluation. Inspection underlies the Common Criteria (ISO 15408), but it relies on subjective human judgment in the sense that the attention of the human inspectors may be guided through the use of tools and agreed frameworks for inspection. Moreover, the use of human inspectors is expensive, suggesting that inspection as a technique for testing and evaluation does not easily scale to large projects.

4.1.3.4 Threat Modeling

Today, most security certification and testing are based on a "test to the specification" process. That is, the process begins with an understanding of the threats against which defenses are needed. Defenses against those threats are reflected as system specifications that are included in the overall specification process for a system. Testing is then performed against those specifications. While this process is reasonably effective in finding functionality that is absent from the system as implemented (this is known because that functionality is reflected in the specification), it has two major weaknesses.

The first weakness of the test-to-the-specification process is that it requires a set of clear and complete specifications that can be used to drive the specifics of the testing procedure. However, as noted in Section 4.1.1, a great deal of real-world software development makes use of methodologies based on spiral and incremental development in which the software "evolves" to meet the new needs that users have expressed as they learn and use the software. This means that it is an essentially impossible task to specify complex software on an a priori basis. Thus, specifications used for testing are generally written after the software has been written. This means that the implemented functionality determines the specifications, and consequently the specifications themselves are no better than the understanding of the system on the part of the developers and implementers. That understanding is necessarily informal (and hence incomplete), because it is, by assumption, not based on any kind of formal methodology. (The fact that these specifications are developed after the fact also makes them late and not very relevant to the software development process, but those are beyond the scope of this report.)

The second weakness, related to the first, is that this methodology is not particularly good at finding additional functionality that goes beyond what is formally specified. (Section 4.1.3.1 addresses some of the difficulties in finding such problems.)

Weaknesses in a test-to-the-specification approach suggest that complementary approaches are needed. In particular, threat modeling and threat-based testing are becoming increasingly important. In these approaches, a set of threats is characterized, and testing activities include testing defenses against those threats. (This is the complement to threat-based design, described in Section 4.1.1.2.)

This approach can be characterized as, "Tell me the threats that you are defending against and prove to me that you have done so." Research in this domain involves the development of techniques to characterize broader categories of threat and more formal methods to determine the adequacy of defenses against those threats. For those situations in which a threat is known and a vulnerability is present but no defense is available, developing instrumentation to monitor the vulnerability for information on the threat may be a useful thing to do as well. Research is also needed for enabling spiral methodologies to take into account new threats as a system "evolves" to have new features.

4.2 GRACEFUL DEGRADATION AND RECOVERY

If the principle of defense in depth is taken seriously, system architects and designers must account for the possibility that defenses will be breached, in which case it is necessary to contain the damage that a breach might cause and/or to recover from the damage that was caused. Although security efforts should focus on reducing vulnerabilities proactively where possible, it is important that a system provide containment to limit the damage that a security breach can cause and recovery to maximize the ease with which a system or network can recover from an exploitation. Progress in this area most directly supports Provision II and Provision III of the Cybersecurity Bill of Rights, and indirectly supports Provision VII.

4.2.1 Containment

There are many approaches to containing damage:

- *Engineered heterogeneity*. In agriculture, monocultures are known to be highly vulnerable to blight. In a computer security context, a population of millions of identically programmed digital objects is systematically vulnerable to an exploit that targets a specific security defect, especially if all of those objects are attached to the

Internet.[25] If it is the specifics of a given object code that result in a particular vulnerability, a different object code rewritten automatically to preserve the original object code's high-end functionality may eliminate that vulnerability. (Of course, it is a requirement of such rewriting that it not introduce another vulnerability. Moreover, such methods can interfere with efforts to debug software undertaken at the object code level, as well as with legitimate third-party software add-ons and enhancements, suggesting that there are trade-offs to be analyzed concerning whether or not automatic rewriting is appropriate or not in any given situation.)

- *Disposable computing*. An attacker who compromises or corrupts a system designed to be disposable—that is, a computing environment whose corruption or compromise does not matter much to the user—is unlikely to gain much in the way of additional resources or privileges.[26] A disposable computing environment can thus be seen as a buffer between the outside world and the "real" computing environment in which serious business can be undertaken. When the outside world manifests a presence in the buffer zone, the resulting behavior is observed, thus providing an empirical basis for deciding whether and/or in what form to allow that presence to be passed through to the "real" environment. As in the case of process isolation, the challenge in disposable computing is to develop methods for safe interaction between the buffer and the "real" environment.

  One classic example of disposable computing is Java, which was widely adopted because its sandboxing technology created a perimeter around the execution context of the applet code. That is, an applet could do anything inside the sandbox but was constrained from affecting anything outside the sandbox.
- *Virtualization and isolation*. As discussed in Section 4.1.2.3, isolation is one way of confining the reach of an application or a software module.

---

[25]Monocultures in information technology also have an impact on the economics of insuring against cyber-disasters. Because the existence of a monoculture means that risks to systems in that monoculture are not independent, insurers face a much larger upper bound on their liability than if these risks were independent, since they might be required to pay off a large number of claims at once.

[26]Perhaps the most important gain from such an attack is knowledge and insight into the structure of that computing environment—which may be useful in conducting another attack against another similarly constructed system.

4.2.2 Recovery

A second key element of a sound defensive strategy is the ability to recover quickly from the effects of a security breach, should one occur. Indeed, in the limiting case and when information leakage is not the threat of concern, allowing corruption or compromise of a computer system may be acceptable if that system can be (almost) instantaneously restored to its correct previous state. That is, recovery can itself be regarded as a mechanism of cyberdefense when foiling an attack is not possible or feasible. Recent work in embedding transaction and journaling capabilities into basic file system structures in operating systems suggests that there is some commercial demand for this approach.

Because of the difficulty of high-confidence prevention of system compromise against high-end threats, recovery is likely to be a key element of defending against such threats. Illustrative research topics within this domain include the following:

- *Rebooting*. Rebooting a system is a step taken that resets the system state to a known initial configuration; it is a necessary step in many computer operations. For example, rebooting is often necessary when a resident system file is updated. Rebooting is also often necessary when an attack has wreaked havoc on the system state. However, rebooting is normally a time-consuming activity that results in the loss of a great deal of system state that is perfectly "healthy." Rebooting is particularly difficult when a large-scale distributed system is involved. Micro-rebooting (an instantiation of a more general approach to recovery known as software rejuvenation[27]) is a technique that reboots only the parts of the system that are failing rather than the entire system. Research in micro-rebooting includes, among other things, the development of techniques to identify components in need of rebooting and ways to reduce further the duration of outage associated with rebooting. Such considerations are particularly important in environments that require extremely high availability.

---

[27]Software rejuvenation is a technique proposed to deal with the phenomenon of software aging, one in which the performance of a software system degrades with time as the result of factors such as exhaustion of operating system resources and data corruption. In general terms, software rejuvenation calls for occasionally terminating an application or a system, cleaning its internal state and/or its environment, and restarting it. See, for example, Kalyanaraman Vaidyanathan and Kishor S. Trivedi, "A Comprehensive Model for Software Rejuvenation," *IEEE Transactions on Dependable and Secure Computing*, 2 (2, April-June): 124-137, 2005. See also http://srejuv.ee.duke.edu.

- *Online production testing*. An essential element of recovery is fault identification. One approach to facilitate such identification is online testing, in which test inputs (and sometimes deliberately faulty inputs) are inserted into running production systems to verify their proper operation. In addition, modules in the system are designed to be self-testing to verify the behavior of all other modules with which they interact.
- *Large-scale undo capabilities*. An undo capability enables system operators to roll back a system to an earlier state, and multiple layers of undo capability enable correspondingly longer roll-back periods. If a successful cyberattack occurs at a given time, rolling back the system's state to before that time is one way of recovering from the attack—and it does not depend on knowing anything about the specific nature of the attack.[28]

4.3 SOFTWARE AND SYSTEMS ASSURANCE

Software and systems assurance is focused on two related but logically distinct goals: the creation of systems that will do the right thing under the range of possible operating conditions, and human confidence that the system will indeed do the right thing.

For much of computing's history, high-assurance computing has been most relevant to systems such as real-time avionics, nuclear command and control, and so on. But in recent years, the issue of electronic voting has brought questions related to high-assurance computing squarely into the public eye. At its roots, the debate is an issue of assurance: how does (or should) the voting public become convinced that the voting process has not been compromised? In such a context, it is not enough that a system has not been compromised; it must be *known* not to have been compromised. This issue has elements of traditional high-assurance concerns (e.g., Does the program meet its specifications?) but also has broader questions concerning support for recounts, making sure the larger context cannot be used for corruption (e.g., configuration management).

A variety of techniques have been developed to promote software and

[28]Aaron B. Brown, *A Recovery-Oriented Approach to Dependable Services: Repairing Past Errors with System-Wide Undo*, University of California, Berkeley, Computer Science Division Technical Report UCB//CSD-04-1304, December 2003, available at http://roc.cs.berkeley.edu/projects/undo/index.html; A. Brown and D. Patterson, "Undo for Operators: Building an Undoable E-Mail Store," in *Proceedings of the 2003 USENIX Annual Technical Conference*, San Antonio, Tex., June 2003, available at http://roc.cs.berkeley.edu/papers/brown-emailundo-usenix03.pdf.

systems assurance, including formal requirements analysis, architectural reviews, and the testing and verification of the properties of components, compositions, and entire systems. It makes intuitive sense that developing secure systems would be subsumed under systems assurance—by definition, *secure systems* are systems that function predictably even when they are under attack.[29]

An additional challenge is how to design a system and prove assurance to a general (lay) audience. In the example above, it is the general voting public—not simply the computer science community—that is the ultimate judge of whether or not it is "sufficiently assured" that electronic voting systems are acceptably secure.

Some techniques used to enhance reliability are relevant to cybersecurity—much of software engineering research is oriented toward learning how to decide on and formulate system requirements (including tradeoffs between functionality, complexity, schedule, and cost); developing methods and tools for specifying systems, languages, and tools for programming systems (especially systems involving concurrent and distributed processing); middleware to provide common services for software systems; and so on. Testing procedures and practices (Section 4.1.3) are also intimately connected with assurance. All of these areas are relevant to the design and implementation of more secure systems, although attention to these issues can result in common solutions that address reliability, survivability, and evolvability as well.

Software engineering advances also leverage basic research in areas that seem distant from system building per se. Success in developing tools for program analysis, in developing languages for specifications, and in developing new programming languages and computational models typically leverages more foundational work—in applied logic, in algorithms, in computational complexity, in programming-language design, and in compilers.

At the same time, assurance and security are not identical, and they often seek different goals. Consider the issue of system reliability, usually regarded as a key dimension of assurance. In contrast with threats to security, threats to system reliability are nondirected and in some sense are more related to robustness against chance events such as power outages or uninformed users doing surprising or unexpected things. By contrast, threats to security are usually deliberate, involving a human adversary who has the intention to do damage and who takes actions that are decid-

[29]For more discussion of this point, see National Research Council, *Trust in Cyberspace*, National Academy Press, Washington, D.C., 1999.

edly not random. A test and evaluation regime oriented toward reliability will not necessarily be informative about security. The same is true about using redundancy as a solution to reliability, since redundancy can be at odds with heterogeneity in designing for security. Thus, it would be a mistake to conclude that focusing solely on reliability will automatically lead to high levels of cybersecurity.

5

Category 2—Enabling Accountability

The goal of requirements in Category 2 of the committee's illustrative research agenda is that of ensuring that anyone or anything that has access to a system component—a computing device, a sensor, an actuator, a network—can be held accountable for the results of such access. Enabling accountability refers to the ability to hold a party responsible for the consequences of its actions, and in particular that a consequence can be associated with appropriate parties if those actions cause harm. In this broad category are matters such as remote authentication, access control and policy management, auditing and traceability, maintenance of provenance, secure associations between system components, and so on.

5.1 ATTRIBUTION

Computer operations are inherently anonymous, a fact that presents many problems in cybersecurity. When a system is under remote attack, the attacker is generally unknown to the targeted system. When an attack has occurred, anonymous individuals cannot subsequently be held responsible and do not suffer any consequences for the harmful actions that they initiated. And, if all users of a system are anonymous, there is no way to differentiate between authorized and unauthorized actions on a system.

Attribution is the ability to associate an actor with an action. (By contrast, *authentication* refers to establishing the truth of some claim of identity.) The actor is characterized by some attribute(s), such as the name of a user, the serial number of a machine on a network, or some other distinguishing property of the actor. Attribution requires technology that is less inherently anonymous so that association between action and actor is easily ascertained, captured, and preserved.

Attribution should be conceptualized with respect to five important characteristics:

- *Precision.* A single attribute may uniquely characterize an actor, as might be the case with the complete genome sequence corresponding to a specific human being or the manufacturer's serial number on a given machine. But such attributes are by far the exception. Individuals may have the same name; the Media Access Control (MAC) address of a specific network device may not be unique, and even a human being may have an identical twin (whose genomic sequence will be identical in all respects to that of the first human being).
- *Accuracy.* A characteristic related to precision is accuracy, a measure of the quality of attribution, such as the probability that the attribution is correct (i.e., that the value of the attribute is indeed associated with the actor in question). Accuracy is a key issue in legal standards for evidence and in the extent to which it is reasonable to develop linkages and inferences based on those attributes.
- *Lifetime/duration.* As a rule, an association (which generally consists of the actor's attribute, the action, the object acted on, and other relevant data such as the time of the action) need not be preserved forever. For example, a statute of limitations applies to many associations, after which the association can often be discarded. But this example also points out that the duration of preservation depends on the purpose being served. From a legal standpoint, it may be safe to discard the association. But what may be safe from a legal standpoint may not make sense for business reasons (e.g., a business may need to reconstruct what happened in a project long ago), and conversely as well.
- *Granularity.* As a general rule, an action consists of a number of components in a certain sequence. For some purposes, it may be sufficient to make attributions about the action at the highest level (that is, at the level of complete transaction). For example, it may be necessary to determine that an operating system patch came from the operating system manufacturer. However, there may be times when an entity contemplating accepting or executing an action may want to make attributions on individual components of a transaction. Perhaps, in a financial transaction, a gross total would

be attributed to a valid counterparty, but the tax implications might be attributed to a tax lawyer. For instance, one could research the possibility of having different attributions associated with the various results of network service invocations. While complex, this is related to the large body of work on transitive, or delegated, trust. In the first instance, the operating system manufacturer trusts its employees and the operating system patch installer trusts the manufacturer. In the example of the financial transaction, the trust relationship is explicitly broken out among the individual components of the transaction.

- *Security* (specifically, resistance of an attribution to attack and spoofing). Attribution depends on the inability to break the association between action and actor, because in its absence, impersonation can easily occur.

These five characteristics vary depending on the application. For example, for operational defense, duration may be very short, measured in seconds or minutes; for forensics investigation, duration may be measured in years.

There are also a number of systems-level issues for the implementers and/or the operators of attribution-capable systems. For example, where should be the locus of responsibility for the implementation of attribution mechanisms? An operator of a system or network may expect that attribution will be built in to system or network actions. But in a decentralized environment in which many vendors are responsible for providing one component service or another, the party responsible for implementing attribution mechanisms may be difficult to identify (or to hold accountable for such implementation). Note that attribution may be an issue at all levels of a system design (the individual and organization at high levels, the computers or applications at low levels).

Another systems-level issue is the privacy of attribution information. Attribution information can be very sensitive, and thus must be protected against unauthorized or improper disclosure. Similar considerations apply to parties that are allowed to request that attribution be obtained in the first place.[1]

The most important cybersecurity issue associated with attribution is a problem that attribution mechanisms cannot solve—the unwittingly

---

[1]This point raises the issue of how attribution is designed into a system. Under some designs and for some applications, all actions might routinely be attributed and the information stored in a secure database, to be divulged only to parties that provide proper authorization. Under other applications (perhaps applications that are more privacy-sensitive), actions might be attributed only under explicit authorization.

compromised or duped user. As the existence of botnets illustrates, a cyberattacker has many incentives to compromise others into doing his or her dirty work. Even in the instances when attribution mechanisms operate perfectly, they may well identify a cyberattack as originating from a computer belonging to an innocent little old lady from Pasadena. Put differently, there is a big difference between identifying the source or sources of a cyberattack and associating with that attack the name of a human being or beings responsible for launching it.

This is not to say that making such an identification is useless—indeed, it may be an essential step in a forensic investigation—and it is worthwhile to make such steps as easy as possible. And, the widespread deployment of attribution mechanisms may increase the likelihood that the perpetrator of any given attack can be identified.

Assuming that identifying the launch point of an attack is possible, such identification could be used in operational defense to identify the source of a remote attack. Such identification is a necessary (though not sufficient) condition for being able to shut off or block the attack in real time at the source. Two such attacks are a distributed denial-of-service attack and the theft—while it is happening—of a large proprietary (or "trade-secret") digital object. In this case, the objective is to block the compromise in real time, and false positives (that misidentify the attacker) are of less consequence than failure to identify the attack at all.

An area related to attribution that warrants further exploration is the automated capture, maintenance, and use of "information provenance." Provenance is a sequence of attributes that in some way specifies trustworthy information relating to the initial creation and every subsequent modification of some information unit or collection of information units (e.g., a file, an e-mail, and so on). An important characteristic of provenance is that it would be maintained on information across distributed systems; for example, it would flow with an object.

There are many possible uses of provenance. For example:

- A computer program may possess a provenance that in some ways specifies who was involved in its creation. This could solve many problems—for example, finding out which programs may have been written or modified by an individual who is later found out to be untrustworthy. Today, some aspects of provenance may be maintained in a source control system, but usually not in a highly trustworthy fashion.
- Just as with antiques, provenance would tend to provide a greater ability to interpret where information came from, and this may shed light on the value of the information. With the proliferation of information of all types including images, it is increasingly dif-

ficult to separate fact from fiction. For example, a picture with provenance indicating that there has been no modification beyond its initial imaging and also its association with the *New York Times* newsroom might well be more trustworthy than a picture that has been postprocessed and associated with a tabloid.

- E-mail with provenance may enable increased trust of that e-mail. While provenance will by no means prevent the transmission of spam or viruses, the knowledge of the provenance of a forwarded e-mail note (some attributes of the author, his or her computer, any modifiers in a forwarding path, and so on) would provide some confidence to the recipient and would certainly provide forensic benefits in tracking down cyberattackers. Provenance for e-mail could also help to address today's problems of anonymous harassing e-mails, since a sender could be more readily identified.
- Databases implementing provenance could provide a user with the ability to easily determine the data elements that contributed to a given result. This ability might well contribute to the confidence that the user has in that result or might suggest new and fruitful lines of inquiry.

There would seem to be significant research related to utilizing provenance to make systems and information more secure, as one element of security (or more precisely, confidence in security) is knowing the detailed lineage of any given system and its components.

There are also complex and highly interesting questions relating to the implementation of provenance. For example, there are questions as to how one can provide systems support for an extensible set of attributes, how those attributes can be associated reliably and immutably with their corresponding information, how performance issues associated with a large list of attributes can be contained, how to surface provenance information via programmatic interfaces, and how one can handle the coalescing of attributes so that the attribute lists do not grow without bound. It seems likely that storage of attributes would be benefited by the existence of a trusted computing base that would use virtualization to ensure sufficient isolation.

Finally, there are fascinating questions as to how to make provenance valuable to users. Given the massive increase in the amount of attribute data available, there are interesting questions as to how to surface it in ways so that the valuable provenance stands out. There is the possibility that significantly useful, application-specific heuristics will be created that can monitor provenance and detect potential problems. Analysis must also be done on the impact of provenance on privacy.

As an example of research in data provenance, Margo Seltzer has undertaken work on provenance-aware storage systems (PASS).[2] Seltzer points out that although the chain of ownership and the transformations that a document has undergone can be important, most computer systems today implement provenance-related features as an afterthought, usually through an auxiliary indexing structure parallel to the actual data. She argues that provenance is merely a particular type of metadata, and thus that the operating system itself should be responsible for the automatic collection and management of provenance-relevant metadata just as it maintains conventional file system metadata. And, it should support queries about that metadata. An extension of a provenance-aware system, more difficult to implement, would enable queries to be made about entities smaller than a file, such as the individual cells of a spreadsheet or particular paragraphs in a document.

Progress in attribution research increases the ability to provide provenance for electronic information or events (Cybersecurity Bill of Rights Provision V), is an integral element of expunging information (Provision IV), inhibits an attacker's ability to perform denial-of-service attacks (Provision I), and improves the ability to audit systems performing certain critical functions (Provision VII).

5.2 MISUSE AND ANOMALY DETECTION SYSTEMS

Misuse and anomaly detection (MAD) systems refer to a fairly wide range of systems and techniques for detecting suspicious or anomalous activity on (or intrusion into) computers, servers, or networks.[3] Intrusions are most often classified either as misuse (i.e., an attack) or as an anomaly. In general, there are two primary types of MAD systems in use today in organizations large and small:

- *Host-based MAD systems.* These systems operate on a specific host or computer to detect suspicious activity on that particular host—for example, malicious connection attempts or applications doing things that they should not be doing (e.g., a word processor

[2]See http://www.eecs.harvard.edu/~margo/research.html.

[3]For more detailed information on ID systems and related issues, see Rebecca Bace, undated, "An Introduction to Intrusion Detection and Assessment for System and Network Security Management," ICSA Labs white paper, available at http://www.icsa.net/icsa/docs/html/communities/ids/whitepaper/Intrusion1.pdf; and Karen Kent and Peter Mell, 2006, "Guide to Intrusion Detection and Prevention (IDP) Systems (Draft), Recommendations of the National Institute of Standards and Technology" (NIST Special Publication 800-94), National Institute of Standards and Technology, Gaithersburg, Md., available at http://csrc.nist.gov/publications/drafts/Draft-SP800-94.pdf.

trying to modify key operating system or configuration files); and
- *Network-based MAD systems.* These systems focus on network data flows, looking for suspicious packets or traffic.

Often these two types of systems are used together to create a hybrid solution for misuse or anomaly detection. Indeed, each by itself is quite limited.

MAD systems are potentially valuable in that they seek to detect the early stages of an attack (e.g., an attacker's probing of a machine or network for specific vulnerabilities) and can then aid in protecting a machine from (or even preventing) the subsequent stages of the attack. MAD systems also seek to detect telltale signs of suspicious activity or patterns of behavior (whether by a user, an application, or a piece of malicious code) that firewalls or other tools might miss or ignore.

MAD systems are generally quite complex and require significant effort to manage properly. They are not a fix-all solution for computer or network security; MAD systems cannot compensate or account for weaknesses such as design flaws and software bugs, and cannot compensate or account for weaknesses in organizational authentication policies, data management practices, or network protocols themselves. From a technical standpoint, one of the most significant difficulties of developing usable MAD systems is the fact that the behavior of an intruder may be nearly indistinguishable from that of a legitimate user; intruders often take great care to make their behavior look innocuous. For instance, MAD systems are "trainable" by attackers. A patient attacker can gradually increase the incidence of events to be later associated with an attack to the point where the MAD system ranks them as "normal," whereas springing the specific events on the system would cause it to alarm.

As a result, when MAD systems are made very sensitive, they are notorious for generating many false positives (sounding alarms when none are warranted) and thereby inconveniencing legitimate users; when they are made less sensitive in order to avoid inconveniencing legitimate users, they are notorious for failing to sound alarms when intruders or misuse is in fact present. An aggravating factor is that attackers are constantly at work devising and refining ways to elude known MAD systems—for example, using so-called "stealthy" scans to avoid the notice of some MAD systems. Reconciling the tension between false positives and false negatives is thus a central area of MAD system research.

Another challenge in the development of MAD systems is that of finding methods that function efficiently in large systems. Many approaches to misuse and anomaly detection generate enormous amounts of data, which must subsequently be analyzed. (In the extreme case, an audit log that allows the reconstruction of a user's activities is a MAD system that only collects data; automated tools for log analysis that search for suspicious patterns of behavior can then be regarded as a kind of post hoc MAD system.) Moreover, the collection and analysis of such large amounts of data may degrade performance to unacceptable levels, suggesting that a hierarchical abstraction process may be needed for more efficient performance.[4]

Related is the challenge of integrating MAD systems with network infrastructure itself, making MAD a standard feature in some deployments. In addition, MAD systems must address the very difficult problem of uncovering possible patterns of misuse or anomalies that may occur in a distributed manner across the systems of a large network. That is, certain behavior may not be suspicious if and when it occurs in isolation, but the identical behavior may well be suspicious if it occurs on multiple systems at the same time. Today, understanding how to correlate behavior that is non-anomalous in the small to infer an indication of anomalous behavior in the large is quite problematic. The problems are even more severe in an environment in which qualitatively different exploitations might be occurring in different systems orchestrated by a single hostile actor. Despite more than two decades of research in this area, significant problems remain concerning the interpretation of the audit and network packet data, in particular, involving the early recognition of patterns of multiple simultaneous attacks or outages, identifying the sources and identities of attackers, and discerning the intent of the attacks.[5]

Privacy problems must also be addressed, because the audit and network packet data can contain sensitive information.[6]

Progress in MAD system research supports Provision I, Provision III, Provision IX, and Provision X of the Cybersecurity Bill of Rights.

---

[4]P.A. Porras and P.G. Neumann, "EMERALD: Event Monitoring Enabling Responses to Anomalous Live Disturbances," in *Proceedings of the Nineteenth National Computer Security Conference*, NIST/NCSC, Baltimore, Md., pp. 353-365, October 22-25, 1997; and P.G. Neumann and P.A. Porras, "Experience with EMERALD to Date," in *Proceedings of the First USENIX Workshop on Intrusion Detection and Network Monitoring*, USENIX, Santa Clara, Calif., pp. 73-80, April 1999, available at http://www.csl.sri.com/neumann/det99.html.

[5]P.A. Porras and P.G. Neumann, "EMERALD: Event Monitoring Enabling Responses to Anomalous Live Disturbances," in *Proceedings of the Nineteenth National Computer Security Conference*, NIST/NCSC, Baltimore, Md., pp. 353-365, October 22-25, 1997; and P.G. Neumann and P.A. Porras, "Experience with EMERALD to Date," in *Proceedings of the First USENIX Workshop on Intrusion Detection and Network Monitoring*, USENIX, Santa Clara, Calif., pp. 73-80, April 1999, available at http://www.csl.sri.com/neumann/det99.html.

[6]Phillip A. Porras, "Privacy-Enabled Global Threat Monitoring," *IEEE Security and Privacy*, November-December 2006, pp. 60-63.

5.3 DIGITAL RIGHTS MANAGEMENT

Digital rights management (DRM) refers to the granting of various privileges depending on the identity of the party who will use those privileges. A common example is the management of privileges for protected content—a publisher may choose to sell the right for an individual to watch a (digital) movie once or an unlimited number of times, but in any case, only to watch it and not to forward or copy it.

Unlike physical objects, if a computer can read some bits (as would be necessary to convert those bits into a human-sensible form like music or pictures), then that computer will also be able to copy those bits an unlimited number of times. Providers want recipients to abide by certain terms of use specified in a contract and want technical assurances that the contract will be enforced. Moreover, permission to copy the bits of a protected work is unlikely to be part of a contract that restricts the use of those bits, since the copies can be used or further distributed for use in ways that do not comply with the contract terms. Thus, a means of enforcement is needed to constrain what is done with the bits. Such enforcement requires software that can be trusted by the provider even though it is executed on a machine that is not similarly trusted.

Since computers are universal—and therefore a computer can simulate any other—the trusted software could well be running in a software simulator rather than directly on the hardware (unless special-purpose hardware is being used). Universality of digital computers is thus problematic, because when the trusted software is run in a simulator, the simulator could make illicit copies of an electronic copy without the trusted software's knowledge of this copying; the illicit copies can then be subsequently used to violate the terms of the use agreement.

Thus, solving the DRM problem is more than a problem of ensuring confidentiality for the content in question—the problem is bigger than how to transmit the electronic content from the owner to the customer in a way that prevents interception by third parties. It is also a problem of (what has come to be known as) trusted computing: how to build a computing environment in which the user is *not* trusted to control certain aspects of its configuration and operation but rather a programmer is trusted to do this.

Recent hardware extensions, such as the Trusted Platform Module (TPM) (see Section 4.1.2.1), can be seen as providing support for exactly this trust and execution model. But TPM and such solutions are not a panacea—many consumers would find it unacceptable to own a general-purpose computer over which they themselves do not have complete control (having ceded some control to the programmers of certain trusted software). So there is a tension between computer owners who feel that they have lost control over their computers and the desire of content providers to enforce their content-usage contracts.

Moreover, DRM schemes may enforce the rights of content owners at the expense of eroding the rights of content users. The most salient example of such erosion is the impact of DRM on *fair use*, which is the principle allowing the small-scale use of limited amounts of copyrighted materials for certain limited purposes.[7] Some DRM implementations eliminate fair use because of the difficulty in algorithmically distinguishing between fair use and illegal copying. Another problem is that DRM schemes often force the user into using the content on only one device—use on a second device requires a second copy. The overall effect of such implementations, especially in the long run, has important public policy implications that are as yet poorly understood.[8]

The economic model for DRM rests on the premise that illegal copies of a work deprive the content owner of the revenues that would be associated with the legal sale of those copies. There is some merit to this claim, and yet it is not the only factor in play. For example, estimating lost revenues in this fashion surely overstates the revenue loss, since some of the copies distributed illegally would be acquired by parties who would not have paid for legal copies in the absence of the illegal copies. Also, by some accounts, unprotected digital content can spur rather than impede sales of that content. These points suggest that the net outcome of widespread DRM implementation is uncertain, and thus the long-term economic rationale for these DRM schemes is poorly understood.

Still another issue with DRM is that DRM technology is usually designed with a failure mode that defaults to "deny access." That is, because DRM technology generally serves the interests of content owners rather than of content users, the operating principle for DRM is to deny access to the content unless the user can provide appropriate authorization for access. Thus, DRM itself introduces a potential security vulnerability to a denial-of-service attack that can be exploited by an adversary clever enough to interfere with the authorization mechanisms involved.

---

[7]*Fair use* is defined by statute in Sections 107 through 118 of Title 17 of the U.S. Code. See http://www.copyright.gov/title17/92chap1.html.

[8]A hardware-based approach is not the only possible approach to digital rights management. Another approach is based on accountability. A content-usage contract could be enforced legally by embedding into every legitimate copy of electronic content a unique identifier (known as a watermark). If an illegal copy is discovered, the embedded identifier can be used to identify the original owner, who has presumably allowed the original version to be copied in violation of the content-usage contract. However, this approach fails if the user can remove the watermark before copying occurs, and there is no reason to believe that it is possible to develop an unremovable watermark. In addition, the identified user could claim that the content was stolen. Finally, this approach requires individual prosecution for every illegal copy found—a major disadvantage when widespread copying is at issue.

Although the most common use today of DRM is the protection of copyrighted works that are sold for profit, the philosophy underlying DRM—that content providers should have the ability to exercise fine-grained control over how their content is used—can be used to support individuals in protecting their own documents and other intellectual property in precisely the same ways. For example, A may wish to send a sensitive e-mail to B, but also to insist that B not print it or forward it to anyone else. Some DRM systems are available today that seek to provide controls of this nature within the boundaries of an enterprise.

This kind of DRM application operates in an environment very different from a copyright-enforcement regime. In a copyright-enforcement regime, the primary concern is preventing the improper large-scale distribution of copyrighted works, whereas the concerns in an enterprise DRM regime are more varied (e.g., individuals may have more concerns about the time periods during which content may be available). Because the particular set of rights relevant to any given recipient is more varied, users must specify in detail the rights they wish to grant to content recipients. Although default settings ease the burden, many users still find enterprise DRM systems cumbersome and clumsy from a usability standpoint. In addition, because the scale of rights enforcement is necessarily much more fine-grained (one improperly forwarded e-mail can become very problematic), there are higher premiums and greater needs for protections against actions such as "screen scraping" as a way of obtaining machine-readable content in violation of the rights mechanism. Finally, both sender and recipient must generally operate within the same enterprise—usually, a sender who wants to engage a recipient outside the enterprise does not have the functionality afforded by the DRM system.

6

Category 3—Promoting Deployment

The goal of requirements in Category 3—Promoting deployment, is that of ensuring that the technologies and procedures in Categories 1 and 2 of the committee's illustrative research agenda are actually used to promote and enhance security. This broad category includes technologies that facilitate ease of use, by both end users and system implementers; incentives that promote the use of security technologies in the relevant contexts; and removal of barriers that impede the use of security technologies.

6.1 USABLE SECURITY

It is axiomatic that security functionality that is turned off or disabled or bypassed or not deployed by users serves no protective function. The same is true for security practices or procedures that are promulgated but not followed in practice. (This section uses the term "security" in its broadest sense to include both technology and practices and procedures.) Yet, even in an age of increasing cyberthreat, security features are often turned off and security practices are often not followed. Today, security is often too complex for individuals and enterprise organizations to manage effectively or to use conveniently. Security is hard for users, administrators, and developers to understand; clumsy and awkward to use; obstructs all of these parties in getting real work done; and does not scale easily to large numbers of users or devices to be protected. Thus, many cybersecurity measures are circumvented by the users they are intended to protect, not because these users are lazy but because these users are well motivated and trying to do their jobs. When security gets in the way, users switch it off and work around it, designers avoid strong security, and administrators make mistakes in using it.

It is true that in the design of any computer system, there are inevitable trade-offs among various system characteristics: better or less costly administration, trustworthiness or security, ease of use, and so on. Because the intent of security is to make a system completely unusable to an unauthorized party but completely usable to an authorized one, there are inherent trade-offs between security and convenience or ease of access.

One element of usable security is better education. That is, administrators and developers—and even end users—would benefit from greater attention to security in their information technology (IT) education, so that the concepts of and the need for security are familiar to them in actual working environments (Box 6.1). In addition, some aspects of security are necessarily left for users to decide (e.g., who should have access to some resource), and users must know enough to make such decisions sensibly.

The trade-off between security and usability need not be as stark as many people believe, however, and there is no a priori reason why a system designed to be highly secure against unauthorized access cannot also be user-friendly. An example case in which security and usability have enhanced each other in a noncybersecurity context is that of modern hotel room keys. Key cards are lighter and more versatile than the old metal keys were. They are easier for the guests to use (except when the magnetic strip is accidentally erased), and the system provides the hotels with useful security information, such as who visited the room and whether the door was left ajar. Modern car keys are arguably more secure and more convenient as well.

The committee believes that efforts to increase security and usability can proceed simultaneously for a long time, even if they may collide at some point after attempts at better design or better engineering have been exhausted. Many of the usability problems of today have occurred because designers have simply given up too soon, before serious efforts have been made to reconcile the tension. All too often, the existence of undeniable tensions between security and access is used as an excuse for not addressing usability problems in security.

One part of the problem is that the interfaces are often designed by programmers who are familiar with the technology and often have a level of literacy (both absolute and technical) well above that of the average end user. The result is interfaces that are generally obvious and well understood by the programmers but not by the end users. Few programmers even have awareness of interface issues, and fewer still have useful train-

BOX 6.1
Fluency with Information Technology (and Cybersecurity)

A report entitled *Being Fluent with Information Technology* published several years ago by the National Research Council (NRC) sought to identify what everyone—every user—ought to know about information technology.[1] Written in 1999, that report mentioned security issues in passing as one subtopic within the general area of information systems. Subsequently, Lawrence Snyder, chair of the NRC Committee on Information Technology Literacy responsible for the 1999 report, wrote *Fluency with Information Technology: Skills, Concepts, and Capabilities.*[2] The University of Washington course for 2006 based on this book (http://www.cs.washington.edu/education/courses/100/06wi/labs/lab11/lab11.html) addresses security issues in greater detail by setting forth the following objectives for the security unit:

- Learn to create strong passwords
- Set up junk e-mail filtering
- Use Windows Update to keep your system up to date
- Update McAfee VirusScan so that you can detect viruses
- Use Windows Defender to locate and remove spyware

Another NRC report, *ICT Fluency and High Schools: A Workshop Summary,*[3] released in 2006, suggested that security issues were one possible update to the fluency framework described in the 1999 NRC report.

Taken together, these reports indicate that in the 8 years since *Being Fluent with Information Technology* was released, issues related to cybersecurity have begun to become important even to the most basic IT education efforts.

---

[1]National Research Council. 1999. *Being Fluent with Information Technology.* National Academy Press, Washington, D.C.

[2]Lawrence Snyder. 2002. *Fluency with Information Technology; Skills, Concepts, and Capabilities.* Addison-Wesley, Lebanon, Ind.

[3]National Research Council. 2006. *ICT [Information and Communications Technology] Fluency and High Schools: A Workshop Summary.* The National Academies Press, Washington, D.C.

ing and background in this subfield. For example, security understandings are often based on physical-world metaphors, such as locking doors and obscuring sensitive information. These metaphors have some utility, and yet considerable education is needed to teach users the limitations of the metaphors. (Consider that in a world of powerful search tools [e.g., Google's desktop, and Spotlight on Mac computers], it is not realistic for those in possession of sensitive information to rely on "trusting other people not to look for sensitive information" or "burying information in sub-sub-sub-sub directories," whereas in the absence of such tools, such actions might well have considerable protective value.) The difficulty of overcoming such limitations suggests that it is simply unrealistic to expect that security should depend primarily on security education and training.

In addition, the extra training and education for security simply do not match the market, with the predictable result that users don't spend much time learning about security. Users want to be able to buy and use IT without any additional training. Vendors want to sell to customers without extra barriers. Couple these realities with the projection that the Internet user population will double in the next decade, with hundreds of millions of new users, and it is clear that we cannot depend on extra education and training to improve security significantly.

If user education is not the answer to security, the only other possibility is to develop more usable security mechanisms and approaches. As a starting point, consider the following example. Individuals in a company may need to share files with one another. When these persons are in different work units, collaboration is often a hassle. Using today's security mechanisms, it is likely that these people would have to go through an extended multistep process to designate file directories that they want to share with one another—managing access-control lists, giving specific permissions, and so on. Depending on the level of inconvenience entailed, these individuals may simply elect to e-mail their files to one another, thus circumventing entirely the difficulties of in-house collaboration—but also making their files vulnerable to all of the security issues associated with the open Internet. It would be much more preferable to have mechanisms in place that aggregate and automatically perform low-level security actions under an abstraction that allows each user to designate another person as a collaborator on a given project and have the system select the relevant files to make available to that person and to no others.

Usable security would thus reduce the cognitive load needed by an authorized user to navigate security and the "hassle factor," thus increasing the likelihood that users would refrain from simply bypassing security measures or would never implement them in the first place. Such issues go far beyond the notion of "wizards," which all too often simply mask an underlying complexity that is inherently difficult to understand.

System administrators are also an important focal point for usable security. Because system administrators address low-level system issues much more often than end users do, they are usually more knowledgeable about security matters and are usually the ones to whom end users turn when security issues arise. But many users (e.g., those in small businesses) must perform their own system administration—a point suggesting that remote security administration, provided as a service, has an important role to play while more usable security mechanisms are not widely deployed.

In addition, the fact that system administrators are more knowledgeable than end users about low-level security issues does not mean that they do not find administering those issues to be a burden. For example, system administrators rather than vendors must make decisions about access control—who should have what privileges on a system—simply because the vendor does not and cannot know to whom any particular user is willing to grant access to a resource. However, this fact does not mean that it should be difficult to specify an access-control list.

Many computer security problems result from a mismatch between a security policy and the way that the policy is or is not implemented, and system administrators would benefit greatly from automated tools that would indicate how their systems are actually configured and whether an actual configuration is consistent with their security policy. For example, administrators need to be able to set appropriate levels of privilege for different users, but they also need to be able to generate lists of all users with a given level of privilege. Some tools and products offer some capability for comparing installed configurations with defined security policies, but more work needs to be done on tools that enable security policies to be described more clearly, more unambiguously, and more easily. Such tools are needed, for example, when security policies change often.

A related though separate point is the extent to which new systems and networks can or should include ideas that involve significant changes from current practice. Though end users are the limiting case of this issue (e.g., "How can you deploy systems that require the habits of 200 million Internet users to change and a whole industry to support them?"), the issue of requiring significant change is also relevant to system administrators, who are fewer in number but may well be as resistant to change as end users are.

In some cases, issues may arise that fundamentally require end users to alter their ways of doing business. Consider the question of whether the end user should or should not make a personal choice about whether or not to trust a certificate authority. One line of argument suggests that such a question is too important to handle automatically. If so, users may indeed be required to change their habits and learn about certificate authorities. But the countering line of argument is that systems that require users to make such decisions will never be deployed on a large scale, regardless of their technical merits, and there is ample evidence that most users are not going to make sensible choices about trusting certificate authorities. One way of addressing such differences is to develop technology that by default shields users from having to make such choices but nevertheless provides those who wish to do so with the ability to make their own choices.

The quest for usable security has social and organizational dimensions as well as technological and psychological ones. Researchers have found that the development of usable security requires deep insight into the human-interaction dimensions of the application for which security is being developed and of the alignment of technical protocols for security and of the social/organizational protocols that surround such security. Only with such insight is it possible to design and develop security functionality that does not interfere with what legitimate workers must do in the ordinary course of their regular work. (That is, such functionality would not depend on taking explicit steps related only to security and nothing else.) For example:

- *Individuals generally have multiple cyber-identities.* For example, a person may have a dozen different log-in names to different systems, each of which demands its own password to access. Different identities often mean that the associated roles differ, for example, by machine, by user identities, by privilege, and so on. It is hard enough to remember different log-in names, which may be necessitated because the user's preferred log-in name is already in use (the log-in name JohnSmith is almost certainly already in use in most large-scale systems, and any given John Smith may use JohnSmithAmex or JohnSmithCitibank or JohnSmithPhone as his log-in name, depending on the system he needs to access). But what about passwords? In order to minimize the cognitive load on the user, he or she will often use the same password for every site—and in particular will not tailor the strength of the password to the importance or the sensitivity of the site. Alternatively, users may plead for "single-sign-on" capability. Being required to present authentication credentials only once is certainly simpler for the user but is risky when different levels of trust or security are involved.
- *Individuals usually don't know what they don't know.* A common approach to security is to hide objects from people who do not have explicit authorization to access them, and to make these objects visible to people who do have explicit authorization. From a business process standpoint, there is an important category that this approach to security does not recognize—individuals who should have explicit authorization for access but do not. Authorization is granted in one of two ways: the individual receives authority unbidden (e.g., a new hire is automatically granted access to his

or her unit's server), and/or the individual requests authorization from some authority who then decides whether or not to grant that authority. The latter approach, most common when some ad hoc collaborative arrangement is made, presumes that the individual knows enough to request access. But if the necessary objects are hidden from the individual, how does he or she know that it is necessary to request access to those specific objects? Such issues often arise in an environment dealing with classified information in which, because of secrecy and compartmentalization, one party does not know what information another party has.

- *Individuals function in a social and organizational context, and processes for determining access rights are inherently social and organizational.* When necessary accesses are blocked in the name of security, individuals must often expend considerable effort in untangling the web of confusion that is the ultimate cause of the denial of access. Individuals with less aggressive personalities, or newly hired individuals who do not want to "make trouble" may well be more reluctant to take such action—with the result that security policies and practices have kept employees from doing their work.

Addressing these social and organizational dimensions of security requires asking questions of a different sort than those that technologists usually ask. Technologists usually seek to develop solutions or applications that generalize across organizational settings—and users must adapt to the requirements of the technology. Focusing on the social and organizational dimension implies developing understandings of what end users are trying to accomplish, with whom, and in what settings. What is the organization trying to achieve? What are the day-to-day security practices of effective employees? What are the greatest security threats? What information must be protected? What workplace practices are functional and effective and should be preserved in security redesigns? These understandings then support and may even drive design innovation at the network, infrastructure, and applications interface levels.

A social and organizational understanding of security is based on posing questions at several distinct levels. In an organization, senior management determines security policy and establishes the nature and scope of its security concerns. But management also shapes a much larger social context that includes matters such as expectations for cooperative work, the nature of relationships between subordinates and superiors, and relationships between support and business units. At the same time, individuals and groups in the organization must interpret management-determined security concerns and implement management-determined policy—and these individuals and groups generally have considerable latitude in doing so. Most importantly, individuals and groups must get their primary work done, and security is by definition peripheral to doing the primary work of the organization. Thus, because there is often conflict, or at least tension, between security and getting work done, workers must make judgments about what risks are worth taking in order to get their work done and how to bypass security measures if that is necessary in order to do so.

It is against this backdrop that the technology infrastructure must be assessed. At the applications and task levels, it is important to understand how data-sharing practices are managed and what interorganizational and intraorganizational information flows must be in place for people to work effectively with others. A key dimension of data-sharing practices is access privileges—how are they determined, and how is knowledge of these privileges promulgated? (This includes, of course, knowing of the privileges themselves as well as their settings.) Technology development so assessed implies not only good technology, but extensive tools that facilitate organizational customization and that help end users identify what needs to be communicated and to whom.

6.2 EXPLOITATION OF PREVIOUS WORK

There is a long history of advances in cybersecurity research that are not reflected in today's practice and products. In many cases, the failure to adopt such advances is explained at least in part by a mismatch between market demands and the products making use of such research. For example, secure architectures often resulted in systems that were too slow, too costly, too late, and/or too hard to use. Nevertheless, the committee believes that some security innovations from the past are worth renewed attention today in light of a new underlying technological substrate with which to implement these innovations and a realization that inattention to nontechnical factors may have contributed to their nonuse (Section 3.4.1.4). These previous innovations include, but are not limited to the following:

- Virtual machine architectures that enable strict partitions and suitable isolation among different users, as discussed in Section 4.1.2.3 (Process Isolation);
- Multilevel security and multilevel integrity that enable the simultaneous processing of information with different classification levels;
- With the exception of the AS/400, System 38 (now the IBM iSeries), capability architectures that have not traditionally been successful but could prove to have valuable lessons to teach; and

- Software engineering practices and programming tools for developing secure and reliable systems.

"Old" but unadopted innovations that solved real cybersecurity problems are often plausible as points of departure for new research that addresses these same problems. As an example of early work that may be relevant today, consider what might be called a "small-process/message-passing" model for computation, in which a user's work is performed using multiple loci of control (generally called threads), which communicate with one another by means of signals and messages. Exemplified by Unix, this model has a demonstrated ability to optimize machine resources, especially processor utilization; while one thread may be blocked waiting on, say, disk access, other threads can be performing useful tasks.

The small-process/message-passing model does, however, have some disadvantages for security. A secure machine must map some set of external attributes, such as user identity, role, and/or clearance into the internal workings of the machine and use those attributes to enforce limits on access to resources or invocation of services. The internal data structures used to enforce these limits is often called the "security state." The security state of a small-process/message-passing structure is diffuse, dynamic, and spread throughout a large number of processes. Furthermore, its relationship to the hardware is tenuous. It is therefore hard to analyze and verify.

An alternative structure is the "large-process" model of computation, an example of which was Multics. In the large-process model, the work being done for a user is tied to a single locus of control, and the security state is mostly embodied in a hardware-enforced structure. This model relies on multiplexing between users to gain efficiency (as opposed to the small-process model, which multiplexes between threads working for a single user) and is efficient only when large numbers of users are sharing a single body of hardware, such as a server. From a security perspective, the advantage of the large-process structure is that the security features of the system are easier to understand, analyze, and verify.

Because hardware resources are increasingly inexpensive, efficient use of hardware is no longer as important as it once was. Designs based on the need to use hardware efficiently have also had undesirable security consequences, and with the dropping cost of hardware, it may make sense to revisit some of those designs in certain circumstances. For example, the multicore processor (discussed briefly in Section 4.1.2.1) holds some promise for mitigating the performance penalties of the large-process model, and permitting the security and verification advantages to be exploited in certain contexts. Although a small-process/message-passing model is sensible for distributed computing (e.g., for Web services) in which administrative control is decentralized, the large-process model makes sense in applications such as a public utility or central server in which security requirements are under centralized administrative control.

6.3 CYBERSECURITY METRICS

Cybersecurity is a quality that has long resisted—and continues to resist—precise numerical classification. Today, there are few good ways to determine the efficacy or operational utility of any given security measure. Thus, individuals and companies are unable to make rational decisions about whether or not they have "done enough" with respect to cybersecurity. In the absence of good cybersecurity metrics, it is largely impossible to quantify cost-benefit trade-offs in implementing security features. Even worse, it is very difficult if not impossible to determine if System A is more secure than System B. Good metrics would also be one element supporting a more robust insurance market in cybersecurity founded on sound actuarial principles and knowledge.[1]

One view of security is that it is a binary and negative property—*secure* is simply defined as the opposite of being *insecure*. Under this "absolutist" model, it is easy to demonstrate the *insecurity* of a system via an effective attack, but demonstrating *security* requires proving that no effective attack exists. An additional complicating factor is that once an attacker finds a vulnerability, it must be assumed that such knowledge will propagate rapidly, thus enabling previously stymied attackers to launch successful attacks.

There are some limited domains, such as the proof of privacy in Shannon's foundational work on perfect ciphers[2] and the proof of safety properties guaranteed by the type systems of many modern programming languages that are successful applications of this approach. But on the whole, only relatively small programs, let alone systems of any complexity, can be evaluated to such a standard in their entirety.

If security is binary, then a system with any vulnerability is insecure—and metrics are not needed to indicate that one system is "more" secure than another. But this absolutist view has both theoretical and practical difficulties. One theoretical difficulty is that the difference between

---

[1]It is also helpful to distinguish between a *metric* (which measures some quantity or phenomenon in a reasonably repeatable way) and *risk assessment* (which generally involves an aggregation of metrics according to a model that provides some degree of predictive power). For example, in the financial industry, risk assessment depends on a number of metrics relevant to a person's financial history (e.g., income, debt, number of years in the same residence, and so on).

[2]Claude Shannon, "Communication Theory of Secrecy Systems," *Bell System Technical Journal*, 28: 656-715, October 1949.

a secure and a vulnerable software artifact can be as small as one bit, and it is hard to imagine a process that is sensitive enough to determining if the artifact is or is not secure.

A practical difficulty is that static-code analysis—predicting the behavior of code without actually executing it—remains a daunting challenge in the general case. One aspect of the difficulty is that of determining if the code in question behaves in accordance with its specifications. Usually the domain of formal proofs of correctness, this approach presumes that the specifications themselves are correct—but in fact vulnerabilities are sometimes traced to incorrect or inappropriate specifications. Moreover, the size of systems amenable to such formal proofs remains small compared to the size of many systems in use today. A second aspect of this difficulty is in finding functionality that should not be present according to the specifications (as discussed in Section 4.1.3.1).

Outside the absolutist model, security is inherently a synthetic property—it no longer reflects some innate quality of the system, but rather how well a given system with a given set of security policies (Section 6.5) can resist the activities of a given adversary. Thus, the security of a system can be as much a property of the adversary being considered as it is of the system's construction itself. That is, measuring the security of a system must be qualified by asking, Against what kind of threat? Under what circumstances? For what purpose? and Under what security policy?

In this context, the term "metric" is not binary. It must be, at the very least, ordinal, so that metrics can be used to rank-order a system along some security-relevant dimension. In addition, the term "metric" assumes that one or more outcomes of interest can be measured in an unambiguous way—that one can recognize a good outcome or a bad outcome when it occurs. Furthermore, it assumes that an improvement in the metric actually corresponds to an improvement in outcome.

Yet another complicating factor is that an adversary may offer unforeseen threats whose impact on the system cannot be anticipated or measured in advance. While the absolutist model—which depends a great deal on formal proof—presumes that all security properties can be specified a priori, in practice it is common that a system's security requirements are not understood until well after its deployment (if even then!). Moreover, if a threat (or even a benign event) is unforeseen, a response tailored to that threat (or event) cannot be specified (although a highly general response, such as "Abort," may be possible, and certain other responses may be known to be categorically undesirable).

For example, the cryptography community has had some success in formalizing the security of its systems. Proving cryptographic security calls for defining an abstract model of an adversary and then using reductions to prove that key security properties have equivalent computational hardness to certain well-known difficult problems. Thus, the strength of a cipher can be parameterized as a function of the adversary's qualitative capabilities (e.g., the ability to inject known plaintext messages into the channel) and quantitative capabilities (e.g., the ability to perform *N* computations in time *M*). However, outside this rarified environment, real attackers bypass these limitations simply by working outside the model's assumptions (e.g., side channel attacks, protocol engineering interactions, and so on). And, sometimes cryptographic primitives can fail, invalidating the model's assumptions, as illustrated by recently discovered problems in the SHA-1 hash algorithm.[3]

Finally, the security of a system tends to be tightly coupled with the particulars of its configuration, which suggests that security can be a highly fragile property. The same software system may be considerably more secure under the care of one administrator than under the care of another.

These challenges suggest that the search for an overall cybersecurity metric—one that would be applicable to all systems and in all environments—is a largely fruitless quest. Rather, cybersecurity must be conceptualized in multidimensional terms, and metrics for cybersecurity must, for example, take into account the nature of the threat and how a system is operated in practice. Users and researchers thus must be clear about the limitations of a given metric (e.g., the metric only applies under the following set of assumptions) and/or create tests that anticipate various classes of adversaries.

Nevertheless, we have strong intuitions that some systems are in fact more secure than others. While security may always be too complex to submit to a precise analysis, it seems likely that even imperfect approaches may provide useful insights for evaluating current and future systems, provided that the necessary qualifiers are taken into account.

To date, most attempts to define security metrics have fallen into one of several broad categories. The first category is operational metrics. This approach, typified by the *Security Metrics Guide for Information Technology Systems* from the National Institute of Standards and Technology,[4] focuses on measurements of the behavior of an IT organization. Thus, at the highest level of abstraction, one might measure the fraction of systems that have certain security controls in place, the number of systems operators with security accreditations, the number of organizational components with incident response plans, and so on. Enterprise IT executives might

---

[3]Xiaoyun Wang, Yiqun Lisa Yin, and Hongbo Yu, "Finding Collisions in the Full SHA-1," *Advances in Cryptology—Crypto'05*; available at http://www.infosec.sdu.edu.cn/paper/sha1-crypto-auth-new-2-yao.pdf.

[4]See http://csrc.nist.gov/publications/nistpubs/800-55/sp800-55.pdf.

also track outcome data (e.g., number of viruses detected inside the organization, number of intrusions from the outside) and control data (number of machines with antivirus software, number of services exposed by firewall, and so on). Operational metrics can be valuable for tracking overall compliance with a security policy and trends in well-established problem classes, but they seem unlikely to be useful in providing finer-granularity insight about software security.

Related to operational metrics are what might be called process metrics; these indicate the extent to which an organization follows some best practice or practices. An example of a process metric is the Capability Maturity Model (CMM), which is intended to measure the quality of an organization's software development processes. In the CMM, organizations are measured from Level 1 (corresponding to a development process that is ad hoc and chaotic) to Level 5 (corresponding to a development process that is repeatable, well-defined, and institutionalized; managed with quantifiable objectives and minimal variation in performing tasks; and optimized to produce continuous process improvement).[5] Process metrics must be correlated with outcome metrics in order to be regarded as successful, and the extent of such correlation is an open question today.

A second broad category of metrics is that of product evaluations. This approach focuses on a third-party evaluation process for products rather than for organizations. These evaluation processes are typically structured around certifications of product security that place a product's security in a categorical ranking based on its passing certain process benchmarks. For example, the Common Criteria specify distinct Evaluation Assurance Levels, which require successfully passing a variety of test regimes ranging from functional system testing to formal design verification. Typically these certifications are based on some combination of software process measures (e.g., what design practices were used in the design of the software) and testing (e.g., validating that unacceptable test inputs are not accepted).

The strongest ratings may require a formal analysis of security for a system's design. However, there are real limits to such metrics for the security field. First, they are largely disconnected from the software artifact itself and can make few statements about the weaknesses of a particular implementation. Second, certification levels are sufficiently coarse that most products can only be successfully evaluated within the same narrow range. Finally, certification is human-intensive and thus can be

[5]The original CMM for software is no longer supported by the Software Engineering Institute. In 2000, the SW-CMM was upgraded to CMMI® (Capability Maturity Model Integration).

very expensive and slow. Under the regime of the *Orange Book,* many software artifacts were no longer marketed or supported by the vendors by the time the certification had been completed. Under the current Common Criteria regime, many small companies cannot afford to get their products certified, thus creating a potential bias that may inhibit a fully open market in secure and security products.

A third category of metrics is post hoc, or outcome, metrics. This is the most data-rich category of security metrics because it is driven by post hoc analysis and characterization of discovered security vulnerabilities or active attacks. Examples of an outcome metric might be the following:

- *The rate (number per unit time) of successful penetration attempts of a system when a given cybersecurity action is in place.* In this example, a lower value is better (assuming that the threat environment remained the same) but is meaningful only for this particular cybersecurity measure.
- *The fraction of known vulnerabilities that a given cybersecurity measure eliminates or mitigates* (Cowan's relative vulnerability metric).[6] In this example, a larger fraction is better, subject to the same qualifiers. (Note that any metric involving the tracking of vulnerabilities over time requires a list of standardized names for vulnerabilities and other information security exposures. Developing and maintaining this list are the purposes of the MITRE Common Vulnerabilities and Exposures effort and have enabled longitudinal vulnerability analyses and a reduction in confusion when communicating about particular problems.) The CERT Coordination Center (CERT/CC) also maintains vulnerability lists that provide common vocabulary, data for classification, and so on.[7]
- *The time that it takes for a particular kind of worm (e.g., a scanner that chooses a target at random once it has been implanted) to infect a certain fraction of the vulnerable population of Internet sites.* Defenses against this kind of worm can then be characterized in terms of their effect on this time (longer times would indicate defenses of greater effectiveness). Staniford et al. present a model of Internet worms that parameterizes worm outbreaks in terms of their spreading

---

[6]Crispin Cowan, "Relative Vulnerability: An Empirical Assurance Metric," presentation at the Workshop on Measuring Assurance in Cyberspace, 44th IFP Working Group, June 2003; available at http://www2.laas.fr/IFIPWG/Workshops&Meetings/44/.

[7]For more information on the CERT Coordination Center, see http://www.cert.org/certcc.html.

rate.[8] Following the model of Moore et al.,[9] defenses can then be evaluated quantitatively as the fraction of susceptible hosts that are protected over a given period of time for a given deployment. In general, this approach is only well suited for evaluating the relative strength of security technologies, and then only when attacks can be abstracted and homogenized.

- *The financial impact of security penetrations when losses are incurred.* Firms cannot make reasonable investment decisions unless they understand the implicit and explicit impact of their security investment decisions. This is a challenging task, but currently the only data available are anecdotal, making the decision to invest difficult to evaluate and compare with other security/nonsecurity investment options.

Software vulnerabilities are widely reported on public mailing lists and archived in both public and private databases (the National Vulnerability Database is one such well-known collection). Each vulnerability is typically tagged with its source and the particular systems impacted and the source of the vulnerability. Attacks are typically gathered from intrusion-detection system logs and honeypot systems designed to detect new attacks (e.g., Symantec's DeepSight and DShield.org are well-known examples of attack-monitoring systems).

Such data can be used in a number of ways:

- *Relative assessments based on counts.* Different systems or versions of systems may be compared on the basis of the number of vulnerabilities or attacks they experienced. This is one of the most problematic use of post hoc data, since it presumes that the vulnerability-discovery process and the target-selection process are random and uniform. In fact, both are unlikely to be true. Particular systems are likely to be targeted more than others owing to popularity (i.e., because the system provides a wider base to attack), owing to familiarity (i.e., there are fewer people with knowledge of unusual systems), or owing to the particular goals of the attacker (i.e., its intended victim makes extensive use of a particular system). Similarly, vulnerability discovery is driven by the same motives as those of attackers as well as by an additional bias from third-party

[8]Stuart Staniford et al., "The Top Speed of Flash Worms," presented at the ACM Workshop on Rapid Malcode (WORM), October 29, 2004, Washington, D.C.; available at www.icir.org/vern/papers/topspeed-worm04.pdf.

[9]David Moore, Colleen Shannon, and k claffy, "Code Red: A Case Study on the Spread and Victims of an Internet Worm," pp. 273-284 in *Proceedings of the 2nd ACM SIGCOMM Workshop on Internet Measurement*, ASM Press, New York, 2002.

security assessment companies that actively search for new vulnerabilities to enhance their offerings and marketing to potential customers.

- *Vulnerability origin studies.* Rescorla first synchronized vulnerability data with particular software versions to analyze the time origin of vulnerabilities in popular open-source operating systems and their "lifetime" distribution.[10] Ozment and Schechter provided a more detailed analysis showing that, at least for the OpenBSD system, most newly discovered vulnerabilities are not in "new" code and have existed for long periods of time.[11] Moreover, they attempt to use reliability growth models to infer changes in the rate of new vulnerabilities being introduced and in the rate of overall vulnerabilities being discovered. While these techniques are necessarily limited (they are inherently "right-censored," since the future is unknown), they suggest a mechanism to identify real trends. This is a nascent area, and there is little doubt that it could be extended to the analysis of particular subsystems, changes in software process, and so on.
- *Defense evaluation studies.* Cowan has argued for using future vulnerability data as a mechanism for evaluating defense approaches.[12] His "relative vulnerability" metric would thus provide a means for comparing different hardening approaches, based on the fraction of subsequent vulnerabilities that were blocked. While this approach cannot predict the impact of completely new attacks, it seems well posed to measure the breadth of defenses intended to address particular classes of vulnerabilities. At the same time, there is a natural symbiosis between attacker and defender, and thus popular defenses will be more likely to induce the creation of attacks that work around them.
- *Reactivity.* Moore et al. first used attack data to infer the rate at which administrators patched systems that were vulnerable to the Code Red v2 worm.[13] Rescorla used a more sophisticated version

---

[10]E. Rescorla, "Is Finding Security Holes a Good Idea?," presentation at the Workshop on Economics and Information Security 2004, May 2004; available at http://www.dtc.umn.edu/weis2004/rescorla.pdf.

[11]Andy Ozment and Stuart E. Schechter, "Milk or Wine: Does Software Security Improve with Age?," *USENIX Security 2006*, 2006; available at http://www.eecs.harvard.edu/~stuart/papers/usenix06.pdf.

[12]Crispin Cowan, "Relative Vulnerability: An Empirical Assurance Metric," presentation at the Workshop on Measuring Assurance in Cyberspace, 44th IFP Working Group, June 2003; available at http://www2.laas.fr/IFIPWG/Workshops&Meetings/44/.

[13]David Moore, Colleen Shannon, and k claffy, "Code Red: A Case Study on the Spread and Victims of an Internet Worm," pp. 273-284 in *Proceedings of the 2nd ACM SIGCOMM Workshop on Internet Measurement*, ASM Press, New York, 2002.

of this analysis to analyze patching behavior for vulnerabilities in popular implementations of Secure Sockets Layer (SSL). Finally, Beattie et al. use patch update data to extrapolate an optimal time to patch (for the purpose of maximizing availability) based on honeypot measures of attack incidence.[14] In general, the effects of software maintenance on security is understudied (indeed, Rescorla provides an argument that patches can harm security[15]), and yet considerable empirical data are available on this topic.

- *Threat assessments.* Different vulnerabilities engender different risks. In particular, some vulnerabilities are easier to exploit than others, some have more significant consequences, some transition more quickly into attacks in the wild, and some persist for longer periods of time. Today threat assessments are largely performed on an ad hoc basis, but there is reason to hope that at least some of this activity could be automated and objectified.

Finally, there are predictive metrics that measure something intrinsic about a given information technology artifact and that are intended to provide an a priori indication of how secure a system is before it is deployed. An example is vulnerability testing/checking metrics that have emerged from recent work enabling the automated detection of classes of security vulnerabilities in software. As opposed to manual penetration testing, automated methods are by design tester-independent and repeatable. Static-analysis approaches include the detection techniques of Wagner et al. for buffer overflows and format string vulnerabilities[16] and the automated analysis and model checking of whole operating system kernels of Engler et al.[17] While these techniques are neither complete nor accurate (they produce false positives), they are able to consume large software systems and identify potential security vulnerabilities. Some systems, exemplified by Ganapathy et al., are even able to analyze binary

---

[14]Steve Beattie et al., "Timing the Application of Security Patches for Optimal Uptime," *USENIX LISA*, 2002; available at http://www.homeport.org/~adam/time-to-patch-usenix-lisa02.pdf.

[15]E. Rescorla, "Is Finding Security Holes a Good Idea?," presentation at the Workshop on Economics and Information Security 2004, May 2004; available at http://www.dtc.umn.edu/weis2004/rescorla.pdf.

[16]David Wagner, Jeffrey S. Foster, Eric A. Brewer, and Alexander Aiken, "A First Step Towards Automated Detection of Buffer Overrun Vulnerabilities," *Network and Distributed System Security 2000;* available at http://www.cs.berkeley.edu/~daw/papers/overruns-ndss00.ps.

[17]Dawson Engler, David Yu Chen, Seth Hallem, Andy Chou, and Benjamin Chelf, "Bugs as Deviant Behavior: A General Approach to Inferring Errors in Systems Code," in *Proceedings of the Eighteenth ACM Symposium on Operating Systems Principles*, 2001; available at http://www.stanford.edu/~engler/deviant-sosp-01.pdf.

programs, discover new vulnerabilities, and identify precise test cases (i.e., exploits).[18] Dynamic testing, via fuzz testers, can manipulate both input and environment to test corner cases known to be a source of security vulnerabilities in the past.

The most sophisticated of these systems can also triage their own output and determine which vulnerabilities are most likely to be exploitable. Using such tools, one can compare this aspect of security across different versions of a software system and evaluate trends in how new detectable vulnerabilities emerge. However, if successful, these tools will become less useful over time as they are introduced into the normal quality-assurance process and the vulnerabilities that they detect are weeded out before deployment.

A similar methodology is possible for detecting confidentiality violations, using static information flow analysis and dynamic taint checking; however, this particular approach has not been explored as a security metric per se (although Garfinkel uses one such technique to demonstrate the presence of information leakage in a commodity operating system[19]).

Another type of predictive metric addresses the attackability of a system. Howard and LeBlanc developed the notion of an attack surface,[20] which is defined in terms of externally visible and accessible system resources that can be used to mount an attack on the system and subsequently weighted according to the potential damage that could be caused by any given exploitation of a vulnerability. Larger attack surfaces indicate a larger extent of potential vulnerability, and vulnerabilities in a system can be reduced by reducing the attack surface. Attack surface measures potential rather than actual aggregate vulnerability. The presumption, supported in part with post hoc data, is that smaller attack surfaces are likely to host fewer exploitable vulnerabilities and will be easier to secure. While Howard and LeBlanc measure the number of potential "attack vectors" in a given system and configuration, Manadhata and Wing have formalized "attack surface" without reference to Howard and LeBlanc's attack vectors.[21] The attack-surface metric appears to have promise, but as of yet it is still largely a manual enterprise.[22]

---

[18]Vinod Ganapathy et al., "Automatic Discovery of API-Level Exploits," in *Proceedings of the 27th International Conference on Software Engineering*, St. Louis, Mo., pp. 312-321, 2005.

[19]Simson L. Garfinkel, *Information Leakage and Computer Forensics*, Center for Research on Computation and Society, Harvard University, February 17, 2006.

[20]Michael Howard and David LeBlanc, *Writing Secure Code*, Second Edition, Microsoft Press, Seattle, Wash., 2002.

[21]P. Manadhata and J.M. Wing, *An Attack Surface Metric*, CMU-CS-05-155, Technical Report, Pittsburgh, Pa., July 2005.

[22]Manadhata and Wing also have made progress on a more semi-automated process for analyzing source code. See P.K. Manadhata, J.M. Wing, M.A. Flynn, and M.A. McQueen,

Research to further develop the types of metrics described above is needed. Outcome metrics would have high utility for characterizing the impact of some cybersecurity measures, whether technical or procedural. Because predictive metrics seek to characterize artifacts themselves, they would facilitate comparative assessments among different software options and configurations. Generalizing across these different types of metrics, the committee believes that some of the most promising lines of research involve the simultaneous use of different combinations of metrics.

For example, an automated analysis of attack-surface metrics might be designed so that the resulting data could direct vulnerability testing, or post hoc metrics might be used to create quantitatively driven threat assessments. In addition, it would be enormously valuable if metrics useful for understanding security behavior and phenomena in detail could be composed into metrics relevant to aspects of overall system behavior. Today, little is known about how to combine metrics of detailed behavior into metrics of larger scope, and research will be needed to advance this goal. Finally, metrics ought to be subject to a continuing validation process in which various metrics are assessed against incidents as they become known, in order to determine what such metrics might predict about the character of such incidents.

A note of caution is also appropriate in the search for cybersecurity metrics. Researchers have sought good metrics for many years, and though many benefits would flow from the invention of good metrics, the challenge in this cybersecurity research area is particularly great, and some very new ideas will be needed if cybersecurity metricians are to make more progress.

6.4 THE ECONOMICS OF CYBERSECURITY

This section provides an economic perspective on why cybersecurity is hard and on why (if at all) there is underinvestment in cybersecurity.[23] Determining the right amount to spend on information security activities in total is linked to efficiently allocating such resources to specific organizational IT activities. For example, organizations need to determine how much to spend on hardware, software, staffing, and personnel training.

"Measuring the Attack Surfaces of Two FTP Daemons," Quality of Protection Workshop, Alexandria, Va., October 30, 2006.

[23]Ross Anderson, "Why Information Security Is Hard—An Economic Perspective," *Proceedings of the 17th Annual Computer Security Applications Conference*, IEEE Computer Society, New Orleans, La., 2001, pp. 358-365.

The committee believes that insight into many problems of cybersecurity can be gained by exploiting the perspective of economics: network externalities, asymmetric information, moral hazard, adverse selection, liability dumping, risk dumping, regulatory frameworks, and tragedy of the commons.[24] As this list implies, the breadth of economic barriers to improving cybersecurity is extensive and nontrivial. These economic factors can result in a potential for market failure—a less-than-optimal allocation of resources. Taken together, their presence creates a complex and interrelated set of perverse incentives for economic actors. These economic factors go a long way toward explaining why, beyond any technical solutions, the provision of cybersecurity is and will be a hard problem—one requiring research and policy solutions beyond funding technology research—to ameliorate.

In contrast to the large body of technical research on cybersecurity, research related to the economics of cybersecurity is still nascent.[25] However, a small but growing body of literature is beginning to provide insights into the necessary elements of the economic analysis essential for addressing policy aspects of cybersecurity. For example, Alderson and Soo Hoo note that most of the public policy initiatives to address the safety and security of the U.S. national information infrastructure have ignored the stakeholder incentives to adopt and to spur the development of security technologies and processes. They suggest that continuing insecurities in cyberspace are in large part the direct result of a public policy failure to recognize and address those incentives and the technological, economic, social, and legal factors underlying them, and argue that the deployment of a more secure cyber infrastructure could be accelerated by careful consideration of stakeholder incentives.[26] Solutions that emerge from such research are likely to be subtle and partial, requiring the cooperation and coordination of technology researchers, engineers, economists, lawyers, and policy makers. Any combination of solutions needs to incorporate a fundamental principle of economic analysis: assign responsibility to parties in proportion to their capabilities for managing the risk.[27]

---

[24]Ross Anderson, "Why Information Security Is Hard—An Economic Perspective," *Proceedings of the 17th Annual Computer Security Applications Conference*, IEEE Computer Society, New Orleans, La., 2001, pp. 358-365.

[25]Lawrence A. Gordon and Martin P. Loeb, "Budgeting Process for Information Security Expenditures," *Communications of the ACM*, January 2006, Vol. 49, No. 1, p. 121.

[26]David Alderson and Kevin Soo Hoo, "The Role of Economic Incentives in Securing Cyberspace"; available at http://iis-db.stanford.edu/pubs/20765/alderson-soo_hoo-CISAC-rpt_1.pdf.

[27]Hal Varian, "Managing Online Security Risks," Economic Science Column, *New York Times*, June 1, 2000; Ross Anderson and Tyler Moore, "The Economics of Information Security," *Science*, 314(5799): 610-613, October 27, 2006.

6.4.1 Conflicting Interests and Incentives Among the Actors in Cybersecurity

There are a number of different actors whose decisions affect the cybersecurity posture of the nation and various entities within the nation: technology vendors, technology service providers, consumers, firms, law enforcement, the intelligence community, attackers, and governments (both as technology users and as guardians of the larger social good). Each of these actors gets plenty of blame for being the "problem": if technology vendors would just properly engineer their products, if end users would just use the technology available to them and learn safe behavior, if companies would just invest more in cybersecurity or take it more seriously, if law enforcement would just pursue attackers more aggressively, if policy makers would just do a better job of regulation or legislation, if attackers could just be deterred from launching attacks. . . .

There is some truth to such statements, and yet merely to state them does not advance the cause of better understanding and solutions. In particular, knowing why various actors behave as they do is the first step toward changing their behavior. Indeed, one could easily argue that from an economic perspective, each of these actors is behaving largely as might be anticipated on the basis of their interests and incentives and that the reasons underlying their behavior are perfectly reasonable from an economic standpoint, despite the negative impacts on cybersecurity.[28]

Consider first the incentives of the attacker. Partly because the incentive structure of the attacker is undesirable from a societal perspective and partly because there is clear moral high ground in going after the bad guy, most regulatory and legislative activity has thus far focused on changing the incentive structure of the attacker to make it more dangerous to conduct an attack.[29] For example, laws have been passed criminalizing certain kinds of activity and increasing the penalties for such activity. Rewards have been offered for information leading to the arrest and conviction of cyberattackers. On the other hand, jurisdictional issues and the anonymity offered by the intrinsically international nature of cyberspace have served to prevent or at least to greatly impede and increase the cost of identifying and prosecuting cyberattackers. In other words, in practice,

---

[28]See, for instance, Hal Varian, "Managing Online Security Risks," Economic Science Column, *New York Times*, June 1, 2000; Alfredo Garcia and Barry Horowitz, "The Potential for Underinvestment in Internet Security: Implications for Regulatory Policy," *Journal of Regulatory Economics*, 31(1): 37-55, February 2007, available at http://ssrn.com/abstract=889071; Tyler Moore, "The Economics of Digital Forensics," presented at the Fifth Annual Workshop on the Economics and Information Security, June 26-28, 2006, Cambridge, England; Ross Anderson and Tyler Moore, "The Economics of Information Security," *Science*, 314(5799): 610-613, October 27, 2006.

[29]Douglas A. Barnes, "Deworming the Internet," *Texas Law Review*, 83: 279-329, 2004.

the disincentives for an attacker are minimal, since the likelihood of punishment for an attack is quite low.

The attacker's incentives are part of a larger underground economy. Broadly speaking, the actors in this economy are those selling attack services (e.g., use of a botnet, stolen credit card numbers); those with the direct malevolent intent paying to use those services (e.g., those who wish to conduct a denial-of-service attack on a site for extortion purposes, those who wish to commit actual fraud); and the victims of the resulting cyberattacks (e.g., the operators of the Web site being attacked, those whose credit card numbers are used for fraudulent purposes [or the banks that absorb the fraudulent charges]).

The existence of this economy makes manifest a decoupling between adversarial or criminal intent and the expertise needed to follow through on that intent, thus expanding enormously the universe of possible malefactors. In other words, attack services (e.g., botnets as described in Box 2.3 in Chapter 2) can be regarded as an economic commodity. For example, if someone needs a botnet for some purpose, that party can obtain the use of a botnet in the appropriate market.

Insight into the underground cyber-economy of attackers potentially yields pressure points on which to focus security efforts. For example, the sellers of attack services must publicize the availability of their services in an appropriate marketplace, and it may be possible to target the sellers themselves. It may also be possible to interfere with the operation of the marketplace itself, by shutting down the various marketplace venues or by poisoning them so that buyers and sellers cannot trust each other.

In addition, many of the constraints on digital forensics practices, essential to law enforcement, are due to conflicting incentives of technology vendors, service providers, consumers, and law enforcement.[30] For example, technology vendors have economic incentives to differentiate their products by making them proprietary—but in a regime in which there are many proprietary products on the market, law enforcement officials must have at the ready a range of forensic tools that together can operate on a wide range of products embedding multiple standards.

Technology vendors have significant financial incentives to gain a first-mover or a first-to-market advantage. They are driven by important features of the information technology market: the number of other people using a product, the high fixed costs and low marginal costs, and the cost to customers of switching to another product (i.e., lock-in).[31]

---

[30]Tyler Moore, "The Economics of Digital Forensics," Fifth Annual Workshop on the Economics of Information Security, University of Cambridge, England, June 26-28, 2006.

[31]Carl Shapiro and Hal R. Varian, *Information Rules: A Strategic Guide to the Network Economy*, Harvard Business School Press, Boston, Mass., 1998.

These network effects have significant consequences for engineering an information system for security.[32] Time-to-market—a key dimension of competitiveness in the industry—is adversely affected when vendors must pay attention to "superfluous" functionality or system characteristics, and functionality or system characteristics that customers do not demand are by definition superfluous. The logic of getting to market quickly runs counter, however, to adding security features, which add complexity, time, and cost in design and testing while being hard to value by customers. In addition, there is often an operational tension between security and other functionality that customers demand explicitly, such as ease of use, interoperability, and backward compatibility—consider, for example, security measures that may make it difficult or cumbersome to respond quickly in an emergency situation.

Information technology purchasers (whether individuals or firms) largely make product choices based on features, ease of use, performance, and dominance in a market,[33] although in recent years the criteria for product selection have broadened to include security to some extent in some business domains. But even to the extent that consumers do consider security, there is an information asymmetry that makes it difficult or impossible for them to distinguish between products that are secure and ones that are not. This leads to the "market for lemons" problem described by Akerlof[34]—buyers are unwilling to pay for something (in this case security) that they cannot measure, so leading vendors to avoid the extra costs of providing something they cannot recover.

Evaluation systems, such as the Common Criteria, have been attempts to remedy this problem. Common Criteria and the European Information Technology Security Evaluation Criteria (ITSEC) require evaluations to be paid for by the vendor seeking evaluation. This introduces the perverse incentive that motivates vendors to shop around for an evaluation contractor with whom a "sweetheart deal" can be negotiated, leading to the potential for suspect certifications.[35] Certification systems may even have the perverse effect of encouraging those most motivated to transfer liability,

---

[32]Ross Anderson, "Why Information Security Is Hard—An Economic Perspective," *Proceedings of the 17th Annual Computer Security Applications Conference*, IEEE Computer Society, 2001, p. 359.

[33]Ross Anderson and Tyler Moore, "The Economics of Information Security," *Science*, 314 (5799): 610-613, October 27, 2006.

[34]George A. Akerlof, "The Market for 'Lemons': Quality, Uncertainty and the Market Mechanism," *Quarterly Journal of Economics*, 84: 488-500, 1970.

[35]Ross Anderson, "Why Information Security Is Hard—An Economic Perspective," *Proceedings of the 17th Annual Computer Security Applications Conference*, IEEE Computer Society, 2001, pp. 358-365. Note that while the meaning of such a certification from a technical perspective may also be suspect, it is beside the point made here.

meet "due diligence" requirements, and take advantage of naïve customers to seek certification. Mechanisms such as online "trust" certifications meant to help users determine the safety of their online activities appear to result in adverse selection that undermines that safety, where untrustworthy sites are significantly more likely than trustworthy ones to seek certification.[36]

End users improve their own cybersecurity postures when they act to protect their systems, for instance by maintaining antivirus software. But if the tasks required to protect their systems are complex or costly and their own risk of a security compromise is minimal, a user has little motivation to spend time or money preventing others from using their systems for nefarious purposes (e.g., as part of a botnet). For example, universities with relatively unprotected networks were used to attack major commercial Web sites but bore only a small amount of the cost (as a nuisance in lost performance).[37] While "concentrated-benefit" users, such as large commercial Web sites, may suffer serious loss, the harm to ordinary users is diffuse and offset by the costs required to take mitigating action.[38] These cases can be recognized as instances of the classic "tragedy of the commons" problem.[39]

Furthermore, from the standpoint of operators, the benefits of successful security can be seen only in events that do not happen, so it is easy to regard resources devoted to security as "wasted." The issue of spending money on insurance premiums is similar, but for the conventional losses against which insurance usually protects, there are at least reasonable risk metrics that make quantitative decisions about insurance spending possible.

Research is needed to accurately characterize the scope and nature of the incentives of these various actors. In addition, understanding the relationships among these actors—that is, the market—is key to finding ways to intervene in the market in order to shape the behavior of its actors.

6.4.2 Risk Assessment in Cybersecurity

Even if the incentive structures for the various actors could be changed, issues of how much to invest in security and what to invest in

---

[36]Benjamin Edelman, "Adverse Selection in Online 'Trust' Certifications," Harvard University, Cambridge, Mass., 2006, draft working paper, available at http://www.benedelman.org/publications/advsel-trust-draft.pdf.

[37]Hal Varian, "Managing Online Security Risks," Economic Science Column, *New York Times*, June 1, 2000.

[38]Douglas A. Barnes, "Deworming the Internet," *Texas Law Review*, 83: 279-329, 2004.

[39]Ross Anderson, "Why Information Security Is Hard—An Economic Perspective," *Proceedings of the 17th Annual Computer Security Applications Conference*, IEEE Computer Society, 2001, pp. 358-365.

would remain. This requires the ability to make sound investments in cybersecurity based on reasonable assessments of the risks.

Individuals and companies do spend large amounts on security. Roughly $100 billion is spent annually on IT security worldwide.[40] But there are few ways to know how much is enough. Indeed, technology solutions can create a false sense of security.[41] Some models for determining appropriate levels of investment at the firm level have been developed,[42] but budgeting for IT security is often driven by such things as the past year's budget, best industry practices, and a list of must-do items, rather than any sound economic principles. While cost-benefit approaches appear to be useful for properly determining levels of investment, they are predicated on an ability to estimate benefits, which requires understanding the risk profile.[43] Firms also excessively discount future costs (see the discussion on behavioral economics below in this section) and costs borne by others (Section 6.4.3), and to the extent that they optimize their operations and investments at all, they do so on a narrow and short-term basis.

A necessary condition for investing rationally in cybersecurity depends on being able to assess the risks of cyberattack and the benefits of countermeasures taken to defend against such attack. Section 6.3 addresses the difficulties in assessing benefits of cybersecurity measures. But assessing risks is also a difficult challenge, especially in a risk environment inhabited at least partly by low-probability, high-impact events. Attempts to construct a business case for cybersecurity often founder because of the unavailability of actuarial data that might help predict in quantitative terms the likelihood of a specific type of attack, and, as discussed below, attacks can change on a short timescale and thereby reduce the utility of such data. In general, such data that are available are not specific enough to drive organizational change, since victims of

---

[40]Kenneth Cukier, "Protecting Our Future: Shaping Public-Private Cooperation to Secure Critical Information Infrastructures," *The Rueschlikon Conference Report of a Roundtable of Experts and Policy Makers*, Washington, D.C., May 2006, p. 12.

[41]Kenneth Cukier, "Protecting Our Future: Shaping Public-Private Cooperation to Secure Critical Information Infrastructures," *The Rueschlikon Conference Report of a Roundtable of Experts and Policy Makers*, Washington, D.C., May 2006, p. 12.

[42]See for instance, Lawrence A. Gordon and Martin P. Loeb, "The Economics of Information Security Investment," *ACM Transactions on Information and Systems Security*, 5(4, November): 438-457, 2002; Soumyo D. Moitra and Suresh L. Konda, *The Survivability of Network Systems: An Empirical Analysis*, CMU/SEI-2000-TR-021, ESC-TR-2000-021, December 2000, available at http://www.cert.org/archive/pdf/00tr021.pdf.

[43]Lawrence A. Gordon and Martin P. Loeb, "Budgeting Process for Information Security Expenditures," *Communications of the ACM*, 49(1, January): 121, 2006. See also, Kenneth Cukier, "Ensuring (and Insuring?) Critical Information Infrastructure Protection," *A Report of the 2005 Rueschlikon Conference on Information Policy*, Switzerland, June 16-18, 2005, p. 7.

various attacks are usually quite reluctant to share information on attacks, concerned about drawing public attention to limitations or deficiencies in their security posture and/or being placed at a subsequent competitive disadvantage in the marketplace.

A major impediment in data collection is the reluctance on the part of owners and operators of IT to collect and share the data necessary for companies to know their risk or for the insurance industry to create a viable market.[44] Indeed, firms have good reasons to avoid disclosing breaches. While economic consequences vary, firms can suffer significant costs.[45] Potential negative impacts from public disclosures of information security breaches include lost market value and competitive disadvantage. That is, if one company releases information about an incident and other companies do not release information about their own incidents, the releasing company may well be disadvantaged by its candor in the marketplace as its competitors call attention to its failings. Firms also fear legal liability and government fines. Indeed, Gordon et al. argue that, absent appropriate economic incentives, it is in a firm's self-interest to *renege* on previously agreed-on arrangements to share cybersecurity-related information, even though information sharing among a group of firms lowers the cost of each firm's attaining any given level of information security and thus yields potential benefits both for individual firms and for society at large.[46]

Thus, one research question suggested by the above discussion is the development of incentives that would promote greater information sharing. Possible incentives that warrant research include providing public subsidies to information-sharing firms that vary according to the level of information sharing that takes place; government-subsidized insurance; and other forms of government regulation. Research would entail an examination of how such incentives should be constructed and evaluated and how to prevent the creation of perverse economic incentives that actually discourage information sharing and/or better cybersecurity.

---

[44]Kenneth Cukier, "Ensuring (and Insuring?) Critical Information Infrastructure Protection," *A Report of the 2005 Rueschlikon Conference on Information Policy*, Switzerland, June 16-18, 2005, p. 22.

[45]Katherine Campbell, Lawrence A. Gordon, Martin P. Loeb, and Lei Zhou, "The Economic Cost of Publicly Announced Information Security Breaches: Empirical Evidence from the Stock Market," *Journal of Computer Security*, 11: 431-448, 2003. This paper examines just one element of potential costs—stock market valuation.

[46]L.A. Gordon, M.P. Loeb, and W. Lucyshyn, "Sharing Information on Computer Systems Security: An Economic Analysis," *Journal of Accounting and Public Policy*, 22(6): 461-485, 2003.

An example of a quantitative cost-benefit analysis was offered by Wei et al. in 2001.[47] Wei and his colleagues developed a methodology, built a model based on cost factors associated with various intrusion categories, and applied the model to investigating the costs and benefits of deploying and using a cooperative intrusion-detection system known as Hummer. The model addressed questions such as "What is the cost of not detecting an intrusion?" and "What does it cost to detect an intrusion?" To address the all-important question of likelihood, Wei et al. used empirical data relating to the frequency with which different categories of intrusion occurred in order to calculate the annual loss expectancy (ALE) (that is, an attack's damage multiplied by its empirically estimated frequency in 365 days of system operation). If a security mechanism prevents a certain kind of attack with probability p, the loss thereby avoided is p times ALE. The net benefit is calculated by subtracting security investment from the sum of all avoided losses over the operational lifetime of the security mechanism installed.

Another reason for the difficulty of risk assessment is that the "likelihood" of a particular attack is a reactive quantity. For example, imagine that the historical record shows that a certain type of attack (Attack A) has accounted for 50 percent of the attacks against a particular operating system recorded in the past year, while another type of attack (Attack B) accounted for only 10 percent of the attacks. Now, imagine that resources have been made available to develop a defense against Attack A and that now such a defense is available and is being deployed. This deployment will have two results—incidents of Attack A will almost certainly be reduced (because adversaries will not waste their time conducting ineffective attacks), and incidents of Attack B will increase, perhaps absolutely or perhaps only relative to the frequency of Attack A. (It is also likely that attacks of still another type, Attack C, will emerge, and attacks of this type will never before have been seen. Indeed, one might well argue that the ability to create attacks of a type never before seen is part of the *definition* of a skilled attacker.)

More generally, decision makers have few ways to understand and quantitatively characterize the space of possible attacks and the evolution of a threat. Since the space of possible attacks is so large, sampling that space is an essential element of tractability. But what are the rules that should govern such sampling? At what level of granularity should attacks be characterized? Thus, an important research area is to find an approach

[47]Huaqiang Wei, Deb Frinke, Olivia Carter, and Chris Ritter, "Cost-Benefit Analysis for Network Intrusion Detection Systems," CSI 28th Annual Computer Security Conference, October 29-31, 2001, Washington, D.C.; available at www.csds.uidaho.edu/deb/costbenefit.pdf.

to the calculus of decision making in cyberspace that does not depend as heavily on actuarial data as do current methods. In addition, this research area would seek to develop more usable characterizations of attacks.

Behavioral economics might suggest research on topics in which human psychological limitations and complications are operative,[48] and consequently how actual human behavior in economic matters deviates, often substantially, from that of the rational actor postulated in neoclassical economic theory. In particular, Tversky and Kahneman have described a mental process known as the availability heuristic, in which individuals assess the magnitude of the risk associated with some harmful event based on whether they can bring examples of harm readily to mind.[49] If people can easily think of such examples, their assessment of risk increases (e.g., their judgments about the likelihood go up).

In the non-cyber domain, Slovic found that people are much more likely to buy insurance for natural disasters if they can recall such disasters in their personal histories.[50] Indeed, policy makers are not immune to the availability heuristic—a great deal of experience in national responses to catastrophic events suggests that such events do much more to force policy makers to pay attention to problems than all the reports in the world.

Applying the availability heuristic to cybersecurity would suggest that if users cannot see a direct and significant impact on themselves from a cybersecurity problem, their awareness and concern about cybersecurity will be relatively low. The converse would also be true: in the aftermath of a "digital Pearl Harbor," public attention to cybersecurity would rise dramatically. Consider, for example, the security of air transport before and after September 11, 2001 (9/11). Prior to the 9/11 attacks, many reports had drawn attention to the weaknesses in flight security—but few changes had been made. After the attacks, airport security was dramatically increased, but in ways that many analysts argue provide only a few genuine enhancements in actual security. Similarly, in the cybersecurity domain, a very important and relevant research question is how research results and best practices in cybersecurity should be disseminated in an

---

[48]Sendhil Mullainathan and Richard H. Thaler, "Behavioral Economics," *International Encyclopedia of the Social and Behavioral Sciences*; available at www.iies.su.se/nobel/papers/Encyclopedia%202.0.pdf.

[49]See, for example, A. Tversky and D. Kahneman, "Judgment Under Uncertainty: Heuristics and Biases," pp. 3-22 in D. Kahneman, P. Slovic, and A. Tversky (eds.), *Judgment Under Uncertainty: Heuristics and Biases*, Cambridge University Press, Cambridge and New York, 2002.

[50]P. Slovic, *The Perception of Risk*, Earthscan Publications Ltd., London and Sterling, Va., 2000.

atmosphere of sudden enthusiasm that would be inevitable after a digital Pearl Harbor.

Gordon et al. go even farther, suggesting that a reactive approach toward the deployment of measures to strengthen cybersecurity beyond some basic minimum may be consistent with an entirely rational (non-behavioral) economic perspective.[51] The essence of the argument is that, given a fixed amount to spend on cybersecurity measures, it may make sense to hold a portion of the budget in reserve and wait for a security breach to occur before spending the reserve. By deferring the decision on spending the reserve, managers may obtain a clearer picture about whether or not such spending is warranted. In a wait-and-see scenario, actual losses do occur if and when a breach occurs, but the magnitude of those losses may be lower than the expected benefits of waiting, and so on balance, it may well pay to wait.

For any given company, the implications of this model depend on the specifics regarding the costs of security breaches, the costs of various cybersecurity measures to be put into place, the likelihood that specific security breaches will occur, and the magnitude of the budget available. Thus, one research theme associated with this perspective would be the development of tools and analytical techniques that would enable reasonable and defensible estimates of all of these various parameters in any given instance.

6.4.3 The Nature and Extent of Market Failure (If Any) in Cybersecurity

As noted in Section 6.4.1, the various actors in the cybersecurity domain may well be acting just as a rational-actor economic model might predict. In this view, users, vendors, customers, and so on are concerned with security at a level commensurate with the risk they perceive: although cybersecurity problems occur, users of information technology learn to adjust their behavior, expectations, and economic models to take into account these problems, and business decisions are being made appropriately for the level of threat that currently exists. In this view, there is no market failure, and allowing the free market in cybersecurity to work its will is the preferred course of action.

To the extent that decision makers do take cybersecurity into account, the natural inclination—indeed, fiscal responsibility—of organizational decision makers is to take only those measures that mitigate the secu-

[51] L.A. Gordon, M.P. Loeb, and W. Lucyshyn, "Information Security Expenditures and Real Options: A Wait-and-See Approach," *Computer Security Journal*, 19(2): 1-7, 2003.

rity problem for their own organizations rather than for society as a whole. (For example, businesses are not required to consider the downside impact of compromising customer privacy—such impact results in costs to the customers rather than to the business.) That is, they must make a business case for their security investments, and any investment in security beyond that—by definition—cannot be justified on business grounds. Thus, beyond a certain level, society rather than the company will benefit, and so security at or beyond that level is a public good in which individual organizations have little incentive to invest.

In short, incentives for deploying a level of security higher than what today's business cases will bear are thus nearly nonexistent. Accordingly, if the nation's cybersecurity posture is to be improved to a level that is higher than the level to which today's market will drive it, the market calculus that motivates organizations to pay attention to cybersecurity must be altered in some ways, and the business cases for the security of these organizations must change.

It is a different—and researchable—question about whether the national cybersecurity posture resulting from the investment decisions of many individual firms acting in their own self-interest is adequate from a societal perspective. This question becomes especially interesting if data and information become available to support business cases for greater cybersecurity investments by individual firms.

6.4.4 Changing Business Cases and Altering the Market Calculus

The business case for undertaking any action is based on a comparison of incremental costs and benefits. Thus, the likelihood of undertaking an action increases if the costs of undertaking it are lower and/or if the benefits of taking it are higher. In the cybersecurity domain, for example, efforts to develop and promote usable security (Section 6.1) can be fairly regarded as efforts both to avoid lower costs (with security measures many of the benefts will come in the form of cost avoidance) and to reduce disincentives to deploying security functionality. In general, the central element of the economic research agenda for cybersecurity is to identify actions that lower barriers and eliminate disincentives; to create incentives to boost the economic benefits that flow from attention to cybersecurity; and to penalize a lack of attention to cybersecurity or actions that cause harm in cyberspace.

The discussions below focus on two complementary approaches to changing business cases—approaches for increasing the flow of relevant information to cybersecurity decision makers and approaches for incentivizing actual change in the behavior of those decision makers.

6.4.4.1 Letting Current Threat Trends Take Their Course

One approach to increasing the flow of information to decision makers is to wait for the threat environment to change. In this approach, individual organizations monitor their cybersecurity environment and alter their approaches to cybersecurity as changes in their environment occur (e.g., as certain kinds of threats manifest themselves in the future). That is, as the threat changes, so too will customer behavior and vendor business cases. Indeed, recent announcements and activities of a number of software vendors indicate that markets have been changing in directions that call for more robust cybersecurity functionality.

Nevertheless, from a public policy perspective, this approach leaves open the possibility of cyberattacks with consequences that ripple and reverberate far beyond individual organizations and affect important societal functions. The reason is that current cybersecurity efforts respond to the current perception of risk, which is driven by the most visible threats of today. History and intelligence information suggest that vastly more sophisticated threats against a wider variety of targets are likely to be in the offing, but that these threats will present little overt evidence to motivate further defensive action on the part of most private organizations and individuals.

Moreover, this approach presumes that organizations can respond to changes in the threat on the necessary timescale. Because new kinds of death emerge relatively infrequently, life insurance companies can adjust their actuarial models and develop new rate structures when new threats emerge. But it is not at all clear that changes in the cyberthreat environment will emerge slowly, and indeed considerable evidence exists that it can change quickly.

6.4.4.2 Use of Existing Market Mechanisms to Improve the Flow of Information

Rational investment in security depends on the availability of accurate information about vulnerabilities, and a number of market mechanisms have been developed (though not all have been deployed) to increase the availability of such information.[52] The availability of information about vulnerabilities depends on two factors. One factor is the identification of vulnerabilities; a second factor is the sharing of information about vulnerabilities once identified.

---

[52]The discussion of this section is based largely on Rainer Böhme, "Vulnerability Markets: What Is the Economic Value of a Zero-Day Exploit?," *Proceedings of 22C3*, Berlin, Germany, December 27-30, 2005.

One market mechanism that has been used to identify vulnerabilities is the bug challenge or bug bounty.[53] Bug challenges and bounties are offered by producers who pay a monetary reward for reporting security problems that someone finds. They require the value of the reward to be greater than the amount that the identifier might realize by exploiting or selling the vulnerability elsewhere. However, the underlying market mechanism suffers a number of imperfections, particularly in the ability for pricing signals to work efficiently, that make it impractical on a large scale.[54] (See Box 6.2.)

Bug auctions based on vendor participation have also been considered.[55] They are similar in concept to bug challenges, although they are based on different theoretical framework. Of course bug auctions could be held independent of vendors, but essentially they act as blackmail for vendors and honest users while providing no useful information about security when no vulnerability is for sale.[56]

Market mechanisms for sharing vulnerability information have also been developed. For example, vulnerability information brokers act as intermediaries among benign identifiers of vulnerabilities, users, and vendors.[57] Because they provide a mechanism for reporting vulnerability information, the U.S. Computer Emergency Response Team (CERT) acts as vulnerability brokers, although it does not profit from reporting vulnerabilities. Some firms have monetized this process by buying information about vulnerabilities and creating business models that offer an advantage of advance knowledge about vulnerabilities to their customers.[58] However, these market-based mechanisms for vulnerability disclosure carry incentives for manipulation (by leaking information) and have been shown to underperform CERT-like mechanisms.[59]

---

[53]See for instance, the Mozilla Security Bug Bounty Program, at http://www.mozilla.org/security/bug-bounty.html.

[54]Rainer Böhme, "Vulnerability Markets: What Is the Economic Value of a Zero-Day Exploit?," *Proceedings of 22C3*, Berlin, Germany, December 27-30, 2005, p. 2.

[55]Andy Ozment, "Bug Auctions: Vulnerability Markets Reconsidered," *Workshop of Economics and Information Security*, Minneapolis, Minn., 2004.

[56]Rainer Böhme, "Vulnerability Markets: What Is the Economic Value of a Zero-Day Exploit?," *Proceedings of 22C3*, Berlin, Germany, December 27-30, 2005, p. 2. See footnote 2 therein.

[57]Karthik Kannan and Rahul Telang, "Market for Software Vulnerabilities? Think Again," *Management Science*, 51(5, May): 726-740, 2005.

[58]See for instance, iDefense Quarterly Challenge, at http://labs.idefense.com/vcp/challenge.php#more_q4+2006%3A+%2410%2C000+vulnerability+challenge.

[59]Karthik Kannan and Rahul Telang, "Market for Software Vulnerabilities? Think Again," *Management Science*, 51(5, May): 726-740, 2005; Ross Anderson and Tyler Moore, "The Economics of Information Security," *Science* 314(5799): 610-613, 2006.

BOX 6.2
Bug Bounties and Whistle-Blowers

The bug bounty—paying for information about systems problems—stands in marked contrast to the more common practice of discouraging or dissuading whistle-blowers (defined in this context as one who launches an attack without malicious intent), especially those from outside the organization that would be responsible for fixing those problems. Yet the putative intent of the whistle-blower and the bug bounty hunter is the same—to bring information about system vulnerabilities to the attention of responsible management. (This presumes that the whistle-blower's actions have not resulted in the public release of an attack's actual methodology or other information that would allow someone else with genuine malicious intent to launch such an attack.) Whether prosecution or reward is the correct response to such an individual has long been the subject of debate in the information technology community.

Consider, for example, the story of Robert Morris, Jr., the creator of the first Internet worm in 1988. Morris released a self-replicating, self-propagating program onto the Internet. This program—a worm—replicated itself much faster than Morris had expected, with the result that computers at many sites, including universities, military sites, and medical research facilities, were affected. He was subsequently convicted of violating Section 2(d) of the Computer Fraud and Abuse Act of 1986, 18 U.S.C. §1030(a)(5)(A) (1988), which punishes anyone who intentionally accesses without authorization a category of computers known as "[f]ederal interest computers" and damages or prevents authorized use of information in such computers, causing the loss of $1,000 or more. However, at the time, a number of commentators argued for leniency in Morris's sentencing on grounds that he had not anticipated the results of his experiment, and further that his actions had brought an important vulnerability into wide public view and thus he had provided a valuable public service. It is not known if these arguments swayed the sentenc-

Another as-yet untried mechanism for sharing information is based on derivative contracts, by which an underwriter issues a pair of contracts: Contract A pays its owner $100 if on a specific date there exists a certain well-specified vulnerability *X* for a certain system. The complementary Contract B pays $100 if on that date *X* does not exist. These contracts are then sold on the open market. The issuer of these contracts breaks even, by assumption. If the system in question is regarded as highly secure by market participants, then the trading price for Contract A will drop—it is unlikely that *X* will be found on that date, and so only speculators betting against the odds will buy Contract A (and will likely lose their [small] investment). By contrast, the trading price for Contract B will remain near $100, so investors playing the odds will profit only minimally but with high probability. The trading prices of Contracts A and B thus reflect

ing court, but Morris's sentence did not reflect the maximum penalty that he could have received.

Those who put on public demonstrations of system vulnerabilities have often said that they did so only after they informed responsible management of their findings and management failed to take remedial action on a sufficiently rapid timescale. Thus, they argue, public pressure informed and generated by such demonstrations is the only way to force management to address the problems identified. However, these individuals are usually (though not always) outsiders to the responsible organization, and in particular they do not have responsibility for overall management.

Inside the organization, management may well have evaluated the information provided by the demonstration and judged its operational significance to be less important than is alleged by the demonstrators. That is, responsible management is likely to have (at least in principle) more information about the relevant operational context, and to have decided that the vulnerability is not worth fixing (especially because all attempts at fixing vulnerabilities run the risk of introducing additional problems).

A further concern is the fear of setting bad precedents. Imagine that an individual launches a cyberattack against some organization and causes damage. When caught, the person asserts that his or her intent was to test the defenses of the organization and so he or she deserves a reward for revealing vulnerabilities rather than prosecution. If the individual could cite precedents for such an argument, his or her own defense case would be much stronger.

One of the most significant differences between the bug bounty and the unauthorized public demonstration of system vulnerability is that in the case of the former, the party paying the bounty—usually the vendor—has demonstrated a receptiveness to receiving the information. But whether other, more controversial mechanisms have value in conveying such information is an open and researchable question.

the probability of occurrence of the underlying event at any time.[60] The derivatives approach requires a trusted third party. This approach shares with insurance underwriters the need to pay upon the occurrence of a breach in order to hedge the risk to which they are exposed.

---

[60]Found in Rainer Böhme, "Vulnerability Markets: What Is the Economic Value of a Zero-Day Exploit?," the concept of the value of derivative contracts reflecting the market's judgment about the security of a system is taken from Lawrence A. Gordon, Martin P. Loeb, and Tashfeen Sohail, "A Framework for Using Insurance for Cyber-Risk Management," *Communications of the ACM*, 46(3): 81-85, 2003; *Proceedings of 22C3*, Berlin, Germany, December 27-30, 2005, p. 3, available at http://events.ccc.de/congress/2005/fahrplan/attachments/542-Boehme2005_22C3_VulnerabilityMarkets.pdf.

6.4.4.3 Private-Sector Mechanisms to Incentivize Behavioral Change

Private-sector mechanisms to incentivize organizations and individuals to improve their cybersecurity postures do not entail the difficulties of promulgating government regulation, and a number of attempts in the private sector have been made for this purpose. Research is needed to understand how these attempts have fared, to understand how they could be improved if they have not worked well, and to understand how they could be more widely promulgated and their scope extended if they have.

6.4.4.3.1 Insurance

Historically, the insurance industry has played a key role in many markets as an agent for creating incentives for good practices (e.g., in health care and in fire and auto safety). Thus, the possibility arises that it might be able to play a similar role in incentivizing better cybersecurity.

Consumers (individuals and organizations) buy insurance so as to protect themselves against loss. Strictly speaking, insurance does not itself protect against loss—it provides compensation to the holder of an insurance policy in the event that the consumer suffers a loss. Insurance companies sell those policies to consumers and profit to the extent that policyholders do not file claims. Thus, it is in the insurance company's interest to reduce the likelihood that the policyholder suffers a loss. Moreover, the insurance company will charge a higher premium if it judges that the policyholder is likely to suffer a loss.

Particularizing this reasoning to the cybersecurity context, consumers will buy a policy to insure themselves against the possibility of a successful exploitation by some adversary. The insurance company will charge a higher premium if it judges that the policyholder's cybersecurity posture is weak and a lower premium if the posture is strong. This gives the user a financial incentive to strengthen his or her posture. Users would pay for poor cybersecurity practices and insecure IT products with higher premiums, and so the differential pricing of business disaster-recovery insurance based in part on quality/assurance/security would bring market pressure to bear in this area. Indeed, cyber-insurance has frequently been proposed as a market-based mechanism for overcoming security market failure,[61] and the importance of an insurance industry role in promoting

---

[61] See, for instance, Lawrence A. Gordon, Martin P. Loeb, and Tashfeen Sohail, "A Framework for Using Insurance for Cyber-Risk Management," *Communications of the ACM*, 46(3): 81-85, 2003; Jay P. Kesan, Ruperto P. Majuca, and William J. Yurcik, "The Economic Case for Cyberinsurance," *Workshop on the Economics of Information Security*, Cambridge, Mass., 2005;

cybersecurity was recently noted at the 2005 Rueschlikon Conference on Information Policy.[62]

Of course, how such a market actually works depends on the specifics of how premiums are set and how a policyholder's cybersecurity posture can be assessed. (For example, one possible method for setting premiums for the cybersecurity insurance of a large firm might be based in part on the results of an independently conducted red team attack.) Furthermore, there are a number of other reasons that stand in the way of establishing a viable cyber-insurance market: the highly correlated nature of losses from outbreaks (e.g., from viruses) in a largely homogenous monoculture environment, the difficulty in substantiating claims, the intangible nature of losses and assets, and unclear legal grounds.[63]

6.4.4.3.2 The Credit Card Industry

A prime target of cybercriminals is personal information such as credit card numbers, Social Security numbers, and other consumer information. Because many participants in the credit card industry (e.g., banks and merchants) obtain such information in the course of their routine business activities, these participants are likely to be targeted by cybercriminals seeking such information. To reduce the likelihood of success of such criminal activities, the credit card industry has established the Payment Card Industry (PCI) Data Security Standard, which establishes a set of requirements for enhancing payment account data security.[64] These requirements include the following:

1. Install and maintain a firewall configuration to protect cardholder data.
2. Do not use vendor-supplied defaults for system passwords and other security parameters.
3. Protect stored cardholder data.
4. Encrypt transmission of cardholder data across open, public networks.

William Yurcik and David Doss, "Cyberinsurance: A Market Solution to the Internet Security Market Failure," *Workshop on Economics and Information Security*, Berkeley, Calif., 2002.

[62]Kenneth Cukier, "Ensuring (and Insuring?) Critical Information Infrastructure Protection," *A Report of the 2005 Rueschlikon Conference on Information Policy*, Switzerland, June 16-18, 2005.

[63]Rainer Böhme, "Vulnerability Markets: What Is the Economic Value of a Zero-Day Exploit?," *Proceedings of 22C3*, Berlin, Germany, December 27-30, 2005, p. 4.

[64]An extended description of these requirements can be found at http://usa.visa.com/download/business/accepting_visa/ops_risk_management/cisp_PCI_Data_Security_Standard.pdf.

5. Use and regularly update antivirus software.
6. Develop and maintain secure systems and applications.
7. Restrict access to cardholder data by business need to know.
8. Assign a unique identifier to each person with computer access.
9. Restrict physical access to cardholder data.
10. Track and monitor all access to network resources and cardholder data.
11. Regularly test security systems and processes.
12. Maintain a policy that addresses information security.

Organizations (e.g., merchants) that handle credit cards must conform to this standard and follow certain leveled requirements for testing and reporting. Compliance with these standards is enforced by the banks, which have the authority to penalize noncompliant organizations and data disclosures caused by noncompliance.

6.4.4.3.3 Standards-Setting Processes

For certain specialized applications, compliance with appropriate security standards are almost a sine qua non for their success. For example, for electronic voting applications, security standards are clearly necessary, and indeed the National Institute of Standards and Technology has developed security standards—or more precisely, voluntary guidelines—for electronic voting systems. (These guidelines are voluntary in the sense that federal law does not require that electronic voting systems conform to them—but many states do have such requirements.)

In a broader context, the International Organization for Standardization (ISO) standards process is intended to develop standards that specify requirements for various products, services, processes, materials, and systems and for good managerial and organizational practice. Many firms find value in compliance with an ISO standard and seek a public acknowledgment of such compliance (that is, seek certification) in order to improve their competitive position in the marketplace.

In the cybersecurity domain, the ISO (and its partner organization, the International Electrotechnical Commission [IEC]) has developed ISO/IEC 17799:2005, which is a code of practice for information security management that establishes guidelines and general principles for initiating, implementing, maintaining, and improving information security management in an organization. ISO/IEC 17799:2005 contains best practices of control objectives and controls in certain areas of information security management, including security policy; organization of information security; information systems acquisition, development, and maintenance; and information security incident management. Although ISO/IEC

17799:2005 is not a certification standard, the complementary specification standard ISO/IEC 27001 addresses information security management system requirements and can be used for certification.[65]

As for the putative value of ISO/IEC 17799:2005, the convener of the working group that developed ISO/IEC 17799:2005 argued that "users of this standard can also demonstrate to business partners, customers and suppliers that they are fit enough and secure enough to do business with, providing the chance for them to turn their investment in information security into business-enabling opportunities."[66]

6.4.4.4 Nonregulatory Public-Sector Mechanisms

A variety of nonregulatory public-sector mechanisms are available to promote greater attention to and action on cybersecurity, including the following:

- *Government procurement.* The federal government is a large consumer of information technology goods and services, a fact that provides some leverage in its interactions with technology vendors. Such leverage could be used to encourage vendors to provide the government with IT systems that are more secure (e.g., with security defaults turned on rather than off). With such systems thus available, vendors might be able to offer them to other customers as well.
- *Government cybersecurity practices.* The government is an important player in information technology. Thus, the federal government itself might seek to improve its own cybersecurity practices and offer itself as an example for the rest of the nation.
- *Tax policy.* A variety of tax incentives might be offered to stimulate greater investment in cybersecurity.
- *Public recognition.* Public recognition often provides "bragging rights" for a firm that translate into competitive advantages; cybersecurity could be a candidate area for such recognition. One possible model for such recognition is the Malcolm Baldrige National Quality Award, given to firms judged to be outstanding in a number of important business quality areas. The award was established to mark a standard of excellence that would help U.S. organizations achieve world-class quality.

---

[65]See http://www.iso.org/iso/en/CatalogueDetailPage.CatalogueDetail?CSNUMBER=39612.

[66]See http://www.iso.org/iso/en/commcentre/pressreleases/archives/2005/Ref963.html.

The desirability and feasibility of these mechanisms and others are topics warranting investigation and research.

6.4.4.5 Direct Regulation (and Penalties)

Still another approach to changing business cases is the direct regulation of technology and users—legally enforceable mandates requiring that certain technologies must contain certain functionality or that certain users must behave in certain ways. This is an extreme form of changing the business cases—that is: comply or face a penalty. The regulatory approach has been taken in certain sectors of the economy: financial services, health care, utilities such as electricity and gas, and transportation are among the obvious examples of sectors or industries that are subject to ongoing regulation.

For many products in common use today, vendors are required by law to comply with various safety standards—seat belts in cars are an obvious example. But there are few mandatory standards relating to cybersecurity for IT products. Indeed, in many cases the contracts and terms of service that bind users to IT vendors often oblige the users to waive any rights with respect to the provision of security; this is especially true when the user is an individual retail consumer. In such situations, the buyer in essence assumes all security risks inherent in the use of the IT product or service in question. (Note here the contrast to the guarantees made by many credit card companies—the Fair Credit Reporting Act sets a ceiling of $50 on the financial liability of a credit card holder for an unauthorized transaction providing proper notifications have been given, and many credit card issuers have contractually waived such liability entirely if the loss results from an online transactions. These assurances have had an important impact on consumer willingness to engage in electronic commerce.)

Such contracts notwithstanding, direct regulation might call for all regulated institutions to adopt certain kinds of standards relating to cybersecurity "best practices" regarding the services they provide to consumers or their own internal practices. For example, in an attempt to increase security for customers, the Federal Financial Institutions Examination Council (FFIEC) has directed covered financial institutions to implement two-factor authentication for customers using online banking.[67] Another

[67]Two-factor authentication refers to the use of two independent factors to authenticate one's identity. An authentication factor could be something that one knows (e.g., a password), something that one has (e.g., a hardware token), or something that one is (e.g., a fingerprint). So, one two-factor authentication scheme calls for a user to insert a smart card into a reader and then to enter a password; neither one alone provides sufficient authentication, but the combination is supposed to do so.

"best practice" might be the use of tiger teams (red teams) to test an organization's security on an ongoing basis. (The committee is not endorsing either of these items as a best practice—they are provided as illustrations only of possible best practices.)

However, regulation is difficult to get right under the best of circumstances, as a good balance of flexibility and inflexibility must be found. Regulation so flexible that organizations need not change their practices at all is not particularly effective in driving change, and regulation so inflexible that compliance would require organizations to change in ways that materially harm their core capabilities will meet with enormous resistance and will likely be ignored in practice or not adopted at all.

Several factors would make it especially difficult to determine satisfactory regulations for cybersecurity.[68] Attack vectors are numerous and new ones continue to emerge, meaning that regulations based on addressing specific ills would necessarily provide only partial solutions. Costs of implementation would be highly variable and dependent on a number of factors beyond the control of the regulated party. Risks vary greatly from system to system. There is wide variation in the technical and financial ability of firms to support security measures.

In addition, certain regulatory mechanisms have been used for publicly traded companies to ensure that important information is flowing to investors and that these companies follow certain accounting practices in their finances. For example, publicly traded companies must issue annual reports on a U.S. Securities and Exchange Commission (SEC) Form 10-K; these documents provide a comprehensive overview of the company's business and financial condition and include audited financial statements. In addition, publicly traded companies must issue annual reports to shareholders, providing financial data, results of continuing operations, market segment information, new product plans, subsidiary activities, and research and development activities on future programs. Audits of company finances must be undertaken by independent accounting firms and must follow generally accepted accounting practices. Intrusive auditing and reporting practices have some precedent in certain sectors that are already heavily regulated by federal and state authorities—these sectors include finance, energy, telecommunications, and transportation.

Research is needed to investigate the feasibility of using these mechanisms, possibly in a modified form, for collecting information on security breaches and developing a picture of a company's cybersecurity posture. As an illustration of the value of regulation, consider that in

---

[68]Alfredo Garcia and Barry Horowitz, "The Potential for Underinvestment in Internet Security: Implications for Regulatory Policy," *Journal of Regulatory Economics*, Vol. 31, No. 1, February 2007; available at http://ssrn.com/abstract=889071.

2002, California passed the first state law to require public disclosure of any breach in the security of certain personal information. A number of states followed suit, and the California law is widely credited with drawing public attention to the problem of identity theft and its relationship to breaches in the security of personal information. An empirical study by Gordon et al. found that the Sarbanes-Oxley Act of 2002 (P.L. No. 107-204, 116 Stat. 745) had a positive impact on the voluntary disclosure of information security activities by corporations, a finding providing strong indirect evidence that the passage of this act has led to an increase in the focus of corporations on information security activities.[69] But such regulatory-driven focus is not without cost and may have unintended consequences, including decreased competition, distortions in cybersecurity investments and internal controls, and lost productivity from increased risk aversion.[70] Thus, research is needed to better understand the trade-offs involved in implementing information-disclosure regulations.

What might be included under such a rubric? One possibility is that a publicly traded company might be required to disclose all cybersecurity breaches in a year above a certain level of severity—a breach could be defined by recovery costs exceeding a certain dollar threshold. As part of its audit of the firm's books, an accounting firm could be required to assess company records on such matters. A metric such as the number of such breaches divided by the company's revenues would help to normalize the severity of the cybersecurity problem for the company's size. Another possibility is that a publicly traded company might be required to test its cybersecurity posture against a red team, and a sanitized report of the test's outcome or an independent assessment of the test's results included in the firm's SEC Form 10-K report. With more information about a firm's track record and cybersecurity posture on the public record, consumers and investors would be able to take such information into account in making buying and investment decisions, and a firm would have incentives to improve in the ways reflected in such information. (These possibilities should not be construed as policy recommendations of the committee, but rather as some topics among others that are worth researching for feasibility and desirability.)

---

[69]Lawrence A. Gordon, Martin P. Loeb, William Lucyshyn, and Tashfeen Sohail, "Impact of Sarbanes-Oxley Act on Information Security Activities," *Journal of Accounting and Public Policy*, 25(5): 503-530, 2006.

[70]Anindya Ghose and Uday Rajan, "The Economic Impact of Regulatory Information Disclosure on Information Security Investments, Competition, and Social Welfare," 2006 Workshop on Economics of Information Security, Cambridge, England, March 2006.

6.4.4.6 Use of Liability

Liability is based on the notion of holding vendors and/or system operators financially responsible through the courts for harms that result from cybersecurity breaches. According to this theory, vendors and operators, knowing that they could be held liable for cybersecurity breaches that result from product design or system operation, would be forced to make greater efforts than they do today to reduce the likelihood of such breaches. Courts in the legal system would also define obligations that users have regarding security.

Some analysts (often from the academic sector or from industries that already experience considerable government regulation) argue that the nation's cybersecurity posture will improve only if liability forces users and/or vendors to increase the attention they pay to security matters. Opponents argue that the threat of liability would stifle technological innovation, potentially compromise trade secrets, and reduce the competitiveness of products subject to such forces. Moreover, they argue that there are no reasonable objective metrics to which products or operations can be held responsible, especially in an environment in which cybersecurity breaches can result from factors that are not under the control of a vendor or an operator.

An intermediate position confines explicit liability to a limited domain. In this view, regulation or liability or some other extrinsic driver can help to bootstrap a more market-driven approach. Believers in this view assert that new metrics, lampposts, criteria, and so on can be integrated with established processes for engineering or acceptance evaluation. Updating the Common Criteria or the Federal Information Security Management Act (FISMA) to include these mandated elements would enable the injection of the new ideas into the marketplace, and their demonstrated value and utility may persuade others not subject to regulation or liability to adopt them anyway.

All of these views on liability were present within the committee, and the committee did not attempt to reconcile them. But it found value in separating the issue into three components. The first is the putative effectiveness of an approach based on liability or direct regulation in strengthening the nation's cybersecurity posture. The second is the character of the actual link between regulation or liability and technological innovation and trade secret protection. The third is the public policy choice about any trade-offs that such a link might imply.

Regarding the first and the second, the committee found mostly a set of assertions but exceedingly little analytical work. Advocates of regulation or liability to strengthen cybersecurity have not made the case that any regulatory apparatus or case law on liability can move quickly enough as new threats and vulnerabilities emerge, while critics of regulation or liability have not addressed the claim that regulation and liability have a proven record of improving security in other fields, nor have they yet convincingly shown why the information technology field is different. Nor is there a body of research that either proves or disproves an inverse link between regulation or liability and innovation or trade secret protection. Substantial research on this point would help to inform the public debate over regulation by identifying the strengths and weaknesses of regulation or liability for cybersecurity and the points (if any) at which a reconciliation of the tensions is in fact not possible. Regarding the third, and presuming the existence of irreconcilable tensions, it then becomes a public policy choice about how much and what kind of innovation must be traded off in order to obtain greater cybersecurity.

6.5 SECURITY POLICIES

With the increasing sophistication and wide reach of computer systems, many organizations are now approaching computer security using more proactive and methodical strategies than in the past. Central to many of these strategies are formal, high-end policies designed to address an organization's overall effort for keeping its computers, systems, IT resources, and users secure. While access control is a large component of most security policies, the policies themselves go far beyond merely controlling who has access to what data. Indeed, as Guel points out, security policies communicate a consensus on what is appropriate behavior for a given system or organization.[71]

Basically, developing a security policy requires making many decisions about such things as which people and which resources to trust and how much and when to trust them. The policy development process comprises a number of distinct considerations:[72]

- Developing requirements involves the often-difficult process of determining just how much security attention to pay to a given set of data, resources, or users. Human resources information, for example, or critical proprietary data about a company's product, might require significantly stronger protections than, say, general information documents on an organization's intranet. A biological research facility might wish to encrypt genomic databases that

[71]Michele D. Guel, "A Short Primer for Developing Security Policies," SANS Institute, 2002; available at http://www.sans.org/resources/policies/Policy_Primer.pdf.

[72]More perspective on developing security policies can be found in Matt Bishop, "What Is Computer Security?" *IEEE Security and Privacy*, 1(1): 67-69, 2003.

contain sequence information of pandemic viruses, allowing access only to vetted requestors.

- Setting a policy entails translating security requirements into a formal document or statement setting the bounds of permissible and impermissible behavior and establishing clear lines of accountability.
- Implementing a policy can be accomplished using any of a range of technical mechanisms (e.g., a firewall or setting a user's system permissions) or procedural mechanisms (e.g., requiring users to change passwords on a monthly basis, reviewing access-control lists periodically).
- Assessing the effectiveness of mechanisms for implementing a policy and assessing the effectiveness of a policy in meeting the original set of requirements are ongoing activities.

Organizations often choose to create a number of distinct policies (or subpolicies) to address specific contexts. For example, most organizations now provide employees with acceptable-use policies that specify what types of behavior are permissible with company computer equipment and network access. Other prevalent policies include wireless network, remote access, and data-backup policies. Having multiple security policies allows organizations to focus specific attention on important contexts (for example, consider the efficiency of having an organization-wide password policy), although harmonizing multiple policies across an organization can often be a challenge.

Determining just how to set one's security policy is a critical and often difficult process for organizations. After all, long before any security policy is ever drafted, an organization must first get a good sense for its security landscape—for example, *what* things need *what* level of protection, *which* users require *what* level of access to *what* different resources, and so on. However, in the beginning of such a process, many organizations may not even know what questions need to be asked to begin developing a coherent policy or what options are open to them for addressing a given concern. One major open issue and area for research, therefore, is how to assist with this early, though all-important, stage of developing requirements and setting a security policy, as well as how to assist in evaluating existing policies.[73]

One approach to the problem of establishing appropriate policies in large organizations is the use of role-based access control, a practice that

---

[73]One interesting framework for developing and assessing security policies can be found in Jackie Rees, Subhajyoti Bandyopadhyay, and Eugene H. Spafford, "PFIRES: A Policy Framework for Information Security," *Communications of the ACM*, 46(7): 101-106, 2003.

determines the security policy appropriate for the roles in an organization rather than the individuals (a role can be established for a class of individuals, such as doctors in a hospital, or for a class of devices, such as all wireless devices). However, since individuals may have multiple roles, reconciling conflicting privileges can be problematic.

Other major open issues and research areas include the enforcement of security policies (as discussed in Section 6.1) and the determination of how effective a given security policy is in regulating desirable and undesirable behavior. These two areas (that is, enforcement and auditability) have been made more significant in recent years by an evolving regulatory framework that has placed new compliance responsibilities on organizations (e.g., Sarbanes-Oxley Act of 2002 [P.L. No. 107-204, 116 Stat. 745]; Gramm-Leach-Bliley Act [15 U.S.C., Subchapter I, Sec. 6801-6809, Disclosure of Nonpublic Personal Information]; the Health Insurance Portability and Accountability Act (HIPAA) of 1996; and so on). Another open question in this space involves the effectiveness of using outsourced firms to audit security policies.

Additional areas for research include ways to simulate the effects and feasibility of security policies; how to keep policies aligned with organizational goals (especially in multipolicy environments); methods for automating security policies or making them usable by machines; how to apply and manage security policies with respect to evolving technology such as distributed systems, handheld devices, electronic services (or Web services), and so on; and ways to reconcile security policies of different organizations that might decide to communicate or share information or resources.

7

Category 4—Deterring Would-Be Attackers and Penalizing Attackers

The goal of requirements in Category 4—Deterring would-be attackers and penalizing attackers, is that of deterring would-be attackers from taking actions that could result in the compromise of a system or network and penalizing attackers who do take such actions. This broad category in the committee's illustrative research agenda includes legal and policy measures that could be taken to penalize or impose consequences on cyberattackers and technologies that support such measures. In principle, this category could also include technical measures to retaliate against a cyberattacker.

The rationale for this category is that in the absence of legal, technical, economic, or other punitive measures against attackers, would-be attackers have few incentives to refrain from launching attacks. (The same rationale applies, of course, in the physical world, where would-be criminals are deterred from criminal activity by the threat of punishment and consequence.) In a penalty-free world, an attacker pays no penalty for failed attacks and can therefore continue attacking until he or she succeeds or quits.

Research in this category thus serves two important but complementary goals. First, such research seeks to develop more effective methods for imposing some kind of penalty on attackers, whether or not they have been successful in their attacks. Second, the availability of such methods increases the likelihood that an attacker will in fact suffer a penalty for hostile actions, and thus the availability of these methods presumably decreases the likelihood that a would-be attacker will initiate such actions. With fewer attackers, the cybersecurity task becomes easier to undertake.

A key characteristic of deterrence is that penalties can be directed at the proper party. Category 2 (Enabling accountability) research supports this goal by focusing on ways to ensure that actions in cyberspace can be associated with specific actors, but that research does not presume that actors will seek to conceal their actions. Malefactors in cyberspace will usually seek to do so, and thus investigators and other interested parties will need forensic tools that allow them to re-establish any deliberately broken bindings between actions and identity.

The following discussion presents illustrative topics within this category.

7.1 LEGAL ISSUES RELATED TO CYBERSECURITY

As noted above, cybersecurity is not just a technical domain. In cybersecurity, as in other areas of life in which security concerns arise, it is not unreasonable to conclude that the tools available to promote and enhance cybersecurity should include a legal dimension. For example, consider the notion of recourse for victims of cybercrime. In most areas other than those involving cyberspace, individuals who are victims of criminal activity can appeal to law enforcement and the courts to punish the perpetrators. But a victim of cybercrime—whether a private citizen, a business, or an organization—often or even usually has little practical recourse.

In principle, of course, cyberattackers can be held accountable for actions that cause harm in cyberspace through criminal or civil penalties. Such action requires a good characterization of what constitutes behavior that warrants criminal penalties, as well as the ability to identify the party responsible (see Section 5.1) and a legal framework that enables prosecutions to take place across all of the political boundaries that may have been crossed in the course of the punishable misbehavior. Many cybercrime perpetrators are outside of U.S. jurisdiction, and the applicable laws may not criminalize the particulars of the crime perpetrated. Even if they do, logistical difficulties in identifying the perpetrator across national boundaries may render him or her practically immune to prosecutions.

Harmonization of national laws (as provided for in the 2001 Council of Europe Convention on Cybercrime) is a good first step toward ensuring the availability of recourse, but there remains substantial legal and policy research to further the cause of harmonization more broadly and to reduce the logistical difficulties entailed in tracking, identifying, and prosecuting cybercriminals across national boundaries. Considerable efforts are underway today at the regional intergovernmental and international governmental level, as discussed in "The International Landscape of Cyber Security."[1]

A second example involves relationships between law enforcement and technology/service vendors. Internet service providers (ISPs) are used by cybercriminals as conduits of their crimes (and sometimes ISPs are willing accomplices). However, law enforcement authorities often have little leverage to persuade or compel ISPs to cut off access to suspicious users or to supply provenance or to trace data for forensics examination. From a law enforcement perspective, data-retention practices for most ISPs are inadequate to support investigative needs. However, providing additional authorities to law enforcement to compel various kinds of cooperation from ISPs (e.g., to enforce longer data-retention periods) has implications for civil liberties and is thus controversial. Legal, policy, and technical research is needed to find ways to protect due process and civil liberties without placing undue barriers in the way of legitimate law enforcement activities.

7.2 HONEYPOTS

The term *honeypot* in computer security jargon refers to a machine, a virtual machine, or other network resource that is intended to act as a decoy or diversion for would-be attackers. A *honeynet* refers to a collection of honeypots on a network. Honeypots or honeynets intentionally contain no real or valuable data (and hence receive no legitimate traffic) and are kept separate from an organization's production systems. Indeed, in most cases, systems administrators *want* attackers to succeed in compromising or breaching the security of honeypots to a certain extent so that they can log all the activity and learn from the techniques and methods used by the attacker. This process allows administrators to be better prepared for attacks on their real production systems. Honeypots are very useful for gathering information about new types of attacks, new techniques, and information on how things like worms or malicious code propagate through systems, and they are used as much by security researchers as by network security administrators.

Honeypots are usually of two main types: (1) a more basic, "low-interaction" implementation that emulates or gives the appearance of a real system or real machines in place; or (2) a more complex, "high-interaction" system containing real tools and applications designed to

[1] Delphine Nain, Neal Donaghy, and Seymour Goodman, "The International Landscape of Cyber Security," Chapter 9 in Detmar W. Straub, Seymour Goodman, and Richard Baskerville (eds.), *Information Security: Policies, Processes, and Practices*, M.E. Sharpe, New York, forthcoming 2008.

gather as much information about attacker activity as possible.[2] Honeypots of the first type can be quite simple to install and manage, although the information they provide on attackers may be limited, and the nature of the honeypot itself may be more susceptible to discovery by a skilled attacker. Honeypots of the second type are considerably more complicated, requiring much more skill to set up and manage, although the richness of information that they are capable of gleaning about attackers and techniques also increases, while the true nature of these honeypots may also be more difficult for attackers to discover.

There are also other, more focused types of honeypots. For example, spam honeypots—basically, vulnerable mail servers set up to attract the notice of those sending out illegitimate e-mail—have been quite useful in helping administrators generate spam "blacklists" for their own real mail servers. Wireless honeypots have also proven useful in detecting and learning from how attackers exploit wireless resources.

Another useful tool along these lines is the *honeytoken*. A honeytoken, like a honeypot, has no legitimate purpose other than to uncover illegitimate activity, so any use or access of a honeytoken can be considered suspicious. For example, consider the following scenario:

> A bogus medical record called "John F. Kennedy" is created and loaded into the database. This medical record has no true value because there is no real patient with that name. Instead, the record is a honeytoken. . . . If any employee is looking for interesting patient data, this record will definitely stand out. If the employee attempts to access this record, you most likely have an employee violating patient privacy [policies].[3]

In any case, just as systems administrators and researchers learn about attackers from honeypots, attackers themselves can learn how to detect honeypots and honeynets as well, thereby avoiding them and maintaining some secrecy regarding the techniques they use. Indeed, one recent paper on the subject likens the relationship between attackers and honeypot administrators to a continual arms race.[4] As one can imagine, as soon as an attacker determines that he or she is actually working with a honeypot, useful interactions are likely to cease. However, even then, researchers and administrators can learn things about how the attacker

---

[2]For additional information on the variety of honeypots in use today and related issues, see the Honeynet Project's home page at http://www.honeynet.org/.

[3]Lance Spitzner, "Honeytokens: The Other Honeypot," *SecurityFocus*, July 7, 2003; available at http://www.securityfocus.com/infocus/1713.

[4]Thorsten Holz and Frederic Raynal, "Detecting Honeypots and Other Suspicious Environments," *Proceedings of the 2005 IEEE Workshop on Information Assurance and Security*, United States Military Academy, West Point, N.Y., June 15-17, 2005.

discovered the nature of the honeypot and how the attacker might try to hide his or her tracks (e.g., altering log files, attempting to damage or crash the honeypot, and so on).

One significant open question with honeypots and honeynets (indeed, this is a broader question within cybersecurity itself) is whether or not one should use honeypot-type resources to strike back at or otherwise affect the resources of an attacker.[5] (This point is discussed further in Section 9.4, Cyber-Retaliation.) In many cases, administrators could use information learned through an attacker's interaction with a honeypot to lessen the danger that the attacker poses to real systems or other machines in the future (e.g., either by "hacking back" at the attacker or even removing or crippling zombie software from the attacking machine).

Another question for some in the computing community involves the ethics of deploying and using honeypots—some consider it a form of entrapment (although U.S. law would seem to argue otherwise).[6]

7.3 FORENSICS

Cyberforensics involves the science and technology of acquiring, preserving, retrieving, and presenting data that have been processed electronically or have been stored in electronic form.[7] Forensic identification is a necessary (though not sufficient) condition for prosecution or of retaliation against parties that take harmful actions. (An essential complement to forensic identification is the existence of a legal framework than allows actions to be taken against cyberattackers; both are foundational elements in a strategy of deterrence that complements defense in supporting cybersecurity.)

Forensics is necessary because, among other things, attackers often seek to cover their tracks. For example, mechanisms for providing provenance (see Chapter 5, "Category 2—Enabling Accountability") are unlikely to work perfectly, suggesting that after-the-fact identification of a perpetrator may be necessary (and may in fact be a somewhat easier task than undertaking real-time identification).

---

[5]For more perspective on passive versus active defense, see National Research Council, *Realizing the Potential of C4I: Fundamental Challenges*, National Academy Press, Washington, D.C., 1999, p. 143; available at http://newton.nap.edu/html/C4I/.

[6]See Michelle Delio, "Honeypots: Bait for the Cracker," *Wired News*, March 7, 2001; available at http://www.wired.com/news/culture/0,1284,42233,00.html.

[7]Michael G. Noblett, Mark M. Pollitt, and Lawrence A. Presley, "Recovering and Examining Computer Forensic Evidence," *Forensic Science Communications*, October 2000, Vol. 2, No. 4; available at http://www.fbi.gov/hq/lab/fsc/backissu/oct2000/computer.htm.

Much of the cyberforensics field has developed largely in response to a demand for service from the law enforcement community to help it deal with the reality that criminals are making more effective and more extensive use of information technology just like the rest of society. Indeed, greater societal use of information technology has expanded the scope of possible opportunities for criminals.

In 1984, the Federal Bureau of Investigation established its Computer Analysis and Response Team to address the needs of investigators and prosecutors to examine computer evidence in a structured and programmatic manner. What was then called computer forensics has evolved to include any evidence in digital form (e.g., audio, video, and data) from digital sources (e.g., computers, faxes, cellular telephones, and so on).[8] Digital forensics is now an integral part of legal investigations, with widespread recognition of its growing importance occurring during the 1990s.[9]

The support for forensic analysis provided by federal agencies such as the Department of Justice and the National Institute of Standards and Technology (NIST) is further recognition of its growing importance. For instance, NIST now maintains the National Software Reference Library, which consists of a collection of digital signatures of known, traceable software applications. By comparing any given file's signature to this collection, investigators can determine if that file is already known—if so, it need not be collected as evidence.[10] NIST's Computer Forensics Tool Testing Program seeks to ensure the reliability of computer forensic tools produce consistent, accurate, and objective results.[11]

Cyberforensics research has moved beyond the initial focus on law enforcement and digital evidence for use in criminal prosecution to include military and business operations. For instance, business needs include forensics for purposes of the investigation of employee wrongdoing and the protection of intellectual property. Practitioners in these areas have different primary objectives (although they may share prosecution as a secondary objective), which affect their analysis and decision-making processes and also affect their perspectives about requirements

[8]Carrie Morgan Whitcomb, "An Historical Perspective of Digital Evidence: A Forensic Scientist's View," *International Journal of Digital Evidence*, Spring 2002, Vol. 1, No. 1.

[9]George Mohay, "Technical Challenges and Directions for Digital Forensics," *Proceedings of the First International Workshop on Systematic Approaches to Digital Forensic Engineering (SADFE'05)*, IEEE Computer Society, 2005.

[10]A description of the National Software Reference Library is available at the program Web site: http://www.nsrl.nist.gov/.

[11]See the Computer Forensics Tool Testing Program Web site for details: http://www.cftt.nist.gov.

for digital forensic research.[12] Meeting statutory standards for evidence creates criteria different from those for producing results in the shortest possible time so that they can be acted on to maintain operations and availability of service, and to protect assets. Moreover, cyberforensics requirements will likely evolve over time, along with the increasingly pervasive use of IT.

One recent example of new forensic requirements is in corporate governance to meet regulatory requirements such as those imposed by the Sarbanes-Oxley Act of 2002.[13] Another factor affecting research requirements is the temporal environment required for forensic analysis—whereas law enforcement's primary focus is on after-the-fact forensics, military and business operations often need real-time or near-real-time forensics. Cyberforensics research must necessarily cover the broad scope of problems that arise from this wide range of requirements.

One working definition of digital forensic science, which reflects this broad scope, was offered by the 2001 Digital Forensic Research Workshop: "The use of scientifically derived and proven methods toward the preservation, collection, validation, identification, analysis, interpretation, documentation and presentation of digital evidence derived from digital sources for the purpose of facilitating or furthering the reconstruction of events found to be criminal, or helping to anticipate unauthorized actions shown to be disruptive to planned operations."[14]

Formalization of the field as the scientific discipline of digital forensic science is still in the early stages, with one of the first formal research papers in the field appearing in 1992.[15] A recent needs analysis survey that focused on law enforcement requirements notes that the national and international judiciary has begun to question the scientific validity of the ad hoc procedures and methodologies applied to digital forensics and is increasingly demanding proof of theoretical foundation and scientific

[12]Gary Palmer (ed.), "A Road Map for Digital Forensic Research: Report from the First Digital Forensic Research Workshop (DFRWS)," *DTR-T001-01 Final*, November 6, 2001, p. 3. Table 1, Suitability Guidelines for Digital Forensic Research, captures differences in these areas.

[13]George Mohay, "Technical Challenges and Directions for Digital Forensics," *Proceedings of the First International Workshop on Systematic Approaches to Digital Forensic Engineering (SADFE'05)*, IEEE Computer Society, 2005.

[14]Gary Palmer (ed.), "A Road Map for Digital Forensic Research: Report from the First Digital Forensic Research Workshop (DFRWS)," *DTR-T001-01 Final*, November 6, 2001, p. 16.

[15]Eugene H. Spafford and Stephen A. Weeber, "Software Forensics: Can We Track Code to its Authors?," *15th National Computer Security Conference*, pp. 641-650, October 1992. A more recent paper that outlines some of the scientific issues in the field is Eugene H. Spafford, "Some Challenges in Digital Forensics," in *Research Advances in Digital Forensics—II*, M. Olivier and S. Shenoi (eds.), Springer, 2006.

rigor.[16] This foundation is required in order to mandate and interpret the standards applied to digital evidence and to establish the qualifications of digital forensics professionals through a certification process.[17] Military and business forensics needs range across a broad spectrum, from traffic analysis tools and instrumentation of embedded systems to handling massive data volume and network monitoring, and they require a similar foundation to deal with increasing complexity and broader application.[18]

The embedding of computational resources in other devices, for instance, seems likely to increase the complexity of digital forensics and the extent of its usefulness. Two examples are the recovering and reconstructing of detail from Global Positioning System units built into cars to determine recent movements of a suspect auto, and the recovery of phone books, notes, and call information from cellular telephones. Accordingly, a number of research areas within this expansive view of digital forensics have been identified:[19]

- *Building a framework for digital forensic science.* This research area includes three elements: definitional work to provide a lexicon with clear terminology, a useful process model for the digital investigation process, and the development of an understanding of the academic and vocational expertise necessary, followed by curriculum development. For example, several models have been developed with increasing levels of abstraction and generalization of the digital investigation process.[20] Definitional work has progressed in the form of ontological models for defining layers of specialization across the areas employing forensic analysis, identifying the necessary elements of a certification process, and domain-specific educational requirements.[21]

[16]Marcus K. Rogers and Kate Seigfried, "The Future of Computer Forensics: A Needs Analysis Survey," *Computers and Security*, 23: 12-16, 2004.

[17]Matthew Meyers and Marc Rogers, "Computer Forensics: The Need for Standardization and Certification," *International Journal of Digital Evidence*, Vol. 3, No. 2, 2004.

[18]George Mohay, "Technical Challenges and Directions for Digital Forensics," *Proceedings of the First International Workshop on Systematic Approaches to Digital Forensic Engineering (SADFE'05)*, IEEE Computer Society, 2005.

[19]Gary Palmer (ed.), "A Road Map for Digital Forensic Research: Report from the First Digital Forensic Research Workshop (DFRWS)," *DTR-T001-01 Final*, November 6, 2001, pp. 33-39. The categories and specific research areas noted are drawn from this paper.

[20]Cf. Mark Reith, Clint Carr, and Gregg Gunsch, "An Examination of Digital Forensic Models," *International Journal of Digital Evidence*, Vol. 1, No. 3, Fall 2002; Brian Carrier and Eugene H. Spafford, "Getting Physical with the Digital Investigation Process," *International Journal of Digital Evidence*, Vol. 2, No. 2, 2003.

[21]Cf. Ashley Brinson, Abigail Robinson, and Marcus Rogers, "A Cyber Forensics Ontology: Creating a New Approach to Studying Cyber Forensics," *Digital Investigation*, 3S: 37-43, 2006.

- *Issues of integrity in digital evidence.* This research would address the need to ensure the integrity of digital evidence, which is inherently fragile and almost always suspect. Several important legal issues arise when seeking to submit digital evidence, affecting whether and what is admissible in court.[22] These include establishing the authenticity, lack of tampering in all of the systems through which the evidence has passed, reliability of computer-generated records (e.g., the possibility that the same digital signature could have resulted from different texts), and authorship. Legal distinctions also arise with differences between human-entered data and computer-generated data. Specific research areas include the development of antitampering methods, the creation of baseline standards of correctness in digital transform technology, and procedural standards for proper laboratory protocols. For example, several methods are in use today—checksum, one-way hash algorithms, and digital signatures—to help to demonstrate that the integrity of evidence has been preserved.[23] Each of these has advantages and drawbacks, ranging from the ease with which they can be applied and maintained to the level of confidence in them and what they prove (i.e., who, when, what). Some work has also been done to understand what requirements cyberforensic analysis tools must meet in order to establish and maintain evidentiary trust: usability by the human investigator (abstracting data to a level that can be analyzed), comprehensiveness (inculpatory and exculpatory evidence), accuracy, determinism, and verifiablility.[24]
- *Detection and recovery of hidden data.* This research area would focus on creating discovery mechanisms that detect and extract digital evidence in all its forms. Specific research areas include the categorization of places and mechanisms for hiding data, mechanisms for the detection of original material, and methods for extracting and recovering hidden data.[25] This line of research would search for ways to identify the who, what, when, where, and how for digital evidence. Merely obtaining data poses a wide variety of technical challenges. For example, the diversity of devices on which

[22]Orin S. Kerr, "Computer Records and the Federal Rules of Evidence," *United States USA Bulletin*, Vol. 49, No. 2, U.S. Department of Justice, March 2001.

[23]Chet Hosmer, "Proving the Integrity of Digital Evidence with Time," *International Journal of Digital Evidence*, Vol. 1, No. 1, 2002.

[24]Brian Carrier, "Defining Digital Forensic Examination and Analysis Tools Using Abstraction Layers," *International Journal of Digital Evidence*, Vol. 1, No. 4, 2003.

[25]One description of the challenges involved in this area can be found in Paul A. Henry, "Anti-Forensics," April 2006; available at http://layerone.info/2006/presentations/Anti-Forensics-LayerOne-Paul_Henry.pdf.

potentially relevant information may be stored means that new protocols and tools must be developed for each device. Relevant information may be buried amidst large volumes of other irrelevant information and may be distributed across many different devices or locations. Information may not even be stored on persistent media (for example, it might be stored in dynamic random access memory [DRAM] and disappear when the system on which it is stored is powered down). The recovery of encrypted data has been a particular concern of both practitioners and researchers.[26] In addition, systems can be designed to support forensic investigation and thereby increase the quantity and quality of forensic information available.[27] Automating the collection process and performing targeted searches using techniques such as data mining could also improve the detection and recovery of useful data.[28] These are aspects of what has been termed "forensic readiness," the extent to which activities and data are recorded in a manner sufficient for forensic purposes.[29] Another aspect of the detection and recovery of data addresses the science and technology of acquiring, preserving, retrieving, and presenting data that have been processed electronically or have been stored in electronic form but in a nonevidentiary context. Outside of this context, the evidentiary requirements of forensic investigation are relaxed. Thus, for example, statistical likelihood, indirect evidence, and hearsay fall within the scope of nonevidentiary forensics.

- *Digital forensic science in networked environments (network forensics).* This research area focuses on the need to expand digital forensics beyond its roots in computer forensics, which focused heavily on stand-alone, media-intensive sources. Specific research areas include understanding the similarities and relationships between computer and network forensics, methods for applying digital forensic analysis in real time, and the development of trusted collection processes and criteria for trusted agents outside of law

---

[26]Eoghan Casey, "Practical Approaches to Recovering Encrypted Digital Evidence," *International Journal of Digital Evidence*, Vol. 1, No. 3, 2002.

[27]Florian Buchholz and Eugene Spafford, "On the Role of File System Metadata in Digital Forensics," *Digital Investigation*, 1(4): 297-308, December 2004.

[28]Brian D. Carrier and Eugene H. Spafford, "Automated Digital Evidence Target Definitions Using Outlier Analysis and Existing Evidence," 2005 Digital Forensic Research Workshop (DFRWS), New Orleans, La., August 17-19, 2005.

[29]George Mohay, "Technical Challenges and Directions for Digital Forensics," *Proceedings of the First International Workshop on Systematic Approaches to Digital Forensic Engineering (SADFE'05)*, IEEE Computer Society, 2005; Eugene H. Spafford, "Some Challenges in Digital Forensics," in *Research Advances in Digital Forensic—II*, M. Olivier and S. Shenoi (eds.), Springer, 2006.

enforcement (e.g., intelligence, network operators) to collect forensic evidence. For example, network geolocation technology would provide a means for determining the physical location of a logical network address. Tools for monitoring and mapping network traffic would allow real-time network management.[30] Related is traffic analysis, which calls for understanding the source and nature of certain kinds of attack and requires techniques, equipment, and legal tools to characterize the huge traffic flows on public and private networks that accompany those kinds of attack. Extracting information about interconnections (e.g., traffic volume, communicating pairs, and network topology as functions of time) can help hunt down enemies and understand interrelationships. Finally, research is needed on the formalization of policies to support network forensics, including systematic application and data retention, logging of system and network information, attack response planning, and network forensic training.[31]

While this and other research marks a clear beginning toward the goal of establishing a discipline of digital forensic science, further progress is possible in all of the areas. Much of the required research is technical in nature, and in many cases the techniques and problems are similar to other technical research areas (e.g., software debugging, data provenance, intrusion-detection, and malware analysis), although such synergies remain largely unexplored. However, there are also legal, economic, and policy research issues. For instance, there are likely economic constraints owing to the lack of incentives for both technology vendors and users related to improving forensic readiness.[32]

The international aspects of digital forensic investigation in a world of global high-speed networks mean that there are some significant legal issues related to the quality, provenance, analysis, and maintenance of data in different legal jurisdictions that have yet to be fully understood and addressed.

---

[30]See, for instance, "Network Geo-location Technology" and "ATM Mapping and Monitoring Tool" at the National Security Agency's Domestic Technology Transfer Program Web site: http://www.nas.gov/techtrans/index.cfm.

[31]Cf. Srinivas Mukkamala and Andrew H. Sung, "Identifying Significant Features for Network Forensic Analysis Using Artificial Intelligent Techniques," *International Journal of Digital Evidence*, Vol. 1, No. 4, 2003; Alec Yasinsac and Yanet Manzano, "Policies to Enhance Computer and Network Forensics," presentation at the Workshop on Information Assurance and Security, United States Military Academy, West Point, N.Y., June 2001.

[32]Tyler Moore, "The Economics of Digital Forensics," presented at the Fifth Annual Workshop on the Economics and Information Security, Cambridge, England, June 26-28, 2006.

One example of a significant policy issue is that of addressing the tension between forensics and privacy. Concerns about privacy have motivated the development of counter-forensic tools. Some initial work has been done to evaluate the effectiveness of existing commercial counter-forensic tools and the operational implications for digital forensic analysis.[33] Yet, policy questions such as understanding and managing the boundary between the legitimate collection and use of digital forensic evidence and the illegitimate monitoring of behavior and activities have barely been asked, let alone answered. Indeed, the question of what is and is not legitimate has still to be answered.[34]

[33]Matthew Geiger, "Evaluating Commercial Counter-Forensic Tools," 2005 Digital Forensic Workshop, New Orleans, La., August 17-19, 2005.

[34]Eugene H. Spafford, "Some Challenges in Digital Forensics," *Research Advances in Digital Forensics—II*, M. Olivier and S. Shenoi (eds.), Springer, 2006.

8

Category 5—Illustrative Crosscutting Problem-Focused Research Areas

While Chapters 4, 5, 6, and 7 address specific focus areas, this chapter presents a number of problems whose solutions will involve research described in all of those chapters.

8.1 SECURITY FOR LEGACY SYSTEMS

Organizations make large investments in making systems work properly for their business needs. If system deployment is complex or widespread, many organizations are highly reluctant to move to systems based on newer or more current technologies because of the (often quite considerable) work that would inevitably be required to get the new systems to work as well as the older systems worked. However, because legacy systems—by definition—embody design and architectural decisions made before the emergence of the current threat environment, they pose special challenges for security. That is, when new and unanticipated threats emerge, legacy systems must be retrofitted to improve security—and this is true even when careful design and attention to security have reduced the number of potential security vulnerabilities in the original legacy system.

In this context, the challenge is to add security without making existing software products, information assets, and hardware devices any more obsolete than is necessary. Research to support this goal has three components:

1. Research is needed to address the relatively immediate security needs of legacy systems, as these systems will be with us for a long time to come.
2. It is worthwhile to expend some significant effort to create new systems and networks that are explicitly designed to be secure, at least for critical systems whose compromise would have high consequences. Research on clean-slate designs for secure and attack-resilient architectures will show what can be achieved when these efforts are relieved of the need to fit into an insecure existing framework, and it may be that new design approaches will make it possible to achieve performance, cost, and security goals simultaneously.
3. Research effort should be explicitly focused on easing the transition path for users of today's information technology applications to migrate to secure-by-design systems in the future—a path that is likely to take years or decades to accomplish even after such "from-the-start secure" systems are designed and initially deployed. (Box 8.1 presents further discussion of this point.)

One key issue in the security of legacy systems is patch management. Tinkering with existing legacy systems—for whatever reason—can result in severe operational problems that take a great deal of time and effort to resolve, but fixing security problems almost always requires tinkering. Therefore, operational managers are often faced with choosing between the risk of installing a fix to some vulnerability (that is, the installation of the patch may disrupt operations or even introduce a new vulnerability) and the risk of not installing it (that is, attackers might be able to exploit the vulnerability). Further, the installation of a patch generally necessitates a set of new tests to ensure both that the vulnerability has been repaired and that critical operational functionality has not been lost. If it has been lost, a new cycle of patch-and-test is needed. These cycles are both costly and inherently time-consuming, and consequently many systems managers avoid them if at all possible. Such dilemmas are exacerbated by the fact that it is often the very release of a fix that prompts an attack.[1]

One area of research thus suggested is the development of a methodology that will help operational managers decide how to resolve this dilemma.

---

[1]This paradoxical situation results from the fact that the release of a fix is publicized so that it can be disseminated as widely as possible. The publicity about the fix can alert would-be attackers to the existence of the vulnerability in the first place, and the fix itself can usually be "disassembled" in order to reveal the nature of the original vulnerability. Because some installations will not install the fix, would-be attackers gain opportunities that would not otherwise become available.

BOX 8.1
Issues in System Migration

One important dimension of security for legacy systems involves strategies for migrating to systems that are more inherently secure. In this context, it is often the case that a migration strategy needs only to preserve existing assets. For example, a user may have a large investment in data files of a given format that are required for a given version of a program. A new version that is more inherently secure may well require files of a different format. One strategy to preserve assets may be to require the new version to open all files in the old format. A different strategy may call for a conversion utility to convert old files to the new format.

The first strategy might be deemed a requirement for backward compatibility—that is, the new system should operate as the old one did in a manner that is as transparent as possible to the user. But all too often, the requirement for full backward compatibility complicates the security problem—backward compatibility may, explicitly or implicitly, call for building in the same security vulnerabilities in an attempt to preserve the same functional behavior. (For example, a large fraction of the Windows XP system code base is included for backward compatibility with Windows 98 and Windows 2000—a fact that is well recognized as being responsible for many vulnerabilities in XP.)

In the second approach, the migration to a more secure system is made easier by the weaker requirement that only the data assets of the earlier generation be preserved (or made usable) for the new system. The duplication of all functional behavior is explicitly *not* a requirement for this approach, although it remains a significant intellectual challenge to determine what functional behavior must and must not carry over to the new system.

Another fact about system migration is that with distributed systems in place, it is very difficult, from both a cost and a deployment standpoint, to replace all the legacy equipment at once. This means that for practical purposes, an organization may well be operating with a heterogeneous information technology environment—which means that the parts that have not been replaced are likely still vulnerable, and their interconnection to the parts that have been replaced may make even the new components vulnerable. The result of this tension is often that no meaningful action for security improvement takes place.

A second area of research relevant to the security of legacy systems is that of program understanding. Program-understanding tools are essential for addressing security issues that arise in legacy systems for which documentation is poor and original expertise is scarce. The reason is that legacy systems continue to play essential operational roles long after their technological foundations are obsolete and after the departure of the individuals who best understand the systems. But as new security issues arise in these legacy systems, a detailed understanding of their internal operation and of how actual system behavior differs from intended behavior is necessary in order to address these issues. Tools that help new analysts understand flows of control and data can facilitate such understanding and the "reverse-engineering" of legacy systems.

8.2 THE ROLE OF SECRECY IN CYBERDEFENSE

Should the inner operations of security mechanisms be kept secret or not? It is widely assumed in much of the unclassified research community—especially the community associated with open-source software—that the correct answer to this question is "No." This answer is based on the idea that secrecy prevents the security community from examining the mechanism in question and in so doing eliminates the opportunity for a rigorous peer review (e.g., finding flaws in results, verifying results independently, and providing [open] building blocks that others can build on [thereby fostering research progress]).[2] There is a further belief in this community that a weak system can usually be compromised without knowledge of what is purportedly secret.[3]

In the classified cybersecurity community, the opposite view is much more prominent. In this view, secrecy of mechanism throws up an additional barrier that an adversary must penetrate or circumvent in order to mount a successful attack, but in no event is secrecy the only or even the primary barrier that should be established. Vendors, even of products for civilian use, also have an interest in keeping implementations secret (under existing trade secret law).

Both points of view have merit under some circumstances, and a number of researchers have sought to reconcile them. For example, Spafford argued in 1996 that unless an exploit is actually being used in a widespread manner, it is better not to publish details of a flaw, because to do so would result in a much larger risk of exposure.[4] This is true even if a fix is available, since the mere availability of a fix does not guarantee—nor even nearly guarantee—that the fix will be installed. Some will not hear of the fix; some will not be able to install it because of certification requirements; some will not have the expertise to install it; some will fear the subsequent breakage of some essential element of system functionality. More recently, Swire has argued that secrecy is most useful to the defense on the first

[2]Spafford goes so far as to argue that open-source development is an issue that is orthogonal to security. See http://homes.cerias.purdue.edu/~spaf/openvsclosed.html.

[3]A related argument applies to data and history. Whether data and development history are protected by national security classifications or trade secrets, their unavailability to the community at large prevents the community from using that data and history to understand why systems fail or the origins of a particular kind of bug or flaw.

[4]Eugene Spafford, "Cost Benefit Analyses and Best Practices," *Practical Unix and Internet Security*, Simson Garfinkel and Eugene Spafford (eds.), O'Reilly Press, Cambridge, Mass., 2003.

occasion of an attack on a computer system but that it is far less effective if an adversary can probe the defenses repeatedly and learn from those probes.[5] The National Research Council itself commented on this tension in 1998 (Box 8.2). Additional research should be done to shed more light on appropriate uses of secrecy in cybersecurity.

Presuming that there are *some* circumstances in which secrecy is an asset to cyberdefense, an additional research question arises: To what extent is it possible to keep any mechanism secret when it is widely deployed? What technological approaches can be used to increase the likelihood that a widely deployed mechanism can be kept secret?

8.3 INSIDER THREATS

The majority of cybersecurity research efforts are focused on making it more difficult for "outside" adversaries to compromise information systems. But, as the cases of Robert Hanssen and Aldrich Ames suggest, insiders can pose a considerable security risk as well. Indeed, much of the past 10 to 15 years of U.S. counterintelligence history suggests that the threat to national security emanating from the trusted insider is at least as serious as the threat from the outsider.[6] Insiders can be in a position to do more harm to services and resources to which they have authorized access than can outsiders lacking such access; these concerns are particularly important in contexts in which safe operation depends on good decisions being made by systems operators. Insiders can also leverage their authorized access to obtain information to extend their access.

The compromised insider presents a more difficult security challenge than that posed by hostile outsiders. The first rule about security is to keep hostile parties away, and the insider, by definition, has bypassed many of the barriers erected to keep him or her away. Moreover, a compromised insider may work with outsiders (e.g., passing along information that identifies weak points in an organization's cybersecurity posture).

Compromised insiders fall into two categories—knowing and unknowing. Knowingly compromised insiders—those that know they are

---

[5]Peter Swire, "A Model for When Disclosure Helps Security: What Is Different About Computer and Network Security?," *Journal on Telecommunications and High Technology Law*, Vol. 2, 2004.

[6]For this report, the term "insider" is used to denote an individual in an authorized position whose actions can materially affect the operation of the information technology systems and networks associated with critical infrastructure in a negative way. Since not all "insiders" pose a threat, the terms "inappropriately trusted insider" or "compromised insider" are used to mean an insider with the willingness and motivation to act improperly with respect to critical infrastructure. The term "outsider" refers to an individual who is not in the position of an "insider."

BOX 8.2
Secrecy of Design

Secrecy of design is often deprecated with the phrase "security through obscurity," and one often hears arguments that security-critical systems or elements should be developed in an open environment that encourages peer review by the general community. Evidence is readily available about systems that were developed in secret only to be reverse-engineered and to have their details published on the Internet and their flaws pointed out for all to see. But open-source software has often contained security flaws that have remained for years as well.[1]

The argument for open development rests on certain assumptions, including these: the open community will have individuals with the necessary tools and expertise, they will devote adequate effort to locate vulnerabilities, they will come forth with vulnerabilities that they find, and vulnerabilities, once discovered, can be closed—even after the system is deployed.

There are environments, such as military and diplomatic settings, in which these assumptions do not necessarily hold. Groups interested in finding vulnerabilities here will mount long-term and well-funded analysis efforts—efforts that are likely to dwarf those that might be launched by individuals or organizations in the open community. Further, these well-funded groups will take great care to ensure that any vulnerabilities they discover are kept secret, so that they may be exploited (in secret) for as long as possible.

Special problems arise when partial public knowledge about the nature of the security mechanisms is necessary, such as when a military security module is designed for integration into commercial off-the-shelf equipment. Residual vulnerabilities are inevitable, and the discovery and publication of even one such vulnerability may, in certain circumstances, render the system defenseless. It is, in general, not sufficient to protect only the exact nature of a vulnerability. The precursor information from which the vulnerability could be readily discovered must also be protected, and that requires an exactness of judgment not often found in group endeavors. When public knowledge of aspects of a military system is required, the

acting on behalf of an adversary—are most likely associated with a high-end threat, such as a hostile major nation-state, and their motivations also vary widely and include the desire for recognition for hacking skills, ideological convictions, and monetary incentives. Knowingly compromised insiders may become compromised because of bribery, blackmail, ideological or psychological predisposition, or successful infiltration, among other reasons. By contrast, unknowingly compromised insiders are those that are the victims of manipulation and social engineering. In essence, unknowingly compromised insiders are tricked into using their special knowledge and position to assist an adversary.

Regarding the knowingly compromised insider, a substantial body of experience suggests that it ranges from very difficult to impossible to identify with reasonable reliability and precision individuals who will

most prudent course is to conduct the entire development process under cover of secrecy. Only after the entire assurance and evaluation process has been completed—and the known residual vulnerabilities identified—should a decision be made about what portions of the system description are safe to release.

Any imposition of secrecy, about either part or all of the design, carries two risks: that a residual vulnerability could have been discovered by a friendly peer reviewer in time to be fixed, and that the secret parts of the system will be reverse-engineered and made public, leading to the further discovery, publication, and exploitation of vulnerabilities. The first risk has historically been mitigated by devoting substantial resources to analysis and assurance. (Evaluation efforts that exceed the design effort by an order of magnitude or more are not unheard of in certain environments.) The second risk is addressed with a combination of technology aimed at defeating reverse-engineering and strict procedural controls on the storage, transport, and use of the devices in question. These controls are difficult to impose in a military environment and effectively impossible in a commercial or consumer one.

Finally, there is sometimes a tension between security and exploitation that arises in government. Intelligence agencies have a stake in concealing vulnerabilities that they discover in systems that an adversary uses, because disclosure of such a vulnerability may lead the adversary to fix it and thus render it useless for intelligence-gathering purposes. If the vulnerability also affects "friendly" systems, a conflict arises about whether the benefits of exploitation do or do not outweigh the benefits of disclosure.

---

[1]See for example, Steve Lodin, Bryn Dole, and Eugene H. Spafford, "Misplaced Trust: Kerberos 4 Random Session Keys," *Proceedings of Internet Society Symposium on Network and Distributed System Security*, pp. 60-70, February 1997.

SOURCE: Adapted largely from National Research Council, *Trust in Cyberspace*, National Academy Press, Washington, D.C., 1998.

actually take hostile actions on the basis of their profiles or personal histories. (For example, it is often hard to distinguish merely quirky employees from potentially dangerous individuals, and there is considerable anecdotal evidence that some system administrators have connections to the criminal hacker underground.) Thus, the identification of compromised insiders must rely on analyses of past and present behavior.[7] (That is, it may be possible to infer intent and future behavior from usage signatures,

---

[7]More precisely, the identification of a compromised insider depends first on identifying behavior or actions that are anomalous or improper, and then on associating an individual with that behavior or those actions. An intrusion-detection system typically flags anomalous behavior, and association of that behavior with an individual depends on higher-level systems issues, such as policies, radio-frequency indentification proximity sensors to autolock machines, authenticated systems logs, and so on.

although the consequences of false positives here may be quite high.) In other words, it is highly unlikely that general means for detecting potential spies and saboteurs will be developed; therefore, barriers to particular *acts* are necessary instead.

The knowledge base about how to defend against compromised insiders is not extensive, at least by comparison with the literature on defending against "outsiders." Still, there is general agreement that a multifaceted defensive strategy is more likely to succeed than is an approach based on any one element. Some of the relevant elements include the following:

- *Technology.* Authentication and access control are two well-known technologies that can help to prevent an insider from doing damage. Strong authentication and access controls can be used together to ensure that only authorized individuals gain access to a system or a network and that these authorized individuals have only the set of access privileges to which they are entitled and no more. As noted in Section 6.5, tools to manage and implement access-control policies are an important area of relevant research; with such tools available to and used by systems administrators, the damage that can be caused by someone untrustworthy and unaccountable can be limited, even if he or she has improper access to certain system components.

  Forensic measures (Section 7.3) and MAD systems (Section 5.2) can also play an important role in deterring the hostile activity of a compromised insider. For example, audit trails can monitor and record access to online files containing sensitive information or execution of certain system functions, and contemporaneous analysis may help to detect hostile activity as it is happening. However, audit trails must be kept for all of the users of a system, and the volume of data generally preclude comprehensive analysis on a routine basis. Thus, automated audit trail analyzers could help to identify suspicious patterns of behavior that may indicate the presence of a compromised insider. In addition, it may be more or less important to audit the records of an individual, depending on the criticality of the resources available to that person; automated tools to decide on appropriate audit targets would be helpful to develop. Note also that maintaining extensive logs may in itself pose a security risk, as they may be used to help re-create otherwise confidential or classified material that is in otherwise restricted data files. For instance, keystroke logs may contain passwords or formulae, and logs of references consulted may be used to reverse-engineer a secret process. Thus, logs may need to be protected to a level as high as (or higher than) anything else on the system.

- *Organizations.* In an environment in which most employees are indeed trustworthy, what policies and practices can actually be implemented that will help to cope effectively with the insider threat? Known organizational principles to deal with a lack of trust include separation of duties and mandatory job rotation and vacations, and are often used in the financial industry. Such principles often generate specific technical security requirements that are often not considered explicitly in technical discussions of security. (For example, separation of duties requires that one person not play two roles—a fact that requires that an organization's security architecture to enforce a single identity for an individual rather than multiple ones.) Research is needed in how to define, describe, manage, and manipulate security policies. Systems can be abused through both bad policy and bad enforcement. Tools are needed to make setting and enforcing policy easier. For example, a particularly useful area of investigation would be to gain a more complete understanding of what sophisticated and successful systems administrators do to protect their systems. Encapsulating that knowledge and codifying it somehow would provide insight into what the best kinds of defense are.
- *Management.* Recent movements toward more-open architectures along with more collaboration and teamwork within and across institutions present management challenges. For example, certain information may be intended for distribution on a need-to-know basis, but given a shift toward more-collaborative exercises, determining who needs to know what and constraining the sharing of information to that end is difficult. In both business and government, there has been a significant movement toward embracing cooperation across organizations and sectors, but this, of course, introduces security problems.
- *Legal and ethical issues.* Many privacy and workplace surveillance issues need to be addressed when an organization determines how to implement tools to decrease the possibility of insider malfeasance. For example, many anomaly-detection systems require the collection of large amounts of data about the activities of individuals in order to establish a baseline from which deviations might detect anomalous behavior.

  Both the fact of such collection and how those data are handled have serious privacy implications, from both a legal and an ethical standpoint. One of the most important of these issues is that it is all too easy for an organization to be both very security-aware and employee-unfriendly at the same time. That is, even if draconian security measures are legal (and they may be of questionable legality), the result may be an environment in which employees feel that they are not trusted, with a concomitant lowering of morale and productivity and perhaps higher turnover. For example, an environment in which employees police one another for violations of security practice may breed distrust and unease among colleagues. Conversely, an environment that provides trusted mechanisms for dispute resolution and justice can promote a greater sense of camaraderie. The interplay between employment laws and the need for system security is also a concern. For example, the termination of suspected individuals may not occur immediately, and thus such people may maintain access while the necessary paperwork goes through channels.

Research is also needed to understand the circumstances under which an insider threat is (or is not) a concern serious enough to warrant substantial attention. Systems are often designed embedding unrealistic assumptions about insiders. For instance, it is common in networked enterprises to assume that one cannot and should not worry about insider attacks, meaning that nothing is done about insiders who might abuse the network. This approach leaves major security vulnerabilities in new networking paradigms in which individual user devices participate in the routing protocol. But in more traditional networking paradigms, individual user devices do not participate in the routing protocol, and thus this particular security vulnerability is of less concern.

As for the unknowingly compromised insider, effective defenses against trickery are very difficult to deploy.[8] Adversaries who engage in such trickery are experts at exploiting the willingness of people to be helpful—a process often known as "social engineering." These adversaries use people to provide inside information, and they use people by taking advantage of situations that cause breakdowns in normal procedures. In short, they help human error to occur.

For example, badges are often required for entry into a secure facility, and passwords are required to access the computer network. However, entry and access can often be obtained in the following manner: Walk up to the door carrying an armload of computers, parts, and dangling cords. Ask someone to hold the door open, and thank them. Carry the junk over to an empty cubicle, look for the password and log-in name that will be on

[8]This discussion of social engineering is drawn largely from National Research Council, *Information Technology for Counterterrorism: Immediate Actions and Future Possibilities*, The National Academies Press, Washington, D.C., 2003.

a Post-it note somewhere, and log in. If you cannot log in, ask someone for help. As one guide for hackers puts it, just shout, "Does anyone remember the password for this terminal? . . . you would be surprised how many people will tell you."[9]

The reason that social engineering succeeds is that, in general, people (e.g., employees of an organization) want to be helpful. It is important to counter social engineering if cybersecurity is to be achieved, but whatever that entails, the solution must not be based on extinguishing the tendencies of people to be helpful. The reason is that helpful people play a key role in getting any work done at all—and thus the research challenge is to develop effective techniques for countering social engineering that do not require wholesale attacks on tendencies to be helpful.

Some of the approaches described above for dealing with the knowingly compromised insider are relevant. For example, compartmentalization or a two-person rule might be useful in combating social engineering. But as a general principle, approaches based on deterrence will not work—simply because deterrence presumes that the party being deterred knows that he or she is taking an action that may result in a penalty, and most people who are trying to be helpful don't expect to be punished for doing so.

8.4 SECURITY IN NONTRADITIONAL COMPUTING ENVIRONMENTS AND IN THE CONTEXT OF USE

As noted in Section 3.4.1.2, cybersecurity research that is situated in the context of use has a greater likelihood of being adopted to solve security problems that occur in that context. This section provides several illustrative examples.

8.4.1 Health Information Technology

Health-related information spans a broad range and includes the medical records of individual patients, laboratory tests, the published medical literature, treatment protocols, and drug interactions, as well as financial and billing records and other administrative information. The deficiencies relate to not having the relevant information (even though it may be available somewhere) at the right time and in the right place to support good decision making. The intensive use of information technology (IT) to acquire, manage, analyze, and disseminate health care information holds great potential for reducing or eliminating these information

[9]See "The Complete Social Engineering FAQ"; available at http://morehouse.org/hin/blccrwl/hack/soceng.txt.

deficiencies, and a variety of reports clearly document the benefits of electronic medical records and computer-based clinical decision-support tools for health care workers.

At the same time, it is also broadly understood that ensuring the privacy and security of personal health-related information is a precondition for the widespread acceptance of health information technologies into clinical practice. Security requirements for such systems span a very large range, including both record-keeping systems and embedded systems that improve or enable the performance of many medical devices and procedures.

Security issues of special importance to health IT systems include the following:

- *Conditional confidentiality.* In general, only pre-authorized individuals should have access to personal health information. However, in emergency situations in which the patient is unable to give explicit consent, medical personnel without previous authorization may need access.
- *Secure diagnostic and treatment systems.* Medical technology (e.g., radiation devices for treating cancer, scanners, pacemakers) are increasingly controlled by computer. Software for these systems must be especially resistant to hostile compromise if their safety is to be ensured.
- *Usability.* Health care providers are particularly sensitive to workplace demands that reduce the amount of time they can spend in actual patient care, and a matter of a few seconds of additional unproductive time per patient can mean the difference between an acceptable system and an unacceptable one. Security functionality, in particular, is notorious for wasting users' time—and thus special attention to user needs in a health care environment is warranted.
- *Record integrity.* Users and patients must be confident that the contents of a medical record are not altered undetectably and that data in transmission are not changed or corrupted.
- *Auditability.* This function ensures that all medical interventions and diagnoses are recorded and associated with a responsible individual, and also that all parties viewing a record can subsequently be audited for having an appropriate need to know. Nonrepudiation is an essential part of auditability for ensuring that a responsible individual cannot plausibly deny responsibility for a decision.

In general, these security and privacy functions do not require technical advances beyond what is known today. Nevertheless, the integration of known security and privacy techniques with the particulars of a very demanding health care environment is an exemplar of the importance of situated research and development.

8.4.2 The Electric Power Grid

The electric power grid is a national infrastructure that links generating stations through transmission lines and distribution lines to the customer loads. High-voltage transmission lines connected in a mesh network bring the power from generating stations to lower-voltage distribution lines that connect to customer loads in a radial topology. The ownership of these elements (generation, transmission, and distribution facilities) in a geographical area may not be shared—in many states, generation has been deregulated, meaning that generators compete with each other in power markets to sell their power.

The hundreds of organizations that own portions of the power grid, and the even more entities (vendors, contractors, market players, and so on) that interact with it, use very large numbers of computers. Some parts of the grid's cyber-infrastructure operate, control, or otherwise directly or indirectly modify the workings of the grid.

The monitoring and control of the power grid are done by computerized control centers. The grid is divided into "control areas"; a control center monitors and controls that portion of the grid using a Supervisory Control and Data Acquisition (SCADA) system. Quite often, the real-time data gathered by the SCADA systems can be analyzed to predict the effects of contingencies (e.g., short circuits that may cause outages of lines or generators, thus overloading other lines or causing other limit violations) and possible remedial actions to guard against such contingencies. The computer systems used to conduct such analysis are known as Energy Management Systems (EMS), and these control centers are often called SCADA-EMS (or simply EMS).

The SCADA systems are connected by communications channels (usually microwave today) to all the substations and generating stations in the control area, and the real-time data are gathered by the SCADA system polling the remote terminal units (RTUs) at the substations. That SCADA system may have communications with other SCADA systems in neighboring control areas or with other control centers in the same area.

In recent years, intelligent electronic devices (IEDs) have proliferated in the substations and generating stations. These microprocessor-based devices perform the usual local functions of control, protection, and switching, but they can also perform other enhanced functions, including the gathering and storage of data at much faster rates. These IEDs are usually accessible remotely, and many utilities use Internet connectivity to conduct normal engineering functions on such substation equipment.

Given the increasing demand for electric power, it is inevitable that the electric power industry will continue to seek ever-higher efficiencies in the existing grid, so as to minimize the expense of constructing new grid elements. Thus, interconnections within the various control centers of the grid must be taken as a given, with all of the vulnerabilities that such extensive interconnections imply.

There is broad agreement that the communications infrastructure that connects the substations to the control area SCADA systems, developed in the 1960s and 1970s, is too slow for today's purposes.[10] Faster communications will allow more wide-area (rather than local) and distributed (rather than central) control, which in turn may require distributed bases of real-time data that are gathered and stored using publisher-subscriber methods and middleware that monitors the quality of service (QoS).

An approach based on deploying a faster but isolated cyber-infrastructure for the power grid is conceptually the simplest. But in addition to its high cost, this approach, at least when taken to its logical extremes, also results in a loss of flexibility and convenience from the standpoint of many engineering and market functions, especially regarding intercommunications, interoperability, and rapid response. An alternative is to develop design guidelines for the evolving cyber-infrastructure that will allow the flexibility of interconnectivity but with controlled and managed risks of penetration. While this approach preserves the lower expenses associated with "piggybacking" on existing infrastructure, it has the major drawback that commercially available computer and communications infrastructures are neither secure enough nor robust enough to support such use.

The new cyber-infrastructure must be able to withstand various contingencies such as malicious threats, human errors, and environmental hazards. (Note that malicious threats may come from disgruntled employees and former employees who have detailed insider knowledge or from enemy nations or terrorists with access to expert knowledge.) Although the power grid must be able to withstand the threat of physical attack on generators and transmission lines, another security concern arises if an adversary can attack the power grid remotely.

In addition, the surprisingly large number of very large scale outages in the United States in the past 40 years raises the question of whether the infrastructure is reliable enough even in the absence of malicious misuse. Indeed, many of those outages could have been triggered maliciously or intentionally, exploiting exactly the same vulnerabilities that were the

[10] United States Department of Energy, Office of Electric Transmission and Distribution, *National Electric Delivery Technologies Roadmap*, January 2004; available at http://www.electricdistribution.ctc.com/pdfs/tech_roadmap.pdf.

cause of the accidental outages. (Some of these outages occurred even though operators had previously insisted that various improvements that had been made in the grid technology would prevent such occurrences in the future.)

The main technical and administrative challenge for the future is not merely to secure the cyber-infrastructure of the grid today, but to guide the evolution of the cyber-infrastructure so that the grid is not vulnerable to cyberattacks and the propagating of accidental effects. As the main purpose of the cyber-infrastructure is to operate the grid reliably, securely, and economically, the advances in communications, computation, and control technologies will continue to push the cyber-infrastructure in directions that accommodate this improved control. A major task is then to determine design factors that meet the cybersecurity and reliability objectives in ways that are consistent with the control and economic objectives of the grid. The entirety of an interconnected grid must be considered as a single system, and developed and analyzed accordingly. This is difficult because of the extent to which the providers are independent and disjoint private entities. However, neither total deregulation nor complete government regulation is compatible with the needs stated above.

Some of the important cybersecurity issues for the grid include the following:

- *Developing lightweight cybersecurity mechanisms.* Computers used for operational control generally run at high duty cycle because of premiums on efficiency and on controlling many systems, and thus there is often little capacity for undertaking activities such as anomaly detection, virus updates, or penetration testing. Although advances in hardware capability could, in principle, mitigate this problem, historically utility operators have adopted a relatively slow refresh rate for technology. Lightweight mechanisms and testing practices that consume minimal system resources while being used on an operational system would be more likely to be used in practice.
- *Developing better forensics for SCADA systems and programmable logic controllers.* For example, logs for these systems generally record physical parameters but not the inbound commands or communications or the originator of those commands. Anomaly detection is also uncommon in these systems, although the highly structured and stylized nature of commands to these systems should make it easier to detect anomalies.
- *Implementing cybersecurity measures that can operate in an interrupt-heavy real-time environment.* Because programmable logic controllers operate multiple devices, the timing of interruptions from

various devices can make program flow highly unpredictable and can thus complicate any security analysis that may be performed.

In general, cybersecurity issues for the electric power grid include (but are not limited to) the possibility of electronically compromising substations operated remotely, tricking operators of control centers into doing harmful things with false or delayed data, managing the high cost of falsely identifying an authorized party as an unauthorized one, and modeling the electric grid in order to understand its vulnerabilities.

8.4.3 Web Services

Web services provide application components and attendant IT resources with defined interfaces that interact over the Web. Any given Web service is also frequently used by multiple organizations.

The commercial objectives are rapid deployment of business offerings, shorter process cycles, synergy between businesses, and customer benefits through integration. One example of Web services is the programmatic interfaces made available through the World Wide Web (WWW) that serve the function of application-to-application communication. These Web services provide a standard means of interoperating between different software applications, running on a variety of platforms and/or frameworks.

WWW services are characterized by their interoperability and extensibility, as well as by their XML-based machine-processable descriptions. A second example of Web services is the Universal Description, Discovery and Integration (UDDI) specification, which defines a registry service for other Web services; this registry service manages information about service providers, service implementations, and service metadata. A third Web service is online storage and distributed data repositories that applications developers can exploit. Web services in general can be chained together in a loosely coupled way to create complex and sophisticated value-added services.

Many of the security issues that arise in Web-based computing are similar to those for local applications, but Web services have a number of additional security concerns that involve networking in an open environment. For example, Web services are loosely coupled in a more or less ad hoc manner. Thus, a dynamically established security model is necessary—that is, the security model is necessarily contextual—and thus requires an integration of intent over all of the components. How should such models be created? What does trust mean in such an environment? What security functionality is required of each component? How is such functionality asserted and substantiated by the application? How are authentication information and storage access rights passed from service to service in a dynamically assembled application? What is the functionality needed in tools for the analysis and specification of security policies for distributed storage?

8.4.4 Pervasive and Embedded Systems

Pervasive computing devices include sensor networks, ad hoc networks (e.g., car-to-car), and human-embedded processors, as well as the devices described in Section 2.1 (Interconnected Information Technology Everywhere, All the Time). Because pervasive computing systems will have programmable hardware processors and will be interconnected, they are subject to all the software and network-based security vulnerabilities that can affect other computing devices (e.g., dedicated computing systems). Furthermore, it is likely that linking together pervasive computing devices will result in the accessibility of significant amounts of potentially sensitive information, personal and otherwise. Such concentration poses both technical risk, because the information can be stolen or corrupted, and social/organizational risk, because the information can be misused by its custodians. The need to protect this information against these risks thus raises the level of security robustness that one might require of the information technology storing this information.

As in many of today's computing devices, the vulnerabilities in pervasive computing will include those that arise from the complexity of the software likely to be used, the likely extensibility of the software built into these systems, and the connectivity of these devices. However, pervasive computing will call for security solutions and approaches to scale upward by many orders of magnitude—to accommodate many more components, many more systems, many more naïve users, many more deployment locations. Pervasive computing systems will also differ from today's systems in several other ways:

- They may be significantly resource-constrained. For example, the battery energy or computing capability may be limited, implying potentially undesirable trade-offs between security and cost or security and performance, as the implementation of security may be costly in computational capability.
- They will be used by people with little knowledge of computing in any form, and thus cannot require a significant degree of attention to the details of security at all. Such users should be, at most, required only to specify the parameters of a desired security policy. Authentication of a person should be handled easily and naturally, without much cognitive effort, and the strength of the authentica-

tion should be matched automatically to the sensitivity of the application. See Section 6.1 (Usable Security) for more on this point.
- They will be smaller in size, which may mean increased difficulty in creating and implementing good human interfaces for security.
- They are far more subject to physical compromise (e.g., they may be unattended) and thus more susceptible to adversarial takeovers in hostile environments, destruction, theft, and loss.
- System architectures for embedded systems need to be flexible enough to support the rapid evolution of security mechanisms and standards and need to provide in situ capabilities for remote upgrade.

One illustrative vulnerability in pervasive and embedded systems (and personal computers [PCs] as well!) arises from the fact that the programming of many such systems depends on the availability of a read-only memory (ROM) chip whose program contents assume control of the system upon power-up. In earlier days, a ROM chip could not be upgraded without the physical access to remove and replace the chip itself. But today, most systems use Flash ROM chips that can be rewritten from software—a feature that greatly facilitates and reduces the cost of upgrades.

A device with a Flash ROM is thus potentially subject to compromise. For example, in 1999, the Chernobyl virus attacked the BIOS chip in many PC-compatible computers, with the result that the program stored in the BIOS memory chip of approximately 300,000 computers was corrupted. Once the programming in Flash ROM has been corrupted, its contents remain even after system restarts, power-off-and-on sequences, and system reinstallation. In other words, Flash ROM corruption defeats many commonly used recovery techniques.

What kinds of problems could be caused by a Flash ROM corruption? Kocher et al. use the example of an antiaircraft radar with an embedded real-time operating system.[11] Within the system are several Flash ROM chips, and a corruption is introduced into one of them. Because the ROM programming is loaded into the system kernel on boot-up, it has trusted access to the entire bus—and its purpose is to cause the radar to ignore certain types of radar signatures.

Physical and side-channel attacks are also possible in systems in which an adversary cannot be denied physical access. Such attacks can be invasive or noninvasive attacks. Invasive attacks against integrated

---

[11]Paul Kocher et al., "Security as a New Dimension in Embedded System Design," *Design Automation Conference*, June 7-11, 2004, San Diego, Calif.; available at http://palms.ee.princeton.edu/PALMSopen/Lee-41stDAC_46_1.pdf.

circuits usually require expensive equipment. Examples include probing and reverse-engineering of the chip. In such attacks, the chip is depackaged and the chip layout is reconstructed through microscopy and the removal of the covering layers. Noninvasive attacks do not require the device to be opened; they include timing attacks, power analysis attacks, fault induction techniques, and electromagnetic analysis attacks.

8.5 SECURE NETWORK ARCHITECTURES

It is often observed that the principles on which the Internet is based were developed in a time in which trust among its users was the order of the day. But such a situation no longer obtains, so an interesting question—with enormous practical relevance—is how a new Internet might be designed and architected with security being a principal feature.

In its purist form, the Internet can be conceptualized as a network that does its best to transmit bits between end-user nodes. These bits are not differentiated from one another, and a bit associated with a virus is delivered in exactly the same way as is a bit associated with a query to a search engine. The processing of these bits, from reassembly to interpretation, is the responsibility of the end nodes. This end-to-end principle, and the lack of intelligence at the center of the Internet, has been a powerful force for innovation and cost-effective network implementation. But this principle—at least in its strongest, most pure form—has come under intense scrutiny, as it is also at the heart of many security difficulties.

In most next-generation Internet conceptualizations, the end-to-end principle is modified to some extent in the name of enhancing security. Clark, for example, argues that any future Internet will have to divide responsibility for security among three elements: the network, the end node system, and the application.[12] As an illustration, he argues that the network ought to be able to quarantine an end node that is behaving antisocially (e.g., if it is infected by a virus that causes known antisocial behavior, or if it is acting as a zombie in a botnet).

A second view of modifying the end-to-end principle is offered by Casado et al. and their Secure Architecture for the Networked Enterprise (SANE) architecture.[13] SANE is an architecture for Transmission Control Protocol/Internet Protocol (TCP/IP) enterprise networks that relies on a logically centralized Domain Controller (DC) with a complete view of

[12]David D. Clark, "Requirements for a Future Internet: Security as a Case Study," Massachusetts Institute of Technology, Computer Science and Artificial Intelligence Laboratory, December 2005; available at http://find.isi.edu/presentation_files/Clark_Arch_Security.pdf.

[13]Martin Casado et al., "SANE: A Protection Architecture for Enterprise Networks"; available at http://yuba.stanford.edu/~casado/sane.pdf.

the network topology to construct routes between any two points on the network. Hosts can only route to the DC, and users must first authenticate themselves with the DC before they can request a capability to access services and end hosts. Once the DC provides a route between two points on the network, that route can only be traversed through a single protection layer that resides between the Ethernet and IP layer. This architecture enables enforcement to be provided at the link layer, to prevent lower layers from undermining it. In addition, it hides information about topology and services from those without permission to see them. And, it requires only one component to be trusted—namely, the DC—in contrast to standard architectures in which multiple components must be trusted (e.g., firewalls, switches, routers, and authentication services).

A different approach is offered by Bryant et al., whose Poly2 architecture separates network services onto different systems, uses application-specific (minimal) operating systems, and isolates specific types of network traffic (e.g., administrative, security-specific, and application-specific traffic).[14] Using separate networks for carrying traffic of different types (and hence different sensitivities) allows for better separation of concerns, reduces interference, and increases confidence in the authenticity of the information. Trust in the overall architecture arises from the separation of untrusted systems and services, which also helps contain successful attacks against individual systems and services.

From a programmatic standpoint, the National Science Foundation's CISE-supported Future Internet Network Design (FIND) initiative is an example of an effort to develop a new Internet architecture from the ground up. (CISE refers to the NSF's Directorate for Computer and Information Sciences and Engineering.) Broadly speaking, the FIND initiative investigates two issues: (1) the requirements for the global network of 15 years from now and (2) how to reconceptualize tomorrow's global network today if it could be designed from scratch. Part of the FIND initiative is of course security. This focus is motivated by the simple observation that Internet security is increasingly worse with time. Clark's arguments on security (above) were presented at a FIND conference in 2005.[15]

8.6 ATTACK CHARACTERIZATION

A problem very closely related to anomaly detection and forensics is that of attack characterization, sometimes also called attack assessment.

---

[14]Eric Bryant et al., "Poly2 Paradigm: A Secure Network Service Architecture," *Proceedings of the 19th Annual Computer Security Applications Conference*, IEEE Computer Society, Washington, D.C., 2003, p. 342.

[15]David D. Clark, "Requirements for a Future Internet: Security as a Case Study," Massachusetts Institute of Technology, Computer Science and Artificial Intelligence Laboratory, December 2005; available at http://find.isi.edu/presentation_files/Clark_Arch_Security.pdf.

Used more or less interchangeably, these terms refer to the process by which systems operators learn that an attack is under way, who is attacking, how the attack is being conducted, and what the purposes of the attack might be.

The first problem is that while the actions of a potentially hostile party may be visible in cyberspace, the intentions and motivations of that party are usually quite invisible. How should a systems operator or owner distinguish between an event that is a deliberate cyberattack intended to compromise an IT system or network and other events, such as accidents, system failures, or hacking by thrill seekers.

A second problem is that a cyberattack may strike multiple targets. How would decision makers know that the same attacker was behind those multiple strikes? Discussed in Section 5.2 (Misuse and Anomaly Detection Systems), this question reflects the issue of large-scale situational awareness. From the standpoint of the defender's perspective, it might well be useful to know if attacks on given sites were in fact correlated in time, in space, in origin, or in type. Collecting such data is difficult enough, since it may be quite voluminous. But analyzing these data to uncover such correlations and presenting the resulting information to decision makers in a comprehensible form present many interesting intellectual challenges.

A third problem is that the identity of an attacker may well be uncertain, for an attacker may well seek to deny provenance or attribution information (Section 5.1, Attribution) that might establish his or her identity. But under some circumstances it may be as important to eliminate certain parties as *not* being responsible for an attack. Consider a large-scale cyberattack that damages key national infrastructure and is also made public. A variety of groups may seek to take credit for such an attack even if they have had nothing to do with carrying out the attack. In these circumstances, policy makers would surely need to be able to distinguish between valid and bogus claims. Ascertaining the identity of an attacker is a forensics problem (Section 7.3, Forensics) writ large, but it also entails pre-incident collection and analysis of possible attack signatures associated with different parties.

8.7 COPING WITH DENIAL-OF-SERVICE ATTACKS

8.7.1 The Nature of Denial-of-Service Attacks

Denial-of-service (DOS) attacks are coordinated attempts to overwhelm a given network resource (e.g., a Web server) with malicious traffic or requests for information to such an extent that legitimate traffic cannot get through. Such attacks are also often distributed in nature, originating from numerous and seemingly unrelated computers (often called zombies, slaves, or bots) from around the Internet (Box 2.3, On Botnets). In most cases, the attacking machines are vulnerable computers that have been infected by malicious software or otherwise compromised by the real attacker (or handler), who controls the attacking machines or botnet from afar either by communicating directly with the machines or by an indirect control method such as passing instructions to the machines through an Internet relay chat (IRC) channel.

Distributed denial-of-service attacks (DDOS) can target the network link or the end node.[16] A DDOS attack on the network link seeks to make the targeted link severely congested. A DDOS attack on an end node seeks to consume the node's resources, such as the central processing unit (CPU) cycles. For example, the attack may cause unnecessary processing (application-level attack) or may seek to consume memory by memory exhaustion. Attacks on an end-node DDOS usually fall into one of two types: bandwidth attacks or resource (or protocol) attacks.[17] Bandwidth attacks can be direct floods of TCP, ICMP, or UDP packets seeking to overwhelm a machine, or they can be so-called reflector attacks in which the attacking machines use spoofed packets to appear as if they are responding to requests from the targeted machine. Resource attacks can entail consuming all available connections on a machine by taking advantage of the way that network communications protocols work (e.g., by using half-open TCP requests) or attempting to crash an intended target outright by using malformed packets or by exploiting weaknesses in software.

All of these DDOS attacks can be quite formidable and difficult to repel. For example, as a recent paper notes, even Internet heavyweights are not immune from them: in "June 2004, the websites of Google, Yahoo! and Microsoft disappeared for hours when their servers were swamped with hundreds of thousands of simultaneous webpage requests that they could not possibly service" in a widespread DDOS attack.[18]

8.7.2 Responding to Distributed Denial-of-Service Attacks

The first step in responding to a DDOS attack is, of course, detecting it—the earlier the better. Administrators use a number of traffic- and network-monitoring tools (e.g., intrusion-detection systems, firewalls, and

[16]Xuhui Ao, *Report on DIMACS Workshop on Large-Scale Internet Attacks*, September 23-24, 2003; available at http://dimacs.rutgers.edu/Workshops/Attacks/internet-attack-9-03.pdf.

[17]Shibiao Lin and Tzi-cker Chiueh, "A Survey on Solutions to Distributed Denial of Service Attacks," (TR-201) RPE report, September 2006; available at http://www.ecsl.cs.sunysb.edu/tr/TR201.pdf, p. 8.

[18]Shibiao Lin and Tzi-cker Chiueh, "A Survey on Solutions to Distributed Denial of Service Attacks," (TR-201) RPE report, September 2006; available at http://www.ecsl.cs.sunysb.edu/tr/TR201.pdf, p. 3.

so on) to stay abreast of the health of their resources. However, inevitably one way of detecting a DDOS attack is by getting a call from a user that a given resource or Web site is unavailable. In any case, once detected, there are today several strategies for addressing a DDOS attack:

- *Respond and block.* This approach involves detecting and characterizing the attack and ideally gaining some kind of "signature" from the attack that can be shared with others who might be affected. This signature can then be used to filter the malicious network traffic, often by the Internet Service Provider (ISP) rerouting traffic for the victim through a "scrubber" node.[19] In practice, if an attack is large enough, ISPs can "blackhole" offending IP addresses or eliminate their routes. That is, the outside path through which the malicious traffic comes can be shut down, thereby keeping at least the targeted service available to local clients. More importantly, this approach avoids collateral damage to other sites downstream of the chokepoint network link.
- *Hide.* In this response, a Web site's true end points are hidden or are set up with very good filters. Traffic is then routed via an overlay network that hides the final destination and spreads the load. An example of this approach has been taken by Keromytis et al. in the design and implementation of Secure Overlay Services.[20]
- *Minimize impact.* This approach involves simply trying to ride a DDOS attack out, either by adding more bandwidth or by using a content distribution network (e.g., Akamai) to lessen the load on a Web site's resources (Box 8.3). Also, tools such as CAPTCHAs[21] can be used to differentiate and filter legitimate traffic from illegitimate traffic. Many Web sites also choose to degrade their services to all users when under such an attack in order to continue providing what are seen as critical services to legitimate users.
- *Make the attacker work.* For attacks aimed at CPU time or memory consumption, a common strategy is to force the attacker to solve

[19]Robert Stone, "An IP Overlay Network for Tracking DoS Floods," in *9th Usenix Security Symposium*, 2000; available at http://www.usenix.org/publications/library/proceedings/sec2000/full_papers/stone/stone.ps.

[20]A.D. Keromytis, V. Misra, and D. Rubenstein, "SOS: Secure Overlay Services," pp. 61-72 in *Proceedings of ACM SIGCOMM*, August 2002; available at http://citeseer.ist.psu.edu/keromytis02sos.html.

[21]CAPTCHAs are an automated means for attempting to determine whether or not a computer or network user is a human being. (CAPTCHA is an acronym for "Completely Automated Public Turing Test to Tell Computers and Humans Apart.") They often involve changing a graphic in such a way that a human can still determine what it shows, while a computer or bot would have trouble. For more information, see http://www.captcha.net.

BOX 8.3
Attack Diffusion

As noted in Section 2.1 (Interconnected Information Technology Everywhere, All the Time) in this report, increased interconnection creates interdependencies and vulnerabilities. Nevertheless, it may also be possible to leverage such interconnections to defensive advantage.

To illustrate the point, consider a denial-of-service (DOS) attack, which fundamentally depends on volume to saturate a victim.[1] Interconnection could, in principle, enable the automatic diffusion of incoming traffic across multiple "absorption servers." (An *absorption server* is intended primarily to absorb traffic rather than to provide full-scale services.) While no one would-be victim could reasonably afford to acquire a large enough infrastructure to absorb a large DOS attack, a service company could provide a diffusion infrastructure and make it available to customers. When a customer experienced a DOS attack, it could use its connectivity to shunt the traffic to this diffusion infrastructure.

At least one company provides such a service today. But the approaches are not without potential problems. For example, the Domain Name System may be used to diffuse requests to one of a number of servers. But doing so reveals the destination address of individual absorption servers, which in principle might still leave them vulnerable to attack. Methods to hide the individual absorption servers are known, but they have potential undesirable effects on service under non-attack conditions. Further, automatic attack diffusion can conflict with occasional user or Internet service provider desires for explicit control over routing paths.

---

[1]David D. Clark, "Requirements for a Future Internet: Security as a Case Study," December 2005; available at http://find.isi.edu/presentation_files/Clark_Arch_Security.pdf.

some sort of puzzle. A good puzzle is hard to compute but relatively cheap to check. Examples include calculating a hash function where some bits of the input are specified by the defender, and the output has to have some number of high-order bits that are zeroes. Most such schemes are based on a 1992 proposal by Dwork and Naor[22]; adaptations to network denial-of-service attacks include TCP Client Puzzles[23] and TLS Puzzles.[24]

---

[22]Cynthia Dwork and Moni Naor, "Pricing via Processing or Combatting Junk Mail," *Proceedings of the 12th Annual International Cryptology Conference on Advances in Cryptology*, 740: 139-147, Lecture Notes in Computer Science, Springer-Verlag, London, 1992.

[23]A. Juels and J. Brainard, "Client Puzzles: A Cryptographic Countermeasure Against Connection Depletion Attacks," pp. 151-165 in *Proceedings of the 1999 Network and Distributed Security Symposium*, S. Kent (ed.), Internet Society, Reston, Va., 1999.

[24]Drew Dean and Adam Stubblefield, "Using Client Puzzles to Protect TLS," *Proceedings of the 10th Conference on USENIX Security Symposium*, 10: 1, 2001, USENIX Association, Berkeley, Calif.; available at http://www.csl.sri.com/users/ddean/papers/usenix01b.pdf.

However, as with most areas of cybersecurity, attackers and defenders are locked in an ongoing arms race trying to stay abreast (or ahead) of each other's techniques and tactics; developments are occurring at a rapid pace. Still, there are no ideal, comprehensive solutions for dealing with DDOS attacks, owing in large part to the sheer number and availability of attacking machines. Indeed, attackers are moving toward using ever-larger numbers of machines in their attacks (i.e., larger botnets), more evenly distributed around the Internet, and are attempting to make their attacks as indistinguishable as possible from legitimate traffic so as to confound the filters and response mechanisms used by defenders.

There are three common motives for denial-of-service attacks: vandalism, revenge, and extortion. The different types of attacks suggest the need for different response strategies.

- Pure *vandalism* in some sense is the hardest to deal with, since it is typically an impulse crime committed without forethought and against more or less any site on the network. Fortunately, the effects are rarely long-lasting. More ominously, this type of attack may have fallen in importance not because of any substantive defensive measures but because of the shift by perpetrators to profit-motivated cybercrime.
- The second cause—*revenge*—is generally more annoying than serious. Typically, one hacker will annoy another; the offended party replies by launching a denial-of-service attack against the offender. These attacks—known as packeting—tend to be of limited duration; however, other users sharing the same access link are not infrequently affected as well.
- Profit-motivated DDOS attacks, and in particular *extortion* attacks, are in some sense easier to deal with. The targets are more predictable and hence can take defensive measures. Nonetheless, there is often insufficient time for a response. One common victim has been sports gambling Web sites, since they sell a time-sensitive product. (While online gambling is illegal in the United States, it is legal in other parts of the world, and U.S. companies often suffer collateral damage when flooding attacks against the gambling sites overload chokepoint network links.) Conventional law enforcement—"follow the money"—may be the most promising avenue, although the perpetrators generally employ money-laundering in an attempt to evade prosecution.

8.7.3 Research Challenges

Research challenges in dealing with denial-of-service attacks focus on how to identify and characterize DDOS attacks and how to mitigate their effects. In the first area, which includes the reliable detection of large-scale attacks on the Internet and the real-time collection and analysis of large amounts of attack-monitoring information, Moore et al. have developed a technique, known as backscatter, for inferring certain DOS activity.[25] The technique is based on the fact that DDOS attackers sometimes forge the IP source address of the packets they send so that the packets appear to the target to be arriving from one or more third parties. However, as a practical matter, these fake source addresses are usually generated at random (that is, each packet sent has a randomly generated source address). The target, receiving a spoofed packet, tries to send an appropriate response to the faked IP address. However, because the attacker's source address is selected at random, the victim's responses are scattered across the entire Internet address space (this effect is called backscatter). By observing a large enough address range, it is possible to effectively sample all such denial-of-service activity on the Internet. Contained in these samples are the identity of the victim, information about the kind of attack, and a timestamp that is useful for estimating attack duration. The average arrival rate of unsolicited responses directed at the monitored address range also provides a basis for estimating the actual rate of the attack being directed at the target.

There are several limitations to this technique. The most important is the assumption that attack packets appear to come from forged source addresses. While this was certainly true of the first generation of DDOS attacks, many attackers no longer bother with such forgery. While the exact extent of forgery is debatable, some experts claim that the large majority of attacks no longer use forged addresses. Two of the reasons are good; one, though, is cause for concern. First, operating system changes in Windows XP Service Pack 2 make address forgery harder. Second, a number of ISPs follow the recommendations in RFC 2827 and block (many) forged packets.[26] Forgery is often unnecessary, however; source address-based filtering near the victim is rarely possible, and there are sufficiently many attack packets that effective tracing and response are difficult.

The second area—mitigating the effects of DDOS attacks—spans a number of topics. One important topic is the development of better filters and router configurations. For example, the optimal placement of filters to maximize benefit and minimize negative impact is not easy to determine. Another example is the development of network-layer capabilities that

---

[25]David Moore et al., "Inferring Internet Denial-of-Service Activity," *ACM Transactions on Computer Systems (TOCS)*, May 2006; available at http://www.caida.org/publications/papers/2001/BackScatter/usenixsecurity01.pdf.

[26]P. Ferguson and D. Senie, *RFC 2827, Network Ingress Filtering: Defeating Denial of Service Attacks Which Employ IP Source Address Spoofing*, May 2000. Also known as BCP 38.

can be used to filter traffic efficiently. An example is the implementation of "pushback" configurations, an approach to handling DDOS attacks that adds functionality to routers so that they can detect and preferentially drop packets that probably belong to a DDOS attack, while also notifying upstream and downstream routers to do likewise.[27] Such an approach requires coordination between various routers beyond that which is available through standard routing protocols.

Another important topic relates to scale. Today's solutions do not scale up to be able to address the numbers of attackers that are seen from today's botnets. Therefore, one major research area is to develop scalable solutions for addressing DDOS attacks or for weathering them (e.g., content distribution networks). Other challenges involve developing ways to ensure that computers and their users are less susceptible to compromise by attackers or malicious code, thereby diminishing the resources available for attackers' use in botnets. Additional DDOS-related research could also be useful in areas such as network protocols, network infrastructure, network flow analysis and control, metrics for measuring the impacts of DDOS attacks, and better forensic methods and techniques for tracing and catching attackers.[28]

Still another topic is organizational and institutional. Because certain promising approaches to dealing with DDOS attacks depend on cooperation between ISPs (some of which may be in different countries and subject to different laws), finding ways to encourage and facilitate cooperation is important.[29] Research on this topic might include how responsibility and obligation for responding to attacks should be shared between ISPs and their customers; what kinds of business service model are needed; how to build formal collaborations for automated coordination among different sites, ISPs, and various agencies; and how to incentivize ISPs to deploy defensive measures.

---

[27]For more information on pushback, see Ratul Mahajan, Steven M. Bellovin, Sally Floyd, John Ioannidis, Vern Paxson, and Scott Shenker, "Controlling High Bandwidth Aggregates in the Network," *Computer Communications Review* 32(3): 62-73, 2002.

[28]For additional information on DDOS attacks, see Jelena Mirkovic et al., *A Taxonomy of DDoS Attacks and DDoS Defense Mechanisms*, Technical Report #020018, University of California, Los Angeles, Computer Science Department, available at http://www.eecis.udel.edu/~sunshine/publications/ucla_tech_report_020018.pdf [undated]; Xuhui Ao, *Report on DIMACS Workshop on Large-Scale Internet Attacks*, Center for Discrete Mathematics and Theoretical Computer Science (DIMACS), available at http://dimacs.rutgers.edu/Workshops/Attacks/internet-attack-9-03.pdf, 2003; and Rich Pethia, Allan Paller, and Eugene Spafford, "Consensus Roadmap for Defeating Distributed Denial of Service Attacks," Project of the Partnership for Critical Infrastructure Security, SANS Institute, available at http://www.sans.org/dosstep/roadmap.php, 2000.

[29]Xuhui Ao, *Report on DIMACS Workshop on Large-Scale Internet Attacks*, September 23-24, 2003; available at http://dimacs.rutgers.edu/Workshops/Attacks/internet-attack-9-03.pdf.

As one example, the entire community of ISPs would benefit from knowing the frequency of DOS attacks. ISPs are aware (or could be aware) of DOS attacks through the measurements that they ordinarily make in the course of their everyday operations, since sustained rates of packet drops by routers, observable via the simple network management protocol (SNMP), frequently indicate the existence of an attack. However, for competitive reasons, this information is rarely disclosed publicly, so the community cannot develop a complete picture of the situation. Research (or at least investigation) is needed to determine mechanisms that would encourage the disclosure of such data to an independent third party and the publication of a sanitized version of these data.

8.8 DEALING WITH SPAM

Spam—what might loosely be defined as unsolicited e-mail sent en masse to millions of users—has evolved from a minor nuisance to a major problem for the Internet, both as a mechanism for delivering attacks (e.g., phishing) and as a means for propagating other types of attack (e.g., viruses). Spam is undesirable from the recipient's standpoint because he or she must continually spend time and effort to deal with unwanted e-mails. In small volume, it would be easy to delete unwanted e-mails that can be identified from the header. But spam e-mail often uses deceptive headers in order to persuade users to open it (e.g., rather than saying "Subject: Viagra for sale," the header will say "Subject: Greetings from an old friend"), and by some accounts, spam accounts for over 90 percent of e-mail sent on the Internet.[30] Thus, it is not unreasonable to estimate that individuals spend hundreds of millions of person-hours per year in dealing with spam. Today, spam threatens to undermine the stability and usefulness of networked systems and to impose significant economic costs and lost productivity.

Spending valuable time dealing with a nuisance is bad enough, but spam can also have serious consequences. For example, spam can clutter one's mailbox so that desired e-mails are missed or other e-mails cannot be received; it forces ISPs or users to implement filters that may inadvertently filter wanted messages. Because spam can prevent a user from doing useful things in his or her computing environment, spam can be regarded as a kind of denial-of-service attack against individual users.

Spam can cause harm. One risk is a form of online identity theft. Because it is easy to forge an electronic return address (so that an e-mail appears to have been sent from the forged address), spam senders often insert legitimate e-mail addresses (e.g., those harvested from online bul-

[30]See, for example, http://www.postini.com/news_events/pr/pr011007.php.

letin boards, chat rooms, and the like) as the purported sender of their spam e-mail. The reputation of the legitimate e-mail user is thus compromised, and the spam also generates for the legitimate user a flood of "mailer-rejection notices" from e-mail systems that reject the spam e-mail for some reason.

A second risk is that spam can compromise the integrity of the user's computing environment, causing it to do things that are undesired from the user's point of view. E-mail systems are often designed to allow users to open and execute e-mail attachments with a simple mouse click, or to access Web pages referenced in an embedded link, or to display images or messages formatted as "rich text." Such functionality increases the convenience and enhances the utility of e-mail for the user. But when spammers exploit these features, the result can be that a hostile attachment is executed, a user-compromising Web page is accessed (merely by accessing it), or a trap door is opened simply by viewing the e-mail.

It is true that clandestine applications can be delivered through many different mechanisms, and in principle there is nothing special about spam e-mail as a delivery mechanism. But in practice, the ease with which e-mail can be delivered suggests that e-mail—and payloads that it carries—will be used aggressively in the future for commercial purposes.[31]

Once compromised, the user's computing environment becomes a platform for active threats such as the following:

- *Divulging the personal information resident on the user's computer.* Especially common would be financial records that are stored by various personal money management systems, but in the future such information may include medical records. Such information could be used to target users with specific and personalized communications that may be threatening. An example of a targeted personal e-mail would be: "Did you know the odds of dying with your disease are much higher now?"
- *Displaying advertisements by surprise* (e.g., pop-under ads).
- *Tracking the user's information-seeking behavior* (e.g., what Web sites have been visited). Today, the use of such traces is most often limited to identifying when a user is visiting a site that was visited in the past, but there is nothing in principle that prevents the entire

[31]It is also true that the root cause of the problems caused by Trojan horses is insecurities in the user's computing environment. Thus, one could argue, with considerable force and reason, that eliminating these insecurities would eliminate Trojan horse problems as well as a host of other problems. On the other hand, it is unrealistic to expect that such insecurities would ever be eliminated entirely. More to the point, users will not be relieved to know that the reason they are suffering from Trojan horses is that their operating systems are insecure.

trace from being made public knowledge. (For example, consider spyware from a group that opposes pornography that reports your use of sexually explicit Web sites to a public database.)

- *Launching attacks on other computer systems without the user's knowledge* (e.g., as part of a botnet).

From an institutional standpoint, spam consumes significant amounts of bandwidth, for which ISPs and network operators must pay. Indeed, large volumes of spam are in some ways indistinguishable from a denial-of-service attack. Thus, spam can have important security implications on a regional or national scale as well as being simply annoying to individual users. ISPs and users may also bear the cost and inconvenience of installing and maintaining filters to reduce spam volumes, as well as of maintaining a larger infrastructure to accommodate the vast amount of spam flowing through their networks (more servers, routers, adminstrators, floor space, power, and so on). (An interesting question is thus how the collective cost to individuals and business compares with the benefits gained collectively by the spam senders and those who actually buy something as a result of the spam.)

Spam is only one dimension of a commercial environment that bombards citizens with junk mail (e.g., catalogs and endless advertising pieces); long, unsolicited voicemails on our telephone mail systems; and unwanted faxes. But spam is different from the others in at least two significant ways. First, the costs per message to transmit spam e-mail and similar electronic messages is much smaller by several orders of magnitude than that for postal mail or telephone calls. Second, spam can be more deceptive than junk snail mail (junk faxes and telemarketing phone calls are annoying but are small fractions of the total fax and phone traffic). Before it is opened, spam e-mail can have the identical look and feel of a legitimate e-mail from an unknown party.

Policy makers at both the federal and state levels are seeking legislative remedies for spam, such as the CAN-SPAM Act of 2003 (17 U.S.C. 103). However, crafting appropriate and workable legislation has been problematic, with at least four separate dimensions that create difficulty:

- *As a commercially oriented activity, some forms of spam do create some economic benefit.* Some small fraction of the spam recipients *do* respond positively to unsolicited e-mail that promotes various products or services. In this regard, it is important to remember that unsolicited commercial e-mail does not consist solely of Nigerian bank fraud messages or ads for Viagra, but also includes ads for cars, software, sunglasses, and vacations. Furthermore, the economics of e-mail are such that if only a very small fraction of recipients of a given spam mailing respond positively, that is sufficient to make the sending of the original spam turn a profit.

- *Defining spam through a legislative process is very difficult.* What is spam for one person may be an interesting curiosity to another. Consequently, it is very difficult to develop regulations that capture the notion of spam in a sufficiently precise manner to be legally enforceable and yet sufficiently general that spam senders cannot circumvent them with technical variations.
- *Spam can be sent with impunity across national borders.* Regulations applying to domestic spam senders can easily be circumvented by foreign intermediaries.
- *Spam is arguably a form of free speech (albeit commercial speech).* Thus, policy makers seeking to regulate spam must tread carefully with respect to the First Amendment.

In the long run, addressing the spam problem is going to involve technology and policy elements. One important technical dimension is the anonymity of spam. Because spam senders realize the unpopularity of the e-mail that they produce, today's spam senders seek a high degree of sender anonymity to make it difficult or impossible for the recipient to obtain redress (e.g., to identify a party who will receive and act on a complaint). Thus, the provenance of a given e-mail is one element in dealing with the spam problem, suggesting the relevance of the attribution research of Section 5.1, "Attribution."

But even if the attribution problem itself is solved, there are complicating factors regarding spam. For example, as far as many people are concerned, the senders of e-mail fall into three categories—those known to the receiver to be desirable, those known to be undesirable, and those of an unknown status. Provenance—at least as traditionally associated with identity—does not help much in sorting out the last category. Moreover, botnets today send "legitimate" e-mail from compromised hosts—that is, if my computer is compromised so that it becomes a zombie in a botnet army, it can easily send spam e-mail under any e-mail account associated with my computer. That mail will be indistinguishable from legitimate e-mail from me (i.e., e-mail that I intended to send). Thus, preventing the compromise of a host becomes part of the complete spam-prevention research agenda.

Yet another technical dimension of spam control is a methodology to examine content as well as origin of e-mails.[32] That is, how can a computer be trained to differentiate spam from legitimate e-mail? Most

---

[32]Joshua Goodman, Gordon V. Cormack, and David Heckerman, "Spam and the Ongoing Battle for the Inbox," *Communications of the ACM*, 50(2): 24-33, 2007.

spam-recognition systems today have at least one machine learning component that performs such differentiation based on examples of both spam and nonspam e-mail. Much of the progress in antispam research has involved improving the relevant machine learning algorithms as spammers develop more sophisticated means for evading spam-detection algorithms. Other relevant factors entail obtaining more examples of different kinds of spam (so that new kinds of detection-evasion techniques can be taken into account by spam detectors) and doing so more quickly (so that spammers have smaller windows in which to propagate their new variants).

Another dimension of spam-detection performance depends on the ability to extract the relevant content from the bits that actually constitute the e-mail. ASCII art, photographic images, and HTML encodings have all been used to evade filtering, with varying degree of success. Indeed, image-based spam, in which an e-mail contains an embedded image of a message, is quite common today. All of these methods are based on the fact that that extraction of the content is computationally intensive and thus impractical to perform on all incoming e-mails.

Spam is, by definition, a collection of many e-mails with identical content. So spam might be identified by virtue of the fact that many copies of it are circulating on the Internet—and there are ways that institutionally based spam filters could be able to identify a given e-mail as being a part of this category. The obvious countermeasure for the spammer is to make each message slightly different, but in a way that does not alter the core message of the spam e-mail, which itself suggests another research problem of identifying messages as "identical in semantic content" despite small differences at the binary level.

The economics of spam are also relevant. If the incremental cost of sending spam were higher, the volume of spam could be reduced significantly. But spammers are not the only parties to send e-mail in bulk—organizations with newsletters, for example, may send large volumes of e-mail as well. The imposition of a small financial cost per e-mail would do much to reduce spam, but it would be difficult to deploy and also would violate long-standing practices that make e-mail an effective mechanism of communication notwithstanding the spam problem. Other ways of imposing cost include requiring a time-consuming computation that makes it more difficult to send e-mails in bulk and requiring a proof that a human is involved in the sending of individual e-mails. How to impose costs on spammers, and only on spammers, remains an open technical and regulatory question.

Finally, as new communications channels emerge, new forms of spam are likely to emerge. For example, spam text messages to mobile and instant message spam are two relatively newer forms of spam. Future spam variants may include exploits related to location-aware devices (e.g., advertisements tied explicitly to the user's location) and spam and spam-like payloads other than text delivered to mobile devices such as cellular telephones. An example of the latter is that with the increasingly popular use of voice-over-IP, junk phone calls (also known as SPIT, for spam over Internet telephony) may come to be a problem in the future. Research will be needed to address these new forms of spam as well.

9

Category 6—Speculative Research

Many of today's most pressing security problems are the consequence of information technologies designed and built when security concerns were largely nonexistent. However, now that these technologies, which include personal computers (PCs) and the Internet, are so widely deployed, the current state of the world does not seem to offer an obvious and direct path to better security.

For this reason, Category 6—Speculative research, is reserved for research ideas that are arguably plausible but which also might be regarded as somewhat speculative and "out-of-the-box" by the mainstream research community. Investment in this category of research should account for only a small fraction of the cybersecurity research budget, but some investment is warranted if only to ensure that groupthink does not suppress ideas that might in fact have merit.

Specific examples of Category 6 research are, almost by definition, controversial. That is, some researcher will propose an idea that he or she believes is worth exploring, and others in the community may argue that such a research direction is not original or new, lacks depth, does not provide insights that suggest opportunities for surprise or success, does not appear to be deployable on any meaningful timescale or for a meaningful user base, poses currently insoluble difficulties, or must be approached with great caution if at all. Indeed, unlike the areas described in Categories 1 through 5 of the committee's illustrative research agenda, the examples of Category 6 research below are controversial in just these ways, even within the committee itself. These examples were selected through a process that required only a few members to support them and should not be taken as ideas that the committee as a whole thinks are worth significant effort or emphasis.

9.1 A CYBERATTACK RESEARCH ACTIVITY

In many domains of security studies, theories of defense and theories of attack are inextricably interwoven. That is, insights on how best to defend are grounded in knowledge of how attacks might unfold, and a deep knowledge of attack methodologies should not be limited to potential attackers. For example, arson investigators know very well how to set fires and agents from the Bureau of Alcohol, Tobacco, Firearms and Explosives know a great deal about how to make bombs. Similarly, a body of cyberattack knowledge that is independent of criminal intent may be very useful to cybersecurity researchers. Although in today's cybersecurity environment, many attacks are simple indeed, such a body of cyberattack knowledge would logically go far beyond the commonplace attacks of today to include at least some of the more sophisticated techniques that high-end attackers might use.

The utility of this approach is suggested by the use of red teams to test operational defenses. Red team testing is an effort undertaken by an organization to test its security posture using teams that simulate what a determined attacker might do. The red team develops expertise relevant to its intended target, conducts reconnaissance to search for security weaknesses, and then launches attacks that exploit those weaknesses. Because red teams have deep knowledge of attack, and in particular know how to look at a system from the outside and how to cross interfaces (such as hardware/software) that may effectively limit the view of insiders, it is possible that greater interaction between red team experts and cybersecurity researchers would prove fruitful.

Many important issues attend the establishment of a research activity intended to develop deep knowledge of cyberattack. For example:

- *How should deep knowledge of cyberattack be acquired?* Cybercriminals and other adversaries develop knowledge by attacking real systems; sometimes their efforts cause real disruptions and loss. It is inconceivable that as a matter of national policy the U.S. government would endorse or support any effort that would result in such harm, and there might well be significant liability issues associated with the conduct of such an activity. The availability of large-scale testbeds for the research community might have some potential for mitigating this particular problem. Moreover, once a plausible attack hypothesis has been developed, it might often be demonstrated on a small subset of the target system that has been temporarily disconnected (or duplicated) for the demonstration.

- *How should such knowledge be shared?* One model is to recruit cybersecurity researchers for "tours of duty" with a "cyberattack institute." Another model is to teach cyberattack techniques as part of cybersecurity education.[1]
- *How should such knowledge be limited?* This issue is the most important one to resolve if this approach is to be pursued. If placed at the disposal of an adversary, knowledge of cyberattack might be very dangerous indeed. Yet if the knowledge is excessively limited, it is useless to the cybersecurity research community at large. This issue is particularly thorny in the context of academic research, in which the dissemination of research results is a sine qua non for advancement. Nondisclosure agreements may be a feasible mechanism to protect knowledge acquired in the case of commercial systems, and security clearances or background checks may be necessary for government systems—although it is easy to imagine that some commercial systems are more sensitive than certain government systems are. Note also that the sensitivity of information about cyberattack increases as knowledge of the specific systems involved increases, suggesting that the study of generic attacks may enable greater information dissemination.

In an environment in which vulnerabilities result from routine implementation and coding failures, it may be that deep knowledge of cyberattack is not needed to develop defenses. But against sophisticated attackers who can target systems that have been hardened against "routine" attacks, deep knowledge of cyberattack may provide a context that can help to drive advanced defensive research.

9.2 BIOLOGICAL APPROACHES TO SECURITY

Biological systems are capable of healing themselves and defending themselves against outside attack. This basic fact has suggested to some researchers that biologically inspired approaches to cybersecurity may be worth some effort in exploring.

What does "biological inspiration" mean? A report of the National Research Council on computing and biology suggests that a biological organism may implement an approach to a problem that could be the

[1]See, for example, George Ledin, Jr., "Not Teaching Viruses and Worms Is Harmful," *Communications of the ACM*, 48(1): 144, 2005.

basis of a solution to a computing problem.[2] But even if an implementation does not carry over well to a computing problem, it may be that its underlying principles do have some relevance.

Researchers exploring biological approaches to cybersecurity argue that the unpredictable pathogens to which an organism's immune system must respond are analogous to some of the threats that computer systems face, and that the principles underlying the operation of the immune system may provide new approaches to computer security.[3] They note, for example, that immune systems exhibit a number of characteristics that could reasonably describe how effective computer security mechanisms might operate in a computer system or network. In particular, the immune system is distributed, diverse, autonomous, tolerant of error, dynamic, adaptable, imperfect, redundant, and homeostatic.[4] To go further, it is necessary to ask whether the particular methods by which the immune system achieves these characteristics have potential relevance to computer security.

For example, Forrest and Hofmeyr have described models for network intrusion detection and virus detection based on an immunological distinction between "self" (regarded as nondangerous) and "nonself" (regarded as dangerous),[5] and at least one company has introduced cybersecurity products based on these models. The primary advantage of the immunological approach in this context is that attacks need not be identified by matching a potential threat to the known signature of a previously identified virus or worm, but rather there would be a behavioral identification of that threat as a "nonself" entity.

Despite some promising results, it remains to be seen how far immunological approaches to cybersecurity can be pushed. Given that the immune system is a very complex entity whose operation is not fully understood, a bottom-up development of a computer security system based on the

---

[2]National Research Council, *Catalyzing Inquiry at the Interface of Computing and Biology*, John C. Wooley and Herbert S. Lin (eds.), The National Academies Press, Washington, D.C., 2005.

[3]One of the first papers to suggest that self-nonself discrimination as used by the immune system might be useful in computer security was by S. Forrest, A.S. Perelson, L. Allen, and R. Cherukuri, "Self-nonself Discrimination in a Computer," *Proceedings of the 1994 IEEE Symposium on Research in Security and Privacy*, IEEE Computer Society Press, Los Alamitos, Calif., 1994, pp. 202-212. This paper focused mainly on the issue of protection against computer viruses but set the stage for a great deal of subsequent work.

[4]This discussion of the immune system is based on S. Forrest and S. Hofmeyr, "Immunology as Information Processing," *Design Principles for Immune Systems and Other Distributed Autonomous Systems*, L.A. Segal and I.R. Cohen (eds.), Oxford University Press, New York, 2001.

[5]S. Forrest and S. Hofmeyr, "Immunology as Information Processing," *Design Principles for Immune Systems and Other Distributed Autonomous Systems*, L.A. Segal and I.R. Cohen (eds.), Oxford University Press, New York, 2001.

immune system is not possible today. The human immune system has evolved to its present state owing to many evolutionary accidents as well as the constraints imposed by biology and chemistry—much of which is likely to be artifactual and mostly irrelevant to the underlying principles that the system embodies and also to the design of a computer security system. Further, the immune system is oriented toward problems of survival. By contrast, computer security is traditionally concerned with confidentiality, accountability, and trustworthiness—and the relevance of immunological processes to confidentiality and accountability is entirely unclear today.

9.3 USING ATTACK TECHNIQUES FOR DEFENSIVE PURPOSES

Viruses and worms exploit vulnerabilities in a system to take control of it. But the payload of a virus or a worm can, in fact, be programmed to harm the system or to benefit it. In particular, it is technically possible to propagate system fixes through such a mechanism. That is, a "white hat" virus could be programmed to exploit a system vulnerability in order to enter that system, and to close that vulnerability through the administration of a system patch or changing certain administrative settings, and finally to self-destruct.

Known for many years,[6] this type of application has advantages and disadvantages. For example, an advantage is that fixes could be propagated very rapidly. But since this approach was first proposed, the disadvantages have been sufficient to prevent its serious consideration. These disadvantages stem from technical, ethical/legal, and psychological reasons.[7] Potential technical disadvantages include the originator's lack of control over how the "white hat" virus or worm will spread, confusion over the intent or purpose of a virus or worm whose behavior may be superficially similar to a nefarious one, waste of system and network resources, and potential escape from any controlled environment. Potential ethical/legal issues include unauthorized data modification, copyright and ownership issues attending to the modification of resident software, and the legitimization of activities that are generally presumed dangerous today.[8] Potential psychological issues include the violation that

[6] An early mention of this idea can be found in Fred Cohen, "Trends in Computer Virus Research," ASP, 1991, available at http://vx.netlux.org/lib/afc06.html; and Frederick B. Cohen, "A Case for Benevolent Viruses," 1991, available at http://all.net/books/integ/goodvcase.html.

[7] Vesselin Bontchev, "Are 'Good' Computer Viruses Still a Bad Idea?," Virus Test Center, University of Hamburg, Germany; available at http://vx.netlux.org/lib/avb02.html. See also Eugene H. Spafford, "Response to Fred Cohen's 'Contest'," *The Sciences*, January/February 1992, p. 4.

[8] For further discussion, see Eugene H. Spafford; "Are Computer Break-ins Ethical?" *Journal of Systems and Software*, 17(1): 41-48, 1992.

may be felt by users regarding the loss of control over their systems that viruses and worms necessarily entail.

9.4 CYBER-RETALIATION

A special case of using attack techniques for defensive purposes arises in the realm of active defense. Traditionally, cybersecurity is based on the notion of passive defense—a defense that imposes no penalty on a would-be attacker apart from the time that the attacker needs to mount its attack. Under such circumstances, the attacker can continue attacking unpunished until success or exhaustion occurs.

The notion of cyber-retaliation as a part of an active defense is intended to make cyberattackers pay a price for attacking (whether or not they are successful), thus dissuading a potential attacker and offering a deterrent to attacking in the first place. But cyber-retaliation raises both technical and policy issues.

From a technical standpoint, the tools available today to support retaliation are inadequate. Identification of cyberattackers remains problematic, as indicated in Section 5.1 (Attribution). Today, the identification of an attacker is an enormously time-consuming task—even if the identification task is successful, it can take weeks to identify an attacker. Furthermore, considerable uncertainty often remains about the actual identity of the attacker, who may be an individual using an institution's computer without the knowledge or permission of that institution. Such uncertainty raises the possibility that one's retaliatory efforts might result in significant collateral damage to innocents without even necessarily affecting the perpetrator. In addition, the technical mechanisms for striking back are generally oriented toward causing damage to computer systems rather than being directed at individual perpetrators.

From a policy standpoint, cyber-retaliation raises issues such as the dividing line between regarding a cyberattack as a law enforcement matter versus a national security matter, the appropriate definitions of concepts such as "force" or "armed attack" as they apply to cyberattacks, the standards of proof required to establish the origin of a cyberattack, and the nature of the appropriate rules of engagement that might be associated with a cyberattack.

These comments should not be taken as denigrating passive cybersecurity measures, which remain central to the nation's cybersecurity posture. Nevertheless, passive defenses have strong limitations, and active defense may provide a more robust set of options if the technical and policy issues can be resolved.

Part III
Conclusion

Part III of this report consists of Chapter 10, which examines why insufficient action has occurred in the cybersecurity arena and provides a set of priorities for the future.

10

Looking to the Future

10.1 WHY HAS LITTLE ACTION OCCURRED?

The Committee on Improving Cybersecurity Research in the United States believes that the cybersecurity threat is real, imminent, and growing in severity. Moreover, as one of the most technologically advanced nations in the world, the United States has much to lose from the materialization of this threat. But this committee is not the first committee—and this report is not the first report—to make this claim.

As early as 1973, the Electronic Systems Division of the U.S. Air Force noted the ease with which then-contemporary systems (such as OS/360 and GCOS) had been penetrated and argued that fundamental design flaws were responsible for allowing these penetrations.[1] In 1974, *Fortune* published an article for the general public presenting a general overview of the vulnerability of multiaccess computer systems to unauthorized tampering, the reliability of access controls, and ways in which systems have been exploited.[2]

In 1991, the National Research Council weighed in. *Computers at Risk* stated:[3]

---

[1]R.R. Schell, P.J. Downey, and G.J. Popek, "Preliminary Notes on the Design of Secure Military Computer Systems," January 1973, HQ Electronic Systems Division, Hanscom Air Force Base; available at http://csrc.nist.gov/publications/history/sche73.pdf.

[2]T. Alexander, "Waiting for the Great Computer Rip-Off," *Fortune*, 90(1): 142-150, July 1974.

[3]National Research Council, *Computers at Risk: Safe Computing in the Information Age*, National Academy Press, Washington, D.C., 1991.

> We are at risk. Increasingly, America depends on computers. They control power delivery, communications, aviation, and financial services. They are used to store vital information, from medical records to business plans to criminal records. Although we trust them, they are vulnerable to the effects of poor design and insufficient quality control, to accident, and perhaps most alarmingly, to deliberate attack. The modern thief can steal more with a computer than with a gun. Tomorrow's terrorist may be able to do more damage with a keyboard than with a bomb.

Computers at Risk was also one of the first reports to suggest that networking between computers would dramatically worsen the cybersecurity situation by enabling problems to propagate electronically and by enlarging the set of potential attackers—and indeed this is exactly what has taken place.

In 1997, the President's Commission on Critical Infrastructure Protection noted:[4]

> [T]he right command sent over a network to a power generating station's control computer could be just as devastating as a backpack full of explosives, and the perpetrator would be more difficult to identify and apprehend. . . .
>
> [Furthermore,] the rapid growth of a computer-literate population ensures that increasing millions of people around the world possess the skills necessary to conduct such an attack. The wide adoption of common protocols for system interconnection and the availability of "hacker tool" libraries make their task easier.
>
> While the possibility of chemical, biological, and even nuclear weapons falling into the hands of terrorists adds a new and frightening dimension to physical attacks, such weapons are difficult to acquire. In contrast, the resources necessary to conduct a cyber attack have shifted in the past few years from the arcane to the commonplace. A personal computer and a telephone connection to an Internet Service Provider anywhere in the world are enough to cause harm. . . .
>
> The Commission has not discovered an immediate threat sufficient to warrant a fear of imminent national crisis. However, we are convinced that our vulnerabilities are increasing steadily, that the means to exploit those weaknesses are readily available and that the costs associated with an effective attack continue to drop. What is more, the investments required to improve the situation—now still relatively modest—will rise if we procrastinate.

[4]President's Commission on Critical Infrastructure Protection, *Critical Foundations: Protecting America's Infrastructures*, October 1997; available at www.fas.org/sgp/library/pccip.pdf.

Two years later, the National Research Council released another report, *Trust in Cyberspace*,[5] which argued that it was necessary to

> move the focus of the [cybersecurity] discussion forward from matters of policy and procedure and from vulnerabilities and their consequences toward questions about the richer set of options that only new science and technology can provide.

Trust in Cyberspace reiterated the emphasis on the security challenges posed by interconnected information technologies and networked information systems. It suggested that the research agenda would be driven in large part by the (then) newly found appreciation of the vulnerability of the nation's critical infrastructure to new forms of attack.

In 2003, the Bush administration released *The National Strategy to Secure Cyberspace*.[6] This report called attention to a threat of "organized cyber attacks capable of causing debilitating disruption to our Nation's critical infrastructures, economy, or national security." It further pointed out that "the attack tools and methodologies are becoming widely available, and the technical capability and sophistication of users bent on causing havoc or disruption is improving." As for the consequences of cyber vulnerabilities, it noted:

> In peacetime America's enemies may conduct espionage on our Government, university research centers, and private companies. They may also seek to prepare for cyber strikes during a confrontation by mapping U.S. information systems, identifying key targets, and lacing our infrastructure with back doors and other means of access. In wartime or crisis, adversaries may seek to intimidate the Nation's political leaders by attacking critical infrastructures and key economic functions or eroding public confidence in information systems. . . .
>
> Cyber attacks on United States information networks can have serious consequences such as disrupting critical operations, causing loss of revenue and intellectual property, or loss of life. Countering such attacks requires the development of robust capabilities where they do not exist today if we are to reduce vulnerabilities and deter those with the capabilities and intent to harm our critical infrastructures.

In 2005, the President's Information Technology Advisory Committee (PITAC) released *Cyber Security: A Crisis of Prioritization*.[7] This report noted:

---

[5]National Research Council, *Trust in Cyberspace*, National Academy Press, Washington, D.C., 1999.

[6]See http://www.whitehouse.gov/pcipb/.

[7]President's Information Technology Advisory Committee, *Cyber Security: A Crisis of Prioritization*, National Coordination Office for Information Technology Research and De-

> The Nation's information technology (IT) infrastructure, still evolving from U.S. technological innovations such as the personal computer and the Internet, today is a vast fabric of computers—from supercomputers to handheld devices—and interconnected networks enabling high-speed communications, information access, advanced computation, transactions, and automated processes relied upon in every sector of society. Because much of this infrastructure connects one way or another to the Internet, it embodies the Internet's original structural attributes of openness, inventiveness, and the assumption of good will. . . .
>
> These signature attributes have made the U.S. IT infrastructure an irresistible target for vandals and criminals worldwide. The PITAC believes that terrorists will inevitably follow suit, taking advantage of vulnerabilities including some that the Nation has not yet clearly recognized or addressed. The computers that manage critical U.S. facilities, infrastructures, and essential services can be targeted to set off system-wide failures, and these computers frequently are accessible from virtually anywhere in the world via the Internet.

The reports mentioned above are only some of those issued in the past 15 years regarding the nation's cybersecurity posture. Taken as a whole and as described in Appendix B, these reports point to an imminent and growing cybersecurity threat. Why then is there not a national sense of urgency about cybersecurity? Why has action not been taken to close the gap between our cybersecurity posture and the cyberthreat?

The notion that no action to promote cybersecurity has been taken in the past 15 years is somewhat unfair. In recent years, most major information technology (IT) vendors have undertaken significant efforts to improve the security of their products in response to end-user concerns over security. Many of today's products are by many measures more secure than those that preceded these efforts. In addition, the sentinel events of September 11, 2001, spurred public concerns about security, and some of that concern has spilled over into the cybersecurity domain.

Nevertheless, these changes in the environment, important though they are, do not change the fact that the action taken in the last 15 years is nowhere near what is necessary to achieve a robust cybersecurity posture. Consider then the consequences of inadequate action, and imagine that sometime in the future the nation experiences what some have called a "digital Pearl Harbor." In the subsequent investigative frenzy, the nation asks, "How could this have happened?"

A digital Pearl Harbor would—by definition—be a surprise. But it would also be a surprise that could have been anticipated. In 2004,

velopment, Washington D.C., February 2005; available at www.nitrd.gov/pitac/reports/20050301_cybersecurity/cybersecurity.pdf. Hereafter, "the PITAC report."

Bazerman and Watkins described a predictable surprise as an event that takes an individual or a group by surprise, despite prior awareness of all of the information necessary to anticipate the events and their consequences.[8] In particular, they identify several characteristics of predictable surprises:

- Leaders know that a problem exists and that the problem will not solve itself.
- The problem worsens over time.
- Solutions for the problem incur significant costs in the present, while the benefits of taking action—although likely larger than the solution costs—are both uncertain and realized in the future.
- Some parties whose efforts are needed to help solve the problem benefit from inaction.

To explain inaction, Bazerman and Watkins posit causes at the individual, organizational, and political levels. Individual causes of inaction are rooted in cognitive biases that lead individuals to discount the future more heavily than is appropriate and thus to undervalue risks. They also prefer to run the risk of low-probability high-consequence events in the future rather than to incur certain but smaller losses in the present. Finally, they find it difficult to take action when they have not personally experienced a problem and cannot imagine what it would mean in practical terms.

Organizations fail to act because they do not have processes in place to scan the environment for all sources of threat, to integrate those sources of information, to respond in a timely manner, or to incorporate lessons learned from those responses into their institutional memory. They also have structural issues that inhibit a coordinated response to the problem and/or have incentives in place that encourage people to behave in a way that damages the ability to achieve organizational goals.

Politically, leaders are reluctant to make decisions that impose certain costs now for benefits that will almost certainly not be realized within their terms of office.

Most of these conditions can be seen in examining the current environment for cybersecurity. Policy makers have been warned repeatedly that there is a cybersecurity problem and that without action the problem will not solve itself. All signs point to a worsening of the cybersecurity problem, and the only argument today is how fast it is getting worse. It is

---

[8] Max H. Bazerman and Michael D. Watkins, *Predictable Surprises: The Disasters You Should Have Seen Coming, and How to Prevent Them*, Harvard Business School Press, Cambridge, Mass., 2004.

simply not credible to assert that the problem is getting better. Putting into place adequate cybersecurity measures, both technical and procedural, will cost in terms of reduced productivity, increased expense, and greater inconvenience, although the costs of such measures are dwarfed by the potential future benefits of avoiding certain kinds of cyber-disasters. And, both vendors and users of information technology benefit from inaction, because they can avoid the costs of changing existing practices.

From the committee's perspective, the lack of adequate action in the cybersecurity space can be largely explained by three complementary reasons:

- *The various cybersecurity reports issued to date have not provided the sufficiently compelling information needed to make the case for dramatic and urgent action.* If so, a sufficiently ominous threat cloud will inspire decision makers to take action. But it is well known that detailed and specific information is usually more convincing than information couched in very general terms—unfortunately, detailed and specific information in the open literature about the scope and nature of the cyberthreat is lacking.
- *Even with the relevant information in hand, decision makers discount future possibilities so much that they do not see the need for present-day action.* In this view, nothing short of a highly visible and perhaps ongoing cyber-disaster will motivate actions. Decision makers weigh the immediate costs of putting into place adequate cybersecurity measures, both technical and procedural, against the potential future benefits (actually, avoided costs) of preventing cyber-disaster in the future—and systematically discount the latter as uncertain and vague.
- *The costs of inaction are not borne by the relevant decision makers.* The bulk of the nation's critical infrastructure is owned and operated by private-sector companies. To the extent that these companies respond to security issues, they generally do so as one of the risks of doing business. But they do much less to respond to the threat of low-probability, high-impact (i.e., catastrophic) threats, even though all of society at large has a significant stake in their actions.[9]

[9]For example, under today's practices, a party that makes investments to prevent its own facilities from being used as part of a DDOS attack will reap few benefits from such investments, because such an attack is most likely to be launched against a different party but will consume few resources locally. But Internet-using society would clearly benefit if many firms made such investments. Making parties liable for not securing their facilities against being illicitly used as part of a DDOS attack (today there is zero liability) would change the incentives for making such investments.

As for the impact of research on the nation's cybersecurity posture, it is not reasonable to expect that research alone will make any substantial difference. Indeed, there is a very large gap between a successful "in principle" result or demonstration and its widespread deployment and use. Closing this gap is the focus of Category 3 research, described in Chapter 6. But, as this report argues, many other factors must be aligned in addition if research is to have a significant impact. Specifically, IT vendors must be willing to regard security as a product attribute that is coequal with performance and cost, IT researchers must be willing to value cybersecurity research as much as they value research into high-performance or cost-effective computing, and IT purchasers must be willing to incur present-day costs in order to obtain future benefits.

10.2 PRIORITIES FOR ACTION

Despite the analysis of Section 10.1, the committee believes that meaningful action is possible to improve the cybersecurity posture of the nation. In certain contexts, it may be that the security risks inherent in using IT may outweigh the benefits of doing so, even after everything possible has been done to improve security in those contexts. (It is, of course, a topic worthy of research in itself to develop a decision-making framework that would help to identify such contexts.)

Nevertheless, for the majority of contexts in which IT is today or will in the future be a necessary enabler, a set of circumstances does give the committee hope that progress is indeed possible. Especially outside the intelligence community, it is increasingly common to find security practitioners and researchers who realize that risk management, rather than risk avoidance, is the name of the game. This realization makes it possible for managers to take pragmatics steps forward rather than waiting for the silver bullet to be found. A more powerful technological base that can support approaches and techniques previously deemed unfeasible for technological reasons is now also available. Most importantly, there is a growing awareness among end users that cybersecurity should be a more serious consideration in their acquisition decisions than it was in the past. This is likely to increase the demand for greater cybersecurity functionality.

The committee has identified the five action items below as warranting the highest priority. Policy makers should carry out the following actions:

- Create a sense of urgency about the cybersecurity problem commensurate with the risks.
- Commensurate with a rapidly growing cybersecurity threat, sup-

port a robust and sustained research agenda at levels which ensure that a large fraction of good ideas for cybersecurity research can be explored.
- Establish a mechanism for continuing follow-up on a research agenda.
- Support infrastructure for cybersecurity research.
- Sustain and grow the human resource base.

10.2.1 Item 1: Create a sense of urgency about the cybersecurity problem commensurate with the risks.

Some lessons can be learned from the nation's response to the Y2K (year 2000) problem. In the early years of information technology, a programming practice arose of recording dates in a six-digit format (mm/dd/yy). If programs embedding this practice were operative at the turn of the century, the result could have been that the year "2000" (recorded as "00") would be interpreted as the year "1900," thus causing many date comparisons to be made incorrectly. Since this programming practice was widespread, and in particular was likely used in many critical systems, concerns arose that many of these critical systems would fail if this problem was not fixed.

Both the extent and the severity of the problem were largely unknown, but the timing of the problem was absolutely clear and unambiguous. In real-time date-dependent systems that used two-digit years, the problem would manifest itself on January 1, 2000, at midnight. In other systems, the problem would manifest itself upon first system startup after January 1, 2000. Consequently, many efforts were made to focus attention on the issue and to effect repairs. These efforts included legislation, public education and awareness, the replacement of old information technology, the development of backup and contingency plans, and insurance policies covering problems resulting from the Y2K problem.

In the late 1990s, the Y2K problem was seen as an urgent one. Moreover, in many ways, the Y2K problem can be regarded as a kind of cybersecurity problem. Plausible arguments existed suggesting that Y2K problems were potentially widespread and serious. Limited testing demonstrated, in a number of systems, the actual existence of Y2K problems. Nevertheless, the actual nature and scope of problems caused by two-digit years were unknown. Y2K problems in one system often had ramifications for the proper operation of other systems to which it was connected. Business considerations, including continuity of operations, insurance, and liability, played important roles in motivating corrective actions.

The national response to the Y2K problem demonstrates that it is possible to take action on a large scale in response to an impending emergency. However, in one very fundamental aspect, the Y2K problem and today's cybersecurity problem are different. The Y2K problem was certain to arrive on a specific date known to everyone (and the nature of the problem was well understood), whereas the arrival date and specific nature of a "digital Pearl Harbor" are highly uncertain. How, then, can a sense of urgency be created in the absence of a natural forcing deadline?

From the committee's perspective, two actions are necessary, both motivated by the discussion of Section 10.1. The first action relates to making more information available. Because it is possible, though in the committee's view unlikely, that the information available to decision makers is inadequate, the compilation of a truly authoritative threat assessment could have salutary benefits. But to be truly authoritative, this assessment would have to draw on the best industry and intelligence data available. Indeed, some of the necessary information is not available today in any meaningful sense, since many victims of cybersecurity incidents are reluctant to discuss these incidents for public attribution, and other data are classified.

Arrangements must thus be made to incentivize these parties to release the information, as discussed in Sections 6.4.4.2 and 6.4.4.5. At the same time, actions must be taken to relieve the concerns of victimized parties about the harm that might result from the release of such information.

The notion of developing measures to increase transparency and provide relevant information so that consumers can make informed decisions is not new, and some steps in this direction have been taken. For example, within the National Security Telecommunications Advisory Committee (NSTAC) context, incident information (e.g., outages, causes) is shared in the relevant community subject to a confidentiality requirement. The InfraGard program is a Federal Bureau of Investigation (FBI)-sponsored effort that brings together businesses, academic institutions, state and local law enforcement agencies, and other participants to share information and intelligence preventing hostile acts in cyberspace. The Department of Homeland Security (DHS) has established "Procedures for Handling Protected Critical Infrastructure Information" that govern the receipt, validation, handling, storage, marking, and use of critical infrastructure information voluntarily submitted to the DHS.[10] Nevertheless, such sharing proceeds somewhat tentatively. Firms have an incentive to free-ride on the information security expenditures of the other members of sharing organizations ("the tragedy of the commons"), and additional incentives need to be developed for firms to fully and truthfully reveal

[10]*Federal Register*, 71(170), September 1, 2006. See http://edocket.access.gpo.gov/2006/06-7378.htm.

security information so that the social welfare benefits of sharing can be accrued.[11] A second reason for a reluctance to share information is that, for a given incident, a fix for the problems that caused it may not be immediately available. Sometimes, even the mere statement that there is a vulnerability in a particular system is enough to prompt special attention to that system from would-be attackers—attention that might result in the discovery of that vulnerability.

A first step toward an authoritative threat assessment could have been the National Computer Security Survey sponsored by the Bureau of Justice Statistics at the Department of Justice (DOJ) and the National Cyber Security Division (NCSD) at the DHS. Conducted by the RAND Corporation, this study was scheduled to be published in 2007, and would have had the advantage of being able to provide legal protection for the information provided by survey respondents. Statutory provisions protect the confidentiality of the information provided, prohibit the sharing of data with other agencies, provide exemptions from the Freedom of Information Act (FOIA), and ensure immunity from legal processes.[12] However, to be truly valuable for understanding the evolving threat and trends, the survey would have to be conducted on a regular and ongoing basis. Unfortunately, this task was terminated before its completion by the DOJ and the NCSD.

Section 10.1 also indicated the possibility—indeed, in the committee's view, the great likelihood—that adequate information on the cybersecurity threat is available today. Thus, the second action calls for changing the decision-making calculus that excessively focuses vendor and end-user attention on the short-term costs of improving their cybersecurity postures.

Calls to change the decision-making calculus are often regarded suspiciously by those who would be affected by such changes—not surprisingly, since their bases for business planning would, by definition, be changed. As noted in Sections 6.4.4.5 and 6.4.4.6, there is enormous political resistance to notions of change that entail direct regulation or liability, resistance that in some cases is well grounded in uncertainty about ultimate effects. This is not to say that it is impossible to take meaningful policy action—only that such action may have to be more indirect and less obvious than some might prefer. Such policy actions might include, for example, encouraging accounting firms and insurance firms to take into

---

[11]See Lawrence A. Gordon, Martin P. Loeb, and William Lucyshyn, "Sharing Information on Computer Systems Security: An Economic Analysis," *Journal of Accounting and Public Policy*, 22(6): 461-485, 2003.

[12]Department of Justice, Bureau of Justice Statistics, National Computer Security Survey Web page, http://www.ojp.usdoj.gov/bjs/survey/ncss/ncss.htm. The law, noted on this Web page, is P.L. 107-347, Title V and 44 U.S.C. Paragraph 3501.

account the cybersecurity postures of their customers when providing audits or setting insurance rates.

The committee recognizes that policy actions are, almost by definition, less compelling for focusing attention and stimulating action than are deadlines imposed by nature. But in the committee's view, even weaker policy actions can stimulate some action, and every little bit helps.

Finally, although the committee did not take a position regarding the desirability of regulation or liability as a way to improve cybersecurity, it did agree that regulation and liability are tools of last resort to promote this end. In other words, the nation should not turn to regulation or liability as an approach to improving cybersecurity until decision makers conclude that other approaches have proven insufficiently effective. In the meantime, while awaiting that judgment, it behooves the research community to consider how the tools of regulation and liability might sensibly be applied should those tools of last resort ultimately prove necessary. The alternative to such interim research is an ill-considered and unresearched regime of liability and regulation that might well be imposed hastily in the wake of a crisis, to the detriment of all. That is, the nation should not turn to regulation or liability as an approach to improving cybersecurity until decision makers conclude that other approaches have proven insufficiently effective.

10.2.2 Item 2: Commensurate with a rapidly growing cybersecurity threat, support a robust and sustained research agenda at levels which ensure that a large fraction of good ideas for cybersecurity research can be explored.

Given the need for breadth and diversity in the research portfolio within the areas of focus described in Part II of this report, the committee believes that the nation is ill served by a funding model that seeks to channel resources to a small number of specific research topics. Instead, it makes more sense to conceptualize the overall research portfolio as one that focuses resources on sustaining the intellectually broad and diverse community capable of (1) generating ideas across a wide waterfront (as one might expect would be needed for a diverse threat) and (2) producing the cybersecurity expertise needed across all points in the IT life cycle, including design, development, implementation, testing, operations, maintenance, upgrading, and retirement. Note further that breadth in the research agenda does not mean that every topic should be funded equally. Rather, it is the merits and rationales of individual proposals, combined with a cognizance of the threat environment and advances in technology, that should determine funding allocations.

With this model, the scale of the necessary funding is set by the amounts needed to sustain this community at appropriate levels and to ensure that a large fraction of good ideas for cybersecurity research can be explored. In this context, a good idea is one that is determined to be good through some kind of evaluative process. In peer-reviewed communities, peer review determines if an idea is "good." In agencies such as the Defense Advanced Research Projects Agency (DARPA), program managers exert much influence in deciding if an idea is good.

Several federal agencies have an important role to play in the cybersecurity research agenda. For two reasons, the committee does not make specific recommendations for which agencies should pursue which specific research topics. First, many of the topics described might well fit into the agendas of multiple agencies. Second and at the same time, the different agencies have different needs—especially mission-oriented agencies. However, the committee does urge that federal decision makers take into account historical strengths and missions of the various departments.

For example, the Department of Energy (DOE) is a logical place to support cybersecurity research efforts that relate to Supervisory Control and Data Acquisition (SCADA) systems, as such systems are an essential element of the electric grid, for which the DOE has much oversight responsibility. The National Institute of Standards and Technology (NIST) and National Security Agency (NSA) have historically undertaken substantial research efforts in cryptography and other security technologies and have developed strengths that should be leveraged in future research to the extent that it can be done on an unclassified basis. With historical efforts in metrology, NIST is also a natural place to focus research on cybersecurity metrics. DARPA has historically conducted substantial research on system-building, and all of the Department of Defense (DOD)—as well as much of the nondefense government portfolio and civilian work—would benefit substantially from advances in secure system building, as discussed in Appendix B (Section B.6.4.2). And, given its investigator-driven focus, the National Science Foundation (NSF) is the obvious agency to develop and sustain a broad national research portfolio.

Different agencies also support different kinds of research communities. For example, NSF tends toward smaller grants for individuals or small teams, with fewer and less specific deliverables. Historically, DARPA has built communities and encouraged large grants to address very hard problems, although recent management changes and policies have begun to change such practices. Diversity in the character of research communities is also to be encouraged, because it is hard to predict what styles of research will result in progress.

As for the magnitude of the budget needed to sustain the committee's principle, the committee notes that for the foreseeable future the cybersecurity threat will only grow. First, the threat is likely to grow at a rate faster than the present federal cybersecurity research program will enable us to respond, and the consequences of failing to provide an adequate response could be quite damaging to the nation.

Second, the PITAC report implicitly enunciated a principle for funding cybersecurity research that the committee finds eminently sensible: most good research ideas should be supported and that proposals based on such ideas should be supported at or near the levels requested.[13]

For these reasons, the committee concludes in general terms that both the scope and scale of federally funded cybersecurity research are seriously inadequate. To execute fully the broad strategy articulated in this report, a substantial increase in federal budgetary resources devoted to cybersecurity research will be needed.

To provide some characteristic orders of magnitude for this discussion, the committee notes that the scale of today's cybersecurity research budgets is probably somewhat larger than $160 million annually. This estimate is based on the PITAC estimate for federally supported cybersecurity research in fiscal year (FY) 2004, both classified and unclassified, of about $160 million. Although the committee was unable to find data to support a similar estimate for FY 2005 or FY 2006, it also knows of no significant change in the budget, a point suggesting that "a little more than the FY 2004" is not an unreasonable guess. (The breakdown of the total $160 million between classified and unclassified research is unknown, although it is obvious that amounts supporting classified research are not accessible to the broad cybersecurity research community at large.)

As a point of comparison, the committee notes a Gartner Group estimate that financial losses stemming from phishing attacks alone exceeded

[13]Specifically, the PITAC report argued for a quadrupling of the NSF budget allocated to the Cyber Trust program ($31 million to $120 million), under which most of the nation's government-supported unclassified basic cybersecurity research is performed. At the time, the PITAC argument was based on a success rate for the Cyber Trust program that was about a factor of three lower than that for NSF as a whole (8 percent versus 25 percent) and the funding of most of the proposals supported at a level significantly below the levels requested. According to Karl Levitt, program manager for the Cyber Trust program, the success rate in 2006 for the Cyber Trust program was about 12 percent—and was accomplished by eliminating for that year the funding for center-level grants and by significantly reducing the funding awarded compared with that requested. The ratio of total amounts awarded to total amounts requested was less than 8 percent, a figure comparable to that of fiscal year 2004. In 2007, the success rate was increased to 20 percent, mostly because the Cyber Trust budget was increased to $34 million, the level that it was at in 2004-2006, but also because of not making center-level awards (Karl Levitt, NSF, personal communications to the committee, November 27, 2006, and June 21, 2007).

$2.8 billion in 2006.[14] The reason that such losses are not more visible is that they are usually absorbed as a "tax" on purchases (that vendors pass along to customers), and they are distributed as small losses and productivity losses over the population. Thus, no one party suffers a huge loss (generally) that shows up in reports. But the overall expense is large.

Another point of comparison is the 2005 FBI Computer Crime Survey, which estimated the cost of "computer security incidents" in the 12-month period from mid-2004 to mid-2005 at $67.2 billion to U.S. organizations.[15] (The raw data for this survey were provided by 2,066 organizations on a self-reported basis, and the $67.2 billion aggregate figure is extrapolated.) It is hard to know how seriously to take this specific figure, which amounts to 0.5 percent of the U.S. gross national product; although statistics on the amount lost to cybercrime are generally of dubious reliability, there is no doubt that aggregate losses are considerable.

The committee does not mean to imply that the dollars that could be saved through better cybersecurity should somehow subsidize a research effort. Yet it is not unreasonable to suggest that the magnitude of such losses should have some bearing on the efforts devoted to cybersecurity research.

Fiscal reality today dictates that discretionary budgets for the foreseeable future will be very tight, if not declining in absolute terms. In the current budget environment, is it "realistic" to recommend budget increases in a program or in a national portfolio?

It is a truism that growth in the budget of any given program comes from one of two sources—an explicit decision to support it with additional appropriations without a corresponding offset somewhere else in the budget, or an explicit decision to increase the program's budget while at the same time decreasing the budget of one or more other programs. But it is also true that no matter how tight budgets are in any given year, some programs grow, others shrink, and still others start anew while others terminate. Thus, growth in existing programs or new program starts reflect political will and a judgment regarding the benefits of such programs relative to other programs.

The committee also makes three caveats about additional funding. First, policy makers should regard cybersecurity research as a continuing and ongoing need that will extend for the foreseeable future. As long as information technology continues to enable economic innovation and to

[14]Gartner Press Release, "Gartner Says Number of Phishing E-Mails Sent to U.S. Adults Nearly Doubles in Just Two Years," November 9, 2006; available at http://www.gartner.com/it/page.jsp?id=498245.

[15]See www.digitalriver.com/v2.0-img/operations/naievigi/site/media/pdf/FBIccs2005.pdf.

be a pillar of prosperity, cybersecurity cannot be seen as a discrete problem to be solved once and for all, but rather as a class of problems that will continuously evolve as new technology and new threats continue to present new issues. As a result, a funding model calling for a one-time increase in cybersecurity research, even a substantial one over multiple fiscal years, is less relevant than one that continues to enable a large fraction of good ideas to be supported in the long term.

Second, additional funding should really be "new money" rather than "relabeled" money or money taken from other computer science research. In the words of the PITAC report, for instance:

> [T]he increase in the NSF CISE budget for civilian cyber security fundamental research [should] not be funded at the expense of other parts of the CISE Directorate. . . . Significant shifts of funding within CISE towards cyber security would exacerbate the strain on these other programs without addressing the existing disparity between CISE and other directorates. Moreover, much work in "other" CISE areas is beneficial to cybersecurity and thus reductions in those other areas would be counterproductive. [For example,] theoretical computer science underpins much encryption research, both in identifying weaknesses and in advancing the state of the art. Algorithms research helps ensure that protocols designed for security can be efficiently implemented. Programming language research can help address security at a higher level of abstraction and can add functionalities such as security assurances to software. Software engineering can help eliminate software bugs that are often exploited as security holes. And new computer architectures might enforce protection faster and at finer granularity.

Nor should cybersecurity research remain in the computer science domain alone. Additional funding might well be used to support the pursuit of cybersecurity considerations in other closely related research endeavors, such as those related to creating high-assurance systems and the engineering of secure systems across entire system life cycles (see the discussion in Section 4.3).

Third, funding should be increased only at a rate consistent with the pace at which qualified researches are trained or move into the field from other branches of computer science. "Boom-and-bust" cycles often do harm to a field, especially when they lead to unwise expenditures.

10.2.3 Item 3: Establish a mechanism for continuing follow-up on a research agenda.

Management of the complete cybersecurity research portfolio across the federal government requires that government decision makers have a reasonably fine-grained understanding of the scope and nature of that portfolio. However, to the committee's knowledge, a picture that is both adequately detailed and sufficiently comprehensive does not exist today. To take just one example, the President's Information Technology Advisory Committee was able to determine the DARPA investment in cybersecurity research and development (R&D) for FY 2004 only within a factor of about four (that is, PITAC determined that figure to be between $40 million and $150 million).

The National Coordination Office (NCO) for Networking and Information Technology Research and Development (NITRD), which supports the planning, budget, and assessment activities of the federal government's NITRD program, tracks the unclassified portion of the cybersecurity research and development portfolio. This portfolio, which accounts for about $175 million in the administration's FY 2007 request, is focused on research and advanced development to prevent, resist, detect, respond to, and/or recover from actions that compromise or threaten to compromise the availability, integrity, or confidentiality of computer-based systems. The NCO supports the Interagency Working Group on Cyber Security and Information Assurance (CSIA IWG), which coordinates programs, budgets, and policy recommendations for CSIA R&D.[16]

The NITRD coordination process is an important first step toward creating the picture that is needed for adequate management of the federal cybersecurity research portfolio. Nevertheless, it could be strengthened in a number of important ways:

- *Distinguishing clearly between research and development.* As presented, the NITRD figures aggregate research and development. Because development efforts are most often focused on short-term deliverables, aggregating research and development does not provide a clear indication of effort devoted to longer-term goals.
- *Including classified research and development in the big picture.* The mere fact that research and development may be conducted under

[16]The CSIA IWG reports to the NITRD Subcommittee of the National Science and Technology Council (NSTC) Committee on Technology. The following NITRD agencies belong to the CSIA IWG: the Department of Defense (Defense Advanced Research Projects Agency, Office of the Secretary of Defense, DOD service research organizations, and the National Security Agency), the Environmental Projection Agency, the National Aeronautics and Space Administration, the National Institute of Standards and Technology, the National Institutes of Health, and the National Science Foundation. The following agencies participate in CSIA IWG activities: the Central Intelligence Agency, the Department of Energy (Lawrence Livermore National Laboratory), the Department of Homeland Security, the Department of Justice, the Department of State, the Department of Transportation (including the Federal Aviation Administration), the Department of the Treasury, the Disruptive Technology Office, the Federal Bureau of Investigation, and the Technical Support Working Group.

classified auspices does not mean that such efforts produce no knowledge of value outside the military, diplomatic, and intelligence communities. It may mean, for example, that researchers and developers may have been asked to conduct their work in the context of specific problems whose details are classified. Thus, classified work is at least potentially relevant to the nation's broad efforts to secure cyberspace. (Note that this notion does not suggest that the detailed spending figures for classified cybersecurity research should be made public or broadly available—but policy makers in both the executive and legislative branches [e.g., in the Office of Management and Budget and in the relevant congressional committees] should have access to the "big picture" of cybersecurity research.)

- *Disaggregating (and publishing) government-wide budget figures associated with different areas of focus.* Individual agencies will often group the contracts and grants they support into broader categories (Box 10.1 presents an exemplary approach). But the major weakness in these agency efforts is that they are not comparable across agencies. That is, any relationship between the categories of one agency and another agency is due mostly to chance. Establishing some common categories (and providing multiple crosswalks among them) that would be relevant across agencies would provide a more informative picture.
- *Tracking budget figures from year to year.* The picture of federal cybersecurity research efforts evolves over time. Thus, efforts must be made to provide comparable analyses from year to year if the time evolution is to be understood.

Note also that the comparability of budget figures in different categories across agencies depends largely on a small number of analysts who are knowledgeable about the subject matter doing the mapping from individual awards to budget categories for all of the agencies involved. The small number is essential, because otherwise an agency is likely to task an individual analyst to do this work for that agency, and this person will use different criteria and judgments for mapping than those that the analyst for a different agency would use. For similar reasons, it is important for the same analysts to do the categorizations from year to year, since doing so will enhance the year-to-year comparability of the resulting figures.

Greater transparency into federal support for cybersecurity research would enable decision makers at all levels of responsibility, and in particular the program managers with direct responsibility for the execution of programmatic responsibilities regarding research, to understand the

BOX 10.1
A Model Categorization for Understanding Budgets

The National Science Foundation (NSF) overview of the fiscal year 2004 awards for the Cyber Trust program and related awards included several substantive categorizations for the same awards, including the following:

- *Topic* (security of next-generation operating systems and networking; forensic and law enforcement foundations; human-computer interface for security functions; cross-disciplinary approaches; theoretical foundations and mechanisms for privacy, security, trust; composable systems and policies; presenting security concepts to the average user; improved ability to certify system security properties; improved ability to analyze security designs and to build systems correctly; more effective system monitoring, anomaly detection, attack recognition and defense; and integrating hardware and software for security).
- *Security life-cycle phase* (understanding what to build; building things right; preventing attacks; detecting/understanding attacks; surviving attacks; system recovery/reconstitution; and forensics/dealing with perpetrators).
- *Security disciplines* (operating system, filesystem, storage security; net security; application/database/Web security; cryptography and applied cryptography; security/privacy/trust modeling and specification; secure system architecture; secure system development; security testing/evaluation; and forensics).

The NSF provided multiple categorizations, noting on the Web site (see the source in this box) that "most research projects have several dimensions, such as the expected time to yield results, where the project lies on scales ranging from empirical to theoretical work, from foundational to applied, and across domains and disciplines of study. Any attempt to group projects into categories will consequently succeed better for some than for others." Accordingly, NSF presents multiple categorizations that constitute a framework for relating projects to each other and that provide an overall picture of the program.

SOURCE: See http://www.nsf.gov/cise/funding/cyber_awards.jsp#other.

big picture of federal activities in this area. One benefit is that program managers would be able to identify more easily excessive redundancy in research.[17] A second benefit is that transparency would facilitate greater

[17]The committee notes that some degree of redundancy in research is not necessarily inappropriate, as it can mean working on different approaches to similar problems. It is true that centralized priority-setting approaches generally seek to eliminate redundancy, but more often than not target all redundancy, whether useful or not. By contrast, conversations between program managers—who are closer to the research actually being performed and thus more knowledgable about the nuances of the research they support—are more likely to be able to identify excessive redundancies.

scrutiny of research projects by the cybersecurity community at large—scrutiny that might help to terminate projects that were clearly going down the wrong path.[18]

10.2.4 Item 4: Support infrastructure for cybersecurity research.

Making progress on any cybersecurity research agenda requires substantial attention to infrastructural issues. In this context, a cybersecurity research infrastructure refers to the collection of open testbeds, tools, data sets, and other things that enable research to progress and allow research results to be implemented in actual IT products and services. Without an adequate infrastructure, there is little hope for realizing the full potential of any research agenda.

The reason is that cybersecurity is a systems and an operational issue. For example, realistic testbeds are needed for demonstrating or validating the operational utility of new cybersecurity technologies. Realistic data sets of sufficient size, realism, and currency are similarly needed for security analysts to understand and characterize the various attacks against which they are defending (while keeping in mind that future attacks may not resemble past attacks).

An infrastructure for cybersecurity research provides invaluable assistance in new ideas at a reasonable scale, in the wild, with real users; insight into appropriate paths to the "tipping point" (the point of acceptance of an innovation after which the entire community feels that it no longer makes sense to refuse to accept it); and ways of exploring the achievement of fundamental change through incremental strategies that do not require all Internet users and all their vendors to change before benefit is realized.

Consider, for example, the need for cybersecurity testbeds. Because a large part of the cybersecurity problem involves the rapid propagation of viruses and worms throughout the Internet, a realistic testbed for testing defenses is necessary. In this context, "realistic" means one of sufficient size and appropriate configuration to be in some sense representative of the Internet as a whole. A testbed enables defenses against viruses and

---

[18]The committee is fully aware of tensions between Category 6 research (speculative research that may be regarded as "out-of-the-box" by the mainstream research community) and research that ought to be terminated. Indeed, supporters of the latter will almost always claim that their research is in the former category. There is no definitive response to such a claim, but it helps to observe that Category 6 research is not intended to be the funding opportunity of last resort for every bad idea in the world, that program managers will need to make informed and reasoned judgments about research to be funded under the Category 6 rubric, and that the amount of funding devoted to Category 6 research is supposed to be a relatively small fraction of overall budgets in any case.

worms to be tested under relatively controlled conditions. Propagation speed, destructiveness, and virulence of an attack can be evaluated in a safe environment (i.e., without consequences for the larger Internet). Most importantly, a testbed can be instrumented quite thoroughly so that the detailed mechanisms of an attack can be better understood. (An example of a cybersecurity testbed is the Cyber Defense Technology Experimental Research [DETER], a joint project of the University of California at Berkeley; the University of Southern California's Information Sciences Institute [USC-ISI]; and McAfee Associates. The DETER network was launched in late 2003 under a 3-year grant from the NSF in cooperation with the DHS.)

Cybersecurity testbeds also include research platforms. A good example of a research platform serving as a testbed is Multics, which served as the focal point for the exploration and demonstration of new ideas over several generations of researchers.[19]

A cybersecurity research infrastructure also includes large-scale data sets that allow researchers to accurately represent certain kinds of attacks flowing across the Internet. In the absence of such large-scale data sets, which ought to be open to any legitimate cybersecurity researcher, the efficacy of a solution may be based on nonrepresentative situations or attacks. An example of an effort to make such data available to the cybersecurity research community is the DHS-sponsored Protected Repository for the Defense of Infrastructure against Cyber Threats (PREDICT) initiative. PREDICT provides cybersecurity developers and evaluators with high-quality, regularly updated, network operations data sources that provide timely and detailed insight into cyberattack phenomena occurring across the Internet, and in some cases will reveal the effects of these attacks on networks that are owned or managed by the data producers.

10.2.5 Item 5: Sustain and grow the human resource base.

Human capital is a particularly important concern for cybersecurity, since people are the originators of new ideas. Recommendation 2 of the PITAC report *Cyber Security: A Crisis of Prioritization* dealt directly with this point. That recommendation stated:

> [T]he Federal government should intensify its efforts to promote recruitment and retention of cyber security researchers and students at research universities, with a goal of at least doubling the size of the

---

[19]Multics (Multiplexed Information and Computing Service) was a mainframe time-sharing operating system begun in 1965 and used until 2000. More information on Multics can be found at http://www.multicians.org/.

> civilian cyber security fundamental research community by the end of the decade. In particular, the Federal government should increase and stabilize the funding for fundamental research in civilian cyber security, and should support programs that enable researchers to move into cyber security research from other fields.

The reasoning underlying this recommendation was, and remains, sound. Today, cybersecurity research is not a broad-based effort that engages a substantial fraction of the computer science research community. For example, only a small fraction of the nation's graduating doctoral students in IT specialize in cybersecurity, only a few professors conduct research in cybersecurity, and only a few universities support research programs in these fields.

The committee aligns itself with the spirit of this recommendation, if not necessarily its specific scale. In times of crisis, calls for new technology usually invoke the memory of the Manhattan Project to build the atomic bomb. But the need to build human capital for the cybersecurity field suggests that it is not the Manhattan Project that provides the right metaphor, but rather the national response to *Sputnik*. The Manhattan Project resulted in the deployment of hardware—whereas a primary result of *Sputnik* was the National Defense Education Act, which focused attention on and generated substantially greater support for increasing science and mathematics education. Analogously, the committee believes that increasing human capital for cybersecurity ought to be an essential part of the national response to the cybersecurity problem.

Consider, then, two key dimensions of the human capital issue in cybersecurity research addressed in the following subsections.

10.2.5.1 Enlarging the Pool of Researchers

Universities are the primary source of human capital—and graduate study is essentially the only source for the researchers of the future. For a field in which new ideas are always needed (and in light of the increasing sophistication of cybersecurity threats), growing the supply of such researchers and exploiting the power of many minds at work are critical for success and essential if we are to have even a remote hope of staying ahead of the curve, or even keeping pace with it.

There are only two strategies for increasing the number of researchers—training new entrants to specialize in the field (that is, graduate students) and enticing already-established researchers in other fields to join the field. Either strategy depends on demonstrating to these prospective new researchers that—in addition to important and interesting intellectual problems—there is a future to working in the field, a point suggesting the importance of research support for the field that is both adequate and stable. Regarding adequacy—increasing the number of researchers in a field necessarily entails increased support for that field, and no amount of prioritization within a fixed budget will result in significant growth in that number. Regarding stability—stable or growing levels of funding act as a signal to potential graduate students about the importance of the field and, by implication, the potential for professional advancement.

Avoiding negative signals to prospective researchers is also important. For example, given the uncertainties of research, funding models for individual research contracts or grants that demand short-term deliverables and that include go/no-go decisions reduce the number of qualified individuals who regard that research field as being worth a career commitment. They also bias the conduct and scope of the research effort. Research that cannot be published or otherwise disseminated is also an inhibitor, given that the potential for recognition by one's peers—whatever the form—is a powerful motivator for many researchers and indeed a career enhancer for those in academia.

Yet another issue is that of making the broadest possible use of available talent. One aspect of such talent is graduate student labor, upon which much of university research is based. Graduate students, who work under the supervision of faculty members, are nevertheless expected to make original contributions to knowledge in their specialties. When the federal government places restrictions on the research work that foreign graduate students can perform, it reduces the pool of talent available to further the research agenda—and given that foreign graduate students constitute a significant fraction of the graduate student population, it diminishes the talent pool significantly.

A second aspect of the talent issue is that of the participation of females and non-Asian minorities in advanced IT education. Apart from issues of simple equity, enhancing diversity in intellectual backgrounds and personal histories of the cybersecurity research workforce is likely to expand the range of approaches proposed and taken to address unsolved problems, an outcome that may well lead to more rapid progress. Moreover, anecdotal evidence from some cybersecurity researchers suggests that a higher percentage of these underrepresented students are involved in cybersecurity research than in other subspecialties within computer science.

10.2.5.2 Enhancing Cybersecurity Knowledge and Awareness in the Future IT Workforce

A number of government efforts to promote the education of security specialists focus on teaching specialists about current technologies, organizational management, and best practices with current products and services. Such efforts are useful, but they do not speak to development of a cadre of computer scientists and engineers and IT leaders that will focus on how to make the *next generation* of products and services more secure.

Today, designers and developers of IT products and services are often not schooled in what it means to design and develop with cybersecurity in mind. Software engineering has not traditionally been conceptualized or practiced with an assumption that there was an active adversary. But now designers and developers must approach their tasks under the assumption that every line of code may someday be attacked. The use of threat-based design and development is a shift in the development of IT products. Education must be seriously revamped if this shift is to take place on a large scale.

Put differently, in the long run, security will require the integration of a cybersecurity perspective in virtually every IT course, with the goal of promoting a security culture throughout the masses of systems designers, developers, and systems administrators and not just in cybersecurity researchers. That is, every software and hardware course of study should integrate the research results from the study of security requirements, architectures, and tools with an eye toward training future IT workers—not just future security experts, but also every IT practitioner, researcher, educator, systems administrator, computer designer, and programmer.

Consider what such revamping of mind-set might mean in the IT life cycle.

- Whereas the old mind-set in hardware and software design focused on performance and functionality, respectively, the new mind-set should also focus equally on security and attack resilience. As an example, current software engineering education stresses some form of object reuse, generalization of interfaces, and modularization, but it does not address the security implications of such features. The various parts of a program that reuse an object may have different security expectations, generalized interfaces may expose too much "attack surface," and modularization itself has the side effect of creating accessible interfaces.
- Whereas security was implemented as an afterthought in previous computer designs, it should be an integral part of the initial designs for future secure and attack-resilient computer architectures, and it should be integrated into every aspect of the hardware and software design life cycles and research agendas.
- Whereas in the old mind-set, design principles help primarily to critique a system after the design has been completed, the new mind-set calls for clear examples of design that demonstrate how such principles can be incorporated into new designs.

- Whereas the response to security breaches was reactive in the old mind-set (e.g., the "patch and pray" approach, with vendors supplying software patches after vulnerabilities are identified or their products are attacked), it should be *proactive* in the anticipation of new types of attacks in the new mind-set.
- Whereas many security products implemented only perimeter security (e.g., firewalls) in the old mind-set, the new mind-set would emphasize pervasive fine-grained authorization. For example, secure computer architecture would include security features in the processor architecture, the hardware platform architecture, the operating system kernel, and the networking protocols; each of these components would be designed and implemented with considerable thought being given to security products.
- Whereas the old mind-set dealt with fault-tolerance, or the resistance to physical aging, deterioration, and transient faults, the new mind-set must also deal with *very intelligent (human) attackers and malicious programs (malware)*. For example, current software engineering education does not emphasize that inputs to a program affecting program flow must always be checked for validity before it is passed to the program, even when data are made available at internal interfaces to program components. Every operation must be considered from the standpoint of how it can be spoofed, tampered with, replaced, or locked up.
- Whereas in the old mind-set, there was time to deal with a security breach, the new mind-set needs to also consider malware such as future viruses and worms that can infect all computers on the Internet in a few seconds. Hence, responses at human operator timescales are woefully inadequate, and more autonomic responses should be researched, and deployed if promising.
- Whereas in the old mind-set, security was treated as mainly a software issue, the new mind-set should consider both hardware and software dimensions of a solution.
- Whereas in the old mind-set, security experts operated in separate domains such as cryptography, network security, operating system security, and software vulnerabilities, the new mind-set should emphasize the integration of these separate areas, cross-pollination of ideas, and working toward the best system solution, given security, performance, cost, and usability goals.
- Whereas in the old mind-set, students are primarily indoctrinated in the importance of correct design and implementation, the new mind-set gives equal emphasis to notions of defensive design and implementation in which the expectation is that programs must deal with user mistakes and malicious adversaries.

- Whereas in the old mind-set, a system is considered secure until demonstrated otherwise by a practical attack, the new mind-set suggests that a system should be regarded as insecure until there is evidence that suggests its resistance to attack.

These comments are not intended to suggest that every designer and developer of IT products, services, and applications must become a security specialist as well. Many of today's security specialists argue, with considerable force and persuasiveness, that security is hard, that only a few folks can get it right, and that if security has to be addressed over and over again in every application, the likely result will be myriad insecure applications. Other parts of this report have suggested that security functionality can be made easier to use (e.g., Section 6.1, Section 4.1.2.1). But the argument for changing the security mind-set across all designers and developers is just that—to create a mind-set that appreciates and acknowledges the value of security and enables the designers and developers to engage in productive and meaningful interaction and dialogue with security specialists in the course of their work.

Also important is eliminating the intellectual mind-set that characterizes many graduates of today's IT educational programs—a "cowboy" mentality antithetical to the disciplined and structured approach needed to design and develop secure systems. In the not-so-distant past, it was fairly routine for the pressure of bringing products and service to market quickly to take precedence over all other considerations, including security. While this mind-set has begun to change, and vendors are realizing that paying attention to security is likely to have some impact on their bottom line, the committee strongly believes that there is a long way to go before a disciplined and structured development effort is routine in all vendors.

In the short run, organizations will adopt this approach if it enables them to ship a security-acceptable product more quickly or cheaply, and they will train their programmers in-house. But in the long run, it is clear that the educational system will—and should—bear most of the burden of integrating security as an important educational element in almost every IT course. This will call for treating security as a co-equal to functionality and performance in most subjects.

The committee believes that those responsible for educating the future IT workforce must work with cybersecurity researchers if the integration of such a perspective is to occur. If a cybersecurity perspective is to become pervasive throughout the IT workforce, it will require a much larger number of faculty specializing in cybersecurity research. The number of such faculty, in turn, is a direct function of the sustained research support available, even acknowledging that not all teaching faculty are research faculty or vice versa.

The direct relationship between faculty size and research support is particularly important if and when departments are contracting. In such times, it is difficult to obtain slots for any subspecialty, and especially so if—as is the case with the cybersecurity specialization—there is not a critical mass of those faculty members already in the department. Thus, targeted funding to support the cybersecurity specialization would be particularly important if the number of such faculty is to grow.

Support for infrastructure is also needed for cybersecurity education. Developing cybersecurity expertise requires hands-on experience with security products, so that their capabilities and limitations can be understood and intuitions developed for when they are or are not helpful. Such infrastructure is often neglected in funding programs, and those that do exist are limited in time, amounts, and schools.

10.3 CONCLUDING COMMENTS

The primary purpose of this report is to formulate a cybersecurity research agenda. But the scope and the nature of this agenda are inextricably intertwined with the character of the threat to cyberspace. Accordingly, this report argues that the threat to cybersecurity is real, significant, and growing rapidly. But because the combination of adversary threats and technical or procedural vulnerabilities of the future is impossible to predict in anything but the most general terms, a broad cybersecurity research agenda (Section 3.4.4, Principle 4: Respect the need for breadth in the research agenda.) is necessary to develop new knowledge that can be used to strengthen defenses against the cyberattacks of tomorrow. Furthermore, the research agenda must examine both technical and nontechnical issues. There is of course a central role to be played by technologists—but they must work hand in hand with organizational specialists, psychologists, anthropologists, sociologists, manufacturing specialists, and many others if the desired outcome—systems that are more secure in the real world—is to be achieved.

In Section 10.2, the committee identified five action items for the nation's policy makers: creating a sense of urgency about the cybersecurity problem commensurate with the risks, supporting a robust and sustained research agenda at levels which ensure that a large fraction of good ideas for cybersecurity research can be explored, establishing a mechanism for continuing follow-up on a research agenda, supporting the infrastructure needed for cybersecurity research, and sustaining and growing the human resource base. If these items are successfully addressed, real progress can be made toward realizing a more secure cyberspace and toward making the Cybersecurity Bill of Rights more a reality than a vision.

Appendixes

Appendix A

Committee and Staff Biographies

COMMITTEE MEMBERS

Seymour (Sy) E. Goodman, *Chair,* is a professor of international affairs and of computing, respectively, at the Sam Nunn School of International Affairs and the College of Computing at the Georgia Institute of Technology. He is also a co-director of the Center for International Strategy, Technology and Policy and associate director for policy of the Georgia Tech Information Security Center. Previously he has been director of the Consortium for Research on Information Security and Policy at the Center for International Security and Cooperation and the School of Engineering at Stanford University. Dr. Goodman is interested in the international diffusion and the national absorption of information technology (IT); the digital divide problems for small, poor and remote villages; and national and international security dimensions of IT. He is contributing editor for *International Perspectives for Communications* of the Association for Computing Machinery (ACM) and has served with many study and advisory groups, including the President's Commission on Critical Infrastructure Protection. He received a B.S. degree in engineering from Columbia University (1965) and a Ph.D. in applied mathematics/mathematical physics from the California Institute of Technology (1970). Dr. Goodman has previously served on several National Research Council (NRC) committees, including as chair of the meeting on Technical Responses to Cyber-attack and their Legal Implications. He also chaired the first large committee (Committee to Study International Developments in Computer Science and Technology) ever to produce a study for the Computer Science and

Telecommunications Board (CSTB); the committee produced the report *Global Trends in Computer Technology and Their Impact in Export Control,* published in 1988.

David Aucsmith is the security architect and chief technology officer for Microsoft Corporation's Security Business Unit, responsible for defining the overall security architecture for Microsoft products. He is currently working on a unified security architecture that spans Microsoft's products and is responsible for government-specific features in the Windows platform. Before joining Microsoft in 2002, Mr. Aucsmith was the chief security architect at Intel Corporation for 8 years. His responsibilities included working on security technology for hardware and software, together with random number generation, cryptography, steganography, and network-intrusion detection. Mr. Aucsmith has been heavily involved in computer security and cybercrime issues for more than 20 years. He is an industry representative to numerous international, government, and academic organizations: he is a member of the advisory board of the National Security Agency, co-chairman of the FBI's Information Technology Study Group, and a member of the President's Task Force on National Defense and Computer Technology. Mr. Aucsmith holds 29 patents for digital security technology. He received a B.S. degree in biochemistry from the University of Georgia, an M.S. in physics from the Naval Postgraduate School, and an M.S. in information and computer sciences from the Georgia Institute of Technology.

Steven M. Bellovin is a professor at Columbia University. He was a fellow at AT&T Labs Research, where he did research in networks and security and why the two do not get along. He has embraced a number of public interest causes and weighed in (e.g., through his writings) on initiatives (e.g., in the areas of cryptography and law enforcement) that appear to threaten privacy. He is currently focusing on cryptographic protocols and network management. Dr. Bellovin is a co-author of the book *Firewalls and Internet Security: Repelling the Wily Hacker* (Addison-Wesley, 2nd edition, 2003), and he is one of the security area directors for the Internet Engineering Task Force. He received a B.A. degree from Columbia University and M.S. and Ph.D. degrees in computer science from the University of North Carolina at Chapel Hill. He was a member of the Computer Science and Telecommunications Board (CSTB) committees that produced the NRC reports *Trust in Cyberspace* (1999), *IDs—Not That Easy: Questions About Nationwide Identity Systems* (2002), *Information Technology for Counterterrorism: Immediate Actions and Future Possibilities* (2003), and *Who Goes There? Authentication Through the Lens of Privacy* (2003). Dr. Bellovin is a member of the National Academy of Engineering (NAE).

Joel S. Birnbaum was formerly senior technical adviser to the chief executive officer (CEO) of the Hewlett-Packard (HP) Company. Dr. Birnbaum's role was to help the company shape its technology strategy and to communicate this strategy to the marketplace. Prior to this, he served as the company's first chief scientist, a consulting position, created for him upon his retirement in February 1999 from his position as senior vice president for research and development (R&D) and director of HP Laboratories. Dr. Birnbaum joined HP in 1980 after 15 years at IBM's Thomas J. Watson Research Center in Yorktown Heights, N.Y., where he had last served as director of computer sciences. His first assignment at HP was as the founding director of the Computer Research Center within HP Labs, which conducted research into new directions in computer architecture, hardware, and software, as well as some novel applications. In 1984 Dr. Birnbaum was named an HP vice president and director of HP Labs. In 1986 he was named general manager of the Information Technology Group. He managed the development of all core hardware platforms and systems software for the Precision Architecture product line, HP's first reduced instruction set computers (RISCs). After the first successful shipment of these systems in 1988, he was named general manager of the new Information Architecture Group, which developed systems architectures for cooperative computing environments, the basis of HP's product line today. In 1991 he was elected senior vice president of R&D and once again director of HP Labs. In this role, as a member of the management staff, he was responsible for coordinating HP's global research and development, directing central research, and acting as the company's chief technical officer. He is a fellow of the Institute of Electrical and Electronics Engineers (IEEE), the ACM, and the California Council on Science and Technology, and a foreign member of the Royal Academy of Engineering. He holds a bachelor's degree in engineering physics from Cornell University and master's and doctoral degrees in nuclear physics from Yale University. He has been granted an honorary doctorate by the Technion University of Israel. Dr. Birnbaum is a member of the National Academy of Engineering.

Anjan Bose is dean of the College of Engineering and Architecture and Distinguished Professor of Electric Power Engineering at Washington State University. He has served as an engineer and manager in industry and as chair and then dean at Washington State University. He also served as the program manager in the Engineering Division of the National Science Foundation (NSF) for a year. Dr. Bose is a researcher in the operation and control of power grids, and his methods and software are widely used in grid control centers around the world. He received the Third Millennium Medal and the Outstanding Power Engineering Educator

Award from the IEEE. He serves on the board of directors of the governor-appointed Washington Technology Council (vice-chair since 2000) and the Indian Institute of Technology Foundation. He served on the committee appointed by the secretary of energy to study electric power blackouts. Dr. Bose is the author or co-author of more than 75 journal articles and book chapters and has served on the editorial board of several IEEE publications. He is active on several national and international technical committees in the field of electric power engineering. Dr. Bose is a fellow of the IEEE. He received a B.S.E.E. degree from the Indian Institute of Technology, Kharagpur (1967); an M.S.E.E. from the University of California, Berkeley (1968); and a Ph.D.E.E. from Iowa State University (1974). He is a member of the NAE.

Barbara Fraser is a senior consulting engineer in the Technology Policy and Consulting Engineering Organization for Cisco Systems, Inc., and is responsible for influencing the security features and characteristics of the company's products. Her primary goal is to help Cisco develop and implement a coherent, achievable network security strategy for all Cisco products. Ms. Fraser's current activities and interests include improving Internet Protocol Security (IPsec) protocols, increasing security in Internet Operating Systems (IOS) software, and improving security testing in Cisco's overall engineering development processes. She participates in Cisco's IPsec Steering Group and is also an adviser to Cisco's Product Security Incident Response Team (PSIRT). Ms. Fraser is an active member of the Internet Engineering Task Force where she co-chairs the IPsec working group. She was editor of the *Site Security Handbook,* and has contributed to a number of other Request for Comments (RFCs). She has been a delegate to the G8 Cybercrime workshops around the world and was also a trustee of the Internet Society. For 10 years prior to joining Cisco, Ms. Fraser was a senior member of the technical staff at the Software Engineering Institute (SEI), located at Carnegie Mellon University. She was one of the early members of the Computer Emergency Response Team (CERT) Coordination Center (CERT/CC). While at the SEI, she led a team that designed and developed a security assessment method and supporting tools, and performed field assessments at major financial institutions, technology producer corporations, and government agencies and organizations. Ms. Fraser earned a B.S. degree in biology at Florida State University and an M.S. in computer science from the University of Central Florida.

James Gosler is a Sandia Fellow for Information Operations Studies. He was commissioned in the U.S. Navy in 1975, and following his active-duty service he became a member of the technical staff at the Sandia National

Laboratories. Early contributions included establishing a performance modeling/simulation program in the data-processing operating systems design area and the development of attack methodologies for both cryptographic and nuclear weapon-systems in the Adversarial Analysis Group. In 1989 Mr. Gosler became Sandia's first visiting scientist to the National Security Agency, where he consulted on computer security concerns and established and chaired key Information Security and Technology (INFOSEC)-related working groups. In 1996 Mr. Gosler entered the Senior Intelligence Service at the Central Intelligence Agency as the first director of the Clandestine Information Technology Office. In 2001 he returned to Sandia as a senior scientist; there he supports national information operations, information assurance, critical infrastructure, and terrorism initiatives. He has completed numerous professional courses and schools, including the National Senior Cryptologic Course, the National Senior Intelligence Course, Harvard's Program for Senior Executives in National and International Security, and the Intelligence Fellows Program. Mr. Gosler received a B.S. degree in physics and mathematics and an M.S. in mathematics.

William Guttman is a Distinguished Service Professor of Economics and Technology at the H. John Heinz III School of Public Policy and Management at Carnegie Mellon University. He was also part of the founding group of Carnegie Mellon's CyLab, one of the world's largest university-based research initiatives focused on dependability and security in software and networked systems, where he serves as co-chairman of the Operations Committee and director of Cylab's Sustainable Computing Consortium. He previously directed the Sloan Software Industry Center at Carnegie Mellon. Dr. Guttman's teaching and research interests include international economic policy as well as competition, innovation, and public policy in the global software industry. Earlier in his career, he served in various advisory capacities at the U.S. Department of State, the World Bank, the International Monetary Fund, and the Organisation for Economic Co-operation and Development (OECD). He is the author of several issued and pending software patents and has written two books on economic policy, among many other academic writings. After receiving a B.A. degree from the University of California, Los Angeles, he was a British Council Scholar and received his master's and doctoral degrees from Balliol College, Oxford University.

Ruby B. Lee is the Forrest G. Hamrick Professor of Engineering and Professor of Electrical Engineering at Princeton University, with an affiliated appointment in the Computer Science Department. She is the director of the Princeton Architecture Laboratory for Multimedia and Security

(PALMS). Her current research is in building security into core computer architecture, protecting critical information, providing hardware "safety-nets" for software vulnerabilities, mitigating information leaks boosted by modern microprocessor architecture features, and designing innovative instruction-set architecture to accelerate software cryptography and cryptanalysis. She is a fellow of the ACM, a fellow of the IEEE, associate editor-in-chief of *IEEE Micro,* and an editorial board member of *IEEE Security and Privacy*. Prior to joining the Princeton faculty in 1998, Dr. Lee served as chief architect at Hewlett-Packard, responsible at different times for processor architecture, multimedia architecture, and security architecture. She was a key architect of the Precision Architecture–Reduced Instruction Set Computers (PA-RISC) architecture used for HP workstations and servers. She pioneered adding multimedia instructions to microprocessors, facilitating ubiquitous and pervasive multimedia. She co-led an Intel-HP architecture team designing new instruction set architecture for multimedia and data parallelism for 64-bit Intel microprocessors. Simultaneous with her full-time HP tenure, Dr. Lee was also consulting professor of electrical engineering at Stanford University. She has a Ph.D. degree in electrical engineering and an M.S. in computer science, both from Stanford University, and an A.B. with distinction from Cornell University, where she was a College Scholar. She has been granted more than 115 U.S. and international patents and has authored numerous conference and journal papers on computer architecture, multimedia, and security topics.

Fernando (Fred) Luiz was most recently division general manager with the Hewlett-Packard Company before retiring in 2002. During a 17-year career, he was a member of the research staff working on the first commercial RISC system at HP Labs; R&D laboratory director; and director of the Distributed Systems Architecture Laboratory. He was also division general manager for HP's UNIX software systems and division general manager for enterprise security. He was also chief input/output (I/O) architect for HP's PA-RISC computer line and a senior technical strategist within HP. From 1987 to 1991, he was with Rolm Corporation, working on the architecture and design of computer integrated telephony systems with interests in the integration of automated and interactive voice sequences into complex and distributed transaction systems. Prior to working at HP, Mr. Luiz was with IBM Corporation for 20 years, as a lead engineer for IBM I/O for disk drives, design and development engineer, principal architect at storage technology, and system and field engineer. He has obtained 10 U.S. patents and several foreign patents. Mr. Luiz has an M.S.E.E. degree, with graduate studies in software tools, communication networks, and business administration and management.

Teresa F. Lunt is principal scientist and area manager of the Security Group and area manager of the Theory Group at Xerox Palo Alto Research Center (PARC), where she heads a project to develop technologies to protect privacy in terrorist-tracking applications. Previously she was assistant director for distributed systems in the Information Technology Office of the Defense Advanced Research Projects Agency (DARPA), as well as program manager of DARPA's information survivability program, where she launched a series of DARPA-funded security programs that continue today. At SRI International, Ms. Lunt led the development of the SeaView multilevel secure database system, the Next-Generation Intrusion Detection Expert Systems (NIDES) intrusion-detection system, and the DISSECT tool to detect inferences of highly sensitive information from less sensitive information. She received an A.B. degree from Princeton University (1976) and an M.A. in applied mathematics from Indiana University (1979). She is a member of the current NRC Panel on Survivability and Lethality Analysis and a former member of the NRC Committee on Network-Central Naval Forces.

Peter G. Neumann is principal scientist with Stanford Research Institute (SRI) International's Computer Science Laboratory. He was at Bell Laboratories in Murray Hill, N.J., in the 1960s, during which time he was heavily involved in the Muliplexed Information and Computing Services (Multics) development jointly with the Massachusetts Institute of Technology and Honeywell International, Inc. He is concerned with computer systems and networks, security, reliability, survivability, safety, and many risk-related issues such as voting-system integrity, crypto policy, social implications, and human needs including privacy. He moderates the ACM Risks Forum, edits the monthly "Inside Risks" column in *Communications of the ACM*, chairs the ACM Committee on Computers and Public Policy, co-founded People For Internet Responsibility, and co-founded the Union for Representative International Internet Cooperation and Analysis. He is a fellow of the ACM, IEEE, American Association for the Advancement of Science (AAAS), and SRI. He has taught at Stanford University; the University of California, Berkeley; and the University of Maryland. He received A.B., S.M., and Ph.D. degrees from Harvard University (1954, 1955, and 1961, respectively); he also holds a doctorate from Darmstadt. Dr. Neumann was a member of the CSTB committees that produced the NRC reports *Cryptography's Role in Securing the Information Society* (1996) and *Computers at Risk: Safe Computing in the Information Age* (1991).

Stefan Savage is an assistant professor in the Department of Computer Science and Engineering at the University of California, San Diego. His current research interests focus on large-scale network security, wireless networking, and self-managing distributed systems. Previously he has worked broadly in the field of experimental computer systems, including research on wide-area networking, real-time scheduling, operating system construction, disk array design, concurrency control, and performance analysis. He recently served as co-organizer of the 2003 Center for Discrete Mathematics and Theoretical Computer Science (DIMACS) Workshop on Large-Scale Internet Attacks, as founding program chair of the ACM Workshop on Rapid Malcode (WORM), and as founding program co-chair of the ACM/USENIX Symposium on Networked Systems Design and Implementation (NSDI). Professor Savage holds a B.S. degree in applied history from Carnegie Mellon University (1991) and a Ph.D. in computer science and engineering from the University of Washington (2002).

William L. Scherlis is a professor in the School of Computer Science at Carnegie Mellon University (CMU), a member of CMU's International Software Research Institute, and the founding director of CMU's Ph.D. program in software engineering. He is principal investigator of the 5-year High Dependability Computing Project with NASA. His research relates to software evolution, software assurance, and collaboration technology. He served 6 years at DARPA, with responsibilities including research and strategy in computer security, high-performance computing, and information infrastructure, before departing in 1993 as senior executive responsible for coordination of software research. He has served as program chair for a number of technical conferences and has more than 70 scientific publications. He holds an A.B. degree from Harvard University and a Ph.D. in computer science from Stanford University. He chaired the CSTB committee that produced the NRC report *Information Technology Research, Innovation, and E-Government* (2002) and its two workshop summaries.

Fred B. Schneider is a professor in the Department of Computer Science and director of the Information Assurance Institute at Cornell University. Dr. Schneider's research is intended to support the construction of concurrent and distributed systems for high-integrity and mission-critical settings. He is co-author, with David Gries, of the introductory text *A Logical Approach to Discrete Math* (Springer-Verlag, 1997) and author of the monograph *On Concurrent Programming* (Springer-Verlag, 1997). A member of the editorial board for *IEEE Transactions on Dependable and Secure Computing*, Dr. Schneider is also associate editor-in-chief for *IEEE Security and Privacy* magazine and co-managing editor for Springer-Verlag Texts and Monographs in Computer Science. He was a member of the 1995 DARPA/Innovative Space Based Radar Antenna Technology (ISAT) study on defensive information warfare. He currently serves on the NSF Computer and Information Science and Engineering (CISE) Advisory Board and the Griffis Institute's board of directors. A consultant to industry, Dr. Schneider serves on technical advisory boards for Cigital, Inc., Fortify Software, Intel Corporation, Microsoft Corporation, and Packet General Networks; he also serves as a consultant to DARPA and in a senior technical advisory position with Fast Search and Transfer ASA ("FAST") on matters of reliability and security. He is a fellow of the ACM and AAAS and the recipient of a doctor of science [honoris causa] degree from the University of Newcastle-upon-Tyne (2003). Dr. Schneider holds a B.S. degree from Cornell University (1975) and a Ph.D. from the State University of New York, Stony Brook (1978). He is a current board member of CSTB and chaired the CSTB committee that produced the NRC report *Trust in Cyberspace* (1999).

Alfred Z. Spector is currently a technology consultant and was recently vice president of strategy and technology for IBM's software business, responsible for technical and business strategy, various technical and business initiatives, standards, and software engineering across the worldwide software group. Prior to that, he was vice president of services and software in IBM research, responsible for IBM's worldwide services and software research. Before that, Dr. Spector was the general manager of Marketing and Strategy for IBM's AIM business, with responsibility for a number of IBM software product families including Customer Information Control System, WebSphere, and MQSeries, and the general manager of IBM's Transaction Systems software business. Dr. Spector was also founder and CEO of Transarc Corporation, a pioneer in distributed transaction processing and wide-area file systems, and an associate professor of computer science at Carnegie Mellon University. He is a member of the Computer Science and Telecommunications Board of the National Research Council. He remains active in the field of distributed computing, but his interests have inevitably broadened due to his recent job assignments. Dr. Spector received his Ph.D. in computer science from Stanford University and his A.B. in applied mathematics from Harvard University. He is a member of the National Academy of Engineering, a fellow of the IEEE and ACM, and the recipient of the 2001 IEEE Computer Society's Tsutomu Kanai Award for major contributions to state-of-the-art distributed computing systems and their applications.

John Wankmueller is vice president for electronic security and technology at MasterCard International. He is responsible for the global security architecture and technologies used in emerging channels and MasterCard's electronic commerce infrastructure. Mr. Wankmueller is currently working on the security infrastructure for payments involving consumer-owned mobile devices as well as biometric verification methods. Previously he worked on the design and development of the Secure Electronic Transaction (SET) specification jointly created by MasterCard, Visa, IBM, Microsoft, GTE, and others. Mr. Wankmueller helped develop MasterCard's integrated chip (smart) card business plan to migrate MasterCard products to integrated circuit (IC) chip technology. He also originated MasterCard's first centralized neural network fraud detection technology project. In 1994 he initiated MasterCard's efforts to create a secure payment standard over open networks like the Internet. Prior to joining MasterCard, Mr. Wankmueller was a staff member in AT&T's research and development area. He holds a bachelor's degree in mathematics from Fordham University New York and a master's degree from New York University.

Jay Warrior leads distributed systems research at Agilent Laboratories. He has more than 15 years of experience creating new networking-technology-based business opportunities for Honeywell, Fisher Rosemount systems, and HP/Agilent. He has led multiple efforts in networking standards setting and currently chairs the IEEE standards working group that developed IEEE 1451.1, a U.S. standard for network-independent interfaces for smart sensors to enable easy support of multiple communication protocols within products. In 1999 he received the IEEE Standards Association Award for his efforts. At HP and Agilent Laboratories, Dr. Warrior led the team that developed an Internet-based distributed system technology that was incorporated into two cellular infrastructure monitoring product lines. He was a laboratory scientist and program manager in the Distributed Measurement and Control Program at Hewlett-Packard Laboratories. Dr. Warrior recently co-founded Sensor Networking Applications and Technology Forum (SNAFUnet) and established Java Distributed Data Acquisition and Control (JDDAC), a joint effort between Agilent Laboratories and Sun Microsystems creating open source Java technology for sensor networks.

STAFF MEMBERS

Herbert S. Lin is senior scientist and senior staff officer at the Computer Science and Telecommunications Board, National Research Council of the National Academies, where he has been study director of major projects on public policy and information technology. These studies include a 1996 study on national cryptography policy (*Cryptography's Role in Securing the Information Society*); a 1992 study on the future of computer science (*Computing the Future: A Broader Agenda for Computer Science and Engineering*); a 1999 study of the U.S. Department of Defense systems for command, control, communications, computing, and intelligence (*Realizing the Potential of C4I: Fundamental Challenges*); a 2001 study on workforce issues in high technology (*Building a Workforce for the Information Economy*); and a 2002 study on protecting children from Internet pornography and sexual exploitation (*Youth, Pornography, and the Internet*). Prior to his NRC service, he was a professional staff member and staff scientist for the House Armed Services Committee (1986-1990), where his portfolio included defense policy and arms control issues. He also has significant expertise in mathematics and science education. He received his doctorate in physics from the Massachusetts Institute of Technology (MIT).

Kristen Batch is an associate program officer with the NRC's Computer Science and Telecommunications Board. She is currently involved with several projects focusing on emerging wireless technology and spectrum policy, biometrics technologies, and privacy in the information age. While pursuing an M.A. in international communications from American University, she interned at the National Telecommunications and Information Administration, in the Office of International Affairs, and at the Center for Strategic and International Studies, in the Technology and Public Policy Program. She also earned a B.A. degree in literary and cultural studies and Spanish from Carnegie Mellon University and received two travel grants to conduct independent research in Spain.

Jennifer M. Bishop, program associate, began working with the NRC's Computer Science and Telecommunications Board in 2001. She was involved in several studies, including those on telecommunications research and development, policy consequences and legal/ethical implications of offensive information warfare, and assessing the information technology research and development ecosystem. She also maintained CSTB's databases, managed the CSTB Web site, produced *Update*, the CSTB newsletter, and designed book covers and promotional materials. Prior to joining CSTB, Ms. Bishop worked for the City of Ithaca, New York, coordinating the Police Department's transition to a new Structured Query Language (SQL)-based time accrual and scheduling application, a project that grew out of her experience maintaining the police records databases. Her other work experience includes designing customized hospitality industry performance reports for Smith Travel Research, and freelance publication design. She is interested in the social and cultural impacts of information technology, including researching and developing effective information design for education and lifelong learning. In her spare time, Ms. Bishop is a visual artist working in oil and mixed media. She holds a B.F.A. degree from Cornell University's College of Architecture, Art, and Planning.

Charles N. Brownstein was the director of the NRC's Computer Science and Telecommunications Board from January 2004 to September 2005. He joined the NRC in 2004 from the Corporation for National Research Initiatives (CNRI), where from 1994 to 2004 he directed the Cross Industry Working Team and did independent research with support from NSF and DARPA. His interests are in innovation, applications, and impacts of information technology, Internet performance, and the technology-policy interface. Dr. Brownstein joined CNRI in 1994 after a 20-year career at NSF. There he served in positions including program director for telecommunications policy and IT applications, division director for information science and technology, deputy assistant director and assistant director of NSF for CISE, and director of the Office of Planning and Assessment. His federal achievements are recognized by Presidential Meritorious and Distinguished Senior Executive Service awards and by NSF's Distinguished Service Award.

Janice M. Sabuda is a senior program assistant at the NRC's Computer Science and Telecommunications Board. She currently supports all CSTB activities and is involved in several studies, including Improving Cybersecurity Research in the United States, Information Technology and the States: Public Policy and Public Interests, Planning Meeting on Fundamental Research Challenges in Computer Graphics, Privacy in the Information Age, and Radio Frequency Identification (RFID) Technologies: A Workshop. Previously, she focused on the congressionally requested study that resulted in *Youth, Pornography, and the Internet* (2002) and the project that resulted in *Global Networks and Local Values* (2001). Prior to joining the CSTB in August 2001, Ms. Sabuda worked as a customer service representative at an online fundraising company and as a client services analyst at a prospect research firm. She is currently pursuing a certificate in event management from the George Washington University Center for Professional Development. She received her B.S. (1999) in business administration from the State University of New York College at Fredonia.

Ted Schmitt is a program officer for the NRC's Computer Science and Telecommunications Board. He is currently involved in the CSTB projects providing a comprehensive exploration of cybersecurity and the use of IT to enhance disaster management. Before joining CSTB, Mr. Schmitt was involved in the development of the digital publishing industry and played an active role in various related standards groups. Prior to that, he served as technical director at a number of small technology companies in Germany, Sweden, and the United States. He started his career in 1984 as a software engineer for IBM, earning two patents and several technical achievement awards. Mr. Schmitt received an M.A. in international science and technology policy from George Washington University. He received a B.S. degree in electrical engineering in 1984 and a B.A. in German in 1997 from Purdue University, and studied at the Universität Hamburg, Germany.

Appendix B

Cybersecurity Reports and Policy: The Recent Past

B.1 INTRODUCTION

Since September 11, 2001, many cybersecurity activities have been undertaken by the federal government,[1] the research community, and private industry. This appendix reviews these activities, providing a snapshot of the efforts undertaken to address cybersecurity concerns over the past several years. Specifically, federal cybersecurity policy activity since 2001 is reviewed. A number of federal government reports that detail cybersecurity risks and challenges that need to be overcome are summarized. Also summarized are best practices and procedures, as well as options for making progress, as identified in these reports. Efforts for improving public-private collaboration and coordination are identified. Reports aimed at elaborating the necessary elements of a research agenda are also reviewed. The final section reviews the current federal research and development (R&D) landscape and describes the particular focus and the types of support being provided at various federal agencies with cybersecurity responsibilities.

Several general impressions about the state of cybersecurity and some common themes about the type of actions required to improve it can be drawn from the various activities summarized here. First, there are

[1]The Congressional Research Service issued the report *Computer Security: A Summary of Selected Federal Laws, Executive Orders, and Presidential Directives* on April 16, 2004; the report outlines the major roles and responsibilities assigned various federal agencies in the area of computer security. See http://www.fas.org/irp/crs/RL32357.pdf.

no "silver bullets" for fixing cybersecurity. The threats are evolving and will continue to grow, meaning that gaining ground against these threats requires an ongoing, society-wide, concerted and focused effort. A culture of security must pervade the entire life cycle of information technology (IT) system operations, from initial architecture, to design, development, testing, deployment, maintenance, and use. A number of focus areas are particularly important to achieving such a culture: collaboration among researchers; coordination and information sharing among the public and private sectors; the creation of a sufficiently large and capable core of research specialists to advance the state of the art; the broad-based education of developers, administrators, and users that will make security-conscious practices become second nature just as optimizing for performance or functionality is; making it easy and intuitive for users to "do the right thing"; the employment of business drivers and policy mechanisms to facilitate security technology transfer and the diffusion of R&D into commercial products and services; the promotion of risk-based decision making (and metrics to support this effort).

Second, several areas for research focus (or areas to support such research), consistent with those identified in this report, are identified across nearly all of the activities summarized in this appendix. These areas are authentication, identity management, secure software engineering, modeling and testbeds, usability, privacy, and benchmarking and best practices. Understanding the intersection between critical infrastructure systems and the IT systems increasingly used to control them is another common theme for research needs.

Finally, taken together, the activities reviewed give an overall sense that—unless we as a society make cybersecurity a priority—IT systems are likely to become overwhelmed by cyberthreats of all kinds and eventually to be limited in their ability to transform societal systems productively. This future is avoidable, but avoiding it requires the effective coordination and collaboration of private and public sectors; continuous, comprehensive, and coordinated research; and appropriate policies to promote security and to deter attackers. Given the global nature of cyberthreats, it also requires effective international cooperation. This survey does not focus on activity under way that aims to further international cooperation. However, considerable efforts are under way at the regional intergovernmental and international governmental levels.[2]

---

[2]See, for example, Delphine Nain, Neal Donaghy, and Seymour Goodman, "The International Landscape of Cyber Security," Chapter 9 in Detmar W. Straub, Seymour Goodman, and Richard Baskerville (eds.), *Information Security: Policies, Processes, and Practices*, M.E. Sharpe, New York, forthcoming 2008.

B.2 CYBERSECURITY POLICY ACTIVITY SINCE 2001

The U.S. Congress passed the Cybersecurity Research and Development Act[3] in November 2002. Section 2(2) of the act noted the ubiquitous and pervasive nature of information and communications technology, stating that revolutionary advancements in computing and communications technology have interconnected critical infrastructures "in a vast, interdependent physical and electronic network." Section 2(2) pointed to the increased societal dependence on that infrastructure, stating that "exponential increases in interconnectivity have facilitated enhanced communications, economic growth, and the delivery of services critical to the public welfare, but have also increased the consequences of temporary or prolonged failure." Section 2(4) found that that computer security technology and systems implementation lack the following:

- Sufficient long-term research funding;
- Adequate coordination across federal and state government agencies and among government, academia, and industry; and
- Sufficient numbers of outstanding researchers in the field.

The Cybersecurity Research and Development Act of 2002 called for significantly increasing federal investment in computer and network security research and development to improve vulnerability assessment and technological and systems solutions, to expand and improve the pool of information security professionals, and to improve information sharing and collaboration among industry, government, and academic research projects. The National Science Foundation (NSF) and the National Institute of Standards and Technology (NIST) are called on to create programs necessary to address these issues. The act authorized appropriations for both agencies to support the specified programs, though appropriations were never made to match authorized levels.

The Bush administration noted its support for the legislation as it was developed,[4] and issued *The National Strategy to Secure Cyberspace*[5] in February 2003. The report noted that securing cyberspace is a difficult strategic challenge and emphasized the need for a coordinated and focused effort, taking in federal, state, and local governments, the private sector, and individual Americans. It calls on the newly formed Department of

---

[3]Cybersecurity Research and Development Act of 2002, P.L. No. 107-305.

[4]Office of Management and Budget, H.R. 3394—Cyber Security Research and Development Act, February 5, 2002; available at http://www.whitehouse.gov/omb/legislative/sap/107-2/ HR3394-r.html.

[5]The White House, *The National Strategy to Secure Cyberspace*, February 2003; available at http://www.whitehouse.gov/pcipb/cyberspace_strategy.pdf.

Homeland Security (DHS) to take the leadership role and become the federal Center of Excellence in addressing the five priorities it identified for cyberspace security: a national response system, a threat and vulnerability reduction program, awareness and training programs, the securing of government-administered systems, and international cooperation. Research and development for cybersecurity are not heavily emphasized in the report, and the roles of NSF and NIST are not mentioned.

The Federal Information Security Management Act of 2002 (FISMA) established a "comprehensive framework for ensuring the effectiveness of information security controls over information resources that support Federal operations and assets."[6] NIST was designated as the agency responsible for setting guidelines and procedures to be met by all federal agencies with regard to securing their information systems.

The National Infrastructure Advisory Council (NIAC) was created by executive order in October 2001 to make recommendations to the president regarding the security of cyber and information systems of the U.S. national security and economic critical infrastructures. NIAC became part of DHS in February 2003 under Executive Order 13286.[7] The council is chartered to examine ways that partnerships between the public and private sectors can be enhanced to improve cybersecurity.[8] Members of NIAC represent major sectors of the economy—banking and finance, transportation, energy, information technology, and manufacturing. The council also includes representatives from academia, state and local governments, and law enforcement. It is intended that NIAC work closely with the president's National Security and Telecommunications Advisory Committee (NSTAC).

Homeland Security Presidential Directive 7 (HSPD-7): "Critical Infrastructure Identification, Prioritization, and Protection," issued in December 2003, aims to establish "a national policy for Federal departments and agencies to identify and prioritize United States critical infrastructure and key resources and to protect them from terrorist attack."[9] The directive makes DHS responsible for coordinating overall efforts aimed at enhancing and protecting critical infrastructure, including cyber infrastructure. As part of that responsibility, DHS is required to create a National Plan for

---

[6]Federal Information Security Management Act of 2002, Sec. 301 of the E-Government Act of 2002, P.L. No. 107-347.

[7]See http://www.fas.org/irp/offdocs/eo/eo-13286.htm.

[8]U.S. Department of Homeland Security (DHS), Charter of the National Infrastructure Advisory Council, July 1, 2005; available at http://www.dhs.gov/interweb/assetlibrary/NIAC_Charter.pdf.

[9]Homeland Security Presidential Directive 7 (HSPD-7), "Critical Infrastructure Identification, Prioritization, and Protection"; available at http://www.whitehouse.gov/news/releases/2003/12/20031217-5.html.

Critical Infrastructure Protection. The department is directed to work with the Office of Science and Technology Policy (OSTP) to coordinate inter-agency R&D for enhancing critical infrastructure. DHS is also required to develop an annual R&D development plan jointly with OSTP.

DHS issued the *National Infrastructure Protection Plan* (NIPP) in June 2006, as required by HSPD-7; the plan provides "an integrated, comprehensive approach to addressing physical, cyber, and human threats and vulnerabilities to address the full range of risks to the Nation."[10] The NIPP provides the framework and sets the direction for implementing this protecting of critical infrastructure. The plan is meant to provide a roadmap for identifying assets, assessing vulnerabilities, prioritizing assets, and implementing protection measures in each infrastructure sector. The NIPP delineates roles and responsibilities among all stakeholders. It is part of DHS's effort to take a leadership role and act as the federal Center of Excellence concerning infrastructure protection. In addition, each sector has developed a Critical Information/Key Resources Sector Specific Plan (SSP). The SSPs were published in May 2007. DHS is the lead agency for the development of the IT and Communications SSPs, and there is a cyber component to each of the remaining 15 SSPs.

The National Plan for Research and Development in Support of Critical Infrastructure Protection,[11] issued jointly by DHS and OSTP in April 2005, specifically addresses R&D not covered in the February 2005 interim NIPP. It is required to be updated annually, as specified in HSPD-7. The plan notes, in this initial version, a focus on (1) creating a baseline, including the identification of existing major R&D efforts within federal agencies, and (2) highlighting long-term goals of federal R&D for critical infrastructure. It identifies nine themes that encompass both cyber and physical concerns: detection and sensor systems; protection and prevention; entry and access portals; insider threats; analysis and decision-support systems; response, recovery, and reconstitution; new and emerging threats and vulnerabilities; advanced infrastructure architectures and systems design; and human and social issues.

The plan provides examples of federal agency efforts already under way or that are part of near-term planning for each of the nine themes. Priority focus areas for each theme are also specified. Three long-term strategic goals are identified:

---

[10] See http://www.deq.state.mi.us/documents/deq-wb-wws-interim-nipp.pdf.

[11] Department of Homeland Security and Office of Science and Technology Policy, "The National Plan for Research and Development in Support of Critical Infrastructure Protection," 2005; available at http://www.dhs.gov/interweb/assetlibrary/ST_2004_NCIP_RD_Plan FINALApr05.pdf.

- A national common operating picture for critical infrastructure,
- A next-generation computing and communications network with security "designed-in" and inherent in all elements rather than added after the fact, and
- Resilient, self-diagnosing, and self-healing physical and cyber infrastructure systems.

The plan states that future versions will "more strongly integrate both technical and budgetary aspects of R&D efforts" and provide all stakeholders with information about progress toward solutions, alignment of efforts to meet evolving threats, and discovery of needs and vulnerability gaps.

The Energy Policy Act of 2005[12] addresses the need for cybersecurity standards to protect the energy infrastructure. It includes a requirement that the Federal Energy Regulatory Commission (FERC) establish an Electric Reliability Organization (ERO) to establish and enforce reliability standards for the reliable operation of existing bulk-power system facilities, where "reliable operation" is understood to mean prevention of instability, uncontrolled separation, or cascading failures of bulk-power systems as a result of a sudden disturbance, including a cybersecurity incident. The North American Electric Reliability Corporation (NERC)—a voluntary industry group composed of electrical utilities—which sought the provisions specified in the act, was certified by the FERC as the ERO on July 20, 2006.[13]

B.3 IDENTIFYING EXPOSURES, BEST PRACTICES, AND PROCEDURES

A number of recent reports have addressed continuing cybersecurity exposures of critical infrastructures. Collectively, they identify the nature of the exposures as well as a number of challenges that must be overcome to address them. Several of the reports make recommendations regarding best practices and procedures necessary to reduce the risks from cyberattacks. More generally, they recommend that available cybersecurity technology be more systematically adopted throughout existing critical infrastructure systems.

---

[12]The Energy Policy Act of 2005, P.L. No. 109-058; Sec. 1211, "Electric Reliability Standards," contains the passages relevant to cybersecurity.

[13]Federal Energy Regulatory Commission, "Order Certifying North American Electric Reliability Corporation as the Electric Reliability Organization and Ordering Compliance Filing," July 20, 2006; available at ftp://www.nerc.com/pub/sys/all_updl/docs/ferc/20060720_ERO_certification.pdf.

In March 2004 the U.S. General Accounting Office (GAO) issued *Critical Infrastructure Protection: Challenges and Efforts to Secure Control System.*[14] GAO undertook the study resulting in the report at the request of the House Committee on Government Reform and its Subcommittee on Technology, Information Policy, Intergovernmental Relations and the Census. The committee and subcommittee had asked GAO to report on potential cyber vulnerabilities, focusing on significant cybersecurity risks associated with control systems, potential and reported cyberattacks against these systems, key challenges to securing control systems, and efforts to strengthen the cybersecurity of control systems.

The GAO report found that several factors have contributed to the escalation of the risks of cyberattacks against control systems, including the adoption of standardized technologies with known vulnerabilities, the connectivity of control systems with other networks, insecure remote connections, and the widespread availability of technical information about control systems. It also found that securing control systems poses significant challenges. These include "the limitations of current security technologies in securing control systems, the perception that securing control systems may not be economically justifiable and conflicting priorities within organizations regarding the security of control systems." The GAO report identifies the need for greater collaboration and coordination among government agencies and with the private sector. It recommends that DHS implement the responsibilities outlined in the *National Strategy to Secure Cyberspace,* specifically calling on DHS to "develop and implement a strategy for coordinating with the private sector and other government agencies to improve control system security, including an approach for coordinating the various ongoing efforts to secure control systems."[15]

In April 2004 NIAC issued the report *Best Practices for Government to Enhance the Security of National Critical Infrastructures.*[16] The report notes how much convergence there is between physical and information infrastructures and indicates the need to view security as including both physical and cyber issues. The NIAC report concludes that, while market forces are the most powerful drivers of change, government intervention can be appropriate and beneficial in certain areas. It focuses on four infrastructure sectors and finds that a deep understanding of sector dynamics is critical for effective government intervention.

---

[14]See http://www.gao.gov/new.items/d04354.pdf.

[15]See http://www.gao.gov/new.items/d04354.pdf.

[16]See http://www.dhs.gov/interweb/assetlibrary/NIAC_BestPracticesSecurityInfrastructures_0404.pdf.

Also in April 2004, the U.S.-Canada Power System Outage Task Force issued its *Final Report on the August 14, 2003 Blackout in the U.S. and Canada*.[17] The report found that, while the blackout was not caused by a cyberattack, the potential opportunity exists for cyber compromise of the Energy Management System (EMS) and supporting information technology infrastructure. It also noted that a failure in a software program not linked to malicious activity may have significantly contributed to the power outage. In all, the task force report made 15 recommendations related to the cybersecurity aspects of protecting the EMS. It called for the following:

- Cybersecurity management standards and procedures,
- Planned and documented corporate-level security governance and strategies,
- Implementation of detection controls,
- Improvement of diagnostic and forensic capabilities,
- Scheduled risk and vulnerability assessments,
- A central point for sharing security information,
- The establishment of clear authority to influence corporate decision making, and
- Procedures to prevent or mitigate inappropriate disclosure of information.

In May 2004, the GAO issued its second study, *Technology Assessment: Cybersecurity for Critical Infrastructure Protection*, in which it found that available cybersecurity technologies were not being deployed to their full extent, while continued R&D was needed for additional technology. The report identified three broad categories of actions that the federal government can undertake to increase the use of cybersecurity technologies:[18]

- Help critical infrastructures determine their cybersecurity needs, such as developing a national critical infrastructure protection (CIP) plan, assisting with risk assessments, and enhancing cybersecurity awareness;
- Take actions to protect its own systems, which could lead others to emulate it or could lead to the development and availability of more cybersecurity technology products; and
- Undertake long-term activities to increase the quality and availability of cybersecurity technologies in the marketplace.

---

[17]Available at https://reports.energy.gov/BlackoutFinal-Web.pdf; see Chapter 9 beginning at p. 131 for a discussion of the cybersecurity aspects of the blackout.

[18]See http://www.gao.gov/new.items/d04321.pdf.

The May 2004 GAO report found a number of cybersecurity research areas in need of continuing attention, including the composition of secure systems, the security of network-embedded systems, security metrics, the socioeconomic impact of security, vulnerability identification and analysis, and wireless security. It also notes that federal cybersecurity research programs are already beginning to address these research areas.

In January 2005 NIST issued a detailed report entitled *Security Considerations for Voice over IP Systems: Recommendations of the National Institute of Standards and Technology*[19] that made nine recommendations for providing secure Voice-over-Internet Protocol (VOIP) services, noting that VOIP introduces potential new cybersecurity risks. The recommendations include the development of appropriate network architecture and the importance of physical controls in preventing unauthorized access to information.

A report from the Environmental Protection Agency's (EPA's) Office of the Inspector General—*EPA Needs to Determine What Barriers Prevent Water Systems from Securing Known Supervisory Control and Data Acquisition (SCADA) Vulnerabilities*—issued January 2005, identified several reasons why vulnerabilities have not been addressed:[20]

- Current technological limitations may impede implementing security measures.
- Companies may not be able to afford or justify the required investment.
- Utilities may not be able to conduct background checks on existing employees.
- Officials may not permit SCADA penetration testing.
- Technical engineers may have difficulty communicating security needs to management.

This report from EPA's Office of the Inspector General recommended that the EPA notify DHS and Congress of problems for which it found no apparent solutions.

The Congressional Research Service (CRS) report *Creating a National Framework for Cybersecurity: An Analysis of Issues and Options*, issued in February 2005, states that "despite increasing attention from federal and state governments and international organizations, the defense against attacks on these systems has appeared to be generally fragmented and varying widely in effectiveness. Concerns have grown that what is needed is a national cybersecurity framework—a coordinated, coherent set of

[19]See http://csrc.nist.gov/publications/nistpubs/800-58/SP800-58-final.pdf.
[20]See http://www.epa.gov/oig/reports/2005/20050106-2005-P-00002.pdf.

public- and private-sector efforts required to ensure an acceptable level of cybersecurity for the nation."[21]

The CRS report identifies various approaches taken, all of which are recommended by one or more of the reports described in this section. These include adopting standards and certification, promulgating best practices and guidelines, using benchmarks and checklists, using auditing, improving training and education, building security into enterprise architecture, using risk management, and employing metrics. It notes that "none of them are likely to be widely adopted in the absence of sufficient economic incentives for cybersecurity." The CRS report also notes concerns about the effectiveness of market forces to provide adequate cybersecurity and the narrow scope of the policy activity in contrast with the apparent need for broad policy actions as called for in the 2003 *National Strategy to Secure Cyberspace* and similar documents. It also identifies the response to the year-2000 computer problem and federal safety and environmental regulations as models for possible federal action to promote cybersecurity, and further notes that the federal government might do the following:

- Encourage the widespread adoption of cybersecurity standards and best practices,
- Leverage the procurement power of the federal government,
- Make the reporting of incidents mandatory,
- Use product liability actions to promote attention to cybersecurity,
- Facilitate the development of cybersecurity insurance, and
- Strengthen federal cybersecurity programs in DHS and elsewhere.

Released in May 2005, the GAO report *Critical Infrastructure Protection: Department of Homeland Security Faces Challenges in Fulfilling Cybersecurity Responsibilities* notes that DHS has become the focal point for critical infrastructure protection. The report identifies 13 responsibilities that DHS has regarding cybersecurity. It states that "while DHS has initiated multiple efforts, it has not fully addressed any of the 13 key cybersecurity-related responsibilities that we [GAO] identified in federal law and policy, and it has much work ahead in order to be able to fully address them." It states that the Interim National Infrastructure Protection Plan is one of several efforts that DHS has undertaken to address its responsibilities for cybersecurity, but notes that DHS has not undertaken a number of critical activities. It cites several organizational barriers and underlying challenges that DHS will need to overcome to assume the key role envi-

---

[21]See http://www.law.umaryland.edu/marshall/crsreports/crsdocuments/RL327770 2222005.pdf.

sioned for it in strengthening the cybersecurity of critical infrastructures and serving as the strong cybersecurity focal point envisioned in federal law and policy.[22]

In September 2006, the GAO report *Coordination of Federal Cyber Security Research and Development* sought to identify the federal entities involved in cybersecurity R&D; actions taken to improve oversight and coordination of federal cybersecurity R&D, including the development of a federal research agenda; and methods used for technology transfer at agencies with significant activities in this area.[23]

The September 2006 GAO report reviews policy actions over the past few years, describes the nature of cybersecurity research support by the various federal agencies, and presents a description of the organization of federal cybersecurity R&D oversight and coordination. It notes several important steps taken by federal agencies to improve the oversight and coordination of federal cybersecurity R&D, including the following: chartering an interagency working group to focus on this type of research, publishing a federal plan for cybersecurity and information assurance research that is to provide baseline information and a framework for planning and conducting this research, separating the reporting of budget information for cybersecurity research from other types of research, and maintaining government-wide repositories of information on R&D projects.

One shortcoming specifically identified in this 2006 GAO report regarding coordination is the continuing lack of an R&D roadmap called for in the *National Strategy to Secure Cyberspace*. (A call for input as a first step to creating such a roadmap was made in April 2006 by the Interagency Working Group on Cyber Security and Information Assurance. See Section B.5, Notable Recent Efforts at Identifying a Research Agenda, below, for a description of this activity.) Overall, the 2006 GAO report found that while progress is being made, key elements of the federal research agenda called for in the *National Strategy to Secure Cyberspace* have yet to be developed.

To strengthen federal cybersecurity R&D programs, the 2006 GAO report recommends that the Office of Science and Technology Policy establish firm timelines for the completion of the federal cybersecurity R&D agenda—including near-term, mid-term, and long-term research—with the following elements: timelines and milestones for conducting R&D activities; goals and measures for evaluating R&D activities; assignment of responsibility for implementation, including the accomplishment of the focus areas and suggested research priorities; and the alignment of

[22]See GAO-05-434; available at http://www.gao.gov/new.items/d05434.pdf.
[23]See GAO-06-811; available at http://www.gao.gov/new.items/d06811.pdf.

funding priorities with technical priorities. The report also recommends that the director of the Office of Management and Budget issue guidance to agencies on reporting information about federally funded cybersecurity R&D projects to government-wide repositories.

In the 2006 report from the Association of Computing Machinery (ACM) entitled *Globalization and Offshoring of Software*, Chapter 6 focuses on cybersecurity risks and exposures presented as a result of the offshoring of software development. The chapter argues that "offshoring exacerbates existing risk and introduces new types of risk by opening more opportunities for incursion, accident, or exposure; and it may greatly complicate jurisdictional issues." This chapter raises a number of issues that it argues must be dealt with to address these risks and exposures. It concludes that the concerns raised need "not lead to a wholesale condemnation and rejection of offshoring but rather to the recognition of the inadequate attention so far paid to these risks" and the need for "prudently cautious, thoughtful, and effective practices in preventing and dealing with these risks."[24]

B.4 PUBLIC-PRIVATE COLLABORATION, COORDINATION, AND COOPERATION

Federal and state governments have taken steps to secure information systems that they manage. FISMA is an example of policy aimed at securing information infrastructure managed by the public sector. Yet, DHS estimates that 85 percent of all critical infrastructures are operated by the private sector.[25] *The National Strategy to Secure Cyberspace* identifies public-private partnership as the cornerstone of securing cyberspace. This emphasis echoes and reinforces that placed on private-sector involvement in Presidential Decision Directive (PDD) 63, the Clinton administration's policy on "Critical Infrastructure Protection," issued in May 1998.[26] This section identifies steps taken by government and the private sector to actively engage private-sector participation, collaboration, and partnership with the public sector.

---

[24]Association of Computing Machinery, Job Migration Task Force, *Globalization and Offshoring of Software*, 2006, especially pp. 6-1 through 6-32; available at http://www.acm.org/globalizationreport.

[25]Department of Homeland Security, Press Release, "DHS Launches Protected Critical Infrastructure Information Program to Enhance Homeland Security, Facilitate Information Sharing," Washington, D.C., February 18, 2004; available at http://www.dhs.gov/xnews/releases/press_release_0350.shtm.

[26]Presidential Decision Directive (PDD) 63, "Critical Infrastructure Protection," May 22, 1998; available at http://www.fas.org/irp/offdocs/pdd/pdd-63.htm.

B.4.1 Information Sharing and Analysis Centers

Presidential Decision Directive 63 created the National Infrastructure Protection Center (NIPC). The NIPC was intended to serve as a national focal point for gathering information on threats to the infrastructures. PDD 63 further recommended the creation of Information Sharing and Analysis Centers (ISACs), meant to "serve as the mechanism for gathering, analyzing, appropriately sanitizing and disseminating private sector information" to both industry and appropriate government agencies.[27] PDD 63 recommended that an ISAC be created for each major infrastructure in the United States. The owners and operators of the infrastructure would determine the design and functions of the center for their sector in consultation with the federal government. The function of the NIPC was integrated into the National Protection and Programs Directorate of DHS as a result of the directives of HSPD-7. Several sector-specific ISACs for the chemical industry, electric power, emergency management and response, financial services, food and agriculture, real estate, state government, surface transportation, telecommunications, and water have been established to allow critical private sectors and infrastructure owners to share information and work with DHS to improve protection of the infrastructure and to coordinate response to threats.

The ISAC Council was created in 2003 "to advance the physical and cyber security of the critical infrastructures of North America by establishing and maintaining a framework for valuable interaction between and among the ISACs and with government."[28] A 2004 white paper from the ISAC Council sought to describe the degree of penetration that each ISAC has had into the infrastructure of the United States.[29] The white paper noted that penetration varied widely from sector to sector, with overall participation at approximately 65 percent of the U.S. private infrastructure. It also noted the importance of government funding support to assist ISACs in reaching numerous small but critical infrastructure owners who are unable to afford ISAC membership and the dedication of resources necessary to participate.[30]

B.4.2 Alliances and Partnerships

In September 2002 the workshop called Accelerating Trustworthy Internetworking (ATI) was held to initiate discussion on how to encour-

[27]PDD 63, "Annex A. Structure and Organization."

[28]Information Sharing and Analysis Centers (ISAC) Council Web site, http://www.isaccouncil.org/about/index.php.

[29]ISAC Council, "Reach of the Major ISACs," White Paper, January 31, 2004; available at http://www.isaccouncil.org/about/index.php.

[30]ISAC Council, "Reach of the Major ISACs," p. 8.

age collaborative activities across academia, industry, and government in the emerging interdisciplinary trustworthy internetworking area. ATI participants included government agencies, private industry, universities, and nonprofit organizations. The goal was to accelerate progress toward high-grade commercial security for Internetworking applications.[31] A second ATI workshop held in January 2004 continued the work of the initial workshop and resulted in the 2004 *Accelerating Trustworthy Internetworking Workshop Report.*[32] The report notes a number of trends emerging since the 2002 workshop. For example:

- The critical role of IT in infrastructure protection has become clearer and has led to an interest in applications drivers that focus on both critical and pervasive scenarios;
- The key role of the private sector—and the importance of relationships among government, universities, industry, and other sectors—in addressing this challenge has been made more clear;
- The need for fundamental (not incremental) cybersecurity improvement goals has been recognized, as has the need for a pervasive trustworthy Internetworking environment to support critical applications;
- There is a growing realization that achieving a trustworthy Internet for these applications may well require a new paradigm, or architecture; hence the reference to trustworthy Internetworking;
- The recently formed Department of Homeland Security has taken responsibility for cybersecurity, and Congress has become increasingly interested in this area; and
- The National Science Foundation and DHS are focusing research resources on cybersecurity. .

The *ATI Workshop Report* states that the "full sustainable potential for scalable and pervasive information technologies cannot be achieved until the architectural framework broadly adopted in *pervasive market driven applications*, also functions as the underlying framework for *critical applications driven by needs of national and domestic security.*"[33] It recommended the development of a collaborative research organization based at a consortium of universities to serve as a "safe place where competing companies can meet with university researchers and set commonalities"

[31] *Accelerating Trustworthy Internetworking (ATI) Workshop Report*, September 3-5, 2002; available at http://www.ati2002.org/.

[32] *Accelerating Trustworthy Internetworking (ATI) Workshop Report*, April 2004; available at http://www.gtisc.gatech.edu/2004site/ati2004/ATI_Report_FINAL_4-25-04.pdf.

[33] *ATI Workshop Report*, April 2004, p. 1. Italics in the original.

and provide a focal point for government involvement. Further objectives included building community-shared "road maps" to encourage support for research collaboration, pilot projects, testbeds, and test-case sharing.

Three major industry alliance groups have formed since the release of the 2003 *National Strategy to Secure Cyberspace*, which emphasized the importance of private-sector participation in improving cybersecurity through the adoption and diffusion of cybersecurity technology. The three groups are the National Cyber Security Partnership (NCSP),[34] the Trusted Computing Group (TCG),[35] and the Cyber Security Industry Alliance (CSIA).[36]

The NCSP, led by the Business Software Alliance, the Information Technology Association of America, TechNet, and the U.S. Chamber of Commerce, was established in 2003 as a public-private partnership to develop shared strategies and programs to better secure and enhance America's critical information infrastructure. NCSP created the following five task forces composed of cybersecurity experts from industry, academia and government: awareness for home users and small businesses, cybersecurity early warning, corporate governance, security across the software development life cycle, and technical standards and common criteria. Each task force produced a report with recommendations for action, published between March and April 2004.[37]

NCSP notes that "like most risks in life, cyber security risks can be mitigated, but not completely eliminated. The nature of the threat is constantly evolving. Not all companies and institutions will share the same level of commitment to protecting their cyber-dependent resources from attack."[38] It advocates increased spending by government agencies to put in place the appropriate people, processes, and technologies in order to demonstrate leadership in cybersecurity. It says that "attempts by government to legislate or regulate cybersecurity would be counterproductive, creating a least common denominator for cyber security practitioners and doing little to stop those intent on wrongfully hacking into systems"; it further notes that industry failure to take proactive steps to demonstrate its commitment to and to make substantial improvements in cybersecurity will open the door for greater government involvement. While NCSP states its intent to continue activities for the foreseeable future, no new activity has occurred since the release of the task force reports in 2004.

---

[34]Information available at http://www.cyberpartnership.org/init-governance.html.

[35]Information available at https://www.trustedcomputinggroup.org/home.

[36]Information available at https://www.csialliance.org/home. Note that this organization is distinct from the Interagency Working Group on Cyber Security and Information Assurance, which goes by the same acronym.

[37]See http://www.cyberpartnership.org/init.html.

[38]See http://www.cyberpartnership.org/about-faq.html.

Also formed in 2003, the Trusted Computing Group is a "not-for-profit organization formed to develop, define, and promote open standards for hardware-enabled trusted computing and security technologies, including hardware building blocks and software interfaces, across multiple platforms, peripherals, and devices."[39] TCG has more than 135 members, including component vendors, software developers, systems vendors, and network and infrastructure companies. It has issued standards for the Trusted Platform Module (TPM) used in personal computers (PCs) and other systems and a software interface specification to enable application development for systems using the TPM. It has also issued a trusted server specification and trusted network connect specification to enable network protection. TCG continues to be active and is developing specifications for storage, peripherals, and mobile devices.

The Cyber Security Industry Alliance, formed in 2004, is a public policy and advocacy group exclusively focused on cybersecurity policy issues. Its membership consists primarily of private-sector information security firms. Its mission is to enhance cybersecurity through public policy initiatives, public-sector partnerships, corporate outreach, academic programs, alignment behind emerging industry technology standards, and public education. Perhaps its most visible effort has been its regular consumer survey to determine the "digital confidence index," which is meant to measure public attitudes regarding the security of information systems. Among other things, the Alliance tracks proposed legislation related to cybersecurity issues—for example, spyware, phishing, identity theft, and privacy.

B.4.3 Private-Sector Support for Cybersecurity Research in Academia

A number of private-sector companies have supported cybersecurity academic research. For instance, Microsoft has funded research in universities on trustworthiness through a request for proposals process for the past few years.[40] Some companies have placed provisions on the results of such research, limiting availability to the sponsoring company for some period of time prior to their being generally available to the wider community or restricting publication of detailed excerpts of the data. Detailed or comprehensive figures about funding levels or the conditions placed on such funding are not publicly available.

---

[39]See https://www.trustedcomputinggroup.org/about/.

[40]Microsoft and the External Research and Programs group announced the recipients of two Request for Proposal Programs, Trustworthy Computing and Virtual Earth Digital Photography. See http://www.microsoft.com/presspass/features/2006/feb06/02-21Research.mspx.

B.5 NOTABLE RECENT EFFORTS AT IDENTIFYING A RESEARCH AGENDA

The academic and policy communities concerned with cybersecurity have held numerous conferences and issued a number of reports aimed at identifying critical elements for a research and development agenda based on the current state of cybersecurity in existing information systems infrastructure.

The 2002 report of the National Research Council (NRC) entitled *Making the Nation Safer: The Role of Science and Technology in Countering Terrorism* dedicated a chapter to cybersecurity.[41] The report outlined a broad IT research agenda for improving cybersecurity and counterterrorism efforts, including information and network security, emergency response, and information fusion. It emphasized that none of these areas "can be characterized by the presence of a single impediment whose removal would allow everything else to fall into place." The report stressed that none of these areas is new, but called for additional research because the existing technologies are not sufficiently robust or effective, they degrade performance or functionality too severely, or they are too hard to use or too expensive to deploy. Finally, the report noted that the research and development agenda is one of the means of leverage that is readily available (beyond constructive engagement with the private sector) to the federal government for influencing progress toward better cybersecurity.

The Institute for Information Infrastructure Protection (I3P), a consortium of academic research centers, government laboratories, and not-for-profit research organizations, was founded in September 2001. I3P identifies as its primary role the coordinating of a national cybersecurity R&D program; helping to build bridges between academia, industry, and government; and reaching out to government and industry so as to foster collaboration and information sharing and to overcome historical, legal, and cultural problems that have prevented some research organizations from working together. I3P issued its *Cyber Security Research and Development Agenda* in January 2003, stating that it sought to "help meet a well-documented need for improved research and development to protect the Nation's information infrastructure against catastrophic failures." This report, which defines an R&D agenda for cybersecurity and says that the agenda will continue to evolve as required, identifies eight areas as underserved and ripe for new or additional R&D:[42]

---

[41]National Research Council, *Making the Nation Safer: The Role of Science and Technology in Countering Terrorism*, The National Academies Press, Washington, D.C., 2002.

[42]Institute for Information Infrastructure Protection (I3P). The 2003 *Cyber Security Research and Development Agenda* is available at http://www.thei3p.org/about/2003_Cyber_Security_RD_Agenda.pdf.

- Enterprise Security Management
- Trust Among Distributed Autonomous Parties
- Discovery and Analysis of Security Properties and Vulnerabilities
- Secure System and Network Response and Recovery
- Traceback, Identification, and Forensics
- Wireless Security
- Metrics and Models
- Law, Policy, and Economic Issues

A brief problem description, existing research and capabilities, and potential research areas are identified for each general area. In addition, I3P maintains a directory of organizations that work in the area of cybersecurity.

The President's National Security Telecommunications Advisory Committee (NSTAC)[43] held a series of Research and Development Exchange Workshops in 2003,[44] 2004,[45] and 2006.[46] The R&D Exchange Workshops are part of what NSTAC sees as its evolving mission, to offer advice to the government on how to protect the information infrastructure from threats and vulnerabilities that might ultimately jeopardize the country's national and economic security.[47] NSTAC is part of the National Communication System (NCS), which became part of DHS. Its work plan includes initiatives that intersect with various programs set forth in the 2000 *National Plan for Information Systems Protection*,[48] "i.e., information sharing, the security and reliability of converged networks, and research and development issues related to converged networks."

The *2004 Research and Development Exchange Workshop Proceedings* identifies five findings regarding the trustworthiness of telecommunications and information systems:

---

[43]The President's National Security Telecommunications Advisory Committee is composed of up to 30 industry chief executives representing the major communications and network service providers and information technology, finance, and aerospace companies. NSTAC was created by executive order to provide industry-based advice and expertise to the president on issues and problems related to implementing national security and emergency preparedness communications policy.

[44]National Security Telecommunications Advisory Committee, *2003 Research and Development Exchange Proceedings: Research and Development Issues to Ensure Trustworthiness in Telecommunications and Information Systems that Directly or Indirectly Impact National Security and Emergency Preparedness*, May 2003; available at http://www.ncs.gov/nstac/reports/2003/2003%20RDX%20Proceedings.pdf.

[45]The *2004 Research and Development Exchange Workshop Proceedings* are available at http://www.ncs.gov/nstac/reports/2005/2004%20RDX%20Workshop%20Proceedings.pdf.

[46]See a summary of the conference objectives and briefing slides, available at http://www.ncs.gov/nstac/rd/nstac_rdexchange_ont.html.

[47]See "How the NSTAC Is Tackling Today's Issues," available at http://www.ncs.gov/nstac/nstac.html.

[48]See http://www.fas.org/irp/offdocs/pdd/CIP-plan.pdf.

- Collaboration is essential for successful R&D initiatives. . . .
- Ubiquitous, interoperable identity management and authentication systems must be embedded into future networks. . . .
- A need to examine interdependencies between critical infrastructures, especially the implications of the intersection between telecommunications and electric power. . . .
- A need to influence business drivers and policy levers and provide other incentives to promote a culture of security. . . .
- Agreement on a common agenda is critical to achieve progress in trustworthiness R&D.

The National Science Foundation sponsored the workshop "Security at Line Speed" in November 2003. The goal of the workshop was to "disseminate information on problems, discuss potential solutions and identify areas requiring additional research" related to coupling the performance requirements of advanced applications with the necessities of prudent network security.[49] The workshop consensus was as follows:

- *Solutions exist, but they are not easy*. . . . There are network architectures and technologies that are useful. . . . There are steps that the research community can take to adapt their protocols and approaches to better fit the realities of the current level of security threats. The use of layered authentication and authorization services offer new opportunities for security. The traditional benefits of education and awareness, mixed with appropriate policies, remain. . . .
- *But they may not be sufficient*. Applied security research, well anchored in the realities of performance issues and network constraints, could significantly advance the future options available. . . . The investment in research and deployment may need to be considerable.
- *The future open networks will require new research*. . . . The state of networking is at a crossroads. If no action is taken, we will continue to see attacks, experience pain and create barriers that will eventually hinder the ability for the network to support the original goal of the Internet. . . .[50]

The NSF workshop report notes the need for new research alternatives requiring basic research to begin to address the need for improvements in network performance and security brought about by the changing reality of how networks are used. It calls for user-level tools that simplify the process of protecting hosts and user education to increase understand-

[49] *Security at Line Speed Workshop: Workshop Findings and Report*, available at http://apps.internet2.edu/sals/files/20031108-wr-sals-v1.1.pdf.

[50] *Security at Line Speed Workshop: Workshop Findings and Report*, available at http://apps.internet2.edu/sals/files/20031108-wr-sals-v1.1.pdf.

ing of the importance of security. It notes the need for the research and creation of tools to assist administrators. Finally, it notes the need for a set of applications communications standards that are coordinated and managed by an objective organization that can support competing efforts.

Also in November 2003, the Computing Research Association (CRA) held the conference "Grand Research Challenges in Information Security and Assurance."[51] Grand Research Challenges seek to inspire creative thinking and vision. As specific examples, CRA cites future research that might emerge from factors such as pervasive networking and mobility; increasing volumes of data; smaller, cheaper embedded computing; and a growing population of user-centric services. The identification of the following four Grand Challenges resulted from the CRA conference:[52]

- The elimination of epidemic-style attacks (viruses, worms, e-mail spam) within 10 years;
- The development of tools and principles that allow large-scale systems to be constructed for important societal applications—such as medical-records systems—that are highly trustworthy despite being attractive targets;
- The development of quantitative information-systems risk management to be at least as good as quantitative financial risk management within the next decade; and
- The provision of end-users with security controls that they can understand and privacy that they can control for the dynamic, pervasive computing environments of the future.

The basis of the Grand Challenges requires the sharing of information on computer security risks—a tactic that the community has been reluctant to adopt, unlike the telecommunications industry, which shares information on outages.[53] The CRA conference presented two alternative futures, depending on whether or not the Grand Challenges can be met. One future envisioned overwhelming unsolicited junk, rampant identity theft, frequent network outages, frequent manual intervention, and largely unchecked abuses of laws and rights. The alternative future envisioned a world with no spam or viruses, uninterrupted communications, user-controlled privacy, and balanced regulation and law enforcement. The CRA conference argued that meeting the challenges (which go beyond those of national defense) requires a focus on long-term research,

---

[51]See http://www.cra.org/Activities/grand.challenges/security/home.html.

[52]See http://www.cra.org/Activities/grand.challenges/security/grayslides.pdf.

[53]Summary of remarks by Richard DeMillo, Georgia Institute of Technology, in a presentation to the NRC committee, Washington, D.C., July 27, 2004.

because the immediacy of the threat focuses too much on near-term needs and an enlarged talent pool.

The Institute for Security Technologies Studies (ISTS) issued *Law Enforcement Tools and Technologies for Investigating Cyber Attacks: A National Research and Development Agenda* in June 2004; the report addresses the highest-priority technological impediments that face law enforcement when it is investigating and responding to cyberattacks and for which research and development might provide solutions. It documents the "continuing, critical, unmet needs of the law enforcement community for solutions to assist in the investigation and prosecution of cyber attacks," and it prioritizes the needs of the cyberattack investigative community that can form the basis for targeted research and development. The ISTS report identifies a number of themes:[54]

- The need to automate tasks in the investigative process,
- Tools that produce evidence-quality data,
- Reducing the cost of available tools,
- Reducing the reliance on insiders or individuals who may be suspects in cyberattacks, and
- The need for continued and expanded public-private partnership, collaboration, and information sharing.

In February 2005 the President's Information Technology Advisory Committee (PITAC) issued a report to the president entitled *Cyber Security: A Crisis of Prioritization* (hereafter, "the PITAC report").[55] The committee was established to provide "the President, Congress, and the Federal agencies involved in Networking and Information Technology Research and Development (NITRD) with expert, independent advice on maintaining America's preeminence in advanced information technologies, including such critical elements of the national infrastructure as high performance computing, large-scale networking, and high assurance software and systems design."[56] The PITAC report stresses how vital the information technology infrastructure has now become for communication, commerce, and control of physical infrastructure. It also stresses that the IT infrastructure is highly vulnerable to terrorist and criminal attacks and that the vulnerabilities are growing rapidly. It cites broad consensus among computer scientists that endless patching is not a solution and that the long-term answer requires fundamentally new security models and

[54]See http://www.ists.dartmouth.edu/TAG/randd.htm.

[55]See http://www.nitrd.gov/pitac/reports/20050301_cybersecurity/cybersecurity.pdf.

[56]See the President's Information Technology Advisory Committee Web site at http://www.nitrd.gov/pitac/.

methods. The report identifies four key issues, all related to cybersecurity research. Specifically, it found the following:

- *Inadequate funding*—Federal R&D funding for fundamental research in civilian cybersecurity is inadequate. Increased funding is needed for NSF to support such research.
- *Lack of researchers and education*—The research community is too small to support the necessary research and education. Increased and stable funding is needed to promote recruitment and retention of researchers and students.
- *Ineffective technology transfer*—Current technology transfer efforts are inadequate to successfully transfer federal research investments into civilian-sector best practices and products. The development of metrics, models, data sets, and testbeds is needed so that new products and best practices can be evaluated. Partnerships with the private sector need strengthening.
- *Lack of coordination and oversight*—Current federal R&D effort is unfocused and inefficient. A focal point for coordinating cybersecurity R&D efforts is needed: specifically, the Interagency Working Group on Critical Information Infrastructure Protection (CIIP).

The PITAC report offers 10 priority areas for increased research focus: authentication technologies; secure fundamental protocols; secure software engineering and software assurance; holistic system security; monitoring and detection; mitigation and recovery methodologies; cyber forensics; modeling and testbeds; metrics, benchmarks, and best practices; and nontechnology issues (psychological, societal, institutional, legal, and economic) that can affect cybersecurity. NSF was singled out by the report for increased funding—a total of $90 million annually—to support fundamental research in civilian cybersecurity.

PITAC was disbanded in June 2005 by the Bush administration. An executive order designated the President's Council of Advisors on Science and Technology (PCAST) to serve in the role of PITAC.[57]

In July 2005 the "OSTP/OMB Memorandum on Administration, FY 2007 R&D Budget Priorities" called for placing high priority on R&D investments in cyber infrastructure protection as well as high-end computing.[58] It specifically called for agencies to work through the National

[57]Executive Order 13385, "Continuance of Certain Federal Advisory Committees and Amendments to and Revocation of Other Executive Orders," September 30, 2005, available at http://edocket.access.gpo.gov/2005/pdf/05-19993.pdf.

[58]Joint Memorandum of the Office of Management and Budget and the Office of Science and Technology Policy, "OSTP/OMB Memorandum on Administration, FY 2007 R&D Budget Priorities," Washington, D.C., July 8, 2005.

Science and Technology Council (NSTC) to generate a detailed gap analysis of R&D funding reflecting the importance of cybersecurity and the need to ensure that areas in need of research be covered in the federal R&D program.

The INFOSEC Research Council (IRC)[59] issued its *Hard Problem List 2005* in November 2005.[60] As the report notes, the hard problems on this list were chosen because they represent fundamental technical challenges that arise in building and operating trustworthy systems, because they are inherently complex, and because of their importance to government missions. They do not (as the report also states) by any means represent the only challenges to the field of IT security. The eight topic areas identified as most relevant over the next 5 to 10 years are as follows:

- *Global-scale identity management:* Global-scale identification, authentication, access control, authorization, and management of identities and identity-related information;
- *Insider threat:* Mitigation of insider threats in cyberspace to an extent comparable to that of mitigation of comparable threats in physical space;
- *Availability of time-critical systems:* Guaranteed availability of information services, even in resource-limited, geospatially distributed, on-demand ad hoc environments;
- *Building scalable secure systems:* Design, construction, verification, and validation of system components and systems ranging from crucial embedded devices to systems composing millions of lines of code;
- *Situational understanding and attack attribution:* Reliable understanding of the status of information systems, including information concerning possible attacks, who or what is responsible for the attack, the extent of the attack, and recommended response;
- *Information provenance:* The ability to track the pedigree of information in very large systems with petabytes of information;
- *Security with privacy:* Technical means for improving information security without sacrificing privacy; and

[59]The INFOSEC Research Council consists of U.S. government sponsors of information security research from the Department of Defense, the intelligence community, and federal civil agencies. The IRC provides its membership with a community-wide forum for discussing critical information security issues, conveying the research needs of their respective communities, and describing current research initiatives and proposed courses of action for future research investments. Further information on the IRC is available at http://www.infosec-research.org.

[60]INFOSEC Research Council (IRC), "Hard Problem List 2005," available at http://www.infosec-research.org/docs_public/20051130-IRC-HPL-FINAL.pdf.

- *Enterprise-level security metrics:* The ability to effectively measure the security of large systems with hundreds to millions of users.

In April 2006 the Interagency Working Group on Cyber Security and Information Assurance (CSIA), under the auspices of the NSTC, issued the *Federal Plan for Cyber Security and Information Assurance Research and Development.*[61] CSIA reports jointly to the NSTC subcommittee on Infrastructure and the NSTC subcommittee on NITRD. The plan is intended to provide "baseline information and a technical framework for coordinating multi-agency R&D in cyber security and information assurance."[62] The scope of the plan is limited specifically to federal R&D objectives. Within this scope the plan is comprehensive in its laying out the breadth of technical perspectives on cybersecurity R&D. It also provides an overview of the threats, threat agents, asymmetric advantages of those agents, vulnerability trends, and infrastructure sectors of particular immediate concern—that is, industrial process control systems and the banking and finance sector.

This *Federal Plan* also aims to respond to recent calls for improving the overall federal cybersecurity R&D program. Specifically, it responds to the following reports and policy actions already discussed: the "OSTP/OMB Memorandum on Administration, FY 2007 R&D Budget Priorities"; *Cyber Security: A Crisis of Prioritization*, the 2005 PITAC report; the 2003 *National Strategy to Secure Cyberspace;* and the Cyber Security Research and Development Act of 2002 (P.L. No. 107-305). Seven broad objectives are identified by the plan as being strategic to federal R&D efforts:[63]

1. Support research, development, testing, and evaluation of cyber security and information assurance technologies aimed at preventing, protecting against, detecting, responding to, and recovering from cyber attacks that may have large-scale consequences.
2. Address cyber security and information assurance R&D needs that are unique to critical infrastructures.
3. Develop and accelerate the deployment of new communication protocols that better assure the security of information transmitted over networks.
4. Support the establishment of experimental environments such as testbeds that allow government, academic, and industry researchers to

[61]National Science and Technology Council, *Federal Plan for Cyber Security and Information Assurance Research and Development*, National Coordinating Office for Networking and Information Technology Research and Development, April 2006; available at http://www.nitrd.gov/pubs/csia/csia_federal_plan.pdf.

[62]National Science and Technology Council, *Federal Plan for Cyber Security,* 2006, p. ix.

[63]National Science and Technology Council, *Federal Plan for Cyber Security,* 2006, p. x.

conduct a broad range of cyber security and information assurance development and assessment activities.
5. Provide a foundation for the long-term goal of economically informed, risk-based cyber security and information assurance decision making.
6. Provide novel and next-generation secure IT concepts and architectures through long-term research.
7. Facilitate technology transition and diffusion of federally funded R&D results into commercial products and services and private-sector use.

These objectives were drawn from a review of legislative and regulatory policy requirements, analyses of cybersecurity threats and infrastructure vulnerabilities, and agency mission requirements. The *Federal Plan* makes a detailed analysis of federal cybersecurity R&D technical and funding priorities for areas broken into eight categories, each with several subcategories. For each subcategory, a definition of the area, its importance, the current state of the art, and the existing capability gap are provided. The eight categories and their subcategories are as follows:[64]

1. *Fundamental Cyber Security and Information Assurance,* including authentication, authorization, and trust management; access control and privilege management; attack protection, prevention, and preemption; large-scale cyber situational awareness; automated attack detection, warning, and response; insider threat detection and mitigation; detection of hidden information and covert information flows; recovery and reconstitution; and forensics, traceback, and attribution.
2. *Securing the Infrastructure,* including secure domain name system; secure routing protocols; IPV6, IPSec, and other Internet protocols; and secure process control systems.
3. *Domain-Specific Security,* including wireless security; secure radio frequency identification; security of converged networks and heterogeneous traffic; and next-generation priority services.
4. *Cyber Security and Information Assurance Characterization and Assessment,* including software quality assessment and fault characterization; detection of vulnerabilities and malicious code; standards; metrics; software testing and assessment tools; risk-based decision making; and critical infrastructure dependencies and interdependencies.
5. *Foundations for Cyber Security and Information Assurance,* including hardware and firmware security; secure operating systems; security-centric programming languages; security technology and

[64]National Science and Technology Council, *Federal Plan for Cyber Security,* 2006, Part II.

policy management methods and policy specification languages; information provenance; information integrity; cryptography; multi-level security; secure software engineering; fault-tolerant and resilient systems; integrated, enterprise-wide security monitoring and management; and analytical techniques for security across the IT systems engineering life cycle.

6. *Enabling Technologies for Cyber Security and Information Assurance R&D,* including cyber security and information assurance R&D testbeds; IT system modeling, simulation, and visualization; Internet modeling, simulation, and visualization; network mapping; and red teaming.
7. *Advanced and Next-Generation Systems and Architectures,* including trusted computing base architectures; inherently secure, high-assurance, and provably secure systems and architectures; composable and scalable secure systems; autonomic systems; architectures for next-generation Internet infrastructure; and quantum cryptography.
8. *Social Dimensions of Cyber Security and Information Assurance,* including trust in the Internet; and privacy.

The R&D priorities identified in the *Federal Plan* are compared with both the IRC and PITAC reports. The generally close alignment between the three reports is called "particularly noteworthy."[65] Authentication, secure software engineering, security throughout the system life cycle, monitoring and detection, modeling and testbeds, metrics, benchmarking and best practices, and privacy are all identified as top R&D priorities in various ways across all three reports.

The *Federal Plan* makes 10 recommendations for federal strategic interagency R&D to strengthen cybersecurity and information assurance in IT infrastructure, noting the need to collaborate and coordinate with the private sector:[66]

1. Target Federal R&D investments to strategic cyber security and information assurance needs. . . .
2. Focus on threats with the greatest potential impact. . . .
3. Make cyber security and information assurance R&D both an individual agency and an interagency budget priority. . . .
4. Support sustained interagency coordination and collaboration on cyber security and information assurance R&D. . . .
5. Build security in from the beginning. . . .
6. Assess security implications of emerging information technologies. . . .

[65]National Science and Technology Council, *Federal Plan for Cyber Security,* 2006, p. 21.
[66]National Science and Technology Council, *Federal Plan for Cyber Security,* 2006, pp. 23-26.

7. Develop a roadmap for Federal cyber security and information assurance R&D. . . .
8. Develop and apply new metrics to assess cyber security and information assurance. . . .
9. Institute more effective coordination with the private sector. . . .
10. Strengthen R&D partnerships, including those with the international partners. . . .

The *Federal Plan* stresses the need for interagency coordination to be strengthened within the context of the continuing mission-specific focus of the various agencies cooperating through NITRD.

In October 2006, CSIA requested input from the computing community on the roadmap for cybersecurity R&D called for in the recommendations (item 7 above).[67] It specifically sought input in four broad topics: R&D strategic issues, R&D technical topics and priorities (as listed in the request), R&D roadmap, and R&D recommendations in the *Federal Plan*. The GAO had noted in a September 2006 report the lack of steps taken to date toward creating such a roadmap.

B.6 THE CURRENT FEDERAL RESEARCH AND DEVELOPMENT LANDSCAPE

This section characterizes the current research activity in cybersecurity being supported by various federal agencies in line with their respective mission focuses. The nature of supported activity in cybersecurity is outlined for each agency. Research focus areas are identified, and a summary of the activities—based on focus area—is provided for each agency supporting or undertaking R&D research.

B.6.1 The Nature of Supported Activity in Cybersecurity

The nature of the activity supported by federal agencies varies depending on the mission of the agency. The following summarizes the *primary* goals of the support that each agency provides for cybersecurity:

- National Science Foundation (NSF)—Basic research, building research capacity.
- Defense Advanced Research Projects Agency (DARPA)—Mission-

[67]Subcommittee on Networking and Information Technology Research and Development, "Invitation to Submit White Papers on Developing a Roadmap for Cybersecurity and Information Assurance Research and Development," October 31, 2006; available at http://www.nitrd.gov/subcommittee/csia/CSIA_White_Papers_Final_103106.pdf.

oriented with the objective of rapid technology transfer for military operational use.

- Department of Homeland Security (DHS)—Development and near-term deployment of useful cybersecurity technologies.
- National Institute of Standards and Technology (NIST)—Standards, guidelines, and certification.
- Department of Energy (DOE)—Provision of a trustworthy environment for access to distributed resources and for supporting collaborative management of those resources.
- National Security Agency (NSA) and intelligence agencies—The unclassified and defensive portion of these agencies' mission is applied research aimed at growing the capabilities necessary to protect national information infrastructure, including support for education aimed at building the necessary domestic cadre of cybersecurity researchers and developers.
- Other agencies (e.g., Federal Aviation Administration [FAA], Department of Justice [DOJ], Department of Defense [DOD])—Mission-specific objectives relating to protecting information systems and infrastructure.

The agencies use a variety of approaches to support research to address their primary goals. Some agencies do all of their research in government laboratories, while others fund a mixture of university or private-industry research. NSF, DARPA, and DHS made recent solicitations directed at supporting cybersecurity research.

NSF supports a broad range of basic research in several areas of cybersecurity research. NSF's Cyber Trust program is dedicated to supporting basic cybersecurity research. It has funded a number of center-scale research efforts of limited scope and duration to provide support for specific focus areas. NSF also supports cybersecurity research through various other programs. DARPA supported one unclassified program directed at cybersecurity in 2004. All research projects in this program focus on one aspect of cybersecurity research. This is consistent with recent DARPA programs addressing cybersecurity. DHS—in keeping with the cybersecurity mission specified for it in the *National Strategy to Secure Cyberspace*—focused on operational aspects of cybersecurity through its National Cybersecurity Division (NCS), although (as noted in the PITAC report) less than 1 percent of its R&D budget is spent on cybersecurity research.

The Homeland Security Advanced Research Projects Agency (HSARPA) solicited proposals for cybersecurity research and development from the academic and private sectors. The focus of this solicitation was on the improvement of existing technologies, the development of new technologies, and technology transfer. DOE cybersecurity research is closely coupled with the science applications that it is focused on supporting—primarily, secure collaborative management of infrastructure resources. The primary focus of NIST's Computer Security Division is cybersecurity tools, standards, best practices, and guidelines. It performs in-house research on cybersecurity in support of this focus.

B.6.2 Interagency Cooperation and Coordination

Several coordinating bodies within the federal government address various aspects of cybersecurity R&D. Two of these, NITRD and CIIP, are under the NSTC. Furthermore, NITRD's Interagency Working Group (IWG) on Cyber Security and Information Assurance was responsible for the creation of the 2006 *Federal Plan for Cyber Security and Information Assurance Research and Development*. As noted previously, this plan was intended to address concerns about the need for more comprehensive coordination of the federal cybersecurity R&D agenda, expressed in the PITAC report and other reports and policy instruments. Several agencies participated in the CSIA IWG: NIST, DOD, DHS, the Department of State, FAA, the Department of the Treasury, the intelligence community, NASA, the National Institutes of Health (NIH), and NSF.

The role of the NITRD program is to provide an interagency coordination function that ensures that unclassified strategic federal IT R&D objectives are covered by the various mission agencies and to provide a mechanism for identifying and addressing gaps in IT R&D. All agencies active in cybersecurity research are included in NITRD. The CSIA *Federal Plan* is meant to provide a framework for coordinating interagency R&D in the context of the NITRD structure.

B.6.3 Research Focus Areas

Creating trustworthy information infrastructure requires addressing many problems. Cybersecurity can be compromised by a weakness in any aspect of a system or network. Thus, cybersecurity research must encompass a broad range of IT disciplines—hardware, networking, and so on. A trustworthy system should aim to be secure by design, but it should also be able to detect, prevent, and survive attacks. The security life cycle begins with architecture and ends with the ability to identify attackers after the fact. The CSIA *Federal Plan* previously summarized provides a sense of the breadth of issues that must be considered in order to comprehensively address cybersecurity.

Current research can be classified in a number of ways—for example, using the categories and subcategories used in the *Federal Plan*. NSF used security discipline and life-cycle classifications for categorizing projects for its 2004 core cybersecurity awards.[68] Categorization is helpful for identifying those areas receiving considerable focus and those that are currently receiving limited funding support, although no conclusions can be drawn directly from relative funding in these various areas about the need for funding in a particular focus area—an area may have been well researched in the past, or may be perceived to hold less promise. The following subsections provide specifics about the nature of cybersecurity R&D at each of the agencies that supported or conducted such research.

B.6.4 Agency Specifics

B.6.4.1 National Science Foundation

The National Science Foundation is the leading agency supporting nondefense basic research in cybersecurity. The Cybersecurity Research and Development Act of 2002 includes specific language regarding NSF's lead role in cybersecurity research and development. It also authorizes appropriations for research.[69] The Cyber Trust program is the centerpiece of NSF's support for cybersecurity research, although the program has not been funded to the fully authorized level.[70] The Cyber Trust program was established in response to the Cybersecurity Act to provide a focal point for cybersecurity activity at NSF.

Since 2004, the Cyber Trust program has awarded more than 100 research grants, including the funding of several center-scale cybersecurity research efforts. Other NSF programs—Information Technology Research, Embedded Hybrid Systems, Small Grants for Exploratory Research, Network Research Testbeds, and Experimental Infrastructure Network—supported awards for cybersecurity research. These programs supported more than 100 additional cybersecurity projects. Projects vary in length from 1 to 5 years, with annual awards ranging from $150,000 to $1.5 million for the center-scale projects. Nearly all the awards include some support for graduate and postdoctoral students. According to Karl Levitt, program manager for the Cyber Trust program, the success rate in 2006 for the Cyber Trust program was about 12 percent—and was accomplished by eliminating for that year the funding for center-level grants and by significantly reducing the funding awarded compared with that requested. The ratio of total amounts awarded to total amounts requested

[68]See http://www.nsf.gov/cise/funding/cyber_awards.jsp.

[69]P.L. No. 107-305, Secs. 4-7.

[70]See the Cyber Trust program home page at http://www.nsf.gov/funding/pgm_summ.jsp?pims_id=13451&org=CISE.

was less than 8 percent, a figure comparable to that of fiscal year (FY) 2004. In 2007, the success rate was increased to 20 percent, mostly because the Cyber Trust budget was increased to $34 million, the level it was in 2004-2006, but also because of not making center-level awards.[71]

The type of research being performed covers a broad range of the categories listed in the *Federal Plan,* although some areas receive significant focus and others relatively little.[72] The Cybersecurity Research and Development Act explicitly identifies a number of areas to receive attention. Each of the areas specified was the focus of at least some projects awarded funding. The act authorized funding of $40 million for FY 2004 and $46 million for FY 2005, excluding center funding, for which separate authorizations were specified. Funding for cybersecurity R&D supported by NSF has grown over the past several years, starting at approximately $30 million in FY 2004; it has not risen to the level recommended by the PITAC report, however.

In addition to awards to eligible individuals, the Cybersecurity Research and Development Act calls for NSF to establish computer and network security research centers to "generate innovative approaches to computer and network security by conducting cutting-edge, multidisciplinary research." The act authorizes center-scale appropriations for FY 2003 through FY 2007, although center-scale awards were eliminated in the FY 2006 solicitation.[73] Center-scale awards are typically 5-year grants, with annual funding ranging from $1.5 million to $4 million. Each center-scale project involves researchers from multiple universities addressing multidisciplinary aspects of each project. Several center-scale projects have been established thus far through the Cyber Trust program, including the following:

- *Security Through Interaction Modeling* will "explore ways to create more effective and usable defenses by modeling these networks of interactions and making the models an integral part of the defenses."[74]
- *The Center for Internet Epidemiology and Defenses* will work "to understand how the Internet's open communications and software vulnerabilities permit worms to propagate, to devise a global-scale

[71]Karl Levitt, NSF, personal communications to the committee, November 27, 2006, and June 21, 2007.

[72]The National Science Foundation did a breakdown of some of the FY 2004 cybersecurity funding. The summary of this breakdown is available at the Cyber Trust Program Web page, http://www.nsf.gov/funding/pgm_summ.jsp?pims_id=13451&org=CISE.

[73]National Science Foundation, Cyber Trust Program Solicitation, NSF 06-517, Washington, D.C., 2006.

[74]NSF Press Release 04-124, September 21, 2004, "NSF Announces Two Cybersecurity Centers to Study Internet Epidemiology and Ecology"; available at http://www.nsf.gov/news/news_summ.jsp?cntn_id=100434.

early warning system to detect epidemics . . . , to develop forensics capabilities . . . , and to develop techniques and devices that can suppress outbreaks before they reach pandemic proportions."[75]

- *The Center for Correct, Usable, Reliable, Auditable and Transparent Elections* will "investigate software architectures, tamper-resistant hardware, cryptographic protocols and verification systems as applied to electronic voting systems."[76]
- *Trustworthy Cyber Infrastructure for the Power Grid* will "create technologies that will convey critical information to grid operators despite cyber attacks and accidental failures. The solutions created are expected to be adaptable for use in other critical infrastructure systems." Both DOE and DHS will collaborate to fund and manage this center. [77]

A major cybersecurity research project funded outside the auspices of the NSF Cyber Trust program is the Team for Research in Ubiquitous Secure Technology (TRUST).[78] TRUST seeks to address a parallel and accelerating trend of the past decade—the integration of computing and communications across critical infrastructures in areas such as finance, energy distribution, telecommunications, and transportation. The center is an NSF Science and Technology Center, chartered to investigate key issues of computer trustworthiness in an era of increasing attacks at all levels on computer systems and information-based technologies. As noted on its Web site, TRUST is "devoted to the development of a new science and technology that will radically transform the ability of organizations (software vendors, operators, local and federal agencies) to design, build, and operate trustworthy information systems for our critical infrastructure." The project takes a highly cross-disciplinary approach, including researchers in relevant areas of computer security, systems modeling and analysis, software technology, economics, and social sciences. Education and technology transfer are also important components. TRUST also receives funding from the Air Force Office of Scientific Research.

B.6.4.2 Defense Advanced Research Projects Agency

In line with its agency mission, the Defense Advanced Research Projects Agency's research focus has been on military applications of infor-

---

[75]NSF Press Release 04-124, September 21, 2004.

[76]NSF Press Release 05-141, August 15, 2005, "NSF Awards $36 Million Toward Securing Cyberspace"; available at http://www.nsf.gov/news/news_summ.jsp?cntn_id=104352.

[77]NSF Press Release 05-141, August 15, 2005.

[78]Detailed information about the project is available at the TRUST project Web site at http://www.truststc.org/overview.htm.

mation security. DARPA began an Information Security research program in 1994.[79] The Information Survivability program, was the initial program, followed by the Information Assurance program. These programs focused on a number of security aspects, including retrofitting security and survivability technology for legacy systems, intrusion detection and response, survivability in the face of attack, high-assurance operating system construction, the composing of trustworthy systems from less trustworthy components, and secure collaboration allowing data sharing and communication over a network.

DARPA expanded its information security investment in 1999. From 1999 to 2003, six programs were funded, covering a range of information security areas and extending research in areas covered by the earlier programs:

- *Composable High Assurance Trusted Systems*—High-assurance operating systems composed out of interoperable subsystems, to provide the required trustworthiness.
- *Cyber Panel*—Monitoring for attacks and allowing operators to manage system security and survivability.
- *Dynamic Coalitions*—Secure communication and data sharing across a network.
- *Fault Tolerant Networks*—Continued network operation in the presence of successful attacks; that is, intrusion tolerance at the network layer and below.
- *Organically Assured and Survivable Information Systems*—Sustained operation of mission-critical functions in the face of known and future cyberattacks; that is, intrusion tolerance at the host and system level.
- *Operational Partners in Experimentation*—Accelerated transition to deployment.

DARPA sponsored three conferences between 2000 and 2003 called "DARPA Information Survivability Conference and Expositions" (DISCEX I, DISCEX II, DISCEX III) to present the findings of the research programs. These programs began winding down in 2003 and had ended by early 2005. Much of the staff focused on information assurance and security left DARPA as these programs wound down and have not been replaced. The institutional knowledge has largely left or become classified.

[79]Much of the discussion concerning past support for cybersecurity at DARPA is drawn from the Information Survivability Conference and Exposition III, Washington, D.C., April 2003; available at http://csdl.computer.org/comp/proceedings/discex/2003/1897/00/1897xi.pdf.

One unclassified program, Self-Regenerative Systems (SRS), focused on information security; it began in 2004 and was scheduled to run for 18 months. This program supports 11 research projects. The funding rate for SRS was approximately 12 percent. Funding projects were about evenly split between universities and the private sector, with four projects being performed jointly by universities and corporations. The overarching theme of the SRS program is on survivability, resilience, and adaptation in the face of attack, with four specific focus areas: code diversity to reduce the impact of exploiting a single flaw across systems; attack masking and recovery; scalable redundancy to achieve survivability and resilience; and detection, prevention, and mitigation from insider threats. Measurable goals have been set for projects, reflecting their applied nature. At least two classified programs are also under way, with largely short-term research and deployment goals. DARPA is also co-funding two projects with NSF.

In recent years, concerns have been expressed about a shift toward classified, shorter-term, and military-mission-focused research in DARPA's cybersecurity portfolio. For example, in 2005, the PITAC report commented as follows:[80]

> DARPA historically used a large portion of its budget to fund unclassified long-term fundamental research—in general, activities with a time horizon that exceeds five years. This provided DARPA with access to talented researchers in the Nation's finest research institutions and helped cultivate a community of scholars and professionals who developed the field. By FY 2004, however, very little, if any, of DARPA's substantial cyber security R&D investment was directed towards fundamental research. Instead, DARPA now depends on NSF-supported researchers for the fundamental advances needed to develop new cyber security technologies to benefit the military. Additionally, the emergence of cyber warfare as a tool of the warfighter has led DARPA to classify more of its programs. The combined result is an overall shift in DARPA's portfolio towards classified and short-term research and development and away from its traditional support of unclassified longer-term R&D.

In the 2 years since the PITAC report was issued, the committee has seen no evidence to suggest a significant change in DARPA's approach to cybersecurity research.

The extent to which DARPA emphasizes classified and short-term

[80] President's Information Technology Advisory Committee, *Cyber Security: A Crisis of Prioritization*, National Coordination Office for Information Technology Research and Development, Washington D.C., February 2005, p. 19; available at www.nitrd.gov/pitac/reports/20050301_cybersecurity/cybersecurity.pdf.

R&D over unclassified longer-term R&D is dependent on many factors, not the least of which is DARPA's interpretation of its mission. The tension between these two different foci has been reflected in many ways, not the least of which is the many changes in the very name of the agency since its birth in 1958.[81] If DARPA continues to emphasize classified, short-term research, that may well raise concerns among academic researchers about the long-term sustainability and future of working in cybersecurity research.

A second possible result of the shift toward short-term, military-mission-focused research is that such a research program may not sufficiently focus on issues relevant to the commercial sector (which develops and operates much of the nation's critical infrastructure). For example, military and intelligence applications often emphasize confidentiality over integrity and availability, whereas the commercial sector is often as concerned or more concerned about integrity and availability. Also, military and intelligence applications are more likely to emphasize risk avoidance, whereas commercial enterprises are more likely to emphasize risk management.

B.6.4.3 Department of Homeland Security

The Department of Homeland Security has both an operational function—preparedness and response—and a research function for cybersecurity. *The National Strategy to Secure Cyberspace* gave DHS the lead role in cybersecurity, calling on it to become the Center of Excellence for response, vulnerability reduction, training and awareness, and securing government cyberspace.[82] DHS created the National Cyber Security Division (NCSD) under the department's National Protection and Programs Directorate in June 2003 in response to the *National Strategy* requirements.[83] NCSD has three operating branches: U.S. Computer Emergency Readiness Team (US-CERT); Strategic Initiatives to advance cybersecurity

---

[81]In 1958, Department of Defense (DOD) Directive 5105.15 established the Advanced Research Projects Agency. In 1972, another DOD directive changed the agency's name to Defense Advanced Research Projects Agency (DARPA). In 1993, DARPA was redesignated the Advanced Research Projects Agency at the direction of President William J. Clinton. In 1996, the Defense Authorization Act for FY 1996 changed the agency's name back to Defense Advanced Research Projects Agency (DARPA). See http://www.darpa.mil/body/arpa_darpa.html.

[82]Discussion in this section is drawn, in part, from the written statement of Donald (Andy) Purdy, Jr., to the House Subcommittee on Federal Financial Management, Government Information, and International Security, July 19, 2005; available at http://hsgac.senate.gov/_files/PurdyTestimony.pdf.

[83]DHS Press Release, June 6, 2003, "Ridge Creates New Division to Combat Cyber Threats"; available at http://www.dhs.gov/dhspublic/display?content=916.

training, education, software assurance, exercises, control systems, critical infrastructure protection, and standards and practices; and Outreach and Awareness.

In July 2005, newly appointed DHS Secretary Michael Chertoff proposed creating a new position of Assistant Secretary for Cybersecurity—moving the responsibility for cybersecurity up one level in the organizational structure, although the position took more than 14 months to fill.[84] Cybersecurity research at DHS is supported through the Science and Technology (S&T) Directorate. The S&T mission includes conducting, stimulating, and enabling research and development. However, the current emphasis is on short- to medium-term needs related to the implementation of the *National Strategy to Secure Cyberspace*, including testing, evaluation, and timely transition of capabilities with approximately 85 to 90 percent of the S&T budget focused on these areas.[85] The remaining 10 to 15 percent of the budget is for the support of long-term, breakthrough research.

The mission of the Cyber Security Research Area—one of 15 S&T research portfolios organized into three categories—is to "lead cyber security research, development, testing, and evaluation endeavors to secure the nation's critical information infrastructure, through coordinated efforts that will improve the security of the existing cyber infrastructure, and provide a foundation for a more secure infrastructure."[86] This broad mission is reflected in the R&D areas that DHS identifies as important to address: secure systems engineering, information assurance benchmarks and metrics, wireless and embedded systems security, critical infrastructure, and cybersecurity education. There is specific focus on technology-transfer issues—moving from research to deployment. Around $300 million has been spent annually on cybersecurity research for the past decade. Yet, the transition path has not existed to produce commercial products from this research. Government funding trends have moved roughly $100 million into classified areas—resulting in even less research available to eventually produce commercial products.[87]

---

[84]See the organizational charts for 2005, http://www.dhs.gov/interweb/assetlibrary/DHS_Org_Chart_2005.pdf, and the proposed structural adjustments, http://www.dhs.gov/interweb/assetlibrary/DHSOrgChart.htm. The position was filled for the first time in September 2006.

[85]Background for the discussion of cybersecurity research missions of the Department of Homeland Security is drawn from presentations given by Douglas Maughan, DHS, to the committee on July 27, 2004, and presentations given at the HSARPA Cyber Security Research and Development Bidder's Conference held on September 23, 2004, in Arlington, Va. (see http://www.hsarpabaa.com/main/Cyber_Security_Bidders_9-13-2004.pdf).

[86]See http://www.dhs.gov/dhspublic/interapp/editorial/editorial_0549.xml.

[87]Statement of Douglas Maughan, HSARPA Program Manager, in a briefing to the committee on July 27, 2004.

The Homeland Security Advanced Research Projects Agency (HSARPA) under S&T created the Cyber Security R&D Center in 2004. HSARPA initiated the Cyber Security Research and Development (CSRD) program in 2004.[88] Program funding supported approximately half of the proposals deemed worthy of pursuing. There was concerted effort to reach out to the private sector for proposals, but few private-sector submissions were received.[89]

The DHS S&T cybersecurity agenda includes several other activities in addition to the Broad Agency Announcement for CSRD. The Cyber Defense Technology Experimental Research project—funded and run jointly with NSF—provides an experimental testbed to facilitate national-scale cybersecurity experimentation. The Protected Repository for Defense of Infrastructure against Cyber Threats is aimed at providing cybersecurity researchers with sufficient access to data necessary to test their research prototypes. Significant steps are being taken to protect the data against privacy concerns and to protect the data providers from abuse. A joint government-industry steering committee has been formed to address issues related to Domain Name Service Security (DNSSEC). Two workshops were held in 2004. NIST provided additional funding for this activity. The Secure Protocols for Routing Infrastructure activity is similar to the DNSSEC activity, with a government-industry steering committee and workshops. Cyber economic assessment studies are being undertaken—in keeping with the focus on technology transfer—to examine cost-evaluation methods for cybersecurity events and to enhance understanding of business cases and investment strategies that promote cybersecurity and risk prioritization. Two Small Business Innovation Research grants were awarded in 2004 addressing intrusion detection and identification of malicious code.

B.6.4.4 National Institute of Standards and Technology

The Cybersecurity Research and Development Act specifies the role of the National Institute of Standards and Technology in cybersecurity research.[90] The Computer Security Division—one of eight divisions in the Information Technology Laboratory—is the focal point at NIST for

[88]Homeland Security Advanced Research Projects Agency (HSARPA) Broad Agency Announcement (BAA) 04-17; available at http://www.hsarpabaa.com/.

[89]Discussion of committee members with Douglas Maughan, HSARPA Program Manager, on May 25, 2005.

[90]See Secs. 8-11 of the Cybersecurity Research and Development Act of 2002 (P.L. No. 107-305).

cybersecurity. CSD describes its mission as improving information security in four ways:[91]

- Raising awareness of IT risks, vulnerabilities, and protection, particularly in new and emerging technologies;
- Researching, studying, and advising agencies of IT vulnerabilities, and devising techniques for the cost-effective security and privacy of sensitive federal systems;
- Developing standards, metrics, tests, and validation programs to promote, measure, and validate security in systems and services; to educate consumers; and to establish minimum security requirements for federal systems; and
- Developing guidance to increase secure IT planning, implementation, management, and operation.

Four focus areas reflect this mission: Cryptographic Standards and Applications; Security Testing; Security Research/Emerging Technologies; and Security Management and Guidance.[92] CSD performs in-house research and provides services to DHS, NSA, and other agencies to support their cybersecurity missions.

CSD's Computer Security Resource Center (CSRC)[93] acts as a focal point for raising awareness about cybersecurity. CSD issues reports, such as *Security Considerations for Voice Over IP Systems*, to raise awareness of IT risks in emerging technologies. NIST runs the National Vulnerability Database (NVD) with funding from DHS's National Cyber Security Division. NVD is "a comprehensive cyber security vulnerability database that integrates all publicly available U.S. Government vulnerability resources and provides references to industry resources."[94]

The bulk of NIST's efforts (~$15 million) are focused on setting guidelines, evaluation tools, and standards for non-national security computers, and providing assistance to improve partnering of industry and academia. For instance, NIST provides coordination and guidance for how federal agencies implement and meet Federal Information Security Management Act requirements. It provides security self-assessment tools, organizes workshops, and gives training sessions and awareness meet-

[91]Statement of Edward Roback, National Institute of Standards and Technology, in a briefing to the committee, July 27, 2004. See also http://csrc.nist.gov/mission.html. The statement "Cybersecurity Research and Development" by Arden Bement, Jr., NIST Technology Administration, before the U.S. House Committee on Science, May 14, 2003, provides additional background information for this section.

[92]See http://csrc.nist.gov/focus_areas.html#sret.

[93]See http://csrc.nist.gov/index.html.

[94]See http://nvd.nist.gov.

ings. It develops encryption standards and cryptography toolkits. The Common Criteria process,[95] run by NSA under the National Information Assurance Partnership,[96] provides a means for the evaluation of information technology products for conformance to the International Common Criteria for Information Technology Security Evaluation.

NIST performs intramural cybersecurity R&D focused on Internet Protocol Security (IPSec), mobile networks and devices, access control and authentication mechanisms, and improved automation testing. It also provides funding—jointly with DHS—for I3P[97] run by Dartmouth College's Institute for Security and Technology Studies. In 2001 NIST provided nine research grants under its Critical Infrastructure Protection Grants Program. Funding for this program was not reauthorized, although the Cybersecurity Research and Development Act calls for the establishment and support of research fellowships.

NIST also supports cyber forensics and law enforcement. It maintains the National Software Reference Library, sets standards for forensic tools and methods, and does some testing of tools and devices for forensic analysis.

The Intelligent Systems Division of the Manufacturing Engineering Laboratory at NIST formed the Process Control Security Requirements Forum in 2001 to address cybersecurity issues related to SCADA systems. In October 2004, the Forum—composed of vendors, system integrators, end users of industrial control systems, and NIST staffers—issued the first draft of the System Protection Profile for Industrial Control Systems, which is "designed to present a cohesive, cross-industry, baseline set of security requirements for new industrial control systems."[98]

B.6.4.5 Department of Energy

The Office of Science (SC) at the U.S. Department of Energy supports cybersecurity R&D focused on "providing a trustworthy environment for access to distributed resources and for supporting collaborations."[99] Research projects are conducted at universities as well as at the Lawrence Berkeley National Laboratory. Cybersecurity research is tightly coupled with science applications that are the primary mission at DOE. In particular, much of the focus of cybersecurity research is on distributed

---

[95]See http://csrc.nist.gov/cc/.

[96]See http://niap.nist.gov/.

[97]See http://www.thei3p.org/.

[98]See http://www.isd.mel.nist.gov/projects/processcontrol/.

[99]Written comments provided by Daniel Hitchcock, Department of Energy, to the committee at a meeting on July 27, 2004.

authorization and secure collaboration using shared resources. From the perspective of the security life cycle, DOE efforts emphasize attack prevention and intrusion detection.

In FY 2005 DOE provided support, along with DHS, for an NSF-funded center-scale project—the Center for Trustworthy Cyber Infrastructure for the Power Grid—which will support 19 researchers across three universities with creating secure network protocols that enable efficient sharing of supply and demand information.

B.6.4.6 National Security Agency

The National Security Agency focuses largely on applied research to meet the needs of DOD and the intelligence community. Approximately 120 internal researchers work on cybersecurity. About 50 percent of the NSA budget for cybersecurity goes to nonacademic organizations doing classified research; 10 to 15 percent of the budget supports academic organizations. In his statement before the House Select Committee on Homeland Security Subcommittee on Cybersecurity, Science and Research and Development, then-NSA Director of Information Assurance Daniel G. Wolf noted that the agency now spends the bulk of its time and resources "engaged in research, development and deployment of a full spectrum of Information Assurance technologies for systems processing all types of information."[100] He identified a number of priority areas for research, including assured software design tools and development techniques, automated patch management, resilient systems, attack identification, and attribution. He expressed concerns about foreign hardware and software being used in critical systems and noted NSA's work on a Trusted Microelectronic Capability.

NSA provides support for civilian cybersecurity research in various ways, including funding and technical advice to NSF, DARPA, NIST, and DHS.[101] NSA sponsors the Information Assurance Technical Framework Forum (IATFF) to foster dialogue between U.S. government agencies, industry, and academia. The IATFF document provides guidance for protecting information and systems. NSA supports several other outreach programs for system security assessment, security design and evaluation,

[100]Statement by Daniel G. Wolf, Director of Information Assurance, National Security Agency, before the House Select Committee on Homeland Security, Subcommittee on Cybersecurity, Science and Research and Development, hearing titled "Cybersecurity—Getting It Right," July 22, 2003; available at http://www.globalsecurity.org/security/library/congress/2003_h/030722-wolf.doc.

[101]The discussion of National Security Agency support for cybersecurity research is drawn from the presentation to the committee by Grant Wagner, NSA Information Assurance Research Group, on July 27, 2004.

and security professional certification. NSA developed Security Enhanced Linux (SELinux) as an enhancement to the Linux kernel that implements mandatory access control and role-based access control. SELinux was released to the Linux community for enhancement and extension.[102]

One of the major priorities for NSA is the growth of a vibrant civil service cybersecurity research community. To that end, NSA is a supporter of education and capacity building in cybersecurity. The NSA, jointly with DHS, sponsors 75 designated centers as part of its Centers for Academic Excellence in Information Assurance Education (CAE/IAE) Program. This program is part of the broader National Information Assurance Education and Training Program, which also supports the national Colloquium for Information Systems Security Education and the National Information Assurance Training and Education Center.[103] No independent assessment of the CAE program has been conducted to determine if the requirements are appropriate, applied appropriately, or whether the program is actually helping to achieve its stated goals. Some individuals associated with schools in the program have questioned the lack of clear delineation between programs that conduct research and graduate education and those that are primarily vocational in nature. Nonetheless, the program has succeeded in bringing attention to educational efforts as little else has done.

B.6.4.7 Disruptive Technology Office, Office of Naval Research, and Air Force Research Laboratory

The Disruptive Technology Office,[104] Office of Naval Research (ONR), and Air Force Research Laboratory through its Air Force Office of Scientific Research (AFOSR) all support cybersecurity research related to their intelligence and military missions. These agencies have been a source of funding continuity, supporting significant unclassified education and research in cybersecurity, as well as funding classified research. AFOSR, for instance, supports the Information Assurance Institute at Cornell University. It also supports, with NSF, the TRUST Center (described above). ONR manages a major Multidisciplinary University Research Initiative program (funded from the Office of the Secretary of Defense) on "secure mobile code."

[102] See the NSA SELinux Web page at http://www.nsa.gov/selinux/.

[103] See http://www.nsa.gov/ia/academia/cisse.cfm and http://niatec.info/.

[104] Formerly known as the Advanced Research and Development Activity (ARDA).

B.6.4.8 Federal Aviation Administration

The Federal Aviation Administration's cybersecurity efforts are focused on its mission of providing for the safety and security of the FAA infrastructure. Its cybersecurity research activities "leverage developments by other agencies."[105]

B.6.4.9 National Aeronautics and Space Administration

NASA has no project current or planned directly related to cybersecurity. It does support research, such as the High Dependability Computing Project, which addresses another aspect of trustworthy computing—system reliability. The project Web site notes that "dependability is a major challenge for all complex software-based systems. Aspects of dependability include safety critical reliability, software safety, high security, high integrity, and continuous operation."[106]

[105]National Science and Technology Council, *Federal Plan for Cyber Security*, 2006, p. 113.
[106]High Dependability Computing Project (HDCP); see http://hdcp.org.

Appendix C

Contributors to the Study

Although the briefers listed below provided much useful information of various kinds to the Committee on Improving Cybersecurity Research in the United States, they were not asked to endorse the conclusions or recommendations of this study, nor did they see the final draft of this report before its release.

BRIEFERS AND PRESENTERS TO THE COMMITTEE
JULY 27, 2004
WASHINGTON, D.C.

Lee Badger, Defense Advanced Research Projects Agency
Richard DeMillo, Georgia Institute of Technology
Peter Freeman, National Science Foundation
Elizabeth Grossman, House Committee on Science (majority staff)
Robert Herklotz, Air Force Office of Scientific Research
Daniel Hitchcock, Department of Energy
Gary Koob, High Confidence Software and Systems Coordinating Group
Carl Landwehr, National Science Foundation
Chan Lieu, Senate Committee on Commerce, Science and Transportation (minority staff)
Douglas Maughan, Department of Homeland Security
Edward Roback, National Institute of Standards and Technology
Brian Shaw, Central Intelligence Agency

Grant Wagner, National Security Agency
Brian Witten, (formerly) Defense Advanced Research Projects Agency

BRIEFERS AND PRESENTERS TO THE COMMITTEE
MARCH 10, 2005
WASHINGTON, D.C.

Djenana Campara, Chief Technology Officer, Klocwork, Inc.
Beki Grinter, Associate Professor, College of Computing, Georgia Institute of Technology
Robert Rigby, Director, Managed Security Services, Security Operation Center, MCI

BRIEFERS AND PRESENTERS TO THE COMMITTEE
JULY 19, 2005
MOUNTAIN VIEW, CALIFORNIA

Alan Karp, Hewlett-Packard, Inc.
Lawrence Roberts, Anagran, Inc.
William Worley, Secure64, Inc.